Puns

Tant d'histoire pour quelques calembours

(So much history/such a hoo-ha over a few puns)

Raymond Queneau, *Les Fleurs bleues*, Paris, Gallimard, 1978, pp. 13–14

Puns

WALTER REDFERN

Basil Blackwell

First published 1984
Reprinted 1985

Basil Blackwell Publisher Ltd
108 Cowley Road, Oxford OX4 1JF, UK

Basil Blackwell Inc.
432 Park Avenue South, Suite 1505,
New York, NY 10016, USA

British Library Cataloguing in Publication Data

Redfern, W.D.
    Puns.
    1. Puns and punning—History and criticism
    I. Title
    809.7   PN6149.P85

ISBN 0-631-13793-9

*Also included in the Library of Congress Cataloging in
Publication Lists*

Typeset by Katerprint Co. Ltd, Oxford
Printed in Great Britain by The Bath Press, Avon

Contents

Acknowledgements   vi

Introduction   1

1   Shaky Foundations   9

2   The Motions of Puns   22

3   Making History I   33

4   Making History II   58

5   The Extended Family   82

6   Rounding Up   103

7   Puns Out and About   130

8   Across the Rivers and into the Trees   156

Conclusion   175

Notes   186

Select Bibliography   218

Index   229

Acknowledgements

Just as jokes belong to nobody in particular, so several of the ideas and the examples I use here must have been lifted, thieving-magpie fashion, from my favourite script-writers. All and Sundry. I have acknowledged debts where I was aware of them.

I am especially indebted to the following for advice, criticism and materials: André Blavier, Brigid Brophy, Philippe Cullard, Michael Edwards, Gaston Ferdière, Henri Fluchère, Paul Hammond, Patrick Hughes, Charles Kestermeier, SJ, Molly Mahood, Violette Morin, Robin Robbins, Geoffrey Strickland and Michael Wood.

My heartfelt thanks to Lorraine Standing for doing the bulk of the typing, with assistance from Jill Guiton; and to the General Editor, David Crystal, for support and counsel.

A part of chapter 7 has appeared in *Language and Communication*, and I am grateful to its editor for permission to redeploy this material. For extended studies of punning in action over whole works, interested readers might consult my articles: 'Vallès and the Existential Pun', *Mosaic*, IX (3), 1976, pp. 27–39; 'Between the Lines of *Billy Budd*', *Journal of American Studies*, XVII (3), 1983, pp. 357–65; and 'Applying the Tourniquet: Sartre and Punning' (to appear in *French Studies*).

All translations of French quotations are my own. In them, I have sometimes managed, and sometimes failed, to find English equivalents for puns in the original. In the cases of failure, I have spelled out the alternative meanings of a word or phrase.

This book is devoted to my wife Angela. Living with me, while on and off it may have been a laugh a minute, must have been at times no joke. She enriches the life that feeds the works.

Introduction

Quand on m'a dict ou que moy-mesme me suis dict: 'Tu es trop espais en figures'
... 'Oui, fais-je' ... 'J'ay faict ce que j'ay voulu: tout le monde me reconnoit en
mon livre et mon livre en moy.'

(When I have been told or have told myself: 'Your style is too figurative,' I reply:
'Yes, that is what I intended. Everybody recognizes me in my book and my book in
me.')

Montaigne[1]

Despite my job, teaching French Studies in England for the past twenty years
and more, I have not gone native, nor am I any longer, if I ever was (born in
Liverpool) a true Brit. I float, somewhat adrift, between the two cultural shores,
like the pun itself between acceptability and rejection, nonsense and point,
decency and obscenity. I spend much of my professional and amateur time
astride, or hanging in between, two languages. Rather than intimacy with either,
this position promotes a certain distance from both. 'La langue étrangère, en
fait, c'est – comme dans le calembour – le langage saisi comme étranger' ('A
foreign tongue in fact, as in the pun, is language itself experienced as foreign').[2]
Either this 'foreign language' is precisely one such, or, using the phrase
metaphorically, it describes the speech, for example, of adults overheard by
young children. My bipartite study of wordplay in French and English leads me
to see and hear my native language as to some extent alien. But the goal is a
double entente cordiale. Like any white man (though puns appeal to all colours), I
necessarily speak with a forked tongue. The Latin word *bilinguis* means split-
tongued, double-tongued.

'Liverpudlian' plays self-mockingly on the idea of 'pool'. I was born in
Liverpool. I would be flattering myself if I claimed that you need to be a
comedian to survive there. But Liverpudlians do, like punsters, switch things
about: they breathe through their mouths and talk through their noses. They
are physiological, existential twisters. My intellectual formation and deformation continued at St John's College, Cambridge, although I was not then aware
of the ancient repute of the place. Steele: 'The Monopoly of Punns in this
University has been an immemorial Privilege of the Johnians.'[3] Swift: '*Cam,*

where this art is in highest Perfection'.[4] Blackmantle: 'The men of Cambridge, in particular, have ever, from their foundation, been distinguished by their excellence as paragrammatists.'[5] John Henley: 'Puns are a main education in Cambridge; and practis'd and profess'd in all Exercises and Conversation.'[6] Addison, more sniffily: 'A famous University of this Land was formerly very much infested with Punns; but whether or no this might not arise from the Fens and Marshes in which it was situated, and which are now drain'd, I must leave to the Determinations of more skilful Naturalists.'[7] And finally, an anonymous graffitist, mephitically:

As learned Johnian wracks his Brain –
Thinks – hems – looks wise, – then thinks again; –
When all this Preparation's done,
The mighty product is – a Pun.
So some with direful strange Grimaces,
Within this dome distort their Faces;
Strain, – squeeze, – yet loth for to depart,
Again they strain – for what? a Fart.
Hence Cantabs take this moral trite.
'Gainst Nature, if ye think or sh-te;
Use all the Labour, all the Art,
'T will ne'er exceed a Pun, or Fart.[8]

The range of the pun, and this study, goes from bog to God, for, as Beckett reminds us, 'In the beginning was the pun.'[9] Maurice Charney speaks of 'the existence of almost continuous unrelieved and uninterrupted word-play in daily life'.[10] Language, in schools and higher education, is often nowadays taught ludically: the play of, and play with, language. If we ask who puns, Kris and Gombrich reply that 'play with words, punning and nonsense talk is one of the most beloved tools of comic creation in many civilisations.'[11] For Colman, 'quibbling [is] one of the occupational diseases of academe.'[12] Has he shut his ears to what is said on the docks, in the armed services, in playgrounds, offices, and on the streets? The inveterate researcher Gershon Legman talks of 'the education group that favours puns in general'.[13] He ignores the banners which pun, especially on names, brandished by working-class football crowds or militant demonstrators. Lichtenberg seems less divisive and more accurate when he claims that 'where the common people like puns and make them, the nation is on a high level of culture.'[14] The sad fact, of course, is that most of the sources are printed and so rarely capture popular habits. If recorded, slang does provide some clues. Pierre Guiraud mentions 'des formes souvent assez fines (du calembour) qui ont laissé des traces dans la langue de l'argotier' and cites: the concierge nicknamed *cloporte* (= woodlouse; *clôt-porte* = doorman). Most of the modern slang words for the police in French derive from *roue* – the wheel of torture – by punning. 'Le calembour est souvent une substitution homonymi-que destinée à créer un mot secret.'[15] A student of homosexual language comes to similar conclusions: 'Slang is a tricky piece of pun acrobatics; the more subculture one contacts, the more meanings slang words project'; and he offers 'señoreater' (Mexican homosexual), and 'Dickless Tracy' (a policewoman, or a gutless cop).[16] From my own plebeian origins I dredge up that, in Liverpool, the reluctant lover is called Father Christmas, because he comes but once a year, or that a defective condom is a 'Welsh letter' (because it has a leek in it), or a 'Scotch letter' (when it has been repaired). On the docks there, the nickname for a workmate cadging loans is 'the Destroyer' (because he is always chasing subs).

According to Oliver Wendell Holmes, women are excluded: 'There is no such thing as a female punster.' He then qualifies his remark: 'On reflection I found that I never knew nor heard of one, though I have once or twice heard a woman make a single detached pun, as I have known a hen to crow.'[17] No doubt he chose not to remember the spirited besting of the men by the women in *Love's Labour's Lost*. Surely Blackmantle is correct to declare: 'Lettered and unlettered, all alike, pun away.'[18] Swift's chief accomplice in the art of punning, Thomas Sheridan, indissolubly links the two sexes in this history of the phenomenon:

> Once on a time, in merry mood,
> Jove made a pun, of flesh and blood;
> A double two fac'd living creature,
> Androgynos, of two-fold nature.
> For back to back with single skin,
> He bound the male and female in;
> So much alike, so near the same,
> They stuck as closely as their name.
> Whatever words the male exprest,
> The female turn'd them to a jest;
> Whatever words the female spoke,
> The male converted to a joke:
> So in this form of man and wife,
> They led a merry punning life.
>
> . . .
>
> 'That's right', quoth Jove; with that he threw
> A bolt, and split it into two.
> And when the thing was split in twain,
> Why then it punn'd as much again.

'T is thus the diamonds we refine
The more we cut, the more they shine;
And ever since your men of wit,
Until they're cut, can't pun a bit.
So take a starling when 't is young,
And down the middle slit the tongue,
With groat or sixpence, 't is no matter,
You'll find the bird will doubly chatter.[19]

Ubiquity, equality, fissiparity, double-talk, intoxication: some of my major categories are already present in this poem.

The question of reputation is crucial. 'The lowest and most grovelling kind of wit which we call clenches', sneered Dryden against Ben Jonson.[20] Like other linguistic modes frequently looked down on but as widely practised – slang, obscenities, incorrect grammar or mispronunciation – wordplay often gets a bad press, even from its defendants. In an otherwise alert effort to get the point of puns, Lionel Duisit describes them as the 'least literary' of figures. Shakespeare, Donne, Hugo, Joyce? 'Le calembour ne peut avoir de statut linguistique que marginal,' he maintains, and even more strangely: 'Tout intellectuel est désarçonné par le spectacle du calembour' ('The only literary status the pun can have is a marginal one.' 'All intellectuals are thrown at the sight of a pun').[21] Although puns are a fact of life, moral majoritarians have ever wanted to abort them. Many are fathered on myriad progenitors. The old one about the punster claiming to be able to pun on any topic, but climbing down when the king suggested himself (since the monarch is not a subject), has been variously attributed to Thomas Killigrew, David Purcell, Dr Johnson and the Marquis de Bièvre – and incidentally runs counter to the notion that puns are untranslatable. Like jokes in general, many puns roam the world like so many bastards in search of their begetters, and are recognized and adopted by successive foster-parents. I will tackle later the dubious genealogy of both 'pun' and 'calembour'.

I will not apologize for anything in this study. Many have defended puns and many have attacked them. Yet I must admit that much of my material is second-hand. Puns are bastards, immigrants, barbarians, extra-terrestrials: they intrude, they infiltrate. Hence the warding-off rejoinder of the straight man: 'I don't wish to know that.' They will not go away. The twister Baudelaire saw straight, when he argued that the comic sense engendered by the Fall of Man must be exploited in the fight-back towards wholeness. The artist, he said (but in this area we are all experts, 'orfèvres en la matière') 'n'est artiste qu'à la condition d'être double et de n'ignorer aucun phénomène de sa double nature' ('is an artist only so long as he is double and faces up to all the implications of his double nature').[22] Likewise, Sir Thomas Browne saw man as an 'amphibian' (in its figurative sense of 'having two modes of existence, of doubtful origin'). Gilman glosses: 'By wedging opposing perspectives into a single image, [the witting artist] is partially able to repair the split suffered in the Fall – to approximate the unity of the divine mind.'[23]

For Freud, there was 'an intimate connection between all mental happenings'.[24] If this is so, some illumination might ensue when human behaviour is studied via wordplay. Diderot examined the deviant for a better understanding of the norm. Indeed, what have we all been doing, since the Fall, except measure the good by reference to the bad? Bad puns may tell us what makes a good pun. Conversely, perhaps an anthology of good examples would instruct us more successfully than any taxonomy ever could, for it would be proof in action. Yet neither taxonomy nor anthology appeal to me. I hope to wear my jargon-suit lightly (I read once of the 'nondisambiguational pun').[25] None of the laboratory tests I have read has added to my understanding or appreciation. As Bergler has said of such humourless researches into humour: 'One gathers the impression that investigators, utterly unable to come to grips with the essentials, have turned with relief to the only sure source of laughter, tickling, and concentrated on that. The emphasis seems unjustified to me – as unjustified as it would be to investigate the problem of crying by concentrating on onions, a sure source of tears.'[26] The other extreme is jokiness, as typified by Evan Esar's *Comic Encyclopaedia*, which lists the following wordplay on 'pun': punster, punmonger, punsmith, punslinger, punnophile, pundit, copropunster, uropunster, pornopunster.[27] The only suchlike I will annex is Rabelais' falsely apologetic self-description, the 'puny rhypographer' – 'a little man, whose vision and whose attention directed his descriptive art to low and sordid things, busy presenting – what? – a world of giants'.[28]

I am not infatuated with taxonomy, which shares more than its stem with taxidermy. In the best study I have so far read, *Upon the Pun*, by Patrick Hughes and Paul Hammond, the distinguos of the authors might be more useful to readers more enamoured of classification than I am. They might have recalled Molly Mahood's timely and salutary reminder in her study of Shakespeare's wordplay: 'Naming the parts does not show us what makes the gun go off.'[29] To be fair, Hughes and Hammond constantly enlarge their categories, widen their polarities chiasmus-wise, and end up proclaiming, like 'Pataphysicians, that the opposite is also true. Their joint effort is a medley of the clerkly and the earthy, the cathedra and the catheter (which can of course take the piss out of the lot of us). More soberly, Esar relates his own experience: 'The variety of puns must be infinite. Years ago I began to write a book on the subject and had little difficulty with its history, literature and other phases. But when I came to record the different types of puns, I gave up after identifying dozens of different species, for it seemed an endless task.'[30] One admission I myself must make at the outset: the theory of puns is often better than the practice.

With its Franco/English basis, my approach is two-pronged. It is binary also because the pun is double-think. Even to talk of wordplay involves, drags in by the scruff of the neck, playing with words, just as Orwell maintained that even to conceive of double-think embroiled double-think.[31] It can be argued that we are programmed to play with language. The speaker 'reçoit de la communauté qui l'intègre un "système de langage" avec un "mode d'emploi", mais aussi un mode de "contre-emploi", qui permet en même temps d'affirmer la maîtrise du mode d'emploi' ('receives from his community a "language-system" with "directions for use", but also with directions for "mis-use", which allow him at the same time to assert his mastery of the directions for use').[32] Perhaps we have heard more than enough of self-referential literature in the modern age. But language itself seems more indisputably self-aware. It is hardly surprising, since we all have a say in inventing it, that language is as self-obsessed as us humans. It talks of itself and with itself non-stop. For the wordplayer, life is language, and the world is a book. Surely this is one of the multiple forms of love. Logolators or, in the fullest sense, philologists. The word 'punster', like others with the same ending, usually devotes a fairly low form of life: monster, hamster, Westminster. I would say that the dislike, the fear sometimes, of wordplay tells us a good deal, as do attitudes towards the human body, about puritanism. Of such sniffers at words, such misologists, we might say that their imaginations are nasty, British and short. The pun is a sixth sense, an intuition of hidden depths or traps. (I thought of calling this book *More Senses than One*.) Puns keep us on the alert, and responding to them reveals that we are alert.

This study does not aim to be conclusive but rather, like many puns, suggestive. There are gaps of varying magnitudes; I have blind spots, or rather continents. I leave to its fanatics the whole area of 'recreational linguistics', the subculture of puzzles, word-games. I have had problems, too, of structure, for puns above all are overlap. What goes here, as the bishop said to the actress, could equally well go there and vice versa. Like asymmetric testicles (the norm), and despite Benjamin Franklin's warning, my chapters hang separately rather than together. I will use the terms 'pun' and 'wordplay', like levers on French trains, indifferently, and in the spirit of Valéry's comment on the term 'Symbolisme': 'Le pouvoir excitant du mot est ici illimité. Tout l'arbitraire de l'esprit est ici à son aise' ('the stimulating power of this word knows no bounds. The whole arbitrary nature of the mind is on confident display here').[33] 'Pun', indeed, as has been pointed out, is a post-Renaissance word, and an inaccurate but convenient tag for a whole variety of rhetorical devices which play on words.[34]

We seem to be, happily, in the realm of the arbitrary. Lacan is reported to have asked Chomsky whether he believed puns were intrinsic to language or merely accidental features of particular ones. Chomsky's reply was that scientific linguistics had to study similarities in language, not the differences between them, whereupon Lacan responded: 'I am a poet.'[35] I myself would opt for the intrinsic, because of the availability of homophones and the undeniable ambiguity of all language, which so often proves inadequate, uncontrollable, misusable. Surely a phenomenon so widespread must correspond to some fundamental, universal structure and impulsion.

Hughes and Hammond quote 'Anon Jr' (Anon is obviously an anagram of Onan, who was, like the pun, secretive and devious): 'The fact that people and trees and elephants and cars all have trunks just proves that there are more things than there are words.[36] Consequently, language (and its receiver) are always doubling up. Hence puns. The scholiast's gloss on Aristotle and Anon Jr reads as follows: 'For names are finite, and so is the sum total of formulae, while things are infinite in number. Inevitably, then, the same formulae, and a single name, have a number of meanings.'[37] While Aristotle valued highly the ability to recognize differences in apparently similar things and noted in his *Rhetoric* the effectiveness of jokes which depended on a shift in the meaning of a word, he also had reservations; he sensed danger. It seems that his view of wordplay is one-sided, 'since he is chiefly concerned with the possible ambiguity and lack of clarity which may result from *homonymia* and *amphibolia* if these devices are employed unintentionally, and with the deceptive argument which may result if they are used intentionally. He is not eager to pursue the poetic possibilities.'[38]

Puns as humour, puns as insight, puns as sophistry, puns as poetry. They do not have to be funny, and the epithets 'serious' or 'uncomic' have often been applied to them by literary critics studying specific instances of their use. St Bernard was presumably not seeking a laugh when he said: 'Non doctores sed seductores, non pastores sed impostores' (these incidentally, like most, are approximate puns, which is yet another reason for not expecting precision here). Interpretations will be loose, in fact gelastic. (Of a hackneyed vaudeville routine, we could say: 'Her knickers fell down: an example of tired gelastic.') Meredith appears to dislike all three categories he details in his study of comedy:

> We have in this world men whom Rabelais would call 'agelasts'; that is to say, non-laughers – men who are in this respect as dead bodies, which, if you prick them, do not bleed . . . It is but one step from being agelastic to misogelastic, and the *misogelos*, the laughter-hating, soon learns to dignify his dislike as an objection in morality. We have another class of men who are pleased to consider themselves antagonists of the foregoing, and whom we may term 'hypergelasts'; the excessive laughers . . . and to laugh at everything is to have no appreciation of the comic of comedy.[39]

Meredith is preaching moderation, which puns seem often to evade. Yet they are moderators in a better sense. Henry Erskine, responding to the cliché that punning is the lowest form of wit, said: 'It is . . . therefore the pun is the foundation of all wit.' At its best it can remind us of unarguable truths we might otherwise prefer to forget. 'Au plus eslevé throne du monde si ne sommes assis que sus nostre cul' ('On the loftiest throne in the world we still have to sit on our arse').[40] "Throne" must be one of the most ancient, rectifying, double meanings.

1

Shaky Foundations

My premise is that puns illuminate the nature of language in general. They are a latent resource of language, and certain temperaments simply will not resist trying to mine and exploit this rich ore, because (like Everest) it is there. The economy of puns make them an inexpensive way of striking gold, albeit often of the fool's variety. This latency, however, hampers mere self-indulgence. The punster always works within limits. He cannot invent puns which are not already potential in language. He merely unearths, sometimes dusts off, this treasure trove. (In this regard, punning is an uncovering, though as we will see in the case of irony, taboo and euphemism it can also be a cover-up job.) Both English and French retain the opposite meanings of the notion of 'invention': creation and discovery; French speaks of 'l'inventeur d'un trésor' in the *Code Civil*. In sixteenth-century French, *rencontrer* had both the sense of 'to meet' and the transitive sense of 'to joke, to make puns'. But should we talk of opposites? Is it not more a matter of interchange, interplay? With *rencontrer*, 'an added meaning of meeting up with thieves might suggest . . . loss, exchange, gain.'[1] When you mix with thieves, who loses honour? Punning appeals to those who take risks, but also to those who expect and value their money's worth, and indeed bonuses, from language. So long as some wager is involved, and not simply the complacently Tory, mercantilist attitude of a Max Müller:

> Our poets make poems out of words, but every word, if carefully examined, will turn out to be itself a petrified poem, a reward of a deed done or a thought thought by those to whom we owe the whole of our intellectual inheritance, the capital on which we live, with which we speculate and strive to go richer and richer from day to day.[2]

As with Emerson's view of words as 'fossil poetry', I remain chilled at the prospect of desporting in a morgue. Finds are flukes; puns are coincidences. Their makers practise linguistic serendipity. Lest we get over-excited, let us recall Augier's sober thought: 'Le hasard fait de sots calembours' ('Chance produces stupid puns').[3]

Let the linguistic scientist speak: 'Unless one is a poet or regards language as a plaything, one tends to regard ambiguity as an undesirable, if not pathological state in language.' Presumably because it upsets the computers. He goes on: 'When the ambiguity in a sentence can be isolated to one word, then we have a pun: for example, "Australians are the finest people in the world because they are chosen by the best judges in England".'[4] He forgets amphibology, where a whole sentence can mean two or more different things. An anodyne example: 'the boxes are free' (the seats are empty; the containers cost nothing). Or more insidiously: 'Nothing is good enough for you.' For Duisit, 'le mode amphibologique [est] une systématisation des effets qui se dégagent du calembour' ('The amphibological mode is a systemisation of the effects produced by the pun').[5] Whether in the short or the longer unit, ambiguity is celebrated – at least by those not blinkered by delusions that language can be scientifically controlled – as a richness. In French, *intelligence* means both intellect and complicity (as in 'être d'intelligence avec quelqu'un'). Barthes explains his pleasure at such finds:

> Chaque fois qu'il rencontre l'un de ces mots doubles, R.B. . . . . garde au mot ses deux sens, comme si l'un d'eux clignait de l'oeil à l'autre et que le sens du mot fût dans ce clin d'oeil, qui fait qu' un même mot, dans une même phrase, veut dire en même temps deux choses différentes, et qu'on jouit sémantiquement de l'un par l'autre.

> (Every time he comes across one of these double words, R.B. hangs on to its two meanings, as if one of them were winking at the other and the meaning overall lay in this wink, so that the same word in the same sentence can mean two different things simultaneously, and we can take our semantic pleasure from one through the other.)[6]

Experimental psychologists have shown quantifiably what most people know instinctively and by experience: that it is authoritarian personalities who most dislike and reject ambiguity. Hence the double meaning practised in all forms of underground literature. However, as well as pointing outwards in this way, wordplay always points inwards and refers to the duplicity of language itself. This is clearly dangerous territory. The *quiproquo*, one of the multifarious forms of punning, can extend to a whole situation: a misreading as well as an alternative reading superimposed on reality. While a fertile source of drama, this can have disastrous consequences in everday life. For normal business, no doubt it is understandable that nouns like equivocation or sophistry, and verbs like see-saw, palter, teeter, and have it both ways, should be regarded with suspicion.

Whatever its glories and perils, this human tendency for double-dealing seems thus far eternal. Jacobs point to the inclination of Anaximander and Heraclitus 'to dwell on the intrinsic ambiguity of language', and sketches in the enduring history of this habit:

Later, the Sophists exploited this duplicity for eristic purposes by first supporting one aspect of an ambiguity and then another by means of paradoxes. This literary mannerism generally flourishes in an age in which the objective view of life has broken down and the need is felt to justify the subjective criteria of judgment. Poets and artists also prefer the binocular vision of the universe implied in ambiguity because it enables them to bring to the surface some unexpected neglected aspect which would rouse us from our mental torpor, as the paradoxes of Nietzsche or Wilde.[7]

Language has shaky foundations. 'Langue fourchée' in French is ambiguous: it can mean wilful deceit or innocent mistake.

Language does have two sides, just as it is comprised of [sic] both acoustic images and concepts; it looks at ideas and it looks at itself, turning a side to things and a side to the speaker . . . Words may not only have dual meanings; they are dual in their very essence.[8]

Two-faced, double-tongued: Janus and jackdaws are favourite analogies.

Perhaps I am most truly interested in why and how people of all ages associate ideas on the basis of verbal affinities. 'Le démon de l'analogie' is the only Satan I believe in.[9] While Saussure was undoubtedly correct in maintaining that the mind 'naturally discards associations that becloud the intelligibility of discourse'[10] – though politicians, some teachers and writers, and liars are dishonourable exceptions to this rule – when we talk to ourselves, at least, we are under no such inhibition. On the most passive level, 'there is pleasure in phonetic free association not unlike the joys of daydreaming.'[11] The associative mind clearly revels in similarities, recurrences, echoes, reminders, assonances and rhymes. Perhaps we revel so much because we are not supposed to. After quoting Jean-Paul Richter's 'Joking is the disguised priest who weds every couple,' Freud goes on to add Vischer's: 'He likes best to wed couples whose unions their relatives frown upon.'[12] Analogy has itself analogies, with love, for instance, spiritual or physical. The appeal, the call, between different words of similar sound resembles those elective affinities between sundered souls in the old Celtic myth, or the sexual tug between bodies.

Proust was much taken with that Celtic myth. Though in search of certainties, though a snob, Proust was the first to agree that, just as 'il n'y a pas de sots métiers' ('all trades are equally valid'), so accident is a main motive-force of language. Quoting a Proust passage on the fortuitous ways languages develop – mistranslation, mispronunciation, erroneous etymology, false connections of all kinds – Queneau glossed: 'Il y a peu de fautes stériles' ('Most mistakes are productive').[13] Frédéric Paulhan explains along similar lines:

Parmi toutes les méprises fécondes . . . est celle qui a fait rapprocher dans l'esprit de l'homme les choses, les idées désignées par un même son ou par des sons à peu près semblables et qui s'appellent naturellement l'un l'autre. Cette opération est l'essence même du calembour; elle a été l'un des plus puissants facteurs de l'esprit humain.

(Among the most fruitful mistakes is that which brings together in the human mind the things or the ideas designated by the same sound or by closely related sounds which call out naturally to each other. This operation is the very essence of the pun; it has been one of the most powerful factors of the human mind.)

After promisingly admitting that 'le jeu de mots est "naturel" à l'esprit humain,' Paulhan, like many in the face of other 'natural functions', gets sniffy. He goes on to argue that puns are inferior, accidental and need to be apologized for, and, instead of seeing that they *overlap* with many other forms of language, sets up too mechanistic a polarity between them and those forms. He often talks as if punning were some kind of mechanical fault, like a record sticking or rails jamming and provoking a derailment. But he does have the grace to admit that when we are concentrating we shut out all potential other meanings, but that when we relax, in dream or if illness upsets our normal control, puns come into their own. Finally he brushes aside the temptation to think of 'le langage comme étant en fait une méprise perpétuelle, et, en principe, un calembour continuel' ('language as being in fact a perpetual misunderstanding and to all intents and purposes a continual pun').[14] Another who alternates between puffing the pun and huffing at it is Koestler. Despite calling it 'infantile', he does link punning with dreams, and with poetic and scientific intuitions which lead to inventions.[15] The pun exclaims 'Eureka!' ('You doan smella so good youself,' as Chico Marx responded).

In their splended book, *Adhocism*, Jencks and Silver continually suggest links between verbal juggling, bifurcating thought and the invention of the new from the old, in science, art or daily life: 'If general spurs to creativity do exist, they are such omnipresent motives as playfulness and dissatisfaction. Only these are strong enough to overcome the status quo of customary association.'[16] Taking the cue from Picasso's 'I don't search, I find' and T. S. Eliot's 'The bad poet borrows, the good poet steals,' they comment: 'Both epigrams point to a coded and loaded world. All one has to do is stumble upon these ready-made subsystems and combine them in a new way.'[17] They cite the war-time invention of limpet-mines, put together from Woolworth bowls, aniseed balls and rubber contraceptives, as practical adhocism. They might have added that it is an approximate scientific, or concrete, pun, as all the constituents imply bodily overlap with each other. Their distinction between random and purposeful creativity corresponds to mine between pointless and pointed wordplay. The whole business has affinities with a mixed bag of activities or phenomena: improvised jazz, serendipity, retrieval and recycling, hybridization. It is essentially a new life, or second life: an injection of dynamism. Similarly, one aspect of Joyce's experimentalism (equally present in the poetry of Francis Ponge) is the habit of allowing or encouraging entries in dictionaries or Roget's *Thesaurus* to set off trains, convoys, of associations. Thus the dictionary the home of the discontinuous (and as such the natural stamping ground of those especially taken with words-in-themselves), contributes to a continuous motion, a proliferation finally controlled by the experimenter. The search for the semantic density of words and the fabrication of new objects can thus be related.

Playfulness and dissatisfaction: first, play. Cultural historians like Huizinga tell us that play with words, which can naturally take other forms than punning – insult-competitions, lying-tournaments, bragging-matches (*joutes de jactance*) – is one of the most beloved practices of human beings the world over and throughout recorded time.

> You can deny, if you like, nearly all abstractions: justice, beauty, truth, goodness, mind, God. You can deny seriousness, but not play . . . The play-concept as such is of a higher order than is seriousness. For seriousness seeks to exclude play, whereas play can very well include seriousness.

Lest it seem that, in his infectious excitement, Huizinga pleads for total anarchy, he repeatedly stresses in fact that, despite its freedom, play quickly assumes frameworks and rituals. He even foresees the objection that Caillois and Benveniste raise: 'We would merely be playing with words were we to stretch the play-concept unduly.'[18] While finding Huizinga's book remarkable, Benveniste complains that 'il annexe au jeu absolument toute activité humaine soumise à des règles. On ne voit plus dès lors à quoi s'opposerait le jeu, ni, par suite, en quoi il consisterait' ('he annexes to play absolutely every human activity subjected to rules. As a result, it is hard to see what could be the opposite of play or, consequently, what it would consist in itself').[19] No doubt my own approach will attract similar objections. The fact is, as Swift put it so pungently, in spuriously deriving 'pun' from the French *punaise* ('a little stinking Insect, that gets into the Skin, provokes continual Itching, and is with great Difficulty removed'), puns, like fleas, get everywhere.[20]

Second, dissatisfaction. Just as many punning epitaphs are probably counterfeit, so the vast amount of spurious wordplay (i.e. wordplay unconnected with real-life situations) suggests that there is a near uncontrollable urge in many humans to overlay, to add to, the given; to rewrite the script of linguistic existence. This includes the urge to turn things round, to put the cart before the horse, thus reminding us of the reversible world we need to think we live in. So often we start from the verbal and invent the factual. It is fitting that a device exploiting ambiguity should be itself shot through with ambivalence. This is no doubt behind the view of wordplay as homeopathic medicine or inoculation with the virus: 'If you engineer a small breakdown of language, by dislocating and misusing words, it might have the force of a magic spell against major breakdowns of language, logic and civilisation.'[21] It is clearly an agent of disorder, a disturbing influence. It breaks the conventions of orthodox speech or writing. It can deflate or inflate, like the *démesure* and *rabaissement* alternately or concurrently practised by Rabelais. 'Puns and double meanings emphasise the unstable nature of language, its dynamic qualities which are so difficult to control. One can never really be sure of saying what one means.'[22] While a pun may never, unlike the CIA in its more hopeful moments, aim to destabilize a régime, it can make an individual, like Hemingway's fortunate heroine, feel the ground move beneath. It can ruin lazy expectations, subvert the inertia of language and thought. Iconocataclysm, to coin a word, can be ludic: 'Don't destroy the idols in anger,' urged Sade, 'break them up in play.'[23] Less brutally and more winningly, Nietzsche built a pun into his recommendation: 'I would believe only in a god who could dance. And when I saw my devil I found him serious, thorough, profound and solemn: it was the spirit of gravity – through him all things fall.'[24] Apart from these sublime heights, it is clearly important to play with language, in order to test its powers. We need to play before being, while being, or after being, serious. As much as anything else, a pun is language on vacation.

Its subversive capability can backfire. A truly compulsive punner like San Antonio ('Il faut que je jeux-de-mote' – 'I can't stop word playing') engineers a kind of autodestructive art, a breaker's yard where we may cease to recognize familiar objects:

> Comme dans les toiles [de Picasso] où chaque trait s'exaspère de, et sur lui-même jusqu'à rendre son objet in-regardable, les pages de San Antonio sont en bien des endroits illisibles; les calembours déforment le récit et les personnages jusqu'à menacer leur vraisemblance narrative ... Le calembour double (au sens également traître du mot) le récit, ligne par ligne, de mots inconséquents: il le déréalise, côtés noir ou rose; il le déforme.
>
> (As in Picasso's paintings, where each brush-stroke gets all worked up on and around itself until it makes the object un-viewable, the books of San Antonio are in many places unreadable. The puns deform the story and the characters and threaten their believability. The pun subtitles/doubles the text (in the equally treacherous sense of the word) line by line, with irrelevant words; it reduces its reality, on both the tragic or the lyrical levels: it perverts it.)[25]

The line here between mastery and self-defeat is stretched to breaking point, as is that between high artifice and artificiality. As Queneau's mentor Vendryès reminds:

Par définition, le calembour n'est pas naturel; c'est une forme d'art, et qui réclame une attention spéciale, comme toute production artistique. Ceux qui s'adonnent à cet exercice connaissent bien la nécessité de préparer le terrain, de mettre en éveil l'esprit de l'auditeur, lequel, une fois prévenu, se tient comme aux aguets pour surprendre le trait d'esprit.

(By definition, the pun is not natural; it is an art-form and demands special attention, like any artistic product. Those who engage in this activity are well aware of the need to prepare the ground, to alert the listener's mind which, once it has been forewarned, is on the look-out for the witty shaft.)[26]

This is the undeniable set-up, but the dramas it can lead to can produce vivacity. Duisit argues that the pun resembles Gide's 'acte gratuit':

C'est-à-dire, la quintessence de l'artificialité. L'acte gratuit pouvait, au nom d'une superbe plénitude, remplacer toute l'action, comme le trait d'esprit remplace, à la limite, toute l'intelligence. Quel animal pourrait comprendre un calembour?

(That is, the quintessence of artificiality. The gratuitous act might, in its search for richness of being, replace action itself, just as the witticism, in the last resort, can replace the whole of intelligence. What animal could understand a pun?)[27]

The notion of 'foregrounding', that is calling attention more to language than to what it signifies, seems unavoidable: 'Verbal play reminds us of the artifice of the work we are experiencing, distances us from its mimetic referents.'[28] This is the *Verfremdungseffekt*, that aesthetic BO:

Wit . . . is the dexterous performance of a legerdemain trick, by which one idea is presented and another substituted . . . A juggler is a wit in things. A wit is a juggler in ideas – and a punster is a juggler in words.[29]

One of the many synonyms for puns has been 'catches'. We are caught out, thrown, and, as on a switchback, the jolt can breed laughter, nervous or otherwise. 'The sounds punned upon conceal a trap-door or a sliding panel.'[30] The pun is a verbal practical joke, a cheat (though often a sweet one) in that it tries to pass off similarity as identity, as when Joyce in *Finnegans Wake* talks of the 'hoax that jokes bilked', where the plays on the terms involved cancel each other out. The trickster-figure, who features in so many cultures, reminds by his very Protean changeability that language is all-powerful: 'The joker as god promises a wealth of new, unforeseeable kinds of interpretation. He exploits the symbol of creativity which is contained in a joke, for a joke implies that anything is possible.'[31] Still, let us remember that punning can spring from uncertainty as much as from overconfidence.

We must remind ourselves of this when we come, somewhat tardily, to definitions. The pun is indeed a slippery customer, a bar of soap in our communal tub. Even that tome of reliable meaning, the British Library catalogue, implicitly makes house-room for puns:

> Words etymologically distinct but identical in form are treated as though they were the same word and are grouped under the same heading, for instance: SEE – See. A monthly magazine of the film. – The See of Canterbury – See und Land.[32]

No wonder other portly institutions can occasionally go daft when it comes to the defining of puns. In the *Grand Larousse Universel du XIXe siècle*, several pages are squandered on an entirely joky treatment of the topic. Joke-dictionaries, offering spurious but engaging definitions, often operate by punning: 'Opéra-bouffe: Nourrit rarement son mélomane' ('Comic opera: rarely nourishes its fans' – *bouffe* = food); 'Calembour: Pointe à pitre' ('Pun: fool's joke' – Point-à-Pitre = capital of Guadaloupe); 'Quintessence: Super-carburant des intellectuels' ('Quintessence: intellectuals' five-star petrol'); 'Atom: one thing that is every bit what it's cracked up to be'.[33] This last item is a sublime tautology, a self-definition which chases its own tail.

Etymology: the genealogy of the word for pun in both English and French is highly dubious, which befits this trope which many consider illegitimate. Best guesses, in English, focus on the possible relation of pun to *punto* or *puntiglio*. Skeat links the word with the verb to *pun*: 'to pound words, beat them into new senses'.[34] These two liken the pun first to a sharp point, then to a bludgeon – a further ambivalence, which does however capture some of its varied effects. For Spitzer weaving his erudite way through *conundrum, quandary, calembour* and *calembredaine*,

> a word meaning whim, 'pun' easily behaves whimsically – just as in all languages, throughout the world, the words for 'butterfly' present a kaleidoscopic instability. The linguist who explains such fluttering words has to juggle, because the speaking community itself (in our case, the English as well as the French) has juggled.[35]

As for French derivation, the most serious is Pierre Guiraud's: like *calembredaine*, from a verb *caller* (= *bavarder*) + *bourder* (= *dire des blagues* – to chatter, to tell jokes).[36] The word breeds or embraces: *calembour, calembredaine, carambolage, cambriolage, cabrioles* (pun, jest, cannon (in billiards) burglary, capering). Some would derive *calembour* and *calembredaine* from each other, in a kind of infinite regress. A 'popular' (i.e. false-scholarly) etymology was 'calamaio-burlare' (= to play with an ink-well). Less phonetically far-fetched, and a punning explanation in itself, is the suggestion *kalos burgos* (= 'beau tour'). *Burgos* does not exist but *purgos* does and means 'tower' (*tour* in another way).[37] Another old favourite links *calembour* and the Pfaffe von Kalemberg, who may have been a trickster at the court of the Austrian Duke Otto of Steiermark, and who became or perhaps always was legendary. Finally, Sardou tied the word with *calambour* (a fragrant resinous heart-wood), and spun a yarn about an abbé, trying to improvise a song at a social gathering and desperately using 'du bois de calambour' for a rhyme. His jamming on the word so amused the listeners that it passed into proverbial usage and eventually to its present meaning.[38] As a dictionary-maker at the start of the nineteenth century, we see Nodier protesting: 'Calembourg: Mot nouveau qu'il faudrait bien se garder d'admettre dans la langue, si le mauvais genre d'esprit qu'il désigne pouvait s'anéantir avec lui' ('Pun: New Word which we should refrain from accepting into the language, if only the poor kind of wit which it designates could be obliterated along with it').[39] No protectionism has ever succeeded in keeping out this permanent illegal immigrant.

When it comes to distinctions between puns and plays on words, it appears that the French are keener on distinguos and classification than the messy British. 'Le jeu de mots', proclaims Bally, 'est la réalisation discursive de l'homonymie sémantique, le calembour la réalisation discursive de l'homonymie phonologique.'[40] Guiraud parts playing *with* words and playing *on* words, but places, rather strangely, rebuses in the former category and anagrams in the latter.[41] Caradec puts himself squarely in the Surrealist tradition, when he claims that 'le calembour est le jeu de mots par excellence. Il en a la gratuité nécessaire' ('The pun is wordplay par excellence. It has the same essential gratuitousness').[42] The best extant English study of puns, by Hughes and Hammond, hovers between Surrealist preferences (for them, puns are 'irrational, capricious, arbitrary', whereas plays on words are 'rational, erudite') and an attempt at Gallic taxonomy. Here, luckily perhaps, they get entangled in their own discourse on the 'untangled pun', and rarely let the scholastic better the gelastic.

One time when the two traditions agree is in the term and notion of 'doublet': one of a pair; one of two words from the same root but differing in meaning (e.g. in French *humeur/humour*). In addition, in English, this word doubles up over a range of contexts: a word printed twice by mistake; a combination of two lenses; a brace of birds shot down with a double-barrelled gun; the same number on both dice; a counterfeit gem; and a garment – all senses but the last having some overlap with our purposes in this book. Some distinctions are unavoidable, for instance that between polysemy (one word used in different senses, like 'doublet') and homophony (several words distinct in meaning but sounding alike); or between homonyms, single words for different things, and their opposite synonyms, different words for single things. It might be argued, however, that to pun is to treat homonyms as synomyns. Franklin holds

homonyms to be 'inherently humorous'.[43] Further subdivisions include heteronyms, words identical in spelling, but different in both sound and meaning
(tear = weeping, tear = rip): these are used especially in off-rhymes, either
hymnal or comic; and homographs, words identical in spelling and pronunciation, but having different origins and meanings (as in race = rush and nation).

 A(n)tanaclasis, traductio, adnominatio, paronomasia, adfictio, skesis, polyptoton:
these are some of the rebarbative terms bandied about by traditional rhetoric.
Many commentators have remarked on the state of extreme confusion between
each of them. Homegrown words for puns have proliferated over the ages:
clinch, quibble, carwhitchet, fetch (i.e. a long stretch, a far-reaching effect), and
bring in variety, if not defining clarity. Perhaps the key notion of rhetoric is that
of decorum – the right thing in the right place, and the pun is obviously anti-
decorum, though it often adjusts its dress, for secrecy and the greater final
effect. As Barthes reminds us, there is in rhetoric, as in literary history, a
persistent counter-tradition or anti-rhetoric, 'une rhétorique noire: jeux,
parodies, allusions érotiques ou obscènes, plaisanteries de collège'. He stresses
that this is no fortuitous coincidence but a deliberate one, 'où deux tabous sont
levés: celui du langage et celui du sexe' ('A black rhetoric: games, parodies,
erotic or obscene allusions, schoolboys' jokes, where two taboos are circumvented: language and sex').[44]

 Transgression, overlap, approximation. The last named is built into the
Greek word *paronomasia* (naming alongside, providing a near-relative to). One
near-relative to paronomasia, coincidentally, is the rare word *paronomesis*, which
means illegality. Paragram is the term for a play on words involving the
alteration of one or more letters – one of the commonest forms of punning.
Hughes and Hammond use the term 'assonant pun' for this variety (as in
'There's a vas deferens between children and no children') which is both self-
evident, tautological, and yet rams a point home. Paronym is another word for
such near-misses (or transvestites). Strangely or not, these approximations are
more pointed, often, than 'perfect' puns: 'en attendant dodo' ('waiting for bye-
byes' – a pithy comment on this play);[45] 'a pornographer is one who offers a vice
to the lovelorn.'[46] The divine Peter-pun is more perfect, too perfect, in French
(*Pierre–pierre*). Such puns can often be too exact, suggest the *déjà vu*, and the
listener may well think not 'I wish I'd thought of that,' but rather 'I'm glad I
didn't.' Spontaneity, though not essential, is prized. Many puns are nonce-
words, special usages for special occasions, one-offs. They are makeshift, with
all that implies of improvisation and rerouting. The French tend to use
paronomase rather more for clang-effects (as in 'tu parles, Charles').[47] But many
'perfect' puns are thus echoic and unproductive. 'Why are red ribbons so very
common in France? Because their name is Legion.'[48] Such puns are
pachydermous. I relish, at the other extreme, an absolutely terrible but lovable
pis-aller like this one: a man forgets to buy his wife her favourite anemones for

her birthday. The shop has only some greenery left, which he purchases. But the forgiving wife exclaims on his return: 'With fronds like these, who needs anemones?'[49] This is another kind of reversal: a formula normally used in a hostile context is here twisted for reuse in a conciliatory one. Apparently forced into a corner by the question: 'How do we ever get *new* verbal creations such as a poem?' the behaviourist Watson replied: 'The answer is that we get them by manipulating words, shifting them about until a new pattern is hit upon.' He went on to use the analogy of the dress-designer, Patou, working with lengths of material on a model, until satisfied (by his own standards and the acclaim of bystanders) that he had created something new and fetching.[50] This is protracted adhocism, and few poets or even punsters can rely on such a sycophantic and patient audience while they play hit-or-miss. 'A tied pub is presumably a trussed house.'[51] This is a pleonastic pun; the second part simply rephrases the first. It is like uninspired design.

We are all approximate people; as such the off-pun is our natural idiom. Maybe we shudder at Quasimodo (who might have been even more aptly named Grossomodo), because he makes full use of his limited resources, whereas we make limited use of our wholeness. It is too comforting to claim that, one-eyed, hunch-backed, crook-shanked, 'Quasimodo n'était guère qu'un à-peu-près' ('Quasimodo was only a near-miss').[52] Like the fearless Quasimodo, the approximate pun goes out on a limb. Outcasts are not to be spurned. After praising Ogden Nash's understanding of 'the athletic grace of distant miscegenated rhymes', Charney says: 'Perhaps half-puns and quarter-puns, like partial rhymes, make more teasing, and poignant examples than the more obvious, full-blooded puns.'[53] Even bad puns can be good, or bad. Fowler lays down the law against dogmatism very eloquently:

> The assumption that puns are *per se* contemptible, betrayed by the habit of describing every pun not as a *pun*, but as a *bad pun* or a *feeble pun*, is a sign at once of sheepish docility and desire to seem superior. Puns are good, bad, and indifferent and only those who lack the wit to make them are unaware of the fact.[54]

The nearest Hughes and Hammond get to value-judgements is the term 'bathos'. Their reluctance to make them is understandable, and it may be that they were working on the premise of a related book:

> Often consideration of a poor example [of a paradox], by virtue of its imperfection, tells one more than consideration of a prime example, in its perfection. For us, all the paradoxes in this book add up to a definition of what a paradox is.[55]

This is no doubt an accommodating view, but if paradoxes, or puns, are not accommodating, they lose much of their distinctiveness: hold-alls, catch-alls.

Such reluctance to exclude I find more engaging that the pious sentiments of the following, which argues that the kind of criticism appropriate to high literature is inadequate for dealing with bad puns.

> The frequent use of the bad pun by the greatest of all English writers, Shakespeare, makes it difficult to dismiss out of hand. The delight afforded to those of all classes by the bad pun cannot be explained in high literary terms. It may be that this play on words, and the distortion of language that is frequently involved, is a means whereby individuality is expressed, due order and the rational are subverted, and personal independence asserted, while at the same time – in the response it evokes – a sense of community is shared. Though the bad pun cannot be accounted for in the terms of high art, its cultural importance (in the anthropological sense) and its popularity – transcending class distinctions – are of great significance. The paradox of the bad pun epitomises some of the peculiarities and problems posed by popular literature. Thus, although by high-literary standards the language of popular literature is often weak, analysis appropriate to high literature may not reveal its essential qualities, and what is different is not necessarily inferior.[56]

No doubt Jews and blacks would concur. Why is this writer not harsher on both Shakespeare and the masses? Like his style, much punning is merely verbal hiccups, echolalia: 'Que vit le paysan au bal? Le villageois vit la joie.' There *are* blunt, toothless, lame or hobbling puns, just as there are pointed or vigorous ones. 'Bad puns', says Fadiman, 'depress us as do waxworks, and for the same reason – they are artifice acting like art.'[57] More fully, Stanford argues:

> Nothing is more futile than the irrelevant pun that is based on only a verbal similarity and brings out no contrast, innuendo, or congruity of meaning. Nothing is a clearer sign of incompetent writing than word-play that distracts rather than concentrates the reader's attention.[58]

Tony Tanner takes this on to an even bleaker, and more troubling level (which I will study in detail later):

> There is a curious kind of linguistic desolation engendered by the totally empty pun that doesn't have in it the slightest trace of any semantic shock ... We all know how purely empty, pointless puns ... can suddenly introduce a dead patch into a conversation, as though language had suddenly gone deaf to its obligations and forgotten its purposes ... Compulsive punning ... is not only embarrassing and exhausting but is undoubtedly a symptom of some kind of pathological state – perhaps impotence, regression, or profound insecurity.[59]

It is sometimes argued that wilful bad punning can ascend to a kind of verbal 'high camp'.

These, then, are the shaky foundations of this study. Latitudinarianism will be the mode and mood. I place face to face two Gallic opponents on this matter. The one: 'C'est l'à-peu-près, calembour suprême qui s'avance le plus dans la voie de l'absurde' ('It is the approximate pun which is supreme and the nearest to absurdity').[60] I am not overly drawn to the absurd as an automatic value. And the other, complaining of 'des bavures, une portion du mot en excédent et dont rien ne justifie la présence sinon un pscittacisme puéril' ('overlays, a portion of the word left over and whose presence is unjustifiable except as childish parrot-talk').[61] How can we speak 'sans bavures'? We dribble as we drivel. We are forever 'loosely speaking'; our coverage is, at best, to *some* extents and purposes. 'Trying to define humour is one of the definitions of humour,' as Saul Steinberg averred.[62] Similarly, trying to lasso the pun involves more lunges than contacts. There can be no single definition of this double agent. To use Anthony Burgess's splendid coinage, the pun is by essence 'multiguous'.[63] A glance at a dialect dictionary makes the point: 'PUN: (Devon): a child's pinafore; (Lincolnshire): a funnel-shaped vessel used mainly for heating beer and milk; (Northants): a slow, inactive person; (Scotland): a sham'.[64] Let us not pin puns down. 'A pun . . . is a process.'[65] Better to keep it, and ourselves, on the move, and to pass to its functioning.

2

The Motions of Puns

We found in the previous chapter that the etymology of the words *pun* and *calembour* was not much help. It is time to turn mobile. My gait will be oscillating, because wordplay is self-evidently a matter of polarities. There is an indissoluble link, if I may speak with a po-face, between punning and the number two. (Even 'number one' intriguingly mashes together: one's own self or interests, urination, flogging, first lieutenants, and party leaders). All humour, and much intelligence, entails an ability to think on two planes at once. Eyes need bifocal vision, or squint. Ears need to hear diphthongs – overlaid or mutually contaminating sounds. Bringing together and splitting: splicing can mean either. In the pun, there are always two or more levels, manifest and latent, in some kind of coexistence, sequence, alternation or tension. As metaphors seem unavoidable, it is tempting to speak of sparks jumping a gap, of hinges, of the intersection of two surfaces. But is it not sad that we thus fall back on mechanistic images for such a dynamic phenomenon? Freud resorted to hydraulics: psychic damming, overspill, condensation; and Bergson attempted, against his own avowed proclivity, to petrify the mobile, for, despite his 'élan vital', he seems to have automated our vocabulary. If, as I agree, wordplay allows language 'to move with something like the freedom reality enjoys', and at the same time, or alternately, is 'a verbal situation in which we have simultaneously two different experiences. Our lives consist of moments like that,'[1] then perhaps we may play static and dynamic metaphors off against each other, starting inevitably with that of 'play'.

'Play' and *jeu/jouer* enjoy multiple uses: to desport oneself, to act, to gamble, to be flexible (as when we talk of *le jeu*, or the play, of a mechanism). All of these contain the idea of room for manoeuvre, the French term even more eloquently than the English:

> La lune joue sur les flots et le chaton avec une feuille morte; les facteurs jouent et le bois joue [i.e. warps]; le pâtre joue du flageolet et le mandarin de l'éventail; les blancs jouent et gagnent, Talma aussi; ma mémoire me joue des tours; le spéculateur joue à la baisse et, le dimanche, joue aux boules; je suis joué par mon adversaire, mais ma pièce est jouée aux Français; le sicaire joue du couteau et ensuite joue de malheur.

(Moonlight plays on the waves and kittens with falling leaves; factors exert pressure and wood warps; the shepherd plays his pipes and the mandarin flirts his fan; white is bet and wins, and Talma acts in a play; my memory plays tricks on me; the speculator gambles on a fall in prices and on Sunday plays *boules*; I am outwitted by my rival, but my play is performed at the Français; the thug wields his knife but then runs out of luck.)[2]

Because of the *play* of a hinge, a door *works* loose. Benveniste sums up the plurivalency, the self-contradiction: 'Le même vocable (*le jeu*) semble signifier à la fois mouvement ou contrainte ou artifice ou facilité en exercise' ('The same word (*le jeu*) appears to signify at the same time movement or constraint or artifice or ease of manoeuvre').[3]

Wordplay, or turns on words. The key movement of the pun is pivotal. The second meaning of a word or phrase rotates around the first one. Or branches off from it; puns are switch words, like pointsmen at a junction. The action of Claude Simon's novel *La Route des Flandres* hinges on a change from the word *saumure* (brine) to Saumur (the military garrison). This pivotal wordplay enables the story to bifurcate (and later to double back on itself). This is part of the process of self-propelling spread so essential to Simon's fictional imagination and world. Ricardou calls this kind of pun 'transitaire et structural'.[4] It generally involves a shift of emphasis ('Did you hear about the plastic surgeon who fell asleep in front of a roaring fire? He melted'). This betokens a sidestepping or kangaroo mind. Trains of thought benefit from being rerouted. The advertisement for toilet-paper which boasted that it was 'Tops for Bottoms' was playing on an ancient tradition of inverting usual hierarchies as a means of focusing attention. Puns are each-way bets, and Elizabethan slang used 'reverence' for faeces.[5] Linguistic history itself goes in for such about-faces: 'excrement' used to mean 'moustache'. Laughter, and fresh ways of looking, alike depend often on the clash or merger between two universes, 'a differential gap, i.e. an awareness of an identity within the difference, or of a difference between the identity'.[6] Puns often have the same logic as Carroll's Alice: ' "Then you should say what you mean", the March Hare went on. "I do", Alice hastily replied; "at least – at least I mean what I say – that's the same thing, you know." '[7] Many puns are situational. They ply between two contexts, switching one for the other.

Two butterflies are on a daisy in a polo field with poloists bearing down upon a ball at rest just beneath them; the caption, a speech of one of the butterflies, connects the language of teenagers incongruously with the situation of pastoral: 'The first one to fly off is chicken'.[8]

Similarly, the chiasmus, or 'Crosse-Copling' as Puttenham termed it,[9] exchanges opposites, works a pointed criss-cross: 'Some co-eds pursue learning, others learn pursuing.'[10] By such rearrangements, meaning is inflicted.

Schopenhauer takes a stern, killjoy and impossibly precise view of all this:

> Just as the witticism brings two very different real objects under one concept, the pun brings two different concepts, by the assistance of accident, under one word. The same contrast appears only familiar and more superficial, because it does not spring from the nature of things, but merely from the accident of nomenclature. In the case of the witticism, the identity is in the concept, the difference in the reality, but in the case of the pun the difference is in the concepts and the identity in the reality, for the terminology is here the reality.[11]

Schopenhauer is in effect distinguishing here between the pointed and the pointless pun (i.e. mere sound-coincidence). No doubt much of the argument for and against punning arises from confusing the two types. As for myself, believing in overlap, I must accept some confusion; and, in the process, we may at times find some point even in apparent pointlessness, just as nonsense can teach wise lessons.

John Gross, in his study of Joyce, talks of 'fission and fusion';[12] Joel Sherzer writes: 'What is interesting about puns is that they can operate both ways – cohesively or disjunctively.'[13] My version would read 'centripetally or centrifugally'. Whichever metaphor is selected, puns clearly make a twofold attack. They make us stretch our minds and double our attention. The opposite (but therefore related) business to 'far-fetched' is: pushing something too far; extending and contracting are interrelated. Do puns distract, or concentrate, the attention? No doubt the worst do the former and the best do both. An example of splitting, of fission, and near the knuckle: 'Britons never shall be slaves, only Europe peons.'[14] An example of fusion (and the equivalent in punning to a mixed metaphor): René Crevel on the clichés surrounding literary reputations and prizes: ' "On cherche un écrivain et on trouve un homme." Cette formule, nous la laissons à tous les mijoteurs, cuiseurs, distributeurs, amateurs du Gâteau Littéraire, dont elle est le four banal'. (' "You look for a writer and find a man." We leave this cliché for all those who cook up, tout and plug the Literary Cake, for which it is the communal oven/common-or-garden flop').[15]

Fission and fusion – such nuclear proliferation also has its dangers (madness, for one). 'Le jeu de mots est une petite révolution: il provoque souvent l'explosion d'une vieille structure et y installe, en son lieu, de nouvelles formes possibles.'[16] An explosive play occurs in these lines from Hugo (and we should bear in mind that le chien is the hammer of a gun and bander le chien is to cock a pistol): 'Tous nos héroïsmes viennent de nos femmes. Un homme sans femme, c'est un pistolet sans chien. C'est la femme qui fait partir l'homme.'[17]

Defending himself against the charge that his pages swarmed with puns, Thomas Hood affirmed his intention 'to persist in using the double barrel as long as meanings will rise in coveys'.[18] Crosbie advises: 'Never point a pun at a friend. It might be loaded.'[19] Like all would-be aggressive activities, wordplay can backfire on us (or chase and swallow its own tail):

> Hard is the job to launch the desperate pun,
> A pun-job dangerous as the Indian one
> ... Like the strange missile which the Australian throws,
> Your verbal boomerang slaps you on the nose.[20]

As well as moving off, or back, puns can of course mark time, run on the spot. Repetition, as Queneau remarked, is 'une des plus odiférantes fleurs de la rhétorique'.[21] We talk of 'thumping' puns, and the other meaning of the verb 'to pun' is 'to hammer home', as when Thersites says in *Troilus and Cressida*: 'He would pun thee into shivers with his fist.'[22] The better pun does not labour the obvious; it belabours the latent. Similarly, in Zen teaching, the master with his stick does not force truths into the mind of his disciple; rather, 'the truth is beaten out of him.'[23]

Punch-lines often pun, as Legman ruefully admits in describing:

> the development of the modern joke-form in the 'facezia', which has supplanted the longer and more leisurely folktale almost entirely, in certain societies, since the time of Poggio in the mid-15th century. This unique characteristic of the *facezia* or joke ... is the punch-line – so well named.[24]

True: we are in a hurry, and hardly want the build-up to the conclusion: 'Be temperate: our first parents ate themselves out of house and home.'[25] We are too obsessed with wrapping up, sealing, with 'strong completion'; with finishing off. But as well as one-off, punchline puns, there are many examples of progressive, elaborated punning. René Crevel orchestrates an extended, splendidly sacrilegious series, to underline an attack on Christianity for trying to desex the universe. It comes in a chapter titled 'Jésus (Famille et complexes, famille de complexes, complexe de famille)', a programme in itself. Mary is embracing the dying figure on the Cross: 'A feindre cette tendresse posthume, la femme se venge de ce par quoi l'homme en *vie*, en *vit*, l'asser*vit*, prétendit l'asser*vir*, au moins la *cloua* sur sa paillasse'. ('By putting on a show of this posthumous affection, the woman avenges herself on what the man, in his lifetime, in his erection, used to enslave her, claimed to enslave her, or at least nailed her to her bed' [*vit* = penis]).[26] A frequently punning author makes us read in slower motion and backtrack: an irritating but salutary reminder that we normally consume too rapidly, guess too much, miss a great deal. In so doing, we get an overview of the text instead of *suffering* it (as when we listen doggedly to a story of personal woe by someone we respect. We go through it, as far as we can, with them).

In addition to metaphors of mobility, we need also those of stasis and arrangement. Punning is the art of superimposing, and therefore of weighting: a didactic and a rhetorical device. Words are loaded, like dice. Like a bus or a sandwich, the pun is a double-decker. As in an air-jam, meanings are stratified, stacked vertically. As a result, we get simultaneous, competing references in the same unit. 'Puns, as Eisenstein observes, are telescoped montage, or montage by juxtaposition.'[27] The pun overstates by understatement. Like irony (devious emphasis), litotes (negative stress), euphemism (dysphemism is full frontal assault) and 'mental reservations', punning is language and mind at their most jesuitical. The dual-purpose word *cant* fits in well here, for the Romance-derived meaning is a beggar's whine and then hypocrisy, whereas the Germanic one is edge, tilt. Wordplay suits natures that are neither preponderantly straightforward nor esoteric. Its realm is that of the sly, the glancing, the teasing, the oblique. It is neither exclusively virile nor epicene, but androgynous: the area where man and woman overlap, the area of congress.[28] Coyness can, of course be prurience, or give rise to it. We are familiar now with the notion of explicit and implicit codes in literature or in general social discourse. Wordplay, and the study of it, can give access to the implicit. Obliqueness is allusive, and so trackable. Winks give games away. And, as always, we must remember the sheer pleasure of well-ordered roundaboutness, as in Legman's analogy with a 'three-cushion carom in billiards'.[29]

As the lisping guru said, 'There are many words. Take the pith of them.' Punning on *maux*, Valéry wrote: 'Entre deux mots il faut choisir le moindre' ('Choose the lesser of two evils/words').[30] The pun, like a contraceptive, is a labour-saving device. It conserves energy, space and time. In case this makes it sound too cosily domestic, it equally well involves spending. There is a more than verbal continuity between *thrift* and *spendthrift*; saving is hard work. Yet the idea of the least effort beguiles: saving one's breath, economizing on space. 'Small effort, large effect – which may be why those who snob [the pun] always sound as if trying to imply that they never have to make their own beds.'[31] As well as being a labour-saving device, the pun is also a bargain: two meanings for the price of one word or phrase; a bonus. 'Besides the contextual meaning of a word, we are made aware of the word itself, and through the form of a word, of other possible and, if the pun is a good one, appropriate meanings.'[32] In this era of retrenchment, we should welcome the value-for-money of the pun. But then the poor tend to avenge themselves by verbal inflation; Diderot's Jacques the Fatalist held that the only luxury afforded the plebs was the gift of the gab.

Much of this was dress-rehearsed by Freud in *Jokes and their Relation to the Unconscious*. Having summarized the economizing tendencies (condensation, multiple use), he has the honest grace to think against himself. He quotes 'the way in which some housewives economise when they spend time and money on a journey to a distant market because vegetables are to be had there a few farthings cheaper'. In so doing he casts doubt on the validity of his own metaphors. He goes on: 'Is not the economy in words uttered more than balanced by the expenditure on intellectual effort? And who saves by that? Who gains by it?'[33] He thus anticipates Greig's criticism that, while saving on words is economical, there is no real correspondence between this and 'economy of psychic expenditure' since the latter involves extra effort – to see and to take the point; it is an active, not a passive phenomenon. For Greig, the whole process entails not economy but speed, and thus, he adds, 'wit is notoriously fatiguing.'[34] This is undoubted. As Pascal knew, succinctness takes time; compression is long-winded. Double messages are overloaded and can cause overloading. Though Freud himself realized the deficiency of his image, he can be further defended by arguing that he was trying to economize, that is to rescue or isolate a unity amid the plethora of material. And his honesty led him to keep on *multiplying* his examples, stretching his categories further and further to see if they would still fit. His fuller formula is more convincing: 'Economy in expenditure on inhibition or suppression'. This is an awkwardly negative way of expressing his own obsession with the phenomenon of 'damming up'. Any agent of release is therefore welcomed to the fold, and a few pages later he equates 'economy' and 'relief', and later again prefers the second term. After the housewife practising false economy by shopping around, he moves to an analogy with a business enterprise.[35] As it grows, economizing (while still important) is less crucial; investment produces expansion, spending money to make money (with of course the risk of throwing good money after bad!). As Batlay commented, we might swop Freud's term 'economy' for 'enrichment': 'Ce qui revient au même: par l'épargne on s'enrichit' ('which comes to the same thing: by saving you grow richer').[36]

While it saves labour, wordplay puts to work. The pun is often an epigram or wisecrack: the sting-in-the-tail, as in Ambrose Bierce's definition of the Sabbath, with its nice play on *rested/arrested*: 'A weekly festival having its origin in the fact that God made the world in six days and was arrested on the seventh'.[37] If needed brevity be the soul of wit, the pun is the antithesis of the shaggy-dog story, which 'is only told in a society which has been saturated with joke stories. The joke of the tale that goes on in a declining spiral to a nadir of pointlessness lies in the dashed expectations of the listeners.'[38] A joke about bad jokes: a metajoke. Pure perversity, like practical jokes; the build-up, then the let-down. Thus the set-up pun (like the criminal 'sting') climaxing the contrived anecdote, of the type 'Putting all your Basques in one exit', is too laborious a cheat. For George Mikes, 'even the best joke necessarily remains the one-yard sprint.'[39] On this score, the shaggy-dog story would approximate more, if only quantitively, to high art. In fact, many such stories do end with a clinching pun or exaggerated bathos.

'Unlike children, puns should be heard, not seen.'[40] Many prefer the idea of a listening public, an audience, to that of a reading public, when it comes to puns; and such distinguish between the orthographic and the auditory or phonological varieties. 'All plays on words, good or bad', claims Greig, 'depend for their effect on the conjunction of similar sound with different meaning, and require us to attend to both sound and meaning.'[41] But *how* do we 'attend'? I suspect that, often, we read sounds, or perhaps simultaneously read-and-mutter. In addition, many a purely acoustic pun evaporates on emission to become an 'aboli bibelot d'inanité sonore' ('a useless trinket of sonorous inanity').[42] As Hugh Kenner points out, 'Printing and its by-product lexico-graphy enforced a uniformity of spelling which gave each word a stable identity to the eye, whatever its equivocal status for the ear.'[43] When he wrote this, around 1964, Kenner assumed that we were still under the thrall of a print-culture. Nearly twenty years later, there are signs of a move towards (anarchic) phonetic spelling. It remains to be seen whether this drawing together of the graphic and the phonic will abort or engender punning. I suggest the latter, as there would be fewer ways of writing the same (or increasing) number of words, and so multiple duty would rule. Poetry, at least, in Valéry's paronomasic formula, will perhaps go on being 'cette hésitation prolongée entre le son et le sens'.[44] McLuhan sounds unduly prescriptive when he states:

> The reader's eye not only prefers one sound, one tone, in isolation; it prefers one meaning at a time. Simultaneities like puns and ambiguities – the life of spoken discourse – become, in writing, affronts to taste, floutings of efficiency.[45]

Even, or especially, lawyers do not believe that. The venerable 'hare' pun ('Is that thine own hare, or is it a wig?'), which combines 'an absolute identity of sound with an equally absolute and therefore ludicrous disparity of meaning'[46] – a gloss which covers over the cracks in the material – is just as feeble in its oral as in its written manifestations. Finally, one factor which does justify distinctions between written and heard puns: heteronyms, or spell-alikes (*bow*: to bend, *bow*: weapon) which are pronounced differently, are much rarer than homophones, or sound-alikes, in punning.

'Maybe you don't like the merely acoustical pun – think only the pun with a point or meaning is worth while.'[47] As well as concision, puns entail incision: a cutting-edge or a point (we saw earlier that *punto* or *puntiglio* are amongst the best guesses as to derivation). Puns can be biting, or of course toothless, gummy. Hughes and Hammond evince a preference for what they call the 'arbitrary pun' over the 'erudite' play on words. Their cultural heritage leans towards Surrealism, and they take little account of the pointed variety; for them, this kind is no doubt overly rational. Let me slip this one in, as the actor said to the bishop. My own favourite concerns the doctor MP who, bewailing in the House the faecal beaches of Britain, said: 'You can no longer actually swim off our coasts. All you can do is go through the motions.' This is true double duty: dual sound, coalesced meaning, a whole speech in miniature. The need to pronounce those last four words in a deliberate voice mimes the clogged activity in question. Similarly: 'It takes a lot of excises to keep Uncle Sam fiscally fit.' While stating the obvious (that taxes are essential to the national economy), the sound and rhythm, a bit breathless, as after chin-ups, mimes and thus underlines the topic. A third perfect double function: 'Said the circus manager to the human cannonball who wanted to leave: "You can't quit! Where will I find another man of your calibre?" '[48] One reading slots inside the other like the artist in his gun-barrel. But what are we to make of this pun: 'What does a rabbit take for its throat? Coney-linctus'? Meaningless? Far-fetched? Designed merely to smuggle in a taboo word? Or does it have some validity, some point? For instance: eating people is right; imbibing a woman is good for you (and her). 'A critic is a man who pans for gold':[49] this is a good working pun, since a critic does sieve, and is paid for an often destructive activity.

So far, I have considered puns primarily as stimulus, as attack. But what of reception, response? Nearly all of us pun on occasion, even if only to the extent of realizing when we have made an involuntary one that we have indeed punned. It could be that the sometimes guilty pleasure we derive from punning stems from a kind of instinctive word-association itself: the sense that twists on words are connected in some fashion with ethical twisting. As a result, the punster simultaneously begs for a pat on the back and dreads a punch on the nose. Hence the defiance in his apologetic stance, the mixture of brazen summoning and cautious warding off.

As for the receiver (who, like the fence for stolen goods, is in a fishy position), he often utters nervous laughter, uncertain whether or not to plump for the obscene or dangerous meaning, and afraid of being thought dense or prudish. If he laughs, he frequently becomes an accomplice in the assault on a taboo. The deliverer, for his part, often either leers, or enunciates slowly, idiot-fashion, to underline the subsidiary meaning. It may well be this special voice, articulating unnaturally, which alienates audiences. Perhaps it reminds too much of parents' weary explanations or schoolteachers' ponderous sarcasms.

At its best, of course, the pun abolishes these barriers of resistance. Like all art, it requires distancing, the right distance. Too great, and the pun is 'far-fetched'. Too short, and it is not worth a detour. The right timing, too. You need a double-take ('Come again,' as the actress said to the bishop), but a quick one. We need to twig, to catch or cotton on, to dig, to get (the hang of), to rumble, to savvy, to tumble to, to smell a rat, 'soupçonner anguille sous roche', to read into, or between, the lines; even intransitively the rising pun can dawn on us. Surely all these implications: penetration, intuition, decoding, are pleasurable and boosting. Playing with the idea of *double entente*, Balzac coined the phrase 'des mots à double détente', where the twin ideas of explosion and release coexist. Puns, which rely on linguistic accidents, aim for a coincidence of ideas. There are many mismatches. Dowden said that Shakespeare's 'thought is more rapid than the language',[50] and this can create imbalance between interlocutors. The deliverer can 'see it coming', and so, in another sense, can the receiver of a poor pun. The jest's prosperity lies in the ear of the beholder and the eye of the listener.

Oblique, the pun counts on allusions being spotted. In the response to my appeal to *Guardian* readers for help with this study, one honest reply stated: 'Why do I like puns? In part it is a form of intellectual snobbery because it shows an ability to think laterally; in part it is companionable in that if you understand a pun or one of yours is understood, it implies a rapport.'[51] Another view puts this more piously and speciously:

> Observez un faiseur de calembours. Son goût pour l'association de mots le prédispose tout naturellement à la communion d'idées et lui confère, partant, d'exceptionnelles vertus de sociabilité. C'est quelqu'un de plus sensible à ce qui rapproche qu'à ce qui sépare. Bref c'est un conciliateur né.

> (Watch a punster. His taste for word-association predisposes him quite naturally to the sharing of ideas and grants him in consequence exceptional qualities of sociability. He is someone who is more alive to what brings together than what drives apart. In short, he is a born conciliator.)[52]

As I believe punning to have more often than not some aggressive charge, I find this view of the ecumenical pun hard to swallow. Similarly, Paul Jennings' rather bland assumption that 'puns are made in convivial company, aware of the quicksilver nature of language,'[53] leaves out the gallows, concentration-camps, death-beds and mental hospitals, in all of which, as we will see later, punning sustains or kicks against life. Molly Mahood, as so often, strikes the right note in defining the necessary responsive company, 'which will not be critical of our absurdity nor shocked by the disclosure of normally inhibited feelings; [in it] we pun freely and intentionally.'[54] Batlay pulls the bonds even tighter, when she speaks of 'cette fraternité (comme dans les sociétés secrètes) qui isole sur un plan supérieur ceux qui se comprennent à demi-mot' ('This brotherhood (as in secret societies) which sets apart on a higher level those who know how to take a hint').[55] Blackmantle takes the all-inclusive, undeceived stance: if the pun is good, he states, 'you laugh at the pun; if bad, at the punster; and in either case, he is almost certain to laugh himself.'[56]

Yet, by common consent, puns make people groan, squirm, flinch, grimace or wince, as we do of course when we witness a physical collision, a painful conjunction, taking place. We feel wounded, but where, and why? Grotjahn says soberingly:

> The listener admires the pun more for the effort and ingenuity which goes into it than because he enjoys the wit. The pun usually does not liberate enough repressive energy to make us really laugh; as a rule, we groan.[57]

This genuflection to Freud (who had a better sense of humour than his disciples) at least stresses the *physical* element which seems essential to wordplay. But I am less keen on Ludovici's implicit reduction of the human to the simian or canine:

> We show teeth at a pun, in the first place because the repetition of similar sounding words in one sentence is, as Bergson points out, sometimes unintentional and a sign of absent-mindedness (that is to say, inferior adaptation). Alexander Bain also suggested two further reasons. In the grasping of a pun there is self-glory (superior adaptation) at having noticed the play on words, and there is triumph over the degradation of a nobler word.[58]

For his part, Koestler demonstrates the limitations of the stimulus-response, behaviourist approach when he writes:'Laughter is a reflex but unique in that it has no apparent biological purpose. One might call it a luxury reflex. Its only function seems to be to provide relief from tension.'[59] This is a luxury? A more moderate objection comes in Eastman's remarks: 'Even in the most loose and foolish of hilarious discourse, a pun comes a little alien, like the attempts at congeniality of a drunkard or of a person whose reason is slightly touched.'[60] Eastman seems to object to punning as making us too separately conscious of words. I am reminded of the old story of the person who, having had explained to him how the muscles and bones of his body actually operated, was then unable to get out of his chair; analysis seen as break-down, disabling.

> Puns have two evil Ends:
> Sometimes they gain us Foes,
> Sometimes they make us lose
> Our Friends.[61]

Whatever the risks involved, many persist. It could be that, obscurely, wordplayers sense that they tread on very basic territory: meaning, communication, the nature of reality itself. A French view ventures out on this limb:

> Le calembour est une tautologie distendue qui miroite de signification, une incantation explosive qui joue de la répétition pour mieux la détruire et entraîne l'esprit sur la pente du Même pour mieux laisser prévoir l'irruption de l'Autre.

(The pun is a stretched tautology, shimmering with meaning, an explosive incantation which plays on repetition all the better to destroy it, and drags the mind along the slope of the Same the better to leave room for the break-in of the Other.)[62]

On the same lines, 'les anciens grammairiens disaient: homonymie, un mot pour deux idées; polysémie, deux idées pour un mot.'[63] Is this not as broad as it is long? Double or quits? Wordplay depends on formal identity and semantic difference. The mind begins to boggle. Let us turn to Robert Frost:

> T. S. Eliot and I have our similarities and our differences. We are both poets and we both like to play. That's the similarity. The difference is this: I like to play euchre; he liked to play eucharist.[64]

Freud quoted Kuno Fischer's finding that, in a large number of joking judgements, differences rather than similarities were found.[65]

'The *Paronomasia*, or Pun, is well known in ordinary conversation, and in comic writing, but rarely enters into serious composition.'[66] Just how wrong Bain was in this claim will be amply indicated in the next chapter.

3

Making History I

The worship of the word must be pagan and polytheistic. It cannot endure one god.[1]

This chapter will have the semblance of chronology but, like history itself, will proceed in fact by lurches, anticipations, cross-leaps, back-pedals and stalls. The pun, like the great god Pan, gets everywhere and will not be confined. There will inevitably be a good deal of name-dropping, but perhaps some Augean stable-boy will sweep up at the end.

The movement, in human development, cannot be from serious to playful, from perfection to decadence. Everything was mixed from the start. Hence the primordial importance of the myths of Chaos and of Babel. The pun was at home in such beginnings. 'In all the wild imaginings of mythology, a fanciful spirit is playing on the border-line between jest and earnest,' advances Huizinga and, later, he talks of 'boundless exaggeration and confusion of proportions, carefree inconsistencies and whimsical variations'. At this level belief almost certainly, he maintains, must have been tinged with humour.[2] Across the world, according to Blyth,

> in ancient Sanskrit literature there is an almost unbelievable amount of punning. Puns were the delight of a small number of great men with unsolemn minds. They felt that the universe was humorous, that the words which express it have some 'metaphysical' correlation and parallelism with it, so that mere rhyme itself reveals or rather hints at occult relations unsuspected by the solemnities of common sense and the logic of philology in prose.[3]

We should not assume that such wordplay was always an in-game for scholars (though as we will see later, it was sometimes this). As Clastres points out:

> the fact must be taken into account that a myth can simultaneously speak of serious things and set those who hear it laughing . . . It is not unusual for these ['primitive'] cultures to entrust their myths with the job of entertaining the people by de-dramatising, as it were, their existence.

Thus the transmission of both culture and amusement can produce a gay science.[4] I do not want to topple any more unnecessary matter into 'that luckless dustbin of pseudo-scientific fantasies – the mind of primitive man',[5] but I would quarrel with any linear account, such as Mercier's: 'It seems likely that plays on words were given magical significance before they were thought of as comic . . . I am convinced that the evolutionary sequence from word play to wit holds good in all languages.'[6] This denies not only the coexistence of seriousness and play, but of the primitive in the sophisticated and vice versa.

Preferring to believe in mess, overlap and struggle, I am more attracted by Lévi-Strauss' proposal of the links between mythology and *bricolage* – a concept which brings together some of the themes already considered: obliqueness, mobility, adhocism, parasitism, creativity.

> Dans son sens ancien, le verbe *bricoler* s'applique au jeu de balle et de billard, à la chasse et à l'équitation, mais toujours pour évoquer un mouvement incident: celui de la balle qui rebondit, du chien qui divague, du cheval qui s'écarte de la ligne droite pour éviter un obstacle. Et, de nos jours, le bricoleur reste celui qui oeuvre de ses mains, en utilisant des moyens détournés par comparaison avec ceux de l'homme de l'art. Or, le propre de la pensée mythologique est de s'exprimer à l'aide d'un répertoire dont la composition est hétéroclite et qui, bien entendu, reste tout de même limité; pourtant, il faut qu'elle s'en serve, quelle que soit la tâche qu'elle s'assigne, car elle n'a rien d'autre sous la main. Elle apparaît ainsi comme une sorte de bricolage intellectuel.

> (In its old sense, the verb *bricoler* is used for ball-games and billiards, hunting and riding, but always in order to describe an extraneous movement: a ball bouncing, a dog darting off, a horse swerving from the straight line to avoid an obstacle. And nowadays the *bricoleur* works with his hands, using materials to hand, unlike the craftsman. Now the essence of mythical thinking is to express itself with the help of a repertoire of heterogeneous material but which, of course, remains limited; however, it has to use this, whatever the task it sets itself, for it has nothing else at its disposal. Thus it appears as a kind of intellectual *bricolage*.)[7]

Punners are such intellectual do-it-yourselfers, verbal handymen, using whatever is 'at hand', recycling odds and ends.

Against Huizianga's joyous celebration of the humorous part of mythology, Max Müller nearly a century before proposed that mythology:

> is in truth a disease of language. A myth means a word, but a word which, from being a name or an attribute, has been allowed to assume a more substantial existence. Most of the Greek, the Roman, the Indian and other heathen gods are nothing but poetical names, which were gradually allowed to assume a divine personality never contemplated by their original inventors.

All of this was 'the bane of the ancient world'.[8] Such men see myth as 'the product of men's vain, futile and misguided attempts to express the inexpressible and to verbalise that which is ineffable'.[9] An opposite tack, in which the modern is devalued in comparison with the ancient, is taken by Regnaud, for whom in modern languages,

> dans tous les cas, le calembour est artificiel, c'est un effet voulu, personnel, sans attaches directes avec les lois qui président au développement général du langage, et qui par cela même reste isolé et infécond. Il amuse un instant par la surprise qu'il cause à l'esprit, et c'est tout.

> (In every case, punning is artificial, it is a chosen and personal product, with no direct links with the laws governing the general development of language, and therefore remaining isolated and unproductive. It entertains for a moment by the jolt it gives the mind, but that is all.)

Whereas plays on words in the Hindu Rig-Veda 'sont naturels et sortent des entrailles mêmes du langage, sans que la volonté de celui qui les produit y ait généralement la moindre part' ('are natural and emerge from the very entrails of language without the will of the person producing them having any say in the process'). This is less flattering than it sounds, for Regnaud's premise concerning the evolution of languages causes him to see the Vedic hymns as a primitive stage and this 'natural' punning as a passive phenomenon: 'Loin d'être complices des erreurs qui en résultent leurs auteurs en sont dupes et se sont pris aux illusions dont ils étaient les agents inconscients' ('Far from being accomplices to the errors which result, their authors are duped by them and caught up in the illusions for which they were the unwitting agents'). Thus 'agni' (fire, especially sacrificial flames, but also 'the brilliant one', and thus a god). He does not go as far as Müller and talk of an inherent malady in early language, as he finds it 'natural' to slide from the idea of shining to burning, and then to suffering.[10] The element of *chiding* is equally apparent, however, in both views, which are perhaps less diametrically opposed than it seemed at first.

Both see, in effect, such communication as *lapsus linguae*, dependent on *lapsus mentis*, and while involuntary punning is part of the total story, it is only part. The whole area of slips will be studied extensively later, but I wish now to stress the deliberate cultivation of double meaning, again from the earliest times. On a more serious level than conundrums, oracles have worked by inserting word-games into predictive riddles. 'The Delphic oracle, telling a general both to stay at home and not to stay at home, employed a pun: "Domine, stes" sounds the same as "Domi ne stes." The enquirer took the latter meaning, went out to battle and was killed.'[11] Punners always like to have it both ways, as the actress and the bishop said in unison. 'For goddes speken in amphibologyes.'[12] No doubt the divine motive was more to flummox than to enlighten, but, beyond that, a kind of purely verbal affinity seems to have been at play. As Heraclitus declared: 'The Lord whose oracle is in Delphi neither declares nor conceals but gives a sign.'[13] On omens and divination in Mesopotamia, Oppenheim writes:

> Only exceptionally are we able to detect any logical relationship between portent and prediction, although often we find paronomastic associations ... In many instances, subconscious association seems to have been at work, provoked by certain words whose specific connotations imported to them a favourable or an unfavourable character, which in turn determined the general nature of the prediction.[14]

Commenting on the same phenomenon among the Assyrians and Babylonians, Conteneau mentions also the factor that Sumerian, a learned language, was written mainly in ideograms, and these, principally monosyllabic in value, often have several meanings, as in modern Chinese, for the same sign. In these circumstances, he finds it hardly surprising if some presages were deduced from puns.[15]

If the universe and its superior beings, the Gods, were often felt to be having fun at human expense, it is expectable that the ambiguity of language should be deified, as it was in the classical shapes of Hermes/Mercury 'the rogue-god, who presides over language'.[16] In the *Cratylus*, talking part jokingly to Hermogenes, Socrates says: 'I should imagine that the name Hermes has to do with speech, and signifies that he is the interpreter, or messenger, or thief, or liar, or bargainer; all that sort of thing has a great deal to do with language.'[17] Very true, but that is a great deal of meaning for one name to house. Hermes did indeed start in life by thieving, acted as courier and protector of travellers, presided over trade both legal and crooked, and embodied eloquence, so necessary for all such activities. Not only the pun then, but language in its wider use has dubious ancestry. Hermes' legendary fleetness of foot was no less essential to his life-style and his survival, and the two chief aspects are interconnected: 'The messenger of the gods, Hermes, is also the god of speech because he is always on the move ... The classical Greeks recognised the difference between the continuous nature of speech and the discrete nature of language.'[18] From the twin source we get 'mercurial' and 'hermetical', which both have their points of contact with wordplay. Hermes had characteristic protean qualities. Though on the very day of his birth he stole Apollo's cattle, he was later adopted as the patron of herds and flocks. Small wonder that he has often been likened to the trickster figure of numerous other cultures, and like such figures he enjoyed or suffered from the frequent divine attribute of a split personality. Another composite mythological creature was Chiron the centaur, a great pedagogue whose pupils included Hercules, Achilles, Theseus and Jason. One of the several French variants for portmanteau-word (as we will see, a prime source of wordplay) is *mot-centaure*. Puns and pedagogy, puns and duality (man/beast, low/lofty):

> The Janus word makes of human speech a slippery instrument. It is, however, the reflection of the double nature of man himself, of the contradiction that lies at the very heart of humanity. In Eden man knew no ambiguity, but when he fell, he became Janus-faced, a *parvus mundus* of opposites, perilously poised at the juncture of nature and spirit, the riddle of the crossroads, the glory and jest of the world.[19]

Man is an oxymoronic pun. The Metaphysical poets, Pascal and Baudelaire might agree on this.

The Judaeo-Christian tradition is not unique in making God an intensely verbal creator, giving the world a verbal fillip. With the later institutionalization of religion, perhaps the most famous of all puns came into operation: that on Peter/*petra*, as the cornerstone of Christianity. 'There is indeed a common human tendency to endow proper names with connotation by punning or fanciful etymology,' notes Caird. He goes on with the example of Jacob, whose 'name is derived from the word for "heel" and explained by the curious circumstance of his birth [i.e. holding on his twin Esau's heel]; in modern terms, he was Heel by name and spent most of his life living up to it.'[20] Against the common explanation that Adam was so called because of the ground (*adamah*) from which he originated, Driver comments: 'Adam may be called . . . "red", whether because his skin was reddish-brown like that of Esau and the youthful David . . . or, though not so probably, from the red earth from which he came . . . and which he tilled.' Asking the crucial question whether the story stems from the name or the name from the story, Driver continues:

> Some of the stories about the patriarchs seem to rest on the meanings of their names and to have been invented 'to point a moral and adorn a tale' . . . Playing on words . . . seems to have begun merely as a literary device to embellish or add point to a story but it clearly comes to serve an entirely different end, namely that of imparting esoteric information to interested readers.[21]

This latter argument is pursued by John Allegro. He sees Judaeo-Christianity as secretly devoted to the cult of a sacred fungus, and, tracking backwards, states that the Sumerian Gu-tar, 'top of the head', or penis, was the most common Semitic name for the mushroom *phutr* (Arabic), *pūtrā* (Aramaic), portrayed in the New Testament myth as Peter (a common variant today, also, for the penis).[22] In this reading, Peter is not a foundation-stone but a channel for coded information. A more traditional explanation of Biblical linking of names and events is that:

phonological recurrence, the repetition of similar words linking related things, imparts a ritualistic, almost litany-like quality [which helps] to convey the sense of an underlying order and purpose in the flux of divine history.[23]

Clearly all such punning on names is much more than mere decoration. Ulysses' famous wordplay ('My name is Nobody') in the Polyphemus episode is essential to his survival, and, in addition, represents an in-joke on the whole business of naming (cf. 'My name is Legion'). Moreover, it is prophetic. After pretending to be 'Nobody' in the cave, on his return to Ithaca, Ulysses has to become a real nobody, by disguising himself as an old beggar in his own house. So many people have chewed over significant names for so many centuries that the aptest name for the game would seem to be onomastication.

'There was a belief that words represented the real inwardness or essence of things, as the etymology of the word etymology shows. Some Greeks said that words were the shadows of things. They had as intimate a relation to the things represented as did the shadow of a man to the man himself,' writes McCartney in a study of verbal aspects of ancient homoeopathy, e.g. that a diet of hare's flesh conferred grace or charm; *lepus* begat *lepos*. He quotes additional Japanese evidence. The use of *imori* (a kind of red-bellied newt) for the production of amuletic love-powder is probably derived from a pun on *imo* ('woman' or perhaps 'darling') and *ri* ('victory' or 'gain'). McCartney then comments:

> Statements to the effect that such usages are puns or word-plays or verbal confusion are entirely beside the point ... The things illustrated in this paper were in no wise trivial or jocular in the eyes of their originators or users. For them it was medicine, curative, prophylactic, and, if I may so use the word, causative. Such magic is distinct from medicine only in the eyes of enlightened persons.[24]

The first of these two phrases is perhaps explained by the second: McCartney equates punning with unseriousness. The age-old and persistent links made between *omen*, *nomen* and *numen* surely reveal both an inveterate leaning towards playing with words, and a proper deference towards mystery and the ineffable. Hugo, as always, piles it on thick. In a spirit-session, after asking who was there, Hugo heard Androcles' Lion answer, in a clanging tongue-twister: 'Omen, lumen, numen nomen meum'.[25] Among many 'primitive' peoples, the name of a deity has often been regarded as his (or her) manifestation and thus treated with the greatest veneration, to the point of refusing even to utter it. And on a more personal level, people in many cultures have been averse to disclosing their own names to outsiders.

This whole complex of beliefs runs counter to the 'conventional' view of language (i.e. that all names and indeed all words are only arbitrary conventions), for such a theory rules out predestined proper names. Shakespeare, however, is more in tune with how most minds actually work when, in *Richard II*, he writes: 'O how thy name befits thy composition.' Heraldry, too, registers the same tendency: tell-tale names, *redende Namen*, *armes parlantes*. All of us think in terms of significant, appropriate (or indeed inappropriate) names, so that as well as saying 'Rejoicing in the name of –', we might also say 'Squirming under the name of –'. As Violette Morin has acutely seen in her study of San Antonio's use of the give-away name, which she calls 'patronyme métaphorique' (e.g. the sexy Scottish policeman called MacHeckett – *ma quéquette*, my dick), it is a device of economy and disruption:

> Il faut avouer que le patronyme métaphorique est un système de digression idéal dans le doublage: non seulement il est un perturbateur constant de supports, mais également un accélérateur improvisé pour la vitesse du récit: il est la concentration minimale de toutes les pages qu'utiliserait un romancier 'sérieux' pour décrire le passé ou pressentir l'avenir de ses personnages.

> (It is undeniable that the metaphorical patronym is an ideal system of digression in doubling up; it is not only a constant disturber of referents but also an improvised accelerator of the narration; it is the shorthand form of all the pages that a 'serious' novelist would take to describe the past or hint at the future of his characters.)[26]

Valéry nicely describes but hardly explains the phenomenon of meaningful names:

> Peut-être ce nom même de La Fontaine a-t-il, dès notre enfance, attaché pour toujours à la figure imaginaire d'un poète je ne sais quel sens ambigu de fraîcheur et de profondeur, et quel charme emprunté des eaux? Une consonance, parfois, fait un mythe. De grands dieux naquirent d'un calembour, qui est une espèce d'adultère.

> (Perhaps this very name of La Fontaine, from our childhood onwards, has associated for good with the imaginary figure of the poet some ambiguous sense of freshness and depth and all the delightful associations of water. A consonance can sometimes create a myth. Great gods have been born from a pun, which is a kind of adultery.)[27]

For Valéry, then, the name comes first, and then has meanings read into it, is pillaged or 'remotivated' (cf. Dupriez on the rhetorical device of *adnominatio*: 'Remotivation du nom propre par étymologie, ou métanalyse ou traduction').[28] In this chicken-and-egg, cart-and-horse dilemma, McCartney hovers:

> In citing examples, especially from the plant world, one cannot be absolutely sure that the magical or supernatural power previously ascribed to an object was not the cause of its name instead of the name's being the cause of the belief.[29]

It does in fact seem to me likely that legends were invented to explain names and vice versa: names devised to suit the legendary adventures of eponymous heroes. There is the ambiguity of the word *name* itself, which means both an identity and a reputation – a distinction and an adjunct – but both well-nigh inseparable. Just as history was said by Marx to repeat itself as farce, so great heroes spawn their own burlesques. Puttenham seems to hint at this when he talks of 'Prosonomia, or "The Nicknamer" ' (i.e. plays on proper names, as in Alphonse Allais' 'Lepère et Ternel', making the Almighty into a business outfit). Puttenham adds that he also understands by his term 'words that pleasantly encounter, and (as it were) mock one another by their much resemblance.'[30] Names and people can be made to match, just like names and things. The belief in significant names is an attempt to create a fully significant universe, from which the arbitrary or the meaningless are banished. Puns, by finding relationships everywhere, operate in this pantheistic fashion.

Staying with the ancient world, I will now cheerfully miscegenate the Presocratics and the Sophists. Philosophers can hardly complain if, in order to bring them back to earth, we occasionally tug on their legs, these 'vieux coqs de l'argument debout sur leur *ergo*' ('old roosters of argufying, on their high horses' – *ergot* = cock's spur; *ergo* = therefore).[31] Wittgenstein once said that 'a serious and good philosophical work could be written that would consist entirely of jokes (without being facetious).'[32] Heraclitus is traditionally known as 'the riddler' or 'the obscure'. For example, in fragment LXXXIX (D. 48): 'The name of the bow is life; its work is death.' *Biós* is the old word for 'bow' and *bios* the usual word for life. Apparently, therefore, the bow is misnamed.

> But that judgement implies the error of taking the opposition of life and death as irreducible, by failing to see 'how it agrees in variance with itself.' The life-signifying name for the instrument of death points to some reconciliation between the opponents, some fitting together as in the unity of Day and Night. (XIX, D. 57)

As so often with deliberate ambiguity, there is a strong dose of pedagogical intent present here: the desire to put the receiver to work. Plain tales are not enough. For such listeners, ' "when their souls do not speak the language," [Heraclitus] must resort to enigma, image, paradox, and even contradiction, to tease or shock the audience into giving thought to the obvious, and thus enable them to see what is staring them in the face.' If some of this strategy sounds akin to that of the Delphic oracle, Kahn points out that:

> the task of understanding an oracle consists in rejecting various possibilities and selecting the one appropriate message. With meaningful ambiguity in poetic discourse, however, there can be no single interpretation that is alone correct: the meaning is essentially multiple and complex.[33]

Burnyeat comments in his review of Kahn's edition on:

> The semantic richness of the word 'logos' . . . That one word encapsulates a
> whole philosophy of difference in sameness and sameness in difference: the
> content of the *logos* is paradigmatically exemplified in the word 'logos' itself.

We are in the realm of the double-think, and at times seem to be heading
beyond language altogether. For instance, when Heraclitus calls the sea both
the purest and the foulest water, he may be denying that 'the boundaries of
sameness and difference marked out by the words of our language have any
claim to absolute validity'.[34] We have already mentioned the affinity of wordplay
with overlap, continuum, the crossing of frontiers, approximation, and the
coexistence of opposites.

Freud talks of 'sceptical jokes' (i.e. those which question our capacity for
knowledge itself), and Feibleman of 'humour at the expense of the problems of
knowledge . . . best exemplified by puns or plays on words'.[35] Stanford equates
Lewis Carroll with the Sophists: 'Dizzy with word-play, they were pleased to
indulge in the ingenious technique without worrying about the preposterous
conclusions.'[36] Davis asserts that 'the paronomasia or pun is the sophism of
equivocation,' and quotes an agèd example: 'Two men ate oysters for a wager;
one ate ninety-nine, but the other ate two more, for he ate a hundred and
won.'[37] Though he on other occasions relished puns, Coleridge held that 'to
expose a sophism and to detect the equivocal or double meaning of a word is, in
the great majority of cases, one and the same thing.'[38] It was not only the pupils
of Sophists but theatre-goers who responded to this tradition: 'Undoubtedly,'
claims Stanford,

> it was the quickness of the Athenian audiences to appreciate subtler plays on
> words and their delight in exercising this faculty that encouraged their dramatists
> and sophists to exploit the various types of ambiguity as much as they did. The
> adult's pleasure in appreciating an ambiguity is a natural development of the
> child's fondness for riddles.[39]

Cicero was for many centuries valued as the prime Roman exponent of the
pun, but I myself find another Latin writer, strongly shaped by Greek thinking,
much more interesting in this regard: Lucretius. He has the authentic punster's
reverence for the *tantamount*. As Snyder has written, 'Fire and firewood, says
Lucretius (11. 907ff.), are composed of slightly different combinations of atoms
just as the two Latin names of the substances, *ignis* and *ligna*, are formed from
slightly different combinations of letters.' We have seen before how wordplay
often seeks to mime reality in some way. Thus, when Lucretius puns on the
name of the venerable poet Ennius (Ennius–*perennis*), 'the letters (elementa) of
the name reflect the atoms (elementa) which constituted the man.' This

practice of playing with the letters or several meanings of words both illustrated the theory of the atoms and emphasized the reality as registered in names and other words. In short: philosophical punning. Punning is indeed a matter of chance but, it seems to some, a necessary chance, a purposeful randomness such as Lucretius observed at work in the universe. An essential factor of his world-picture is the *clinamen*, or swerve. Puns are oblique; they sidestep. A final example, the play on *materies/mater*:

> Just as *materies* contains the letters m-a-t-e-r, so also matter and its atomic structure function as the mother of things; *materies* is the *mater* from which all forms of plant and animal life arise, Lucretius implied, for nothing can spring up suddenly out of nothing.

Snyder concludes that Lucretius used the structure of words as a kind of parallel to the structure of the universe and attempted to reinforce this parallelism through the use of wordplay.[40]

Valéry said of a pebble that it is 'de la même matière que sa forme: matière à doutes' ('of the same matter as its form: a matter for doubts').[41] It is so smooth that he wonders whether it is a natural or an artificial object; it is thus two-faced, and the twist on *matière* underlines this. Puns play between form and matter. Puns are parallel, as well as tangents. Of course, the argument whereby you try to back up an idea by finding a support for it within language itself (e.g. via etymologies) is a circular one. But what do we ever do except circle round truth, or mystery? Even then, the sense of mystery can at least be shared with others (for wordplay needs a responsive audience), and in this way Heraclitus' complaint can be countered: 'Although the *logos* is shared, most men live as though their thinking were a private possession.'[42] Great, and dirty, and punning, minds think alike.

Leaping eclectically across the centuries, we reach Petrarch who immediately returns us to the ancient play on names and projects us towards the personal hallmark mode, where 'le nom poétique est un auto-graphe, lisible et déchiffrable' ('the poetic name is an autograph, readable and decodable').[43] An intricate code where secretion of another's name helps to boost the poet's own name, or fame: encomium and self-congratulation conjoined. Thus, on the one hand,

> word play does on a small scale what poetry does with the form of language as a whole. Word play shows the poet's sensitivity to the most distant relationships. The whole of nature thus can become the mirror of a beloved object. Petrarch is defended for playing on the name of Laura (*l'aura*, breeze, *lauro*, laurel, *l'auro*, gold).[44]

On the other hand, as Rigolot points out, Laura is never mentioned by name, even though the whole collection centres on the magic of her name, which, as in Proust, seems to connote her essence. Perhaps, indeed, it is because of this magic that the name is not spelt out, but rather circumscribed, circumlocuted. It is too precious to be squandered on direct utterance. As Flaubert warned, gold idols should not be touched, lest the gilt comes off on our sticky fingers. Rigolot sums up wittily: 'Si Pétrarque ne multiplie pas "sauvagement" les procédés mimétiques du langage, c'est qu'il sait que, dans le jeu où l'or (Laure) résiste mal à l'inflation, la voie la plus sûre est celle de l'*aurea mediocritas*' ('If Petrarch does not multiply of his own accord the mimetic processes of language, it is because he knows that in the game where gold (Laura) easily falls victim to inflation, the safest way is that of "golden mediocrity" ').[45]

A later series of poets, 'les Grands Rhétoriqueurs', ignored such discretion. Men such as Marot and the well-named Guillaume Cretin used not only punning rhymes, but punning hemistiches and indeed whole lines (holorhymes). Here is an example of the first from an anti-woman poem:

> Je fus bien mal-heureux, tout haut je le confesse
> Quand je touchay sur vous, tetin, cuisse, con, fesse.

> (It was unhappy for me, as I confess aloud,
> When I touched your tit, thigh, cunt or buttock proud.)[46]

As wordplay proliferated in the fifteenth and sixteenth centuries, the very terms for it were given extensions, as Tabourot notes:

> Les amphibologies ou amphibolies qui sont équivoques à deux ententes que nos bons pères ont surmommé des entend-trois. Dont nous avons encore ce proverbe ordinaire, que quand quelqu'un feint ne pas entendre ce que lon luy propose, et respond d'autre, on dit qu'il fait de l'entend-trois.

> (The amphibologies or amphibolies which are double-meaning equivoques; our forefathers called them triple-hearers. And so we have this everyday proverb – when somebody pretends not to understand what is said to him, we say he plays the triple-hearer.)[47]

A variation on deliberate and tendentious mishearing is the trick of taking phrases literally instead of as they are commonly understood. This is, as Martin Gardner remarks, typical of the creatures behind the looking-glass and a basis for much of Lewis Carroll's humour. I am none too convinced, however, when Gardner calls this 'a variety of nonsense'.[48] When the King exclaims at Alice's ability to 'see Nobody', the deliberate mistake harks back to the French monk Radulfus Glaber who, having discovered the great Nemo in a number of

Biblical, Evangelical and liturgical texts, composed a *Historia de Nemine*: 'Thus, in the Scriptures, *nemo deum vidit* (nobody has seen God) in his interpretation, became "Nemo saw God." Thus, everything impossible, inadmissible, is, on the contrary, permitted for Nemo.'[49]

Rabelais' well-known outburst against rebuses (e.g. 'un lict sans ciel pour un licentié' – 'a bed without a canopy/a licentiate') is clearly, by its very hyperbole, ironic, and celebrates where it seems to castigate:

> Qui sont homonymies tant ineptes, tant fades, tant rusticques et barbares, que l'on doibvroit atacher une queue de renard au collet et faire un masque d'une bouze de vache à un chascun d'iceux qui en vouldroit dorenavant user en France, après la restitution des bonnes lettres.
>
> (These puns are so inept, stale, clodhopping and barbarous that anyone trying to use them in France henceforth, since the Revival of Letters, should have a fox's tail tied to his collar and a cowpat smeared on his face.)[50]

That Rabelais is preaching against what he himself practises is clearly exposed by Bakhtin when he comments: 'All these ambivalent images [of the Sileni-boxes] are dual-bodied, dual-faced, pregnant. They combine in various proportions negation and affirmation, the top and the bottom, abuse and praise.'[51] This inside-out and topsy-turvy world is that of carnival, feasts of fools, and puns. In such a world, people let their hair down, but do not necessarily cease using their minds. The Greeks had a lovely, wobbly word for the serio-comic: *spoudaiogeloion*, and the Renaissance resurrected the spirit behind those letters. In Colie's words:

> Folly (to say nothing of Erasmus) is engaged in *serio ludere*, playing with the crucial problems of intellectual, moral, and spiritual life, playing also with the men who take them too seriously as well as with the men who do not take them seriously enough.

A linked mode is the macaronic which:

> involves the kind of wit demonstrated in puns, calembours, conundrums, clerihews, and even limericks: its violation of linguistic convention and expectation depends upon profound control of just that convention. Macaronic is only occasionally *serio ludere*, but its play derives from a great deal of serious application in the past.

Renaissance paradox, 'antique and antic', also seems close kin.[52] The term 'paradox' is in itself paradoxical, self-contradicting, for it can mean a statement which seems false but is true, or which seems true but is false. Many words are in themselves paradoxical, in that they house opposite meanings: fast (rapid

motion or standing still), cleave (separate or fuse), stain (colour or discolour), overlook (to look over, or to fail to do this). Paradoxes, for Colie, 'make an equation of two things manifestly unlike'. Furthermore, it is 'self-contained, self-sufficient, self-referential, yet it needs an audience to register the brilliance and be surprised by it'. But when Colie asserts that 'the parodoxical form denies commitment,' when she sees in effect parodoxes, like puns, as wind-hoverers, I think of Orwell, Sartre, Silone, and demur.[53] There is disagreement about the connection between humour and paradox. For Hugh Kenner in his study of Chesterton, 'all humour rests on paradox, because every good joke is capped by the unexpected.'[54] For C. P. Wilson, conversely, 'paradoxes are unfunny . . . The typical response to paradox is not amusement: few jokes are genuinely paradoxical: by definition, the paradox defies resolution, while jokes are characteristically resolved – "got", "understood." '[55]
Kenner realizes that both he and Chesterton tread on treacherous ground:

> The pun is the foundation of his humour and through his analogical perceptions inextricably mixed with his thought; dangerous because word-play of all the forms of paradox balances most precariously on the knife–edge between the perfunctory and the profound.

For Kenner, Chesterton is heir to a long tradition, 'for, to perceive puns is ultimately to perceive a totality of words and things and feelings analogically'.[56] And analogy, like punning, senses likeness at the core of difference.
It is Zen which shows most darkly the ties between verbal play and paradox:

> There has probably never been a religious movement more sweepingly iconoclastic than Zen . . . For before true liberation can occur, all idols must be overturned or stood upside down . . . To take things too seriously, let alone absolutely, however significant they might otherwise seem, is to be dependent upon them and therefore caught in the wheel (the vicious circle) of attachment, desire and bondage.

A permanent, if curiously bodiless, Carnival. The indirection of Zen is suitable for the oblique pun.

> The profusion of puns, idiomatic turns upon words, paradoxes and enigmatic sayings, startling gestures and acts . . . all have the same general intent of calling an abrupt halt to an unenlightened plane of perception, and projecting the hearer onto a more fundamental plane of experience. The disciple is never allowed to rest in an intellectual understanding or an attachment to names and forms.

The previously noted concision and pedagogical pointedness of wordplay appears here again: 'A great deal of Buddhist teaching is lightly compressed in the small chambers of the riddle or pun.'[57]

If Zen gets too embroiled in the double bind, then what of those who see analogies between puns and mathematics? Lewis Carroll and Raymond Queneau practised in both areas. Rather nervously, in his study of mathematics and humour, Paulos stresses that his analogies:

> are by no means meant to be funny; they are meant to show the same qualities inherent in a good mathematical proof are similar to qualities inherent in good humour: cleverness and economy, playfulness, combinatorial ingenuity, and logic (particuarly reductio ad absurdum).[58]

After reading a remark by Pierre Guiraud that one day we might see computers generating puns, I asked a computer scientist for his reaction, which I failed to understand, except for the general point that, for the foreseeable future, any computer (and the programme even for this would be complex and laborious) would produce only obvious and uninteresting specimens.[59] On the other hand, in January 1984, ICL advertised that their Information Search Processor could find not only a needle in a haystack, but also a noodle in a hatrack. So, there is hope; or despair.

It is not modesty but realism that convinces me I have little to say on Shakespeare's wordplay, which, like all other aspects of his work, has been comprehensively investigated by others. It may still prove useful, however, to select some of the more telling finds. Dr. Johnson notoriously said: 'A quibble was to him the fatal Cleopatra for which he lost the world, and was content to lose it.'[60] As Mahood points out, Johnson was much more alert to Shakespeare's wordplay than most nineteenth-century commentators, for, on the look-out against puns, he detected more of them.[61] Empson takes over ironically the Doctor's arguments about the wordplay:

> It shows lack of decision and will-power, a feminine pleasure in yielding to the mesmerism of language, in getting one's way, if at all, by deceit and flattery, for a poet to be so fearfully susceptible to puns. Many of us could wish the Bard had been more manly in his literary habits.[62]

Many of Shakespeare's characters have typically split attitudes to the split–tongue. Hamlet can warn 'We must speak by the card or equivocation will undo us,' whereas Richard III, in an aside, gloats 'I moralise two meanings in one word.'[63] Many of them are in fact existential punsters – Richard II, for one: 'Only a double language, painfully aware of the opposite meanings lurking in words, is adequate to Richard's own double condition.' The inverting tendency of puns is seen also on the comic, but no less serious level: 'In Bottom the proper subordination of sense to intellect is over-thrown in a topsy-turvy metamorphosis that puts his "bottom" faculties on "top".'[64]

Shakespeare of course benefited not only from his native genius but also from the luxuriant growth of his mother tongue. Kökeritz charts the changes:

During the Middle English period the possibilities of punning had been vastly increased as a result of the wholesale importation of Romance loan-words into the language. The excessive Latinization of the vocabulary during the Renaissance had the same effect. The consequent wealth of synonyms, which from then on became a permanent characteristic of English, brought with it an increasing differentiation in usage as well as in meaning and connotation, which was eminently favourable to punning and other forms of conscious or unconscious verbal ambiguity, including malapropisms. No less is this true of the revolutionary changes in pronunciation that English underwent at the beginning of the fifteenth century and through which it acquired many new homonyms.[65]

In his various studies of Shakespeare's wordplay, Coleridge picks and rejects, hits and misses. Here he is at a point of equilibrium:

No doubt something of Shakespeare's punning must be attributed to his age, in which direct and formal combats of wit were a favourite pastime of the courtly and accomplished ... But independently of this, I have no hesitation in saying that a pun, if it be congruous with the feeling of the scene, is not only allowable in the dramatic dialogue, but oftentimes one of the most effectual intensives of passion.[66]

A pity that Coleridge snobs the groundlings who no doubt equally coined and registered puns, but the latter part of the statement is amply supported by the general study of Mahood and the particular one of Kenneth Muir. For Mahood, 'wordplay was a game the Elizabethans played seriously.' She illustrates this by, among others, the case of Hamlet: 'At times Hamlet's wordplay does double-duty, by both masking his hostility towards Claudius and affording him a safety-valve for his bitterness at his mother's guilt.'[67] What she demonstrates, in effect, is the reciprocal support of play, interplay (between characters, or between character and creator) and wordplay. Whereas Coleridge had failed to find any wordplay in *Macbeth*, Muir talks of the 'prevalence' of puns there. He goes on to tabulate the:

four main functions of the serious pun in dramatic poetry. First, puns – and especially hidden puns – provide ... an illogical reinforcement of the logical sequence of thought, so that the poetic statement strikes us almost as a remembrance – as Keats said that poetry should do. Secondly, such puns often link together unrelated imagery and act as solvents for mixed metaphors. Thirdly, they made the listener aware of a complex of ideas which enrich the total statement, even though they do not come into full consciousness. Fourthly, they seem to shoot out roots in all directions, so that the poetry is firmly based on reality.

Muir aims to justify what for many is a disabling aspect of wordplay, its self-consciousness, by an analogy with Henry Moore's sculpture, where:

> it is always possible to perceive how his actual medium has influenced the finished work of art . . . In much the same way the artist in words must collaborate with the genius of the language. If he tries to write without due regard to his medium, his work will be thin, artificial and sterile. We can only master language by submitting to it.[68]

Muir's term, 'the uncomic pun', serves of course to stress the seriousness, the relevance, of much play with words, but it disserves when it seeks to dissociate humour and gravity. Stoic wit, for example, is hardly uncomic (e.g. when the blinded Gloucester says 'I see it feelingly,' he must be boosting his disability by reminding himself and others that he retains a discerning intellect, and taking pleasure in so doing).[69] When Gaunt puns about himself on his death-bed and Richard II queries, 'Can sick men play so nicely with their names?', Gaunt replies, 'No, misery makes sport to mock itself.'[70] Mercutio, like the Gnat in Lewis Carroll, expires on a pun ('a grave man').[71] Maurice Morgann strikes a bluff pose on the issue:

> The censure commonly passed on Shakespeare's puns is, I think, not well founded . . . The art which he so peculiarly possessed of converting base things into excellence
>
> > 'For if the Jew cut but deep enough,
> > I'll pay the forfeiture with all my heart'.
>
> A play upon words is the most that can be expected from one who affects gaiety under the pressure of severe misfortunes; but so imperfect, so broken a gleam, can only serve more plainly to disclose the gloom and darkness of the mind; it is an effort of fortitude, which failing in its operation, becomes the truest, because the most unaffected *pathos*; and a skilful actor, well managing his tones and action, might with this miserable pun, steep a whole audience suddenly in tears.[72]

But puns are gaiety amid (potential) good fortune, too. As Mahood notes,

> Most of the witty wordplay in Shakespeare is either wanton or aggressive. The liveliest exchanges are between those pairs of lovers who fight their way to the altar, for their wordplay is doubly tendentious in being at once both hostile and seductive.[73]

Spevack focuses on *Love's Labour's Lost* and comes to similar conclusions:

By nature playful, querulous, and often critical, punning duels are a perfect medium to express the amorous give-and-take, for they embody the paradox in love-game comedy of an underlying love cloaked in a seeming hostility. Thus the verbal sallies represent more than sheer froth: they provide and typify the kind of armed rapport so necessary to the action.

In these duels, the women often beat the men. Yet it is not, ultimately, a combat, but a congress, for:

> when the warring-wooing lovers meet a pun . . . they are voicing a connection, a mutuality, of interest and aim. If one puns, for example, the other must respond in kind or at least act as foil . . . In short, a partner in the pun is as much needed as a partner in life.

Having noted, rightly, that 'wordplay implies sexplay,' Spevack later sets off a nuclear explosion of his own: Berowne's 'light-darkness' speech is 'a bravura conceit in which the word *light* is subjected to a kind of neutron bombardment setting off a chain reaction of linguistic fission'.[74] In Shakespeare's universe, it often seems as though 'the bawdy hand of the dial is now upon the prick of noon.'[75] Shakespeare induces us to 'stand to' on such signals.

Where Shakespeare paraded, Milton camouflaged. 'It is only rarely that decorum permits Milton's word-play in *Paradise Lost* to have the brusque simplicity which we associate with the word "pun" . . . Sombre and quiet equivocation is characteristic of Milton.'[76]
But even he has his moments, as Robin Robbins details acutely:

> When Milton in Book VI of *Paradise Lost* describes Satan as 'scoffing in ambiguous words,' the sardonic fiend has just perpetrated some dozen puns in a nine-line speech, displaying both braggadocio and duplicity. The poet's word play here is in as deadly earnest as the swordplay of the spirits . . . The still unfallen Adam sees sinful Eve as 'Defaced, deflowered and now to death devote' – literally disfigured, deprived of her garden, and given over to death, but at the same time discountenanced, robbed of moral beauty, violated, and doomed by God's vow. Because the narrator himself, working from an exegetical tradition that wrung every drop of meaning from every word of the Bible, respects what Sir Thomas Browne called 'the deuteroscopy, and second intention of words,' he too, in *propria persona*, packs his language with metaphor and allusion.

Robbins calls this practice 'grave paronomasia', and indeed prefers 'ambiguity' to 'pun'.[77] A further example, from *Samson Agonistes*(87), is 'silent as the moon,' which recalls both Selene and *luna silens* – the non-shining phase of the moon; here, 'a familiar Latinate word is used in its unfamiliar Latin sense.'[78] Landor's commentary on the Satan passage mentioned above was: 'It appears then on record that the first overt crime of the refractory angels was punning: they fell rapidly after that.'[79]

Where anti-punsters see falls, champions see ascent. In Donne's 'The Canonization', the line 'Wee dye and rise the same' elicits a punning gloss from Colie: 'In Donne's love-poems, "low things," ' " or lovers' deaths [in the sense of orgasms] are made to stand for the greatest death of all; erection becomes a symbol for resurrection.'[80] Or as the old sea-shanty puts it: 'Hey ho! up she rises, early in the morning!' By this reasoning, incidentally, impotence and atheism are cognate. The affinity of *concept, conception* and *conceit* has often been noted. That is, the very idea of thinking at all has often been wedded to wit, just as *wit* and *intelligence* have been interchangeable. It is indeed possible, as Ruthven argues, to see the conceit as 'a respectably ancient mode of thought like the paradox, for the deftly manipulated paradoxes of religious poets testify to the powers of yoked contraries in evoking ideas which cannot be defined.'[81] Not all religious poets of the age were so convinced as Donne, however, and Herbert for one criticized the 'metaphysical' mode and its assumption that poetic meanings:

> Must all be vail'd, while he that reads, divines,
> Catching the sense at two removes.[82]

But, for many, the tide ran the other way: God was on their side:

> One of God's most brilliant conceits was the Incarnation, although it took a saint rather than a literary critic to see what God was lightly hinting at when the Word became flesh, for it was no less a person than St. Augustine who detected God's wit in allowing the Word to become speechless (*infans*) in the infant Jesus (*Sermones*, CXC).[83]

As well as enjoying divine backing, such writers were steeped in the language of Holy Writ. As Empson noted:

> The study of Hebrew ... and the existence of English Bibles with alternatives in the margin, may have had some influence on the capacity of English for ambiguity: Donne, Herbert, Jonson and Crashaw, for instance, were Hebrew scholars ... Hebrew, having very unreliable tenses, extraordinary idioms and a strong taste for puns, possesses all the practical advantages of a thoroughly primitive disorder.

Elsewhere, Empson redresses the balance by stressing how *natural* such punning could be, as against the traditional charge of being contrived:

It is partly this tact which makes Marvell's puns charming and not detached from his poetry . . . he manages . . . to imply that it was quite easy to produce puns and one need not worry about one's dignity in the matter. It became harder as the language was tidied up, and one's dignity was more seriously engaged. For the Elizabethans were quite prepared, for instance, to make a pun by a mispronunciation, would treat puns as mere casual bricks, requiring no great refinement.[84]

Writing a century or so after the backlash bent on banning puns from sermons, journalism and literature, Coleridge felt moved to remind his readers of this home truth, when he spoke of:

the beauty and true force of nature with which conceits, as they are called, and sometimes even puns, are introduced. What has been the reigning fault of an age must, at one time or another, have referred to something beautiful in the human mind; and, however conceits may have been misapplied, however they may have been disadvantageously multiplied, we should recollect that there never was an abuse of anything but it previously has had its use.[85]

Decorum wielded that backlash. Dryden, no mean punster himself on occasion, spoke dismissively of 'the jingle of a more poor paranomasia', and jibbed at a pun by Horace: 'Certain it is, he has no fine palate who can feed so heartily on garbage.'[86] John Dennis asserted that 'every Equivocal is but ambiguous Falsehood,' and, against the defence that puns are diverting, responded by asking whether those who fart in company might use the same foolish argument to exonerate themselves.[87] Seeking to blacklist quibbling, John Eachard inadvertently begets some, if we remember the old typographical confusion of f and s. 'Such preachers', he writes, 'there lie nibbling and ſucking at an end.'[88]

An even more pervasive decorum, *la bienséance*, in seventeenth century France, sought to keep wordplay at bay. Molière:

> Ce n'est que jeux de mots, qu'affectation pure,
> Et ce n'est point ainsi que parle la nature.

(It's all plays on words and pure affectation and this is not the true voice of Nature.)[89]

But the natural chased away comes back at full gallop. The classical straightjacket, the distaste for the mixture of genres, the obsession with high seriousness, tried to blot out the memory of Rabelais and Montaigne. While there were fewer deliberate puns, later generations (especially of dunned schoolboys) have riposted by planting them on innocent authors. Such wilful mishearings as this: Corneille's line 'Et le désir s'accroît quand l'effet se recule'

('And the longing increases when the target withdraws') becomes warped to 'Et le désir ça croît quand les fesses reculent' ('And desire leaps up when the buttocks retreat'). We have often underlined the obliqueness of wordplay. French classicism, too, valued the slanting approach, but it took most often the forms of litotes, allusiveness, the recharging of restricted vocabulary, than it did of wordplay in the English fashion. In its turn, England caught the virus of decorum.

> The Restoration dramatists were admirably lucid, but their use of language was, in the last resort, unimaginative. The banishing of the pun except for comic purposes was the symbol of a radical defect: it was a turning away from the genius of the language.[90]

But wordplay is a contagious phenomenon, and the anti-quibbler puns in the act of condemning, as Wycherley does on seeking to mock the notorious Mr Swan:

> Tho' Quibblers, Wits, Birds of a Feather are,
> As Goose, and Swan, something alike apear.[91]

Addison sought to codify: 'false Wit', 'true Wit' and 'mixt Wit'. Despite the last-named category, he ignored the area of overlap, and in any pairing (e.g. reason and extravagance) headed unerringly for the safer. He does, decently, acknowledge the longevity of the punning instinct, and even admits that 'the Seeds of Punning are in the Minds of all Men,' but the remedy is at hand: 'Tho' they may be subdued by Reason, Reflection and good Sense, they will be very apt to shoot up in the greatest Genius, that is not broken and cultivated by the Rules of Art.' You can glimpse the gleam of the gelder's knife. This is apparent from one of Addison's own wordplays on 'Squire *Squelkum*, who by his Voice seems (if I may use the Expression) to be cut out for an *Italian* Singer'.[92] Names are *italicized*, nouns capitalized, abstraction abounds. In these conditions, it is not strange that, as James Sully put it, Addison 'was rendered blind by the god of laughter to the real nature of wit, as essentially a mode of intellectual play'.[93] In more detail and more soberly Colie points to a further deficiency in Addison:

> Using Locke's distinction between wit and judgement, Addison categorized as false wit all puns, anagrams, rebuses, lipogrammatic writing, imprese, echo-refrains, (especially macaronic echoes), *bouts rimés*, and shape poems ... for which 'Mr. Herbert' was particularly taken to task. Stylistically, so to speak, the gaming spirit was disqualified as a poet's proper tool.[94]

Dr Johnson, as we have seen when speaking of Shakespeare, had a more nuanced attitude to wordplay, and he probably shared Boswell's opinion that 'a

good pun may be admitted among the smaller excellencies of lively conversation.'[95] Johnson himself created an excellent, if perhaps unwitting, double
entendre, when he called wit 'the unexpected copulation of ideas', for the erotic
impulse in wordplay is ubiquitous. Empson reminds, down-to-earthly, that
'Johnson had been bored by charades recited in coffee-houses, and thought the
Elizabethan pun was the same.'[96] Empson's let-off is, of course, fairly damning.
The French neo-classicists were in chorus, too, for a change, with Voltaire
calling plays on words 'la pire espèce du faux bel esprit' in his entry on wit in his
Dictionnaire philosophique. The abbé Delille wrote:

> Le calembour, enfant gâté
> Du mauvais goût et de l'obscurité,
> Qui va guettant dans ses discours baroques
> De nos jargons nouveaux les termes équivoques,
> Et se jouant des phrases et des mots
> D'un terme obscur fait tout l'esprit des sots.

(The pun, the spoilt child of bad taste and gibberish, which in its baroque modes
goes in search of the equivocal terms of the new cant, and playing on sentences
and words makes out of an unintelligible term a witticism for fools.)[97]

The big difference is that French anti-punsters were reacting against a plague
of society rather than of literature, though both English and French counter-
attacks suggest that punning was prevalent, even if often scorned. Smollett's
subjunctive in these lines is suitably ambivalent:

> Debauch'd from sense, let double meanings run,
> The vague conundrum and the prurient pun.[98]

If, for the Augustans, ambiguity was a vice, it was the more 'vicious' of
eighteenth century writers (Swift, Sterne) who most valued it.

Pope, at least, recognized the existence of the divided as against the seamless,
when he spoke of 'the Paronomasia, or Pun, where a word, like the tongue of a
jackdaw, speaks twice as much by being split.'[99] In the previous century, pulpit
wordplay (e.g. in Bishop Andrewes' sermons) had provoked, as we have seen, a
backlash. For Swift's henchman, Arbuthnot, the opponents of wordplay could
only have sectarian motivation:

> But, dearest Nann, I smell the bottom
> Of all our Anti-Punsters (rott'em).
> It is a Papist-Jesuit Plot,
> By Tory Jacobites begot.[100]

Swift himself put wordplay vigorously to work. Several have commented on the marathon etymological pun on the Aeolists in *A Tale of a Tub*. 'The technique by which he throws a rope around several cognate terms and pulls them down with a low synonym' is a feature of his polemic. For the Augustans, Donoghue continues, 'words were responsible to things; or it was dangerous to think otherwise. The pun . . . is a step in this subversive direction.' Swift's parody of the Augustan tendency takes the form of turning words into physical objects in the Academy of Lagado, or of negating their usual meaning. Donoghue sees the process as one where authorial control is loosened if not abdicated:

> A language committed to the pun pushes the discourse adrift from 'meaning' and, like *Finnegans Wake*, sets it spinning in purely verbal water. Once there, the language develops resources of its own, without responsibility to 'the things' from which it had parted or to the speaker who finds himself abandoned.[101]

Clive Probyn ventures an intricate reconstruction of Swift's punning in *Gulliver's Travels*:

> *Homonym* has two morphemes (*same/name*) and in addition to its lexicographical sense also suggests *man-name*. *Houyhnhnm* cannot be thus easily broken up into morphemes, but if we substitute the phonologically linked homonym by its logical alternative (i.e. *equivocal*) we produce a term which suggests both a literal pun on the horse's characteristic (*horse speaking*) and a critical judgement on their status in Swift's discussion of the nature of man. As symbols the *Houyhnhnms* are ambivalent, and their names indicate their natures.[102]

Such subversive activity is, of course, dangerous also to itself. As David Nokes concludes after his study of Swift's wordplay: 'The punster clouds his meaning in perpetual ambiguities, trusting to neither the word nor the flesh, and always the more ambiguous when his intentions seem most clear.' Swift's habit of literalization, however, can strike home, as when, in *A Tale of a Tub*, he mocks the 'inspiration' of the Dissenters by reducing it to a taking in of wind, 'with every Man a Pair of Bellows applied to his Neighbours' Breech, by which they blew up each other'. Expectably, many of Swift's most pointed puns home in on the fundament. If (and Spanish uses the same word for both *escatológico*), eschatology and scatology are close kin, because both concern the final issue of things, then Swift's contribution is the wise man's rule of *Regarding The End*, which 'plays with all possible meanings of that phrase, from a meditation upon mortality to arse-wiping'.[103] Swift's love of conversation-games, his playing with the complex question of veracity, his faceted irony, his love of inversion and reversal, his black outlook are all inspirations for his punning. It was not always inspired, even though he stressed the 'grand Mistake' of the author of 'God's Revenge Against Punning' (probably Pope), 'that he condemns the whole Art in general without distinguishing Puns into Good and Bad'.[104]

Much of Swift's wordplay, especially in letters or conversation, was naturally playful rather than polemical. Such varieties belong to the spirit as described by Elizabeth Carter, a member of the Blue Stocking circle and friend of Richardson and Johnson, in her projected jeu d'esprit on *The Whole Art and Mystery of Punning*, calculated:

> to furnish the sweet *nepenthe* of nonsense in such copious streams as to water the face of the whole earth . . . To so great a perfection have the authors of this work carried their design, as to lay down rules to divide, subdivide, compound, recompound, decompound, rack, torture, strain, and quodlibetificate any word into a pun by nineteen several ways of false spelling.[105]

Such gaming instinct, wilful distortion and sheer exuberance are to be found in the work and life of the Marquis de Bièvre.

Bièvre was a living legend, and indeed eventually became trapped in the role of a pun-making machine. His simplest statements were conned for their expected hidden meanings. Either he kept a stock of puns, often elaborate, ready for insertion into the appropriate context on cue, or many of those attributed to him were spurious, coined at leisure by others. For instance, when a bishop farted at table, he explained:

> Monseigneur, vous voudriez que ce fût un vent cardinal . . . La chose ayant fait du bruit . . . On croit que lâcher un pet en campagnie est très-mal; mais c'est un *mal-entendu*, car on doit sentir que celui auquel il échappe ne le fait pas de sa tête, et que ce n'est pas sans fondement qu'il en agit ainsi.

> (My lord, you would like to pass it off as a cardinal wind. As the affair made a stink. People think that letting off in company is very naughty, but that's a misunderstanding/an audible naughtiness, for, as we get wind of it, we sense that he who lets rip doesn't put his heart into it, and that he can't fundamentally help it.)

When the Prince de Condé asked Bièvre for a play on his name, the reply was that 'Condé renfermait les jeux de l'amour et du hasard' ('*Con/dé* [cunt, dice] contained the games of love and chance').[106] He wrote a play *Vercingentorixe*, understandably never acted, which contained a pun a line. For example:

> Je sus *comme un cochon* résister à leurs armes,
> Et je pus *comme un bouc* dissiper vos alarmes.

> I succeeded/sweat like a pig in resisting their attack, and I was able/stink like a goat to calm your anxiety.)[107]

The puns are italicized, and subvert or pervert the preceding or following 'fine', i.e. stereotyped style: this is pure burlesque. Grimm's comment, in the

Correspondance littéraire for December 1770, was: 'Il n'y a pas de genre qui demande plus de sobriété que le genre détestable des pointes et des calembours' ('No genre is in greater need of sobriety than the detestable genre of quibbles and puns') Roudaut describes the verses of the type quoted above as split ends: 'Le vers fourche soudain comme un cheveu malade' ('The line splits suddenly like out-of-condition hair').[108] The process is related to that of mishearing, whether accidental or purposeful, and to a long French tradition, later baptized 'queue romantique', or tack-ons (of which the most hallowed is 'Comment vas-tu 'yau de poêle?'). The idea is to make sense bifurcate into nonsense or innuendo. The first speaker can be made to co-operate in the construction of 'une idée parasite et déshonorante, qu'il n'a pas vraiment dite' ('a parastical and degrading idea which was not what he really uttered').[109] The punster bandwaggons. The whole game reflects parodically what Jespersen termed 'metanalysis', in which:

> words or word-groups are by a new generation analyzed differently from the analysis of a former age. Each child has to find out for himself, in hearing the connected speech of other people, where one word ends and the next begins, or what belongs to the kernel and what to the ending of a word (e.g. a *napron* – an *apron*).[110]

During the French Revolution was formed a 'Club des Anes'. Those who belonged were called 'membranes'. A donkey's member is proverbially prodigious, and about the same period came in the adjective *calembourique*, – a pun itself on *bourrique*: ass or dolt. Punning always thus hovers between the exceptional and the stupid. It can sometimes seem accurate of Kant to define the cause of laughter as 'the sudden transformation of a strained expectation into nothing', that is, you reach after something and find it is not there.[111] Jean-Paul Richter acts as a useful hinge between the often vapid or harmless punning of the eighteenth and the more varied wordplay of the nineteenth century.[112] He was perhaps the first to wax lyrical, and indeed cosmic, about the whole phenomenon. Jean-Paul located one of the seductions of puns in the:

> surprise at the element of chance which runs through the world playing with sound and parts of the world. As a wild coupling without priest, every coincidence pleases us, perhaps because the very idea of causality half-hiding and half-revealing itself seems like wit to wed the dissimilar.[113]

The sacerdotal image crops up again, in changed garb, in his study of the 'aesthetic joke, wit in its strictest sense, that priest in disguise who connects all couples [and] uses to this end various nuptial blessings'.[114] The erotic pulse and the flavour of a black mass can be felt in these words. He might have tempered them by noting that punners are often the match-makers of shotgun-marriages. Jean-Paul can be calmer, as when he states that 'a third ground for pleasure in puns is the evidence it gives of intellectual freedom, which can turn our glance from the object to its sign.'[115] Such a diversion, such a reminder that words can come adrift of their bases, is precisely what anti-punners object to.

4

Making History II

Of eighteenth-century English punning – but he should have excluded Swift at least from his sweep – Empson wrote:

> The eighteenth-century use of a pun is always worldly; to join together so smartly a business and a philosophical notion, a nautical and a gastronomical notion, with an air of having them in watertight compartments in your own mind . . . all this belongs to the light-weight tattling figure . . . the man quick to catch the tone of his company, who knows the talk of the town.

The generalization continues its approximate way, only more so, when he turns to the next:

> The nineteenth-century punster is quite another thing . . . I suppose he came in with the Christmas annuals, and supplied something which could be shown to all the daughters of the house.

He has a firmer footing for his bird's-eye view when he concentrates on one characteristic, as when he claims that:

> The pun's most definite examples are likely to be found, in increasing order of self-consciousness, among the seventeenth-century mystics who stress the conscious will, the eighteenth-century stylists who stress rationality, clarity and satire, and the harmless nineteenth-century punsters who stress decent above-board fun.[1]

Hazlitt could not sound less like Jean-Paul Richter:

> Mere wit, as opposed to reason or argument, consists in striking out some casual and partial coincidence which has nothing to do, or at least implies no necessary connection with the nature of things, which are forced into a seeming analogy by a play upon words, or some irrelevant conceit, as in puns, riddles, alliteration, etc. The jest, in all such cases, lies in the sort of mock-identity, or nominal resemblance, established by the intervention of the same words expressing

different ideas, and countenancing as it were, by a fatality of language, the mischievous insinuation which the person who has the wit to take advantage of it wishes to convey.[2]

A similar residue of only reluctant admiration for the phenomenon can be seen in Sydney Smith's:

> Punning grows upon everybody, and punning is the wit of words . . . I have very little to say about puns; they are in very bad repute, and so they ought to be. The wit of language is so miserably inferior to the wit of ideas, that it is very deservedly driven out of good company. Sometimes, indeed, a pun makes its appearance which seems for a moment to redeem its species; but we must not be deceived by them: it is a radically bad race of wit.[3]

Since it breeds everywhere else, we should not be surprised at linguistic racism like this. R. B. Martin's verdict is:

> Either Smith is attempting to disclaim his own notorious addiction to punning, or he actually fails to see that puns may be a formidable weapon against the tyranny of language, and that they may serve to reveal real relationships of considerably greater importance than the mere chance likeness of sound shared by two words or phrases.[4]

Ambiguous reactions to ambiguity became more common in the nineteenth-century, as punning came more into the cultural mainstream. In the previous age, the authors or reporters of puns often felt the need to elaborate, to underline, to tack on – by way either of elucidation or of mitigation. The incidence of laboured, 'corny' punning no doubt continued unabated, as in all ages. 'Why is a nigger like a door? Because he is palpably made for an egress.'[5] The nameless author of a squib called 'The Anti-Punster' couches his defence of the mode in suitably backhanded compliments:

> His singleness of apprehension cannot stand the shock of a double-meaning. He is unconscious that the excellent and the execrable meet together upon a point which genius alone can reach; and that in the art of punning, to be good enough and bad enough are the same thing – the difficulty being as great, and the glory as equivocal. The anti-punster is an incapable.[6]

One of the first men of letters to try to make puns respectable by argument, Charles Lamb, carried on the same tactic of making virtue out of vice, strength out of weakness. 'The puns which are most entertaining are those which will least bear an analysis.' He must have had the more particularly auditory variety in mind when he wrote that 'a pun is not bound by the laws which limit nicer wit. It is a pistol let off at the ear; not a feather to tickle the intellect.' Despite the vigour of the imagery, Lamb was too measured to be a whole-hearted supporter or practitioner. While it is no doubt true to claim that some puns are 'too good to be natural', he shrinks back before the 'superfoetation' of multiple punning: 'When a man has said a good thing, it is seldom politic to follow it up. We do not care to be cheated a second time . . . The impression, to be forcible, must be simultaneous and undivided.'[7] When, in another essay, he elaborates on this last point, he makes it clear how tenuous the whole business really is for him:

> The vigour of puns is at the instant of their birth . . . A pun hath a hearty ear-kissing smack with it; you can no more transmit it in its pristine flavour, than you can send a kiss . . . A pun, and its recognitory laugh, must be, co-instantaneous . . . A moment's interval, and the link is snapped.[8]

His attitude, then, is coherent, but inadequate, for the slight delay is essential to most pointed puns. Lamb preferred, it seems, pointless ones, for immediate and easy consumption.

Lamb was at least, after his mild fashion, championing the pun. A continuous tradition chorused objections to it. A *Westminster* reviewer of 1871 spoke of:

> the evanescent character of wit, and especially that form of wit we call 'punning'. A flash, a sudden contrast, a laugh, and all is over; the heartiness of our laughter being in proportion to our surprise, and we can only be surprised once.[9]

How to explain, then, that a fine mind like Keats's should be so given to punning? Was this just the vestigial child in him? If so, it accompanied him to his death-bed.

> I have an habitual feeling of my real life having past, and that I am leading a posthumous existence . . . Yet I ride the little horse, – and, at my worst, even in Quarantine, summoned up more puns, in a sort of desperation, in one week than in any year of my life.

Although in his letters, he often complained of being sick and tired of bad puns, emanating particularly from Leigh Hunt, he went in heavily himself for what he once called 'such tantrum sentences – or rather ten senses'. When he apologized for his own monsters, he did so unembarrassedly. 'I beg leaf to withdraw all my puns – they are all wash, an base uns.'[10] He was very aware that his mind jumped to conclusions, jumped the gun. 'Keats's mind, so alertly prefigurative', comments Ricks, 'was especially liable to puns and to portmanteaux, often of course quite premeditatedly: his letters are full of conscious effects of which Lewis Carroll or James Joyce would have been proud.'[11]

We have met with Coleridge already in the section on Shakespeare's wordplay. I can agree only with the last sentence of M. West's survey of the pun's fortune between the early eighteenth century and Coleridge:

The gentlemanly English cult of the pun, frowned upon by *The Spectator* but leading a subterranean existence in the eighteenth century (as the lacklustre efforts of the Scriblerians testify) flourished anew with such Romantic devotees as Lamb and Byron, was vitalised by Carlyle, and mechanised by Hood. But Coleridge, its most prominent English theorist, never fully exploited the intellectual energy with which the Schlegels' philosophy of language and the practice of Jean Paul endowed the pun.[12]

Coleridge did not compose his 'intended essay in defence of punning (Apology for Paronomasy, *alias* Punning)' but, under the same heading as this, 'Words and Things', he did state what has been called since Plato's *Cratylus* the 'nominalist' viewpoint, as against the 'conventionalist':

that words are not mere symbols of things and thoughts but themselves things, and that any harmony in the things symbolised will perforce be presented to us more easily, as well as with additional beauty, by a correspondent harmony of the symbols with each other,

i.e. by sound-associations.[13] Barnet sums up Coleridge's mixed response: 'As a man in social situations he enjoyed puns and punning; as a philosopher he detested distortions of language; as a student of Shakespeare he found explanations for some puns and ignored others.'[14] For instance, he maintained that *Macbeth* has no wordplay. His classification of Shakespeare's punning seems woefully one-sided:

Play on words either [due] to 1. exuberant activity of mind, as in Shakespeare's higher comedy; [or] 2. imitation of it as a fashion . . .; or 3. contemptuous exultation in minds vulgarised and overset by their success, [like] Milton's Devils; or 4. as the language of resentment, in order to express contempt – most common among the lower orders, and [the] origin of nicknames; or lastly, as the language of suppressed passion, especially of hardly smothered dislike.[15]

Such a preponderantly negative overview amounts, willy-nilly, to a hardly smothered dislike.

Or it would, if Coleridge, on reading Thomas Hood's *Odes and Addresses to Great People* (1825), had not felt sure they were composed by Lamb and written to congratulate him. 'The puns are nine in ten good – many excellent, – the *Newgatory* transcendent!'[16] In his turn, Hood was devoted to the poetry of Keats. Though the mechanical enters into all punning, and especially Hood's, he does not deserve the dismissive label (e.g. 'cracker-motto ingenuity') with which he is often ticketed and ticked off.[17] While it is no guarantee of excellence, success cannot simply be discounted. For Clubbe, 'the Victorian middle and lower middle classes, where he found the great mass of his readers, relished the domestic sentiment and the puns that pointed a moral.'[18] For Henkle, Hood was fulfilling, and not trying to reform, a demand. Hood had to 'suit the taste of his audience, which is as yet – in the 1830s and 1840s – too uneasy to deal with pain and instability except by treating it as grotesquerie'.[19] Perhaps this coming together of a style and a public response was more of a coincidence, which would be fitting, as punning relies, as we have seen, on this very coincidence. This is, however, too passive a term for what is an active phenomenon: 'The same instantaneous perception of the analogies . . . between apparently incongruous things that was possessed by Dickens, Hood possessed with regard to words and ideas.'[20] As Sutton glosses:

> Hood's most witty puns join ideas of the human and the non-human violently together. Margate Beach is the resort 'Where the maiden flirts, and the widow comes / Like the ocean – to cast her weeds'. In India, the business-like English couples who consigned themselves to wedlock through a marriage plan meet on 'Calcutta's quay / Where woman goes for mart, the same as mangoes'.[21]

The enthusiast Ainger exclaims:

> How utter the surprise, and yet how inevitable the simile appears. It is just as if the writer had not foreseen it – as if it had been mere accident – as if he had discovered the coincidence rather than arranged it. This is a special note of Hood's best puns. They fall into their place so obviously, like the rhymes of a consummate lyrist, that it would have seemed pedantic to go out of the way to avoid them.[22]

Hood was said to think in puns. Even in this study, that is no automatic compliment. D. J. Gray clearly has Hood in mind when he says of Victorian humour:

> Puns and travesty did not enlarge significance by allowing a word or a poetic idiom to introduce a meaning different from and at least as important as that expected. Usually they reduced or frustrated significance by preparing or recalling serious responses which turn out not to be required.[23]

Evasion by the author; frustration, or emotion spared, for the reader. Empson charges that Hood, 'uses puns to back away from the echoes and implications of words, to distract your attention by insisting on his ingenuity so that you can escape from sinking into the meaning'. Empson goes on to qualify the verdict:

Such virtuosity cannot be despised; I have warmed to admiration in copying it out. But the nervous jumping of the style, the air of feeling that all feeling (ahem) is a little better avoided, gives a sort of airlessness to the humour.[24]

I imagine that it was notorious lines such as 'The cannonball took off his legs / So he laid down his arms' which lead critics to diagnose some kind of dissociation. 'His punning', says Clubbe,

> indicated that his mind possessed a fundamental, unresolved dichotomy: he perceived the comic in the tragic and the tragic in the comic. But this discovery of incongruity caused in him distinct unease. Since equivocation came easily to his nature, Hood was, through puns, provided with a defence mechanism by which he could shy away from the full implications of his vision. In his social poems his marked reluctance to affirm in a straightforward manner his beliefs on controversial subjects reveals a basic insecurity; through punning, the outlet his gifts permitted him, he reconciled his embarrassment before unease. Rarely did he stare boldly in the face of a problem, social, political, or other – hence the puns and anti-climactic endings of so many works.

Did Hood suffer from a psychological fear of 'being taken at face value'?[25] Or is he just very English, which of course does not even begin to be an excuse for anything, and afraid of appearing pedantically serious? Do not we, as a nation, try to joke unpleasantness away? To make light, to make small? Poe maintained that Hood's 'main stock in trade was *littleness*', yet went on to contradict this depreciation by admitting that Hood's puns 'leave upon us a painful impression; for too evidently they are the hypochondriac's struggles at mirth – the grinning of the death's head'.[26] Poe should have written this before a mirror, intoning 'De te fabula narratur'.

> Even the bright extremes of joy
> Bring on conclusions of disgust,
> Like the sweet blossoms of the May,
> Whose fragrance ends in must.

Is this not a beautiful, poignant and pointed example of a working wordplay, where the whole dilemma of determination and free-will is memorably caught? The verbal complexity or oscillation seems to match what More calls 'the equivocation of circumstances, or the pun in things themselves'. More goes on to stress the undoubted links of the pun with conceit and metaphor:

> Beauty, these verses would seem to say, is the most fantastic of creatures, submitting to our clumsy speech only in the form of similitude, as indeed it owes its fascination to some obscure similitude the other term of which we seek and never quite grasp; it is the equivocation of matter and spirit.[27]

This is expressed fancifully but makes a real point, for punning is an attempt at an adequate response, and not necessarily an evasion of reaction. Chesterton makes a far more inflated, but fascinating, claim: that Hood 'understood the tragic and poignant use of verbal coincidences. He knew that the most profound and terrible and religious thing in literature was a profound and terrible and religious pun.'[28] A comparison with Nietzsche's wordplay is odious, except that, in *Thus Spake Zarathustra* at least, inveterate punning does not appear pathological:

> Zarathustra laughs at his own failings and punctures his pathos, like Heine ... The puncture, however, does not give the impression of diffident self-consciousness and a morbid fear of self-betrayal, but rather of that Dionysian exuberance which Zarathustra celebrates ... That *Übermut* which Nietzsche associates with the *Übermensch*: a lightness of mind, a prankish exuberance – though the term can also designate that overbearing which the Greeks called *hybris*.[29]

In such company, Hood must indeed seem little, as Poe alleged. But in his seemingly callous, even perverse, serio-comic poems (e.g. 'Sally Simpkin's Lament', where a man is bitten in two by a shark), Hood can hit other targets and 'stir within us a consciousness of our own ambivalent response towards the grotesque in human life'. His wordplay keeps on the move, makes him a moving target; he is always a step ahead of us. 'The psychic charges of his puns seem to travel rapidly through the reader, firing off into release before they can be absorbed into consciousness, before they can be *experienced* in any way.'[30] If I am unsure where that leaves us, why should puns not unsettle? Sutton finds in Hood's better puns 'a distant similarity with Carlyle's concept of "inverse sublimity" as the constituent of humour'.[31] His punning certainly enveloped all he undertook: 'His letters overrun with quibbling conceits; "the equivocation of the fiend!" we are likely to exclaim at the last, in wonder and dismay.'[32] Poe inverts his already quoted demurral into sublimity when he writes:

> But his true province was a very rare and ethereal *humour*, in which the mere pun was left out of sight, or took the character of the richest grotesquerie; impressing the imaginative reader with remarkable force, as if by a new phase of the ideal.[33]

Hood is one of the most intriguing figures in the history of the pun. Lewis Carroll is another. In *Alice in Wonderland*, Humpty Dumpty is of the race of punsters, in his cavalier, piratical attitude towards language, whereas Alice is pedantically, anxiously conservative, grasping at linguistic straws, as children often are. Humpty, however, plays fair to language in one respect: 'When I make a word do a lot of work like that, I always pay it extra': a paternalist boss.

For him, words shape reality; he talks the world round. He is shocked to learn that Alice's name means nothing. 'My name means the shape I am . . . With a name like yours you might be any shape, almost.' This last statement is logically true, for Alice is Protean. We should remember, of course, that Humpty Dumpty's verbal pride precedes his fall. Much of the unsolicited advice with which those she meets hector Alice is troubling but unsound (e.g. the Duchess: 'Take care of the sense, and the sounds will take care of themselves.')[34] Puns have often been compared to guns, but in *Alice* they act more often as silencers, for instance the King's pun which produces a deathly hush in the court-room. Concerning the 'unmistakable marks' of the Snark,

> The third is its slowness in taking a jest.
> Should you happen to venture on one,
> It will sigh like a thing that is deeply distressed:
> And it always looks grave at a pun.[35]

This pseudo-apologetic stance is of course belied by the heavy incidence of punning. The subtitle of *The Hunting of the Snark* is 'An Agony in Eight Fits', which is a splendid play on 'fits': seizures as well as cantos – especially as the poem both (possibly) deals with and induces lunacy. The Gnat, who has, as so many of the creatures she meets, been tormenting Alice with puns and logic-catches, eventually perishes of a pun. He loses 'sighs' until he disappears, probably in a puff of blue smoke up his own fundament.[36]

Such wordplay is functional. We are already familiar with the pun as an agent of deflection or bifurcation. In *Alice*,

> no argument is ever developed. It is immediately undercut, often by a misinterpretation. The word which is misinterpreted acts as a pivot . . . The pun is invaluable as a pivot for redirection . . . Random arguments proliferate on all sides, not as digressions diverging from a central meaning but as offshoots from language itself.[37]

Martin Gardner is surely right to doubt whether Carroll's interest in logic and mathematics is a sufficient explanation for his need 'to be forever warping and stretching, compressing and inverting, reversing and distorting the familiar world'.[38] One theory resorts to Nonsense:

> A pun requires a conscious awareness of the ordinary and expected meaning of the sound on which the pun is made. The writers of nonsense often play with the sound of words, but they rarely pun. Instead they put meaningless sounds into sentences as if they were conventional words . . . or they use the sounds of conventional words without bothering about their meanings.[39]

This is much truer of Edward Lear than of Carroll. Rather than Nonsense, I prefer the analogy with dreams, especially as dreaming is the ground of *Alice*. 'A school of fishes becomes a real school by the dream-law which takes homonymous puns not as jokes but as statements of double fact, and all that follows has to confirm the duality.'[40] In her study of Nonsense, Elizabeth Sewell elaborates on this dream-factor:

> Dream vision is essentially fluid; nothing is reliable, anything may change into anything else, our comfortably numbered time foreshortens into simultaneity, a thing may be two things, or a person two people, at the same moment. The result is that dreams cannot be controlled and so cannot be played with. From this something rather alarming seems to follow: that dreams play with the dreamer, who is ourself. Perhaps this holds good of all the things in experience which we cannot break down and control and play with. They may play with us.[41]

Alice is very much, though she resists womanfully, at the mercy of language games. She is at the beck and call of Lewis Carroll, but he is under her youthful sway. If there is nonsense in *Alice*, it is 'consistent nonsense'. Carroll's people live in a world of alternative sense, a counter-culture. What access do readers have to it? 'The characters Alice meets are in it both physically and mentally; Alice is in it physically but not mentally; while we are in it mentally (though we remember the other) but not physically.' Are we then at a safe distance, from which we can be merely amused? Alexander asks the awkward question:

> Notoriously we laugh to cover our confusion. Are we intellectual prudes, embarrassed when the naked body of our reasoning is shown to us, either because we are staggered by its beauty or shocked by its deformities?[42]

Nobody can tell how confused Dodgson was at the spectacle of girlish naked bodies, but nobody refuses to blow the gaff. Carroll was not entirely Dodgson when he wrote *Alice*, just as, when the caterpillar tells Alice to explain herself, she objects that she cannot, as she is not herself today.

> Why, Dolly, you have made a pun.
> But still a pun I do detest.
> 'Tis such a paltry, humbug jest;
> They who've least wit can make them best.[43]

Carroll? Swift? Shakespeare? For Mahood, the pun continued to attract low credit in the nineteenth-century, despite Coleridge's attempts to justify Shakespeare's puns on psychological grounds, and Byron's attempts to revive Shakespearean wordplay.[44] Across the Atlantic, too, its championing was often ambiguous ('PUN, *n*. A form of wit, to which wise men stoop and fools

aspire'),[45] or shamefaced, as with the sheepish recidivist Oliver Wendell
Holmes, who characterized punning as 'verbicide – violent treatment of a word
with fatal results to its legitimate meaning'.[46] Thoreau opted for discretion. As
Walden is a parable, it naturally lends itself to constant punning, playing all the
time between the levels of literal and metaphorical, and thus producing a kind
of sublime excruciation: 'Of all ebriosity, who does not prefer to be intoxicated
by the air he breathes?' This strategy is existential, rather than merely
rhetorical, for it chimes with 'a certain doubleness by which I can stand as
remote from myself as from another'.[47] In particular, studying Thoreau's
scatology, West says that his:

> excremental wordplay is neither primarily evasive nor primarily subversive. It is in
> the radical sense elusive . . . Hence [*Walden*'s] style relies so heavily upon paradox
> and covert wordplay, explanation of which would frustrate the aim of exercising
> the audience's mind.[48]

Thoreau was as interested in fomenting an attack on 'brain-rot' as he was in
fermenting human waste.[49] I cannot follow Richard Poirier over the top when
he claims that 'as a fantasia of punning, *Walden* is excelled only by *Finnegans
Wake*'. But Poirier's stress on Thoreau's efforts 'to absorb, then to refashion,
then to displace the commonly accepted meanings of words and idioms' does tie
in with the undoubted etymological play of *Walden*. The wit is glancing. At his
best, Thoreau's phrase 'does not call attention to itself . . . Thoreau's best jokes
occur however, precisely where he sounds most harmless, most idiomatically
familiar.'[50] Thoreau's crafty punning is, appropriately for the life celebrated in
Walden, artisanal. And it makes a refreshing counter to Emerson's pompous
work-ethic:

> Fatal to the man of letters, fatal to man, is the lust of display, the seeming that
> unmakes our being. A mistake of the main end to which they labour is incident to
> literary men, who, dealing with the organ of language – the subtlest, strongest and
> longest-lived of man's creations, and only fitly used as the weapon of thought
> and of justice – learn to enjoy the pride of playing with this splendid engine, but
> rob it of its almightiness by failing to work with it.[51]

I think that, in this respect, Thoreau and Emerson heard different drummers.

'Le dix-neuvième siècle fut . . . par excellence, le siècle des jeux d'esprit. On
imprimait des calembours sur les assiettes, sur les pots à tabac, on publiait des
recueils populaires de bons mots' ('The nineteenth-century was above all the
century of witticisms. Puns were inscribed on plates, on tobacco-jars, and
popular collections of jokes were published').[52] Round 1900, there was a vogue
for illustrated postcards with punning mottoes. There remained a certain
coyness, unless when it was thought to be part of the jokiness, in the use of

pseudonyms for collections: Baron de la Pointe, Eugène le Gai, Marquis de Dinenville. The co-founder of *Le Tintamarre*, Commerson (real name: Jean-Louis Auguste) claimed, of himself, that 'dès l'âge de cinq ans trois quarts, Commerson faisait des calembours jusqu'à la dysenterie.'[53] One of his most quoted ones is the mild Spoonerism: 'J'aimerais mieux aller hériter à la poste que d'aller à la postérité' ('I would prefer to collect my inheritance through the post than through posterity'). Many are pointless, and self-confessedly so: 'Il n'y a aucun rapport entre un âne et un musicien; pourtant l'un et l'autre aiment le son' ('There is no connection between donkeys and musicians, yet both of them are keen on oats'). Many are self-evident truisms: 'J'aimerais mieux prêter à rire qu'à la petite semaine' ('I would prefer to lend myself to mockery than at high interest'). He accepted that, on the literary scale, the pun was of the same order as the comb and paper on the musical.[54]

Balzac made higher claims, and surprisingly neo-classical they were, for multiplicity of meaning. In a letter to Louis Aimé in 1844, he wrote:

> Je ne puis vous laisser dans l'erreur sur le sens de cette expression *créer un mot*. Je maintiens que Racine a créé l'acception que je donne à *Décevant*. Les mots sont susceptibles de prendre plusieurs significations; et leur en donner de nouvelles est ce que j'appelle *créer*, c'est enrichir une langue, une langue s'appauvrit en gagnant des mots, et elle s'enrichit en en ayant peu et leur donnant beaucoup de significations.

> (I must make it clear to you what I mean by the expression 'coining a word'. I maintain that Racine created the meaning that I give to *Décevant*. Words can take several meanings and giving them new ones is what I call 'coining'. It enriches a language; a language is impoverished when it acquires new words, and it is enriched when it has few but gives them several meanings.)[54]

Not neologisms, then, but the densification of existing words (presumably by placing them in new contexts, otherwise their extant meanings would remain static). Few but hard-working, limited but resonant: this neo-classical view of lexis would not be shared by champions of Romanticism like Hugo. A cleverly plotted set-up like the following would no doubt have been condemned by Molière as unnatural: 'La Duchesse de R., vaporeuse, mélodieuse, vibrante, gâtant tout par de brusques griffes; c'était une harpie éolienne' ('The Duchess of R., vaporous, melodious, vibrant, but spoiling everything by sudden bitchiness; she was an Aeolian harpy').[55] Hugo was especially addicted to paronomasia in the French sense of approximate sound-association: 'Ils n'ont qu'un cri de marche: En arrière! une route, / La routine' ('They have only one marching chant: "Retreat!" and one route, routine').[56] His qualifications were, as Rochette points out, a formidable vocabulary, an acute sense of sound-links, an open-armed approach to all forms of humour, including the grotesque, a belief in the mixture of genres and a veneration for Shakespeare.[57] Being Hugo, he swivelled between extremes. In *Lucrèce Borgia*, Gennaro deletes the first letter of the name *Borgia* to leave *orgia*; Gubelta warns: 'Voilà un calembour qui fera mettre demain la moitié de la ville à la question' ('That's a pun which will get half the population tortured tomorrow').[58] But his notorious narcissistic rhyme in *Booz endormi*, 'Jérimadeth' ('j'ai rime à deth'), shows him at the gorblimey end of the sublime/grotesque ladder. His characters are often similarly self-congratulatory. As he throws bread into a park lake in *Les Misérables*, '"Les cygnes comprennent les signes", dit le bourgeois, heureux d'avoir de l'esprit' (' "Cygnets contain/understand signs", said the bourgeois, pleased with his wit').[59] In the same novel, in a chapter called 'Sagesse de Tholomyès', the character of this name makes a plea for moderation. After a weakish pun, he pontificates:

Il ne faut pas que trop de stupeur accueille ce calembour, tombé du ciel . . . Loin de moi l'insulte au calembour! Je l'honore dans la proportion de ses mérites; rien de plus. Tout ce qu'il y a de plus auguste, de plus sublime et de plus charmant dans l'humanité, et peut-être hors de l'humanité, a fait des jeux de mots. Jésus-Christ a fait un calembour sur saint Pierre, Moïse sur Isaac, Eschyle sur Polynice, Cléopâtre sur Octave.

(This pun, dropped from the sky, should not be greeted with too much amazement. Far be it from me to insult the pun! I respect it for what it is. The most august, sublime and delightful examples of mankind, and perhaps beyond, have made plays on words. Jesus Christ made a pun on Peter, Moses on Isaac, Aeschylus on Polynices and Cleopatra on Octavian).[60]

This impressive list of guarantors shifts the emphasis, however, from the middle of the road to the top level.

In Flaubert, punning becomes less lordly and playful: excruciation is the Flaubertian mode *par excellence*, as it can be of the pun. Playing with words, and agonizing over them, share the same nuptial couch for Flaubert. Not long before his death, Sartre recalls, he wrote to his niece: 'Suppose que je m'appelle Druche. Tu me dirais: tu es beau, Druche.'[61] This ponderous set-up for a feeble gag (*baudruche* = windbag) reiterates a lifelong taste for making others squirm. In one of his projected 'féeries', a father catches his son boozing in a bar and exclaims 'Tu n'es qu'un pilier d'estaminet' ('You're holding up the walls of this pub'), whereupon the lad changes into a doorpost.[62] Flesh is turned into thing in this cliché twisted by the tail; the person is reified. No wonder that Lukács charged that, despite being moral and sensitive, Flaubert was the instigator of the inhuman in modern literature.[63] Other critics have piled it on even thicker. Tony Tanner starts spinning a yarn: Flaubert shows:

the words in his text beginning to look at each other and discover similarities and repetitions that suggests [sic] the beginnings of some kind of ultimate perverse rapprochement among words themselves, not a marriage but a merging, meanings swallowing each other in hopeless circularity as Binet's lathe seems to swallow clear utterance in its insentient unvarying hum.

The woof starts getting warped:

Binet fills any *trou* with his *tour*, which effectively manufactured *trous*. The phonetic repetitions, the words mirroring each other so that *tour* only requires the displacement of one letter to become *trou* [we can all play that game: 'To bed or not to bed, that is the question'], the odd and unstabilising sense of apparently different phenomena merging into each other, are all surely important aspects of the experience of reading this book.

It is true that Emma Bovary fails to make distinctions, but the dangerous facility of this approach is obvious. When we look for anagrams, we find them unfailingly, and thus we get that much closer to the goal of so many parasite-critics: rewriting the text they are supposed to be explicating. 'Rouen', 'Rouault', 'roue': for Tanner this is 'higher-order punning'.[64] By Flaubert or Tanner? The commentator on wordplay who plays with words should come clean. In partial fairness, I should admit that Flaubert was indisputably in a trance of empathy when writing *Madame Bovary* – the taste of arsenic in his own mouth – and this is precisely the state in which words might well call independently to each other in odd associations and obsessions.

Sartre's different kettle of fishiness is altogether more appetizing. Though he too, like all of us, foists on to Flaubert, he also coincides at times, and then seems truly to speak for, or through, him. Flaubert plainly did flail around all kinds of vicious circles. Sartre's term for these, 'le tourniquet', seems apt, for the tourniquet hurts as it stanches. Flaubert suffered in his own *Schadenfreude*. Hence the desperate gaiety of his *farces et attrapes*. Sartre's gloss on the 'Hôtel des Farces' episode is instructive. What was celebrated was 'la fête de la Merde, lors de la vidange, où l'on entendait résonner dans les couloirs les commandes suivantes: "Trois seaux de merde au 14"' ('The Feast of Shit, when the night-soil is emptied and the following orders can be heard along the corridors: "Three buckets of shit to room 14" '). Sartre comments:

Le calembour – il en a raffolé toute sa vie. L'origine de cette festivité est *verbale*: vidange, vendanges. Quand vient l'époque du vendangeur, on fête le raisin, produit et matériau de travail; pourquoi, lorsqu'on fait la vidange, ne pas célébrer la merde, produit de l'homme et matériau d'horribles travailleurs? A partir de cet à peu-près, Gustave se jette dans l'hyperbole et pantagruélise, la merde coule à flots, on la commande par seaux, on s'en bourre. Après l'anthropophagie, la coprophagie.

(He revelled in puns all his life. The origins of this festivity are *verbal*: slopping out and lopping grapes. At grape-harvest time, the grape is celebrated as the product of and material for labour; when you're slopping out, why not celebrate shit, a product of mankind and material for horrible labourers? From this approximate pun, Gustave launches into hyperbole and does a Pantagruel, shit flows galore, is ordered by the bucketful, people get their bellyful. After anthropophagy, coprophagy.)

While Sartre here annexes, sniffily, some of Flaubert's gusto, his bad-taste gusto, he suggests, as in his study of Jean Genet, that the coprophile can have his cake and eat it. If all criticism is at best approximation, Sartre seems to me here to draw near to Flaubert's imaginative functioning, by seizing on the implications of this 'à peu-près'.

In that 'féerie' we saw the pun mortify the flesh. Sartre sees how, in Flaubert, it can also vivify:

Flaubert s'y plaisait parce que chaque calembour lui découvrait une ambiguïté essentielle du langage et se présentait, obscurément d'abord puis de plus en plus clairement comme un grossier symbole de l'oeuvre littéraire ... Le calembour, somme toute, nous fait découvrir le langage comme paradoxe et c'est précisément sur ce paradoxe que Gustave pressent qu'il faut fonder l'Art d'écrire.

(Flaubert delighted in them because each pun reminded him of an essential ambiguity in language itself and appeared to him, vaguely at first, then more and more clearly, as a rough-and-ready symbol for the literary work. All in all, the pun makes us experience language as paradox, and it is precisely on this paradox that Gustave sensed he had to base his Art of Writing.)

We have seen often already how paradox and punning are devices of economy, and, like Balzac a few paragraphs ago, Sartre harks back to the French classical era: 'Les auteurs classiques s'inspirent du paradoxe, jeu d'idées qui est à leur style ce que le jeu de mots sera pour le style de Flaubert' ('The classical authors were inspired by the paradox, a play with ideas which was for their style what play with words would be for the style of Flaubert').[65] The idea of dense intelligence must appeal to the creator of Bouvard and Pécuchet. In his own voice, Flaubert spoke of his longing to attain 'le comique arrivé à l'extrême, le comique qui ne fait pas rire' ('Comedy at its peak, comedy which is not funny').[66] Sartre, despite temptations, refuses to be totally won over by Flaubert's fascination for any writer, and he says coldly; 'Le calembour flatte son fatalisme'[67] – presumably because puns are accidents of language, *objets trouvés*, passively received, and, as such, appal the voluntarist in Sartre.

Another voluntarist, though not one whose company Sartre would seek for long, is Bergson, author of perhaps the best-known comic theory of all. He invented the malady of 'la trahison des clercs' ('the intellectuals' betrayal')

before even Benda diagnosed it, because he claimed for his study *Le Rire* a
scientific rigour which philosophy, literary criticism and often enough science
itself can hardly justify. Bergson takes a pseudo-industrial stance in his aim to
determine 'les procédés de fabrication du comique'.[68] This automating of
humour is necessary to his doctrine: comedy is a policeman, aggressive,
punitive, corrective. Laughter 'a pour fonction d'intimider en humiliant' (p.
151). There is something inherently and unconsciously comic in Bergson's own
rhetoric: the way he slides from the physical to the figurative or moral:
'Coureurs d'idéal qui trébuchent sur des réalités ('The pursuers of the ideal
who trip over reality'), as he says of Don Quixote-types (pp. 10–11). He keeps
up an act of working towards a finding, whereas patently he knows exactly
where he is going; his argument illustrates a preconceived idea. For him,
society, and its agent, comedy, are powers for conformity, which blackballs
eccentric steps. He conveniently omits the subversive action of dirty or political
jokes. Bergson takes essentially a theatrical view of comedy, based on a one-
sided use of Molière – the more comforting side. Despite admitting that 'il serait
chimérique de vouloir tirer tous les effets comiques d'une seule formule simple'
('it would be ludicrous to try to extract all comic effects from a single, simple
formula'), – for this would be too static for a man who believes his mind is in
tune with the dynamic flux of life – the leitmotif of 'raideur' (inflexibility) means
that Bergson is trapped in his own definition. Hence his foot-shuffling: 'Il y
faudra penser toujours, sans néanmoins s'y appesantir trop – un peu comme le
bon escrimeur doit penser aux mouvements discontinus de la leçon tandis que
son corps s'abandonne à la continuité de l'assaut' ('We must keep it always in
mind but without over-emphasizing it – rather as the skilful fencer must think
of the discontinuous movements of his training while his body gives itself up to
the continuity of attack') (p.28). He is a slippery customer. Yet he can be as
inelastic, to put it mildly, as the human behaviour he mocks. Doesn't a
hunchback, he asks, look as if he's acting a part? Why do we laugh at a negro?
(pp. 18, 31). He is forever papering over the cracks of his scissors-and-paste
job, in his concern for a smooth texture: the blandness of decorum and
conformity ('une âme à la vie harmonieusement fondue, unie, semblable à une
nappe d'eau bien tranquille' – 'a soul whose nature is harmoniously blended, all
of a piece, like a very calm sheet of water' (p.99)). Marx, or most of us, would
hardly agree that the reification of the person is a comic thing. He admits the
existence of *quiproquo*, or *équivoque* in connection with situations, though
ignoring double entendre in words. For him, wordplay is closer to the
vaudeville tradition than to the 'nobler' comedy of character. If he had included
a proper discussion of puns, he would have had to entertain the possibility that
they subvert the automatisms of language, as well as imitating them. As it is,
they are for him the 'least estimable' of the ways of giving more than one

meaning to a phrase. Finally he dismisses the whole phenomenon of wordplay as slacking, never popular with headmasters:

> Le jeu de mots nous fait plutôt penser à un laisser-aller du langage, qui oublierait un instant sa destination véritable et prétendrait maintenant régler les choses sur lui, au lieu de se régler sur elles. Le jeu de mots trahit donc une distraction momentanée du langage et c'est d'ailleurs par là qu'il est amusant.

> (Wordplay reminds us of a slovenliness in language, which can forget for a time its true purpose and claim to control things instead of being controlled by them. Wordplay therefore betrays a temporary linguistic absent-mindedness, and that is how it can be entertaining.) (p.92).

This might be true of mechanical, pointless punning, but what of deliberately aimed wordplay? All in all, his stress on the mechanical seems to have ground down his own spirit, for the last words of *Le Rire* are strangely disabused. Arthur Koestler makes joyful mincemeat of Bergson's renowned theory.

> If rigidity contrasted with organic suppleness were laughable in itself, Egyptian statues and Byzantine mosaics would be the best jokes ever invented. If automatic repetitiveness in human behaviour were a necessary and sufficient condition of the comic there would be no more amusing spectacle than an epileptic fit . . . If 'we laugh each time a person gives us the impression of being a thing', there would be nothing more funny than a corpse.[69]

Max Eastman latches on to the élitist element, the psychic meritocracy, in Bergson's theories: 'The function of this highly discriminating laughter of Bergson's is to aid in the process of Creative Evolution by making life uncomfortable for the clods.' Of such theorists, he adds: 'I suspect them not only of never having seen a baby, but of never having been one.'[70]

Freud, whom we have met already in the discussion of the pun's economy and will meet again when it comes to parapraxes, neurosis and dreams, saw the very limited value of Bergson's categories: 'The uncovering of psychical automatism is one of the techniques of the comic, just as is any kind of revelation or self-betrayal.'[71] Like Flaubert's Bouvard and Pécuchet who, once they had heard of phallic symbolism, saw priapuses everywhere, Freud was a born punner, for he saw double meanings on all sides.

> According to Bergson, laughter defends society by ridiculing the deviant; according to Freud, laughter attacks society by ridiculing conventional values and the status quo . . . In both theories aggression is the primary ingredient.[72]

This is only half the story of Freud, for he was fully aware, too, of non-tendentious verbal humour. In contrast with Bergson's arrogance, Freud's honesty is delightful, as when he admits 'how hard it is for a psychoanalyst to discover anything new that has not been known before by some creative writer'.[73] Max Eastman, while not so harsh on Freud as on Bergson, still maintains that 'what Freud's theory first needs is to be cured of the German habit of explaining the universe every time you explain a fact.'[74]

Whatever his weaknesses, it was Freud who ushered in the Age of Suspicion: we are today the undeceived, or the less deceived. We think we can see through façades, camouflage, the smokescreen of words. We are on the look-out for the wilfully or unconsciously withheld, the further or double meaning. If we caught this from America, the Americans caught it from Freud. He himself would have been suspicious of what lay behind the arras of Raymond Roussel's curious verbal universe, at the turn of the century. Roussel was an infantilist and a neurasthenic, whose charades or rebuses, those dramatized puns, would have given Freud much food for speculation. What, for instance, makes a man take flight not on, but into, language? Burrowing into it. In *Comment j'ai écrit certains de mes livres*, Roussel gives details of his generative method: 'la création basée sur l'accouplement de deux mots pris dans deux sens différents.' One word is forced to mount, or pierce, or swallow, another. Another device was to take a ready-made phrase and to dislocate it into different, splintered words – wrecking meaning: 'J'ai du bon tabac – jade tube onde aubade.' With these smashed eggs, he would then cook up an exotic omelette. This is aleatory art. Puns on the original structure engender the tale itself. Just as the pun Ernest/earnest was probably the mainspring of Oscar Wilde's play, so such plays on words as Roussel's are said to be 'generative', 'transitive' or 'mythopoeic'. The pun gives an initial fillip, like the deist's god, to creation. The pun is the logos. Roussel linked his process with rhyme: 'Dans les deux cas, il y a création imprévue due à des combinaisons phoniques. C'est essentiellement un procédé poétique' ('In both cases there is an unforeseen creation due to phonic combinations. It is essentially a poetic device').[75] For Foucault, the fantastic machines that Roussel's ex-human imagination built are 'le langage rimant avec lui-même', which, if it means anything, suggests a claustrophobic narcissism.[76] It is a jigsaw-puzzle literature, which comes close to being, or at least seeming to be, a world of words with nothing beyond, 'vox et praeterea nihil', as Addison said of punning.

A much more convincing example of generative punning may be found in the work of Claude Simon. He uses puns for fission and fusion. 'One cell of the story material has split into two to increase the complexity and density of the text,' says Alastair Duncan in his study of Simon's novels; 'the narrative has, so to speak, been fashioned from its own rib.' This leads to a proliferation. For Duncan, 'the reader's attention is diverted from any possible reality depicted by the words. He is made to focus instead on the relationship of the words to each other in the text.' But is this not too polarizing a view? What about overlap? The pan-sexuality of Simon's people, as well as of language, is here on display. Meaning is not evicted quite so comprehensively, even if it is true that the reader is 'forced more and more to lend his attention to the text as text, as a play on and with words'. Duncan analyses very well that pan-sexuality:

> The play on sound and sense from 'boufferais des pissenlits' to 'bouffant là où elle pisse' [i.e. the jump from death to cunnilingus]; the implied pun which leads from 'gland' as acorn to 'gland' as sexual organ; the dual reference in 'j'essayai de la mâcher' ['I tried to munch it/her'], where 'la' could stand for 'l'herbe' or Corinne.

Duncan concludes:

> Georges had planned to use language as a means of recapturing the past, but now it has run amok, producing an apparently unlimited range of variants on the theme of metamorphosis. At one level, indeed, the imagery of metamorphosis may be taken to symbolise the power of language to breed from itself in an endless series of transformations by analogy. Georges' recital of past events turns into an exploration of the possibilities of language.[77]

The story forks (fission) but the analogies fuse: a nice example of double duty.

The baroque conjunctions engineered by what Roussel called 'métagrammes' endeared him to the Surrealists. André Breton talks generally in a pretty cheerless fashion about wordplay, but he did value in it the opportunity for demonstrating that words can behave autonomously and indeed dictate thought. One Surrealist offspring, Ionesco, is particularly taken with this hectoring quality of language, as indeed was Lewis Carroll. Automatic writing, or robot-like speech, are both difficult to argue with. As always, Breton lays down the law:

> les jeux de mots méritent l'attention du fait de ces deux caractères distincts: d'une part leur rigueur mathématique (déplacement de lettre à l'intérieur d'un mot, échange de syllabe entre deux mots, etc.), d'autre part l'absence de l'élément comique qui passait pour inhérent au genre et suffisait à sa dépréciation.

> (Plays on words deserve our attention for these two separate reasons: on the one hand their mathematical rigour (the displacing of a letter inside a word, the exchange of a syllable between two words, etc.), on the other, the absence of any comic element, which was supposed to be inherent to the genre and which was enough to get it a bad name.)

His dead hand also lies heavy on his *Anthologie de l'humour noir*. His attempt to celebrate the undeniable erotic vim of wordplay: 'Et qu'on comprenne bien que nous disons: jeux de mots quand ce sont nos plus sûres raisons d'être qui sont en jeu. Les mots, du reste, ont fini de jouer. Les mots font l'amour' ('And let there be no mistake when we say plays on words, for it is our clearest reasons for existing which are at stake. Words, besides, have finished playing. Words make love'), sounds schoolmasterly when placed beside the *practice* of a René Crevel or a Marcel Duchamp (whose pseudonym Rrose Sélavy translates as 'Eros c'est la vie'). Breton pompously enthrones an *idea* of wordplay.[78]

The Surrealist notion of *le hasard objectif* embraces the idea of puns as *objets trouvés*, windfalls, ready-mades. But such material still needs to be put to work; chance encounters have to be organized. *Le hasard* has to be channelled; its hand forced, as for example in their game of 'cadavre exquis' (a kind of fragmented 'Consequences'). They found that this experiment produced more freedom than 'automatic writing', where the individual writer's unfettered assocations were still determined by personal idiosyncrasy; collective arbitrariness appealed more. From a given start, all is supposedly then at the mercy of the inertia of language: logic, sounds, rhythms. We have already seen, however, that puns are perhaps better used to *subvert* this very inertia. Besides, the whole process is much exaggerated, for the writer remains ultimately in majority control, whether he is one or many. Sane people do not speak in tongues. It still could be foolish to ignore the element of automatism in all writing and speaking.

The Surrealists did not have the possible benefit of that religious belief which inspired Gerard Manley Hopkins, who progressed 'by double meanings, entering a word through one, departing through another.'[79] As a result,

the search for relationships that reveal the hidden internal order of creation was for Hopkins a search for 'inscape', signs of the continuing activity of divine ordering. Such signs – a fortuitous similarity in the sounds of words, a random formation of clouds – may have the appearance of chance, but they may also be clues suggesting an underlying design. 'All the world is full of inscape', he wrote, 'and chance left free to act falls into an order as well as purpose' ... Casting sound-echoes and puns in language is thus for Hopkins not simply a game of chance, but divination. In the poem 'Spelt from Sibyl's Leaves', he finds through the sound-associations of charm-melos, and in particular through puns and near-puns, darkly prophetic meanings.[80]

This multi-layered use of wordplay as divination takes us back to where we started, and reminds us in this way that there is no relentless 'progress' in language-use or anything else.

There was no God, in man or the physical universe, for the Surrealists, though they tended to deify their own activities, and to appropriate to themselves the divine gift of serendipity. Divine or Satanic? Breton stressed that wordplay does not seek to amuse, and Michel Corvin added: 'C'est une entreprise désespérée de création inversée. "Démon est l'anagramme de monde",' remarque . . . Torma.'[81] The whole tradition in Modernism, set off by Laforgue and Corbière, of 'la poésie dépoétisée' rests on such inversions.[82] Another Modernist innovation, that of simultaneism (in the work of Cendrars, Romains or Apollinaire) naturally drew upon the pun, that instance of the all-at-once. For me, most Surrealist punning lacks point, and I prefer this variety, which defies possibility more surreally: 'When he got the writing desk home from the auction and opened it, a dozen people fell out. Apparently, it was a missing persons bureau.'[83] The displaced here find an abode.

It was the precursors to or refugees from Surrealism who exploited wordplay more profitably. Alphonse Allais or Boris Vian are especially adept at taking literally set expressions. In his poem 'Xylopages' (the title refers to woodcuts and to wood-boring insects), Allais puns on the militaristic motto 'Fais ce que dois' in this fashion:

> Un général anglais, dans une bataille,
> Eut les deux fesses emportées par la mitraille.
> Il en fit faire une autre paire en bois,
> Mais jamais il ne les paya.
> Moralité
> Fesses que doit!

(An English general in a battle had his buttocks shot away by shrapnel. He had another pair made in wood, but never paid the bill. The moral: Do as you must/He owes for his buttocks.)[84]

Less purely ludic often, Jacques Prévert, in his anticlerical poem 'La Crosse en l'air' (the crozier held on high by the drunk bishop, and the rifle which anarchists encouraged common soldiers to keep reversed when facing strikers), cuts cinematically between the Rue de Rome in Paris, the militaristic Rome of Corneille's *Horace*, and the Papal seat. Elsewhere, 'L'Emasculée Conception, ou qui aime bien châtre bien' ('the Emasculate Conception, or The loving father doesn't spare his child's rod') refers in brief to heavy feathers, the inhuman doctrine of Virgin Birth and a knife-wielding, anti-erotic God.[85]

I placed as epigraph to this book Raymond Queneau's 'Tant d'histoire pour quelques calembours', a sentiment that putative readers may well wish to echo. It is a pun itself, for in *Les Fleurs bleues* you have to wade through a good deal of (admittedly zany) history to get at the scattered jokes; secondly, there is in it such a lot of fuss and all you get is a few puns for your pains. Queneau's apology for punning is always ironic, for he once wrote 'parmi les alcools de ma vie, il y aura eu l'érudition et le calembour.'[86] The two alcohols blend together. Wishing to convey the projection of uncloudy urine, Queneau says 'pisser de façon cartésienne'.[87] In *Les Fleurs bleues* there are, as always in Queneau, floating puns here and there in the text (e.g. 'Le Gaulois fumait une gitane') but the story itself mimes the action of punning. Queneau maintained that it was possible to rhyme (and hence to pun) situations as well as words. In *Les Fleurs bleues*, Auge and Cidrolin (already implicitly linked by the Norman resonance of their names – Vallée d'Auge, *cidre*) – draw closer and closer together over the centuries, approximate and finally overlap. Throughout, neither is sure who is dreaming up the other. In puns too, we often wonder who or what is manipulating whom or what. This novel even has a talking horse given to punning. All the random joking, however, does not conceal the primordial place granted by Queneau to this phenomenon. In his *Petite Cosmogonie portative*, he writes:

> De quelque calembour naît signification.
> Ce petit prend la chose comme elle vient.

(Meaning can be born of any old pun. This little fellow takes things as they come).[88]

He clearly sees wordplay as a way of multiplying the possibilities for manoeuvre:

> Queneau will use a word as a pun, in a vertical sort of mode, or at least in such a manner that several definitions are apt in a given context; he will also bring these meanings out through repetitions in varying contexts, a horizontal mode, which causes this same accretion of meaning by the effect of memory. Both means have the effect of proving an escape from the merely linear addition of word to word.[89]

Polyphonic, polysemic: this again is a Modernist programme. 'Vous faites des calembours? – Qu'est-ce que vous voulez: l'esprit moderne.'[90]

For Michel Leiris, words are not instruments but containers, housing meanings: *syllabe* begets *sibylle*.[91] He and language cannot leave each other alone; it plagues him; he pesters it. Words are his life, to an extent that even Sartre's *Les Mots* never reaches. After comparing his own autobiographical exposure with the performance of a matador, he makes it clear that his existence is a stylistic risk; he is living vicariously. 'La question est de savoir si, dans de telles conditions, le rapport que j'établis entre son authenticité et la mienne ne repose pas sur un simple jeu de mots' ('The question is in this case, does the relationship I establish between the authenticity (of the bullfight) and my own rest on a mere play on words?'). He is naturally undaunted by this prospect. He lives so intensely inside language that he is constantly rewriting it, 'décomposant les mots du vocabulaire, et les reconstituant en des calembours poétiques qui me semblaient expliciter leur signification la plus profonde'.[92] His ambition was to 'faire un dictionnaire en jeux de mots'.[93] This is a process half wilful and half accidental. His text on this is 'Glossaire, j'y serre mes gloses' ('Glossary: where I store my glosses'), in *Mots sans mémoire*. With a head as buzzing with sounds as his, he cannot have failed to think of Molière's Tartuffe ('Serrez ma haire avec ma discipline' – 'Put away my hair-shirt with my scourge'). Glossaries contain all the elements that Leiris needs for verbal masochism (the dominant motif of his autobiography), and untrustworthy sincerity, both characteristic also of Tartuffe.

For many readers, no doubt, the experiments of a Raymond Roussel are already far enough out on a limb. Here is Michel Foucault on Roussel, on him like a succubus or spreading ivy:

> L'identité des mots – le simple fait fondamental dans le langage, qu'il y a moins de vocables qui désignent que de choses à désigner – est elle-même une expérience à double versant: elle révèle dans le mot le lieu d'une rencontre imprévue entre les figures du monde les plus éloignées (il est la distance abolie, le point de choc des êtres, la différence ramenée sur elle-même en une forme unique, duelle, ambiguë, minotaurine), et elle montre un dédoublement du langage qui, à partir d'un noyau simple, s'écarte de lui-même et fait naître sans cesse d'autres figures (prolifération de la distance, vide qui naît sous les pas du double, croissance labyrinthique des corridors semblables et différents). En leur riche pauvreté, *les mots toujours conduisent plus loin et ramènent à eux-mêmes.*

> (The identity of words – the simple fundamental fact in language that there are fewer words which designate than there are things to designate – is itself a two-sided experience: it reveals in the word the locus of an unexpected encounter between the most remote features of the world (it is distance wiped out, the collision-point between creatures, difference coiled up on itself in a form at once unique, dual, ambiguous, Minotaurine), and it shows a doubling-up of language which, from a simple kernel, splits off from itself and incessantly engenders other figures (proliferation of distance, a void opening up under the feet of the double, labyrinthine growth of similar and different corridors). In their rich poverty, *words always lead us on further and lead us back to themselves.*)[94]

This last phrase, which I have italicized, seems to me to enact what is going on in the whole preceding development. The author's language has been cut adrift from any identifiable referent; it is self-generating. It is academic, in the most pejorative sense – that it has lost all contact with reality. Lévi-Strauss describes very pungently how his intellectual formation, or deformation, trained him in effect to treat serious matters ludically (and comic ones pedantically?). In the *classe de philosophie*,

> là, j'ai commencé à apprendre que tout problème, grave ou futile, peut être liquidé par l'application d'une méthode, toujours identique, qui consiste à opposer deux vues traditionnelles de la question; à introduire la première par les justifications du sens commun, puis à les détruire au moyen de la seconde; enfin à

les renvoyer dos à dos grâce à une troisième qui révèle le caractère également partiel des deux autres, ramenées par des artifices de vocabulaire aux aspects complémentaires d'une même réalité: forme et fond, contenant et contenu, être et paraître, continu et discontinu, essence et existence, etc. Ces exercices deviennent vite verbaux, fondés sur un art du calembour qui prend la place de la réflexion, les assonances entre les termes, les homophonies et les ambiguïtés fournissant progressivement la matière de ces coups de théâtre spéculatifs à l'ingéniosité desquels se reconnaissent les bons travaux philosophiques . . . De ce point de vue, l'enseignement philosophique exerçait l'intelligence en même temps qu'il desséchait l'esprit.

(There I began to learn that any problem, whether serious or trivial, can be solved by the application of a method, always the same, which consists in contrasting two traditional views of the question; to introduce the first by the proofs of common sense, then to destroy these by means of the second; and finally to send them both packing thanks to a third which reveals the equally partial character of the first two, reduced by adroit use of vocabulary to the complimentary aspects of one and the same thing: form and content, container and contained, being and appearance, continuity and discontinuity, essence and existence, etc. These exercises swiftly became purely verbal, based as they were on an art of punning which replaced thinking; assonance between the terms, homophonies and ambiguities gradually provided the material for these sensational speculations by whose ingeniousness proper philosophical work can be recognized. From this angle, our philosophical training honed the mind and simultaneously dried up the spirit.)[95]

Here Lévi-Strauss, who of course like the rest of us is not above practising what he preaches against, provides a verdict on the Foucault passage quoted above, which illustrates precisely what is amiss. Barthes (with the saving grace of self-critical irony), Foucault, Lacan and their proliferating neophytes demonstrate the *sliding* potentialities of language ('le glissement progressif des sens'). In such writings, the words seem always to be en route for somewhere else, to take leave of their grounding: the text becomes a pretext for flight.

We have already seen how important wordplay always was for Freud. In his self-appointed successor, Jacques Lacan, punning becomes manic. Clearly, ambiguity, double meaning, repressed meaning, slips, are all crucial to psychoanalysts. I am not convinced by Lacan's attempts, many of which seem mere hiccups ('De ce qui perdure de perte pure à ce qui ne parie que du père au pire') and have led one disbeliever, François George, to counter by calling him 'le père Hoquet' ('Father Hiccup/parrot').[96] Lacan's concept of 'la passe', in which an aspirant analyst gives an account of his training to the master and his sidesmen, is uncomfortably reminiscent of 'une maison der passe', with that decrepit bidet and dubious bar of soap.[97] Lacanism has certainly become a communicable disease. The fact that 'le nom du père', 'le non du père' and 'Les Non-Dupes Errent' are homophonic in French alone should have given him pause for thought before erecting a theory on such a gratuitous basis. He can be defended only on mimetic grounds. For example, Malcolm Bowie suggests:

> By writing 'la langue' as 'lalangue', Lacan inserts several facts of language into the name language bears: it is repetitious; it is an affair of the tongue (*langue* – our tongues beat our palates as we say it); it has a musical tendency (*la* is a note in the tonic sol-fa); it has a capacity to shock or surprise ('Oh là là!') ... The unconscious is speaking in its native tongue.[98]

Patrick Bowles makes a comparable defence, but more critically:

> Directly inspired by the criminals and mystics – almost exclusively women – whose 'syntaxe originale' echoes within the earth's prisons and asylums, Lacan's own 'schizophasie' is often all but indistinguishable from that of his patients, from the 'disorders' of baroque artists like, say, Jean-Pierre Brisset, or from the ecstatic glossolalia of certain saints ... And if Lacan's celebrated word-play rarely rises above the level of inspired idiocy – 'l'Hommelette', 'je père-sévère' – idiocy is indeed its inspiration.[99]

Lastly, Sherry Turkle stresses the tactical nature of such punning. Lacan wants to speak directly to the unconscious and believes that wordplay, where causal links dissolve and associations abound, is the language which it understands.[100]

Lacan's influence has spread beyond psychoanalysis to literary criticism, to semiotics and deconstruction (one of whose *mafiosi* describes it as 'playing on the play within language').[101] Particularly in France over the past twenty years or so, but increasingly too in other cultures, both creative writing and criticism (though the two often merge) have grown ludic, if rarely funny. Fashion has made such cheek chic. Bertrand Poirot-Delpech, after comparing the use of 'ça' in Lacan to that of the blank tile in Scrabble, coins a pun better than any of the master's to describe what is happening to words today: 'Le texte s'est mis aux tics' ('The text twitches with semio-tics').[102] Perhaps when Nathalie Sarraute called this 'l'Ere du soupçon', she intended both meanings: The Age of Mistrust, and the Age of Trifles – of nugatory art and criticism. Wordplay, as we have seen abundantly already and will go on seeing, need not be like this.

5

The Extended Family

Classification of rhetorical devices, from Aristotle through Cicero and Quintilian had, by the time of the Renaissance, produced more confusion than enlightenment. Perhaps all we really need, in terms of rhetorical nomenclature, is the idea of trope: a pun is a figurative use of a word or phrase. Little else is needed, once, as Northrop Frye claims, we accept that 'paronomasia is one of the essential elements of verbal creation.'[1] Some have recognized that punning overspills any boundaries placed around it ('The basic structure of the pun is identical at a deep level with a number of more respectable literary genres, including the allegory, the mystery and the detective story'),[2] and it is this extended family that I now want to interview.

Firstly, word-games, which is what many understand if you use the term 'wordplay'. Puns can be pictorialized in the rebus, as in the one over the entrance to Blenheim House (a lion rending a little cock: *gallus* = cock, or Frenchman). Steele commented: 'Such a device in so noble a Pile of Building looks like a Pun in an Heroic Poem.'[3] According to the *OED*, the modern sense of conundrum as 'riddle in the form of a question' did not come into use till the latter half of the eighteenth century; before that, it meant a pun. Puns can be dramatized in the charade; and of course in crossword-puzzle clues they can drive you mad. In all these instances, they are a kind of code which the reader, spectator or hearer is invited to crack. Conundrums are slightly different from the others, as there is less element of surprise. You expect a pun from the set-up, even if you are unsure what it will be. Question: How do you make an elephant fly? Answer: Well, first you take a gr-r-r-eat big zip . . .[4] The conundrum or joking riddle re-emphasizes and crystallizes what all wordplay aims at: testing. But as Gruner points out,

> losing to a conundrum is not the same thing as losing to a straight riddle. To be sure, the loser has been outsmarted, but *double meaning* was used! . . . The riddle has turned from a 'real' contest of brains to a 'play' contest more like a game than a fight . . . The 'duel' turns not upon wisdom and knowledge of the real world, but upon nonsensical symbolic manipulation of the 'unreal'.[5]

More than nonsense is at stake, for even a sniffer like Bain admits that the conundrum 'pushes to the utmost limits the playing at cross purposes with the meaning of words'.[6] It may be significant that it is children who are primarily interested in punning riddles, for they are serving their apprenticeship with language. That shamefaced relapser, Oliver Wendell Holmes, sums up the conundrum when he imagines encountering, on a visit to an asylum for aged and decayed punsters, a centenarian conundrummer inmate, who asks:

'Why is a-a-a-a like a-a-a-a? Give it up? Because it's a-a-a-a.' The doctor comments: 'He lost his answers about the age of ninety-eight. Of late years he puts his whole conundrums in blank, but they please him just as well.'[7]

This is probably true: it is the pattern, the drum-beat, the formula, that intrigue and not the specific words used. Much the same might often be true of limericks. A final area which leaves me rather cold but excites others (including Saussure) is anagrams, which clearly appeal to the crossword mentality. For me they are a rather debased version of the belief in the magic of names. A refinement is the antigram, in which a name is reshuffled into its opposite: The Louvre – True Hovel; or The Waldorf – Dwarf Hotel.[8] All of these devices reveal how many cross-breeds are the offspring of the illegitimate pun.

Such is part of the popular idea of wordplay. Etymology takes us into deeper waters. 'Consider! and you con the stars for meaning.'[9] Children want to know where babies come from; adults are forever asking the same poser with different subjects. This is the etymological urge, the search for origins, in the hope that, once found, they might explain all subsequence. 'Quoi de plus divertissant et de plus instructif, tout ensemble, qu'un beau calembour étymologique' ('What is more entertaining and more instructive at the same time than a fine etymological pun?') said the French translator of Homer's *Odyssey*, Victor Bérard.[10] Kirk illustrates the ancient interest in significant etymology (i.e. explanation by roots) by stating; 'Aeschylus related the name of Helen to the idea that she "took the ships" (hele-naus), that of Apollo to *apollunei*, "destroy", and that of Zeus to *zēn*, "live".' He adds that this might be dismissed as mere *jeux d'esprits*,

were it not for the much more widespread Egyptian and Mesopotamian occurrences . . . Learned Sumerian priests have undoubtedly put their fingers in this particular mythical pie, but the result is something more than trivial wordplay, for it was evidently believed that names revealed part of the true essence of the things or persons to which they were attached.

In all such speculation, language is posited as central, indeed primordial:

Deucalion and Pyrrha . . . recreate the human race on purely etymological principles; they do so by throwing stones over their shoulders, and the stones turn into people – but that is because the Greek word for stone (*laas*) is similar to that for people (*laos*). From such trivial ideas are myths sometimes made

For example, the birth of Aphrodite in Hesiod's *Theogony* rests on the possible interpretation of her name as 'she who came out of the foam', allied no doubt with the 'foamy appearance of both sperm and spume'.[11]

Raymond Queneau defined the pun as 'la réflexion philologique première', which interestingly makes the comic or parody version predate the serious original.[12] Whereas an orthodox etymologist lists the meanings of a word over the centuries, the punster makes them coexist, as they actually do: the word contains its variant senses; all words are composite, polysemous. To twig etymological puns, you need to have one foot (or rather ear and eye) in one age and the second in another: the straddle position so characteristic of punning. (And if one foot rests on a bar of soap, so characteristic also of that gestural pun, the pratfall.) 'Whatever other definition of man may be hazarded, he is beyond doubt an etymologizing animal, and he must render some account to himself of the origin and reason of the words which he uses.'[13] In *Upon the Pun*, Hughes and Hammond claim that the 'knowing or intuitive erudition characteristic of the play on words makes every man an etymologist,' though later they admit the limitation of everyman's expertise in this area. The question of rightness or wrongness is, besides, of lessened importance. As John Orr reminds: 'Even a wrong etymology is a sound and sense association, and therefore a linguistic fact.'[14] It is not even a question of degrees of literacy. Some of the daftest derivations originate from the most learned minds. The classic example is 'Lucus a non lucendo': a grove is dark because it does not shine. Quintilian argues: 'We must admit the derivation of certain words from their opposites.'[15] Isidore of Seville favoured teleological etymologies: bees (*apes*) are so called because they hold to one another by the feet, or it may be because they are born without feet (*a-pes*).[16] Such pseudo-etymologies are akin to punning (and the approximate pun is at home in the pseudo). We are loth to believe in accidents. Jean Paulhan recalls that *chrétien* and *crétin* are the same word (but adds, fairly, that knowing this we know no more about Christians). He goes on:

> Or de tels calembours ou jeux de mots et tous ceux, stupides ou spirituels, que l'on imagine à leur suite, offrent bien certains traits de l'étymologie: le même brillant dès l'abord, ou l'éclat, et comme cette chaleur subite de l'esprit. On ne sait quoi d'apparemment tranchant et quelle allure de preuve. Oui – mais de preuve trompeuse et passagère à laquelle il faut aussitôt renoncer, où l'étymologie apparente se révèle fausse aussitôt.

> (Now, such puns or plays on words and all those, whether stupid or witty, that are thought up in their wake, do offer certain resemblances with etymology: the same initial brilliance or glitter, and that sort of sudden warming of the mind. Some

apparently sharp-witted and persuasive-seeming quality. Yes, but the persuasive-ness is misleading and fleeting, and it must be rejected at once: the apparent etymology quickly proves itself a fake.)

Despite this warning, he stresses that popular false etymologies often strike chords, and he quotes a neighbour who, on the basis of *paillasse* no doubt, calls a soporific acquaintance un *paillard* (usually = a debauchee).[17] Yvon Belaval links Paulhan and Queneau: 'Si l'étymologie, comme le veut J. Paulhan, est de l'ordre du calembour, on voit que, réciproquement, le calembour est de l'étymologie à l'état naissant' ('If etymology, for J. Paulhan, is part of punning, we can see that, conversely, punning is etymology in embryo').[18]

Caird seems to undervalue our atavistic habits when he remarks that 'We continue to use the word "etymology", even though we no longer believe in what it etymologically stands for.'[19] That is: true science, with the implication that the 'true' meaning of words is their original one. Surely we hark both back and forward. True etymology, if there is such a thing, seeks to displace our attention back in time, to roots, whereas the 'popular' variety tries to update words, to familiarize them where the so-called science estranges them. When the 'folk' (i.e. all of us at some time) mishears or misreads a new word, we tend to corrupt and naturalize it. And, of course, depending on our level of education, we can mangle even standard vocabulary. The natives of Chester-le-Street commonly write, for *register*, 'Red-chester'. A good example of annexation, of trying to make our own language, that often strange and foreign thing, our own. Either we domesticate loan-words or we fail to recognize obsolete or recondite 'native' words and treat them likewise. Economy of effort is obviously at stake in all of this, as is our 'craving for symmetry and likeness'.[20] Divining is both prospective and retrospective: guessing the future and rereading the past; forecasting and dowsing, just as invention implies both finding and creating. Montaigne called this 'deviner à reculons', guessing backwards.[21] Such activities can of course be less than scrupulous:

> Exegetes and existentialists resort to violent methods in order to confer meaning upon a word. The exegetes stuff a word with a significance not its own by extracting from it a meaning they had previously smuggled into it in the manner of a conjuror who draws miles of threaded needles out of his mouth ... Clement of Alexandria [declared] that the sacred books, like the blessed Virgin, are pregnant with hidden truths. The existentialists, on the other hand, do not impose an *alien* meaning on a word but attempt to restore a forgotten aspect or hidden secret by splitting a word wide open, using the hyphen as an axe: *re-sponsible ... at-one-ment*[22]

Writing today, Jacobs would have said 'the Lacanians'. Etymologists claim that they are getting back to basics. Recent deconstructionists claim (and to do so exploit an etymological pun) that they are thus *radicalizing* the way we think about thinking. Like early Church Fathers, they are trying to put the fear of God into us about the things we do most naturally.

Stanford stresses the positive side of etymological wordplay:

> Being free from the restraints of scientific method, amateur etymology gives access to such a wide domain for imaginative speculation on word meanings that few major poets can entirely ignore it. It lends itself to personal, original and satisfying interpretations of language where scientific philology would only chill and sterilize.

He cites some fantasy suggestions: *virgin* – a snare for men; and *cinema* – a place you go without your mother.[23] We have seen earlier how myths might grow from small beginnings. For Goldberg, 'myth is often ex-post-facto etymology; so, too, are heroes often eponymous – that is, invented to explain the word or the name that suggests them.'[24] This kind of creative etymology is sometimes called *ethymologia*. Pierre Guiraud calls the process 'rétromotivation', and believes it to be widespread across the whole of culture. In ancient Greece, he points out, etymology was a type of genealogy on the basis of names, and its function was to establish the origins of peoples and of cities by granting them an eponymous hero (cf.Wace, in the *Roman de Brut*, who makes Bretons derive from Brutus). Such rapprochements were unverified and of course unverifiable. Guiraud links this habit with the genesis of myths: 'Ainsi de l'homonymie en sanskrit de *gavos* (nuage) et *gavos* (vache) serait née la légende du bouvier Cacus, gardien des vaches du ciel' ('Thus from the homonym in Sanskrit of *gavos* (cloud) and *gavos* (cow) may have come the legend of the drover Cacus, guardian of the cows of heaven'). He recalls the Biblical confusion between *malum* (apple) and *malum* (evil), which planted the apple-tree in Paradise. As he stresses, this is not 'pre-scientific' thinking; our present day etymological dictionaries are full of such phantoms. It is not just writers for whom it is true to say that 'les mots engendrent la fable là où la réalité devrait engendrer les mots ... Croyant penser aux choses nous ne faisons que raisonner sur les mots' ('Words beget fables where reality should beget words. Believing we are thinking about things, we merely reason from words'). He makes a splendid development himself on far*ce*, far*cir*, far*ceur* (farce, stuffing, prankster), which begets multiple meanings within meanings, like Russian dolls, like stuffed meat. Poets above all are the exponents of *ethymologia*. Valéry, for Guiraud, is the inheritor of les Grands Rhétoriqueurs: the same primacy given to form as a creative restraint, or rather propulsion, for form can create content; the habit of using words in their root-sense (e.g. 'le ruisseau scrupuleux', i.e. a stream filled with stones).[25] (Other descendants of this rhetorical tradition of formalism are the members of OULIPO.) Such use of the rarer senses of words can obviously lead to esoteric art. If this needs justification, Ponge offers the idea of matching, as a form of homage: 'O ressources infinies de l'épaisseur des choses, *rendues* par les ressources infinies de l'épaisseur sémantique des mots' ('Oh infinite resources of the density of things, *captured* by the infinite resources of the semantic density of words').[26] Linking *voir* and *voyager* in a cranky derivation, he challenges: 'Etymologistes, ne bondissez pas! N'arrive-t-il pas que deux plantes aux racines fort distinctes confondent parfois leurs feuillages? ('Etymologists, do not blench! Doesn't it sometimes happen that two plants with entirely separate roots intertwine their foliage?').[27] Here, poetic etymology, pun and conceit intertwine.

Ponge coined the word 'amphibiguïté': the state, I imagine, of being neither fish nor flesh.[28] Much false etymologizing gives rise to neologisms: 'butcher': 'to butch', a back-formation. In pun-fashion, coinages often stack meanings. As Burgess says of James Joyce, 'The piling on of extra connotations is of the essence of the palimpsestuous – or palincestuous – technique.'[29] Barthes wraps himself amorously, self-lovingly, round his chosen verbal mirrors. In the section 'Etymologies' of *Roland Barthes par Roland Barthes*, he says:

Lorsqu'il écrit déception, cela veut dire déprise ... l'*obligation*, un *lien*; la *définition*, un *tracé de limite*, etc. Son discours est plein de mots qu'il campe, si l'on peut dire, à la racine. Pourtant, dans l'etymologie, ce n'est pas la vérité ou l'origine du mot qui lui plaît, c'est plutôt l'*effet de surimpression* qu'elle autorise: le mot est comme un palimpseste; il me semble alors que j'ai des idées *à même la langue* – ce qui est tout simplement: écrire (je parle ici d'une pratique, non d'une valeur).

When he writes 'disappointment', that means detachment, 'obligation', a bond; 'definition', a setting of limits, etc. His discourse is full of words which he plants, so to speak, at their roots. And yet, in etymology, it's not the truth or the origins of a word that please him, it's rather the effect of superimposition that it allows: the word is like a palimpsest; I feel then that I have words *flush with language* – that is to say, writing (I'm talking of a practice, not a value).)[30]

Neologisms, like Janus the pun-deity, can look either back or forward. They can exploit etymological roots to devise new forms, or concoct these from scratch – when the obvious danger is nonsense. Indeed, it has been pointed out that:

coining new and bizarre words is a common symptom among psychotics, but in only slightly different form it infects scientists and scholars. One should particularly be wary of Greek neologisms when they bear the gifts of apparent – but only apparent – precision.[31]

It was to counter the mystifying jargon of educationalists that the terms 'Pedaguese' and 'Educanto' were invented.[32] So many communicators today operate the closed economy of hermeticism.

> Lacan coins words that have no definitions other than his own and then tends to define them only contextually. Even when Lacan borrows what might superficially seem to be standard technical terms from other disciplines, he often uses them in ways in which their normal definitions are not applicable.[33]

No wonder he was so keen on his punning coinage 'Les Non-Dupes Errent'; it disqualified dissenters.

A list of telling neologisms: 'scripturience' (to describe, by analogy with *prurience*, the *cacoethes scribendi* – the itch for writing); the Abbé Galiani calling the economists of his day, as we might in ours, 'économystificateurs'; the *Canard enchaîné* and its 'fliconoclaste' tradition of police-bashing; Joyce's bilingual 'mielodorous'.[34] In all these examples, two existing part-words are blended: the mixer has, as with the pun, seen the similarities in differences, and telescoped them. Such provoked accidents are, to mix a metaphor, 'l'oxygène du vocabulaire'.[35] These blends have themselves begotten a whole range of names: portmanteau words, meld puns, *mots-sandwiches*, *mots-valises*, *mots-gigognes* (*gigogne* = nest of tables, etc.), *mots-centaures*, *amalgames*, *emboîtement lexical* (lexical interlocking), *collage verbal*. (The French have tended to discard the Carrollian 'portmanteau-word,' as *porte-manteau* nowadays suggests to French eyes a coat-rack rather than a bag, a peg rather than a container.) *Mots-centaures*, 'qui rend exactement la double nature de ces "monstres" ambigus',[36] is a term dramatized in Claude Simon's *Route des Flandres*, in which the transition or overlap between a woman and a horse preoccupies the narrator. Edmond Rostand's *ridicoculiser* buries the cuckold (*cocu*) in mockery. As well as being sometimes a symptom of mental disorder, such forgeries can denote unusual control over language. As Carroll himself said, 'If you have that rarest of gifts, a perfectly balanced mind, you will say "frumious", instead of "fuming-furious".'[37] On Humpty Dumpty's famous definition of portmanteau words, Elizabeth Sewell comments: 'It would fit the pun well enough, in which there are precisely that – two meanings (or more than two) packed up in one word.'[38] A good example is de Quincey's splendid 'anecdotage' where aging and rambling are tied indissolubly.

Like puns, portmanteau words are hybrids, bastards, and of similar vigour. For Finkielkraut, they are a source of creativity, accessible to all.

> Agglutiner au lieu d'opposer . . . Les choses perdent leurs contours; les objets les plus distincts deviennent les éléments de combinaisons aléatoires . . . Les saveurs du pêle-mêle et de la confusion.

(Agglutinate instead of separating. Things lose their outlines; the most distant objects become the elements of random combinations. All the flavour of the pell-mell and the medley.)

He pleads for a linguistic melting-pot. Hugo did not go far enough with his programme of putting 'un bonnet rouge au vieux dictionnaire' ('a Revolutionary cap on the old dictionary'): 'Il faut mêler les mots, les contaminer, les confondre: il faut métisser le vieux dictonnaire' ('We must mingle words, contaminate them, mix them up: the old dictionary has to be miscegenated'). He offers for inspection:

'Chastethé: boisson sédative, recommandée pour endormir l'instinct sexuel': 'constipassion: amour timide, qui n'arrive pas à se déclarer'; and 'orthografle: descente de police effectuée chaque semaine dans le discours des enfants'.

('Chastitea': a sedative drink to calm the sexual instinct; 'constipassion': a held-in love that dare not speak its name; and 'M15spelling': a police-raid each week on children's schoolwork.)

Similarly, he finds in Carroll's stammer a childlike reaction to adult authority: 'La nature, en lui, résistait à la morale du langage'.[39] Francis Huxley tells the lovely story of Carroll's creative misreading of 'romancement' as 'Roman cement'.[40] Learning to speak, hear and write, children are forever reworking the linguistic map.

L'enfant pratique spontanément le néologisme (montrant ainsi qu'il a acquis le mécanisme de l'analogie.) C'est en ce sens qu'on a pu dire que les 'fautes' de l'enfant sont en réalité la manifestation de sa compétence linguistique en cours de formation.

(The child spontaneously coins neologisms, thus showing that he has mastered the mechanics of analogy. It's in this sense that some have argued that children's 'mistakes' are in fact the proof in action of their linguistic competence as it grows.)[41]

There is semantic as well as lexical neologism; we are forever recycling meaning. Slang, for example, often gives a new sense to old words (grass, gay). As with literal counterfeiting, it is best to coin words on the model of existing ones. Thus, to baptize a new dance, it would be better – because more familiar, echoic and less arbitrary – to call it e.g. a twerk (*twist* + *jerk*) than a *grunk* (just a funny sound). Familiarity, is, however, not the only consideration; estrangement, too, has its appeal. Like puns, coinages can defamiliarize a situation and foreground its agents. On the basis of *xénophobes*, Queneau coins the term *xénophones*, speakers of foreign tongues. In a sense, for him, we all speak our native tongue as if it were a foreign lingo. It is a source of perpetual astonishment to us. In a way, it speaks us as much as we speak it. To this end, Queneau makes sparing use of what I would call concertina-words, phonetic coagulations, e.g. 'Imélamin loculdlastar' ('il met la main au cul de la star,' where the graphic agglutination mimes the excitement of the speaker).[42] Barthes gets even more excited over the whole phenomenon. After claiming that homonymy is voluptous, he celebrates Fourier's language in these uplifting terms:

> La parole même de Fourier est sensuelle, elle progresse dans l'effusion, l'enthousiasme, le comblement verbal, la gourmandise du mot (le néologisme est un acte érotique, ce pour quoi il soulève immanquablement la censure des cuistres).

> (The very prose of Fourier is sensual, it proceeds by effusion, enthusiasm, verbal climax, the gluttony of the word (the neologism is an erotic act, which is why it never fails to attract the blue pencil of pedants).)[43]

Many writers have wanted to script-tease (Laforgue: 'voluptés à vif' – 'rapeture on edge'; 'sangsuel' – which translates as 'leecherous'). As well as celebration, neologism can attack, as in Nietzsche's linguistic iconoclasm, for he often seems to believe that 'the worst coinage is still better than the best cliché.'[44] Round Christmas-time, the coinage 'Santaclaustrophobia' might help some to survive.

Another avoidance of plain speaking, if not necessarily of direct communication, is afforded by litotes. Writing small can be a way of belittling a performance, as when we say we are 'underwhelmed'. The British, traditionally, have a name for miniloquence: we make molehills out of mountains, often to such an extent that we seem to have a faith that would move molehills. Litotes is linked with punning, irony, euphemism, conundrums and circumlocution: all indirect modes which express most by specifying least. Each describes a hole which the receiver needs to fill in, or a code to be unscrambled. In intention at least, euphemism fudges issues:

> we know what a euphemism is driving at, but the respectable images it calls to mind block the emotional force of the reference and make it impossible for the mind to focus on anything but vague impressions.[45]

That is one way of looking at it, but the euphemism can equally well be prurient (and certainly more exotic if not erotic) than what it pretends to conceal: e.g. 'to shake hands with the wife's best friend' for 'to urinate'. Here the metaphorical and more physical substitute is more imaginable than the colourless straight, or technical, word. Self-proclaimed prudes, afflicted with logophobia, are particularly aware of this potentiality:

The seventeenth-century *Précieuses* were so haunted by the indecent implications of chance assonances, that they even banned quasi-homonyms (paronyms) capable of arousing dubious associations, e.g. the verb 'in*cul*quer' . . . A group of six American musicians had to be called a 'quartet' since 'sextet' would have been too 'suggestive'.[46]

Such lexical scruples, as in bowdlerization, are generally misplaced, though it is equally true that we often blaspheme for the sheer hell of it. On one view,

because taboo words are so important in language, they must be accorded their due respect, [because] by investing certain words with sweeping emotional overtones, we leave the bulk of language free of apprehension.[47]

This belief that certain words can act as scapegoats for the decorous majority seems a naïvely pious hope, as *contamination*, in its myriad forms, is a central fact of language's life. Unlike cyphers or cryptograms, 'an equivoque or double entendre just pretends to hide its meaning; it wants the insinuation to show through.'[48] Puns are a means of circumventing taboos, as are euphemisms, which play a similar hide-and-seek game with the listener/reader. For Farb, 'The obscene pun is dangerous, because it cleverly attacks the sacredness of taboo words, and it manages to do so with apparent innocence.'[49] Moving beyond the sexual, if we ever can, Edmund Leach maintains more generally:

A familiar type of purely linguistic taboo is the pun. A pun occurs when we make a joke by confusing two apparently different meanings of the same phonemic pattern. The pun seems funny or shocking because it challenges a taboo which ordinarily forbids us to recognise that the sound pattern is ambiguous. In many cases, such verbal taboos have social as well as linguistic aspects.

A readiness to play on sounds, in other words, reveals socially unsound tendencies. Leach goes on:

In seventeenth-century English witchcraft trials it was very commonly asserted that the Devil appeared in the form of a dog – that is, God backwards. In England we still employ the same metathesis when we refer to a clergyman's collar as a 'dog collar' instead of a 'God collar'.[50]

The more prosaic explanation, that it *looks* like a dog-collar, is of course equally apt. There is a tie-up between verbal fig-leaves, superstition and mistrust of language. Litotes, in all its variations, acts as a smuggler of the contraband taboo. The argument that such equivocation does not set out to hoodwink others but allows them to deceive themselves strikes me as jesuitical. Euphemism would seem to be the opposite of the aggressive insult, the dysphemism, or cacophemism – and litotes of hyperbole, if evasion of direct statement did not itself constitute a form, like exaggeration, of undue (if hidden) emphasis.

Overwhelming and underwhelming are not polar opposites. Feinberg argues that, as against Kant's 'sudden transformation of a strained expectation into nothing', the humour of exaggeration 'functions by giving the reader more than he expects, not less'.[51] From childhood we are taught not to exaggerate, and we need a Thoreau to remind us that an equal danger consists in being:

> not extra-vagant enough . . . *Extra vagance!* it depends on how you are yarded . . .
> I desire to speak somewhere *without* bounds . . . for I am convinced that I cannot
> exaggerate enough even to lay the foundation of a true expression.[52]

Like puns, exaggeration underlines, points up. If, as has often been argued, art is by nature a hyperbole, then wordplay is a further upping of art. Freud sounds the warning note: 'The value of phantasy is exalted unduly in comparison with reality; a possibility is almost equated with an actual event.'[53] But wordplay, like art, is precisely concerned with the entertaining of possibilities. Nothing succeeds like excess, we might often think; but for Puttenham, hyperbole is 'the over-reacher or the loud liar'.[54] Etymologically, 'exaggeration' means a building-up. It is also a desire to improve upon. Social reformers, like all interested parties, overstate their case, in order to gain a hearing. This has its black obverse. The cynic, says Jankélévitch, 'croit à la fécondité de la catastrophe . . . Il fait éclater l'injustice dans l'espoir que l'injustice s'annulera elle-même par l'homéopathie de la surenchère' ('believes in the fecundity of catastrophe. He blows the gaff on injustice in the hope that injustice will abolish itself via the homoeopathy of escalation').[55] This sounds to me more like the strategy of the gallows-humourist than of the cynic, who is hardly in the business of amelioration.

Insult, too, goes in for exaggerated wordplay. 'For his admirers Luther himself was "Luter" ("pure") and for opponents "Luder" ("carrion", "sod", "slut").[56] Such name-calling, or 'flyting', reveals a different kind of belief in the magic of names. In Negro ghetto culture among young blacks flourishes the practice of 'sounding', 'the dozens', or 'signifying': ritual insults, often in the form of puns: 'At least my mother ain't no railroad track, laid all over the country'; 'Your mother's like a police station – dicks going in and out all the time.'[57] Such taunting no doubt willingly incurs risks, but because of its ceremonial nature is still presumably in some kind of control. Coprolalia, inveterate swearing, is something else. The sufferers from the 'foul-mouth disease' or the cursing disease (also called Tourette's syndrome after Georges Gilles de la Tourette, the French physician who described it in the 1880s), on the other hand, 'cannot control what they say or when they say it, and they utter such streams of obscenities that they are forced to run off by themselves so that their foul language will no longer be imposed on the unsuspecting'.[58] Such 'bad-mouthing' is a real example of the way in which language can take over from the speaker. All the same, insult-jousts are of such antiquity that it stands to reason that they avert as much as they provoke injury. In an article on the 'failure of insult', the journalist Gustave Frejaville spoke of 'de très simples associations d'idées assaisonnées d'assonances', which, by its very form, enacts a definition of punning as much as of insulting. Edouard in fact uses *injure* rather specially, as a gratuitous game (and evokes Gide's 'acte gratuit'): an oratorical tourney, tit-for-tat. Indeed, he uses it very much as a synonym for exaggeration: stylistic exuberance, rhetorical flourish, and sees the phenomenon as a safety-valve, a therapeutic, standing in lieu of a real fight: 'Employez donc des injures . . . toujours excessives: elles ne sauraient ainsi tirer à conséquence. ('So let your insults always be over the top; then they can't amount to anything').[59] Flyting – a word Legman relishes, for its very sound suggest unponderous gaiety – was, according to Cazamian, 'a humorous exchange of huge opprobrious high-sounding abuse, a kind of serio-comic contest which flourished in the Scottish poetry of the sixteenth century'.[60] W.H. Auden spells it out:

> the comic effect of flyting arises from the contradiction between the insulting nature of what is said which appears to indicate a passionate relation of hostility and aggression, and the calculated skill of verbal invention which indicates that the protagonists are not thinking about each other but about language and their pleasure in employing it inventively. A man who is really passionately angry is speechless and can only express his anger by physical violence. Playful anger is intrinsically comic because, of all emotions, anger is the least compatible with play.[61]

Let us have words, before we come to blows. As well as the serious name-calling against Luther, we can enjoy the gratuitous coinages of Allais, like 'Elie Coïdal'.

Like punning or irony, parody superimposes two levels or schemes of references, so that we hear or see double. Punning is parodic, because parasitical: it needs a target or basis to react against, to work on. Sex in both rears its tumescent head, for parody too is a cod-piece. It is as old as literature, and as social life itself no doubt, and yet is a denigrated mode, like wordplay. 'La parodie s'offre, traditionnellement, comme un double grotesque des genres "élevés" et des ouvrages en renom; au moment où ils culminent, elle les consacre et les sape à la fois' ('Parody, traditionally, stands as a grotesque double of lofty genres and famous works; as they reach their peak, it consecrates and undermines them at the same time'). Contrasting it with caricature, which latches on to physical or moral traits, Abastado continues: 'La parodie au contraire porte sur des systèmes signifiants; c'est un langage au second degré' ('Parody on the other hand bears on signifying systems; it is a metalanguage').[62] Codes, languages, styles, ceremonials, this whole area has been of great interest to structuralist and post-structuralist criticism, with its fixation on cliché, quotation, stereotype and intertextuality. Spoofs clearly presuppose a linguistic collaboration between purveyor and buyer. Looking at the phenomenon more from the perpetrator's viewpoint, Dwight Macdonald notes the tendency of parody towards philistinism, but values in it:

> an intuitive kind of literary criticism, shorthand for what 'serious' critics must write out at length. It is Method acting, since a successful parodist must live himself imaginatively into his parodee. It is jiujitsu,. using the impetus of the opponent to defeat him.

This aspect can be appreciated, I feel, in Proust's splendid pastiches. Macdonald goes on to confess his taste for the bookishness of parody,

> a kind of literary shop-talk . . . And I feel at home with it because an elderly culture like ours is suffused with parody . . . our avantgarde has done a lot of its fighting in the rear . . . Picasso steals everywhere . . . and above all from Picasso; his own fence, he disguises the hot jewels in new settings . . . We are backward-looking explorers.

At the end of his extensive sample, he concludes that this supremely self-conscious mode is 'conservative and classical'.[63] This possibility, the whole subject of twisting for reuse (to be discussed later concerning proverbs and clichés), and all that Macdonald rightly finds in parody have significant links with punning. Macdonald's view that most parody is activated more by admiration than by contempt is, however, countered by Donoghue's study of Swift. Donoghue finds parody to be the ideal form for an artist committed to negation:

> This applies to the configuration of the work as a whole. When we think of the same motives carried down into the details of the writing, line by line, word by word, it becomes clear that the classic form, in this miniature, is the pun. The pun . . . turns things upside down, and rids words of their agreed meaning.[64]

Swift is the dark end of the spectrum of such topsy-turveydom, with Rabelais at the more carnivalesque opposite. Puns too can pull inertia up with a jolt, reverse the direction of a sentence, as parody or burlesque invert a world.

Other tricksiness on the level of, and within, a sentence is represented by zeugma and syllepsis. Here we see language playing with itself in a kind of syntactical doubling-up. It is a psychological tic of Flaubert, with its bitter teaming of the lofty and the nondescript: Léon appreciating indiscriminately in Emma Bovary 'l'exaltation de son âme et les dentelles de sa jupe' ('the loftiness of her soul and the lace on her skirt'). If fits in with Flaubert's pronounced sense of the grotesque, the yawning gaps or over-close juxtapositions which produce excruciation, as when the Abbé Bournisien mentions to a distraught Emma, pregnant with woes, his cure of 'une vache qui avait l'*enfle*' ('a cow with a swollen belly').[65] Zeugma, like the pun, is economical: it contracts two sentences into one, as in this charming example from Hugo:

> Tous les soirs, quand Lisbeth souffle
> Sa chandelle et ma raison.
> (Every night, when Lisbeth blows her candle and my mind.)[66]

Zeugma, too, takes a word (most often a verb, but often a preposition) literally and figuratively; it links unrelated terms – mental with moral, abstract with physical, high with low – and thus generates surprise. It has been called 'yokewit'.

Oxymoron is this, only more so. Like equiparation, it juxtaposes subjects or terms which initially appear to have nothing to do with each other, except by the relationship of opposites: bitter-sweet, *festina lente*, living death, *odi et amo*, serio-comic, sinister dexterity. 'L'oxymore est une figure où l'antithese est niée et la contradiction pleinement assumée ('The oxymoron is a trope where opposites are negated and contradictions fully integrated').[67] Such *coincidentia oppositorum* is the stamping-ground of 'Pataphysicians, Metaphysical poets, religious mystics, or of lovers of paradox like Chesterton, who called one of his books *Tremendous Trifles*. 'The oxymoron combines not only opposites but also impossibilities in its unity'; *docta ignorantia*.[68] I fail to see that any real distinction is being made in the following: 'Paradoxes and oxymorons are logical ambiguities, puns are ambiguities of meaning,' for it must be difficult to attempt logic without engaging meaning.[69] I find Jacobs' description more accurate:

> The oxymoron is strong in the tension with which it compresses far-fetched ideas, in making *extremes meet* (itself an example as well as a definition of the oxymoron). It is a verbal gargoyle which smiles and frowns at once . . . The Janus word is the paradox par excellence, the oxymoron compressed in one word, a one-word adynata.[70]

Odi et amo:

> oxymoron is the rhetorical device used most commonly in the organization of conceits describing the lover's tormented state of mind, for this figure (which unites opposites) is ideally suited to expressing the emotional turmoil experienced by sonneteering lovers.[71]

This forced conjunction of beings – the relationship for instance of Don Quixote and Sancho Panza which is a kind of running oxymoronic pun, a living and working play on the coming together of incompatibles – leads, whether in pun or oxymoron, to a telescoping, osmotic event. Both make bedfellows of unlikely partners.

'Puns of all kinds', claims Wayne Booth, 'are close to stable irony in intending a reconstruction.'[72] Like zeugma and puns, irony, 'the Drie Mock',[73] is double-edged, two-in-one, a bargain. As we have seen in euphemism, litotes and taboo, the pun can, as well as uncovering, be a cover-up, for the punner can take refuge, like the ironist, behind the pretence that he did not intend the other meaning of the double entendre, just as an ironist can protest that he was speaking literally. Irony and pun are transparent dissimulations, for those that have eyes to pierce; both separate the lynxes from the sheep. Both depend on the existence of two orders or levels, of an apparent and assumed meaning, with a play-space in between. Both allow for the possibility that some undiscerning readers or listeners will miss the reserved meaning. Both are potentially subversive, for, under the challenge of such decoying double exposures, 'our minds which naturally seek to relate and synthesize are affronted.'[74] Despite this tension, for the duality in irony is in opposition, any equivocation there, if it is to operate successfully, cannot be ultimately ambiguous. The best irony is a roundabout way of speaking plainly. 'Romantic irony' sets up serious lines followed by afterthoughts which deflate or modify the preceding pretentiousness. This is linked to the classical retort, exemplified by my old English teacher, Joe Ellis, who, when the class was playing him up, would announce: 'I suppose you think I've got one limb in the grave, the other on a bar of soap – but the third can still say Heil Hitler!' This is sarcastic irony, a form of pointed wordplay. There is also the 'dramatic irony' of talking at cross-purposes, as in this Max Miller story. A man has told his wife he is giving a talk on sailing at his club, whereas in fact he has simply told dirty stories. She meets a friend, who mentions what a great evening it was. The wife exclaims: 'I didn't think he knew anything about it. The first time he tried it he was sick, and the second time his hat blew off.' This anecdote is funny, or significant, for neither of the two interlocutors; it makes sense only for the listener in the third apex of the triangle. For Muecke,

> the art of the ironist is most like the arts of the wit and the raconteur; and not only because irony runs the same risks of failure through being too laboured or too subtle, too brief or too long drawn out, mistimed in the telling or ill-adapted to audience or occasion.[75]

Irony plays with parallels. In symbol, myth or allegory, we also see a proposition with a double meaning. The one narrative, the other figurative; a clear idea is expressed under a veil. But the parallel metaphorical meaning does not oppose or invalidate the primary one; they work in tandem.

We reach metaphor. 'The pun is the first step away from the transparent word, the first step towards the achievement of symbolic metaphor.'[76] We have considered conundrums, preciosity and circumlocution; another variety of guessing-game is furnished by that primitive metaphor, the kenning, which can sometimes be a pun.[77] There are punning similes ('A woman is like a tree: she can bear fruit'), which resemble conundrums, except that the puzzle in the latter is stated interrogatively and not categorically. Such punning similes are akin to Wellerisms (to be considered later).

> In the making of speech and language, the spirit is continually 'sparking' between matter and mind, as it were, playing with this wondrous nominative faculty. Behind every abstract expression lie the boldest of metaphors, and every metaphor is a play on words. Thus in giving expression to life, man creates a second, poetic world alongside the world of nature.[78]

Like wordplay, metaphor incites us to think, see and hear on more than one level concurrently, or at least with only a slight time-lag, the time needed to seek the connection. The opposite is literal-mindedness (which can of course have its own saving grace). 'When the pun discovers that two things, two different concepts, or two widely separate experiences bearing the same name also share deeper affinities, it is a metaphor.'[79] The associative faculty of our minds produces such findings: 'The world we carry in our heads is a vast elaborated metaphor ... Look for what happens when people free-associate, and you have a clue to the ganglionic ramifications of metaphors and themes.'[80] As Caird points out, comparison is like classification:

> Both processes depend on our ability to isolate significant resemblances and to ignore other irrelevant characteristics ... Our understanding of a metaphor depends on our ability to detect and concentrate on the point or points of comparison, to the exclusion of all else. The neck of a bottle is not so called because it supports a head of beer.[81]

Like puns, then, metaphors are selective and, as such, similarly approximate, *à peu près*. Both say 'or words to that effect'. (Puns are often mixed metaphors, cocktails, themselves, or, as Muir said of Shakespeare's puns, can act as solvents for them.) Figurative language is 'language which doesn't mean what it says.'[82] But, as with irony and wordplay, such language does say, obliquely, what it means. Meaning in all of these forms is transferred, displaced ('metaphor' means 'to carry over').

Cocteau's insolent claim:

La poésie est un vaste calembour. Le poète associe, dissocie, retourne les syllabes du mot, mais peu de personnes le savent. Peu de personnes sont assez souples pour sauter d'un plan sur l'autre et suivre la manoeuvre foudroyante des rapports,

(Poetry is a vast pun. The poet associates, dissociates, turns around the syllables of a word, but few people realize this. Few people are supple-minded enough to leap from one plane to another and to follow the lightning manoeuvre of connection)

is countered by Annette Thau's calm reminder that, though puns are often close to metaphor, unlike it they can hardly be ambiguous or obscure: 'The text's control of interpretation is complete,' once the point is taken.[83] Both rhetorical forms incur obvious dangers, of which the principal is 'le démon de l'analogie', and thus the jumping to false conclusions. As we have seen already with Lacan, a current tendency is to appropriate the terminology of one discipline (e.g. linguistics) to a wide range of others: politics, literary criticisms, anthropology, sociology, history; technical words in this way are used metaphorically. Analogy can fuse, but also melt differences. Ponge houses both the danger and its antidote. One analogy he must have known to be spurious, for he is talking of *abstract* dimensions, occurs when he states: 'Le mot est un objet à trois dimensions [sight, sound, meaning], donc vraiment un objet.'[84] Yet the same man says: 'Les analogies, c'est intéressant, mais moins que les différences. Il faut à travers les analogies, saisir la qualité différentielle' (Analogies are interesting, but less so than differences. Via analogies we must grasp the differential quality'), and 'il s'agit du dogme singulier de chaque chose' ('it's a question of the unique dogma of each thing').[85]

As do puns, metaphors rest on the principle of interchangeability ('A metaphor makes a mutual comparison between things at once like and unlike').[86] Separates are bracketed with each other. This can lead to indifference, in both senses: equivalence and uncaring. It can have a levelling effect on the things yanked together, and a numbing effect on the receiver. Conceits, which have been defined as 'big-headed ideas', are another area of risk.[87] 'As a neoclassical theory of decorum began to take shape, conceits were excluded from the sublime style and relegated to the low style.' In that backlash, as we have seen, much the same fate befell puns. Earlier, a prime exponent of the conceit, John Cleveland, had given rise to the term *Clevelandism*: 'An art of condensation, an art of "summing whole books into a metaphor and whole metaphors into an epithet," in the words of an admirer, David Lloyd'. Amongst the Metaphysical poets, 'God himself could be imagined as the archetypal conceitist who created a world which St. Augustine calls an exquisite poem.' Even the Augustans were not altogether closed to this magic aspect of language.

When Johnson describes the resemblances in a *discordia concors* as 'occult', he seems to be recalling earlier theories about the transcendental origins of metaphor and the status of conceits in times when the universe was imagined to be a vast net-work of symbolic correspondences.[88]

Whatever the dangers, all of us have secondary notions, mental reservations and ulterior motives: we are all cunning. When we read or listen, we are not passive. We carry over; we are analogizing animals. Language is inconceivable and inoperable without metaphor. And inflexible without wordplay.

Rhyme I remain unsure about, but here are the arguments for its kinship with punning. These range form the relatively indisputable (Rayner Heppenstall: 'Not all rhymes are puns, but we may say that all puns are rhymes') through the categorical Koestler: 'The pun's opposite number is the rhyme . . . The rhyme is nothing but a glorified pun', to attempts to explain the linkage.[89] Michael Edwards writes:

> One may reflect that all rhymes are quasi-puns . . . Tynianov, perceiving that, in poetry, to associate words phonetically is also to relate them semantically, called rhyme a 'rhythmic metaphor'. Yet the pun, surely, is the rhetorical figure behind rhyming.

And Louis Untermeyer:

> The pun is, like certain forms of verse, a form of verbal dexterity, a syllabic matching of sounds that, like rhymes, are similar yet not quite the same. Whatever change it assumes, searching or silly, the pun springs from the same combination of wit and imagination that speeds the poetic process.[90]

For myself, I would acknowledge the reason in rhyme. Particularly appropriate rhymes (e.g. in slogans such as 'I like Ike') can come to seem natural, to have a reason for existence. Onomatopoeia, alliteration, consonance or assonance – all devices in which there is an echo-effect, a chiming or a clanging – seem very close to wordplay: 'Le monde mental/ment/monumentalement'. ('The intellect lies monumentally').[91] Half rhymes, or 'hymn rhymes' would approximate to the *à-peu-près*. Hughes and Hammond talk of the 'assonant pun'. As we saw in the early days of the pun, 'This form of assonance regularly provided the mental mechanism or stimulus for the oracles of the prophets. A basket of fruit *(qais)* becomes a portent of Israel's end *(qes)* (Amos, 8:2).'[92] The pun *is* like the rhyme, in that it calls the sense by the sound; it brings together words which often are thought separate.

As well as operating *like* rhymes, puns can be used *as* rhymes. This is especially visible in holorhymes, which, by analogy with *rimes riches*, are sometimes called *rimes millionnaires*.[93] The most famous of these is:

> Gal, amant de la reine, à la tour Magne, à Nîmes
> Galamment de l'arène alla, tour magnanime.[94]

For Carrière

> Les vers olorimes ne sont en définitive que le goût de la rime riche poussé aux
> extrêmes limites . . . La rime riche, qui si souvent se confond avec le calembour, a
> sévi parti [sic. partout] au XIXe siècle. On trouve par exemple dans *Le Charivari*:
> 'On demande une panacée universelle / Pour guérir une panne assez universelle'.

> (Holorhymes are definitely nothing but the love of rich rhyme pushed to the limit.
> Rich rhyme, so often confused with the pun, proliferated everywhere in the
> nineteenth century, e.g. in *Le Charivari*: 'Required: a universal panacea to repair a
> fairly common breakdown'.)[95]

Hugo himself produced rhymes in three successive lines like:

> mémorable,
> même au râble,
> mais mort, hâble.[96]

Such rhymes are outrageous: Ogden Nash, W.S. Gilbert, Hood and Byron all
practise them; e.g. Byron:

> There's not a sea the passenger e'er pukes in,
> Turns up more dangerous breakers than the Euxine.[97]

On such comic rhyming, Auden commented:

> The effect . . . is as if the words, on the basis of their auditory friendship, had
> taken charge of the situation, as if, instead of an event requiring words to describe
> it, words had the power to create an event.[98]

Rhyming slang, on the other hand, seems to me closer kin to Nonsense than to
punning, for what is the connection between a tram and bread-and-jam, or
apples-and-pairs and stairs? Puns, and rhymes, yodel. They call to each other,
just as we saw in etymological fables that word-conjunctions invent believable
realities. This seems to involve both spontaneity (the sudden catching of
similarities) and ordering (showing the link, underscoring it phonetically). But I
still remain somewhat dubious of this linkage, and would echo this opinion of
Rochette:

> On a dit que la rime était un calembour resté à mi-chemin. Je ne crois pas que
> cette pensée soit exacte; la rime est une condition favourable pour le calembour

mais elle en diffère essentiellement; la rime est un amusement pour l'oreille flattée de ce retour du même son. Le calembour est un plaisir où il entre une part de satisfaction intellectuelle; c'est la surprise de l'esprit qui trouve dans un même signe une double valeur sémantique.

(It has been said that rhyme is a pun halfway there. I don't think this is accurate; rhyme is a favourable condition for the pun but differs from it in essentials. Rhyme is a tickling of the ear which is pleased by the return of the same sound. The pun is a pleasure which has an element of intellectual satisfaction; it is the surprise sprung on the mind, which finds in the same sign a double semantic value.)[99]

One thing seems undeniable:

It is no accident that the best punsters have been poets, for there is a natural affinity between the two. A pun is for the ear as well as the eye; a good pun, like a good rhyme, seems both accidental and inevitable.[100]

It is indeed the poets (Shakespeare, Donne, Hood, Hugo) or the writers of 'poetic' prose (Nabokov, Joyce, Flaubert) who have been most responsive to, and prolific in, punning. For Chesterton, the pun 'may briefly embody the chief essence of art, that completeness of form should confirm completeness of idea'.[101] This is overstating the case, but puns add to polyphony, to fugality. They are a poetic device because they combine economy and richness: density of meaning. (If they are *only* economical, then they are little better than abbreviations, which are rarely poetic.) They are poetic because they are on the magic side of language, 'Le jeu de mots, parce qu'il est, à la lettre, un "jeu", rend au créateur la maîtrise magique du language' ('The play on words, because it is literally "play", gives back to the creator a magical mastery over language').[102] In his *Roots of Lyric*, Welsh states:

We find over and over in the language of poetry lexical puns, syntactical puns, and the sophisticated form of punning that juxtaposes two dictions ... The most significant puns may be as much the result of haphazard coincidences in language as the puns of bad jokes, but some poets, following their intuitions to the *onoma* [name] in *paronomasia*, make puns that reflect not chance but a deep order in the roots of language and a vision of archaic namings.[103]

One student of naming, Lipton, offers a timely reminder of the dangerous seductiveness of this process. Seeking collective nouns for people, animals and so on, on the model of the old hunting catalogues – e.g. 'a sord of mallards' – he admits that he has been tempted to pun (as he indeed does in calling this 'the venereal game'). He offers for a group of male homosexuals 'a basket of fruit', 'a bundle of faggots' (or, in England, 'a packet of fags'). But he argues that, as with the famous Oxford anecdote about 'a flourish of strumpets', 'anthology of pros', such punning coinages are jokes rather than poetry, for they do not say, in Robert Frost's term, 'one thing in terms of another', but say two things. 'Anthology', for example, tells us nothing about whores (where 'a parliament of owls' tells us something about human views on owls). He does allow that, at its best (as in 'the flourish of strumpets'), both joke and poetic revelation can be attained.[104] Taking a wider view, Roman Jakobson unhesitatingly asserts that 'le jeu de mot ou, pour employer un terme plus érudit et à ce qu'il me semble plus précis, paronomase, règne sur l'art poétique' ('Wordplay or, to use a more erudite and I think more exact term, paronomasia, rules over poetics').[105] To come full circle in this study of the extended family, Queneau shows us how we speak rhetoric even unwittingly: '"Ça faut avouer", dit Trouscaillon qui dans cette simple ellipse utilisait hyperboliquement le cercle vicieux de la parabole' ('"That, have to admit", said Trouscaillon, who in this simple ellipsis was using hyperbolically the vicious circle of the parabola/parable').[106] Rhetoric and geometry play off each other.

6

Rounding Up

Round the Twist

We think twice, often simultaneously; we can see double. We have the potentiality, at least, for schizophrenia, and this same potentiality is reflected in the language we make, use, or are used or made by. The double is present in everyday language: to be beside oneself, to laugh at oneself, to go out of one's mind, to come to oneself or to one's senses, to frighten oneself to death, to contradict oneself (as Vigny said: 'Je ne suis pas toujours de mon opinion'),[1] to not be oneself ('I'm not myself today'), and – the ultimate dichotomy – to take one's own life. This is language in the reflexive mode. The punner senses that words or phrases have their alter-ego or Doppelgänger, their often distorted mirror-image, their twin identical or not. An enantiomorph is a mirror-image, and enantiosis means saying (ironically) the reverse of what you mean. 'Enantiodromia' is a term from Heraclitus, and denotes the process (which we earlier saw embodied in his work), whereby things meet with their opposites. It means 'clashing together', which captures the attraction and repulsion present in punning.

There is much area of overlap between look-alikes and sound-alikes, well illustrated in this statement by Gutwirth, a definition which is a pun in itself: 'Le comique du quiproquo étend son domaine du calembour au sosie, de la substitution de lettres à la substitution de l'être ('The comedy of the quiproquo stretches from the pun to the double, from the substitution of letters to the substitution of identities').[2] In its extensive literature, the double, or 'second self', is 'an always contradictory being, a paradox of simultaneous outwardness and inwardness, of difference from and identity with the first self'.[3] The French talk of 'l'état second', a complex dimension composed of hallucination and inspiration. I quoted in an earlier chapter Corvin's view that 'le calembour . . . entraîne l'esprit sur la pente du Même pour mieux laisser prévoir l'irruption de l'Autre' ('the pun drags the mind along the slope of the Same the better to leave room for the break-in of the Other').[4] We might call this the intuition that neither we, nor words, are alone. This can assume a sinister form, as in Stevenson's *Dr. Jekyll and Mr. Hyde*, on which Jean Paris glosses excitedly:

Voilà justement ce que Stevenson illustre à merveille: ce monstre accompli, c'est la pensée même dans sa fonction de 'synthèse disjonctive': tout homme est mot-valise, qui doit pour prendre sens et, ce faisant, en reconnaître le non-sens, commencer par disjoindre ses constituants. *Jekyllhyde* s'appelle aussi bien *Rilchiam.*

(That is just what Stevenson illustrates so splendidly: this perfect monster is thought itself in its function of 'disjunctive synthesis': everyone is a portmanteau-word, and in order to acquire meaning and at the same time to acknowledge its non-meaning, each must begin by breaking up his constituent parts. *Jekyllhyde*'s other name could well be *Rilchiam.*)[5]

Thus bays the Parisian armchair-werewolf. Thoreau, of course, is more serene: 'With thinking we may be beside ourselves in a sane sense.'[6] Here, the double is unthreatening, constructive, contemplative, capable of aesthetic distancing. Puns, like this kind of second self, can detach us from life, offer it to us as a spectacle (this is no more modest than the extremist position Paris lends to Stevenson, for we have seen Thoreau's praise, earlier, of 'extra-vagance').

Puns, like people, are double-tongued creatures; they need someone to hear double. Barthes wrote:

La double entente (bien nommé), fondement du jeu de mots, ne peut s'analyser en simples termes de signification (deux signifiés pour un signifiant); il y faut la distinction de deux destinataires; et si ... les deux destinataires ne sont pas donnés par l'histoire, si le jeu de mots semble adressé à une seule personne (le lecteur, par exemple), il faut concevoir cette personne divisée en deux sujets, en deux langages, en deux espaces d'écoute (d'où l'affinité traditionnelle du jeu de mots et de la 'folie': le 'Fou,' vêtu d'un costume bi-partite (divisé) était autrefois le fonctionnaire de la double entente). Par rapport à un message idéalement pur (tel qu'il s'accomplit dans la mathématique), la division de l'écoute constitue un 'bruit', elle rend la communication obscure, fallacieuse, risquée: incertaine. Cependant, ce bruit, cette incertitude sont produits par le discours en vue d'une communication: ils sont donnés au lecteur pour qu'il s'en nourrisse: ce que le lecteur lit, c'est une contre-communication.

(Double entendre (so aptly called), the basis of wordplay, cannot be analysed in mere terms of meaning (two signifieds for one signifier); it needs the separate idea of two listeners; and if these two listeners are not provided in the story, if the wordplay seems to be addressed to one person only (the reader for example), we must think of this person as split into two subjects, two languages, two listening areas (hence the traditional affinity of wordplay with 'Folly' – the Fool, dressed in a two-part (divided) costume, was in earlier days the main agent for double entendre). In comparison with an ideally pure message (such as is possible in mathematics), split hearing constitutes a 'noise', it makes communication obscure, misleading, chancy – unreliable. And yet this noise, this uncertainty are produced by speech with the aim of communicating. They are given to the reader so that he can be nourished by them; what the reader reads is a counter-communication.)[7]

In this passage, Barthes jumbles up hearing and reading, phonic and graphic, possibly because books talk to him. He suggests that we have to be at least partly mad to register a communication at all. It is true that even technically sane people, such as literary critics, know, like Empson, that 'the practice of looking for ambiguity rapidly leads to hallucinations.'[8]

'In jokelore the proverbial wise fool may be described as an oxymoron who is also a foxy moron.'[9] Lanson held that punning brings together 'les grands artistes et les grands imbéciles'. Cocteau spoke of 'le gâtisme hautain' ('the haughty senility') of Marcel Duchamp's puns.[10] There are grains of stupidity, and of madness, in punning (and it is often, like hysteria, contagious). Paul Jennings talks of 'us paronomasiamaniacs', Esar of 'punnitis', or 'punnorrhea'.[11] I imagine that most people have experienced the occurrence whereby, under stress – or indeed in a state of great relaxation, as in dreams or reveries -- the mind catches wildly or idly at jingling words or phrases, and fears it is losing control. Mahood connects the supposed abnormal and the alleged normal:

> The poet and the psychologist both know that madness is full of meaning, that the puns of mania or the portmanteau words of the schizophrenic are the outer verbal evidence of a strong underlying association of ideas.[12]

Such unconscious or 'irrational' coalescence is closely allied with wilful punning. I am not sure how anyone can prove Frédéric Paulhan's claim that this is commoner among the mentally disturbed than amongst the officially sane.[13] For his part, Coleridge likens punning to 'what is highly characteristic of superfluous activity of mind, a sort of playing with a thread or watch train or snuff box'.[14] Up to a point, this sounds normal, harmless. Beyond a badly specified limit, we may begin to be perturbed.

Before Freud, John Jackson was writing: 'Punning is well worthy of the psychologist's attention. I seriously mean that the analysis of puns is a simple way of beginning the mechanical analysis of the process of normal and abnormal mentation.' From this chilling premise, he develops an intriguing analogy between the visual and the auditory:

> Vision is stereoscopic; in a sense it is slightly diplopic, for there are two dissimilar images although there seems to be but one external object . . . Just as there is visual diplopia so there is 'mental diplopia', or, as it is commonly called, 'double consciousness'.

In the hoary 'hoarse/horse' pun, Jackson claims that 'we have the sensation of complete resemblance with a sense of vast difference.' Seeing double in these ways certainly perturbs us. But Jackson seeks to minimize the worry, and talks, like Coleridge, of 'surplus mind'. Rather dismissively, he describes punning as 'playing at being foolish; it is only morbid in that slender sense.' Before Freud, however, Jackson saw the links of dreaming and punning, for dreaming, he argues, is also diplopic.[15] In the same year, a French alienist noted the incidence of punning in some forms of mental illness: 'Il est à remarquer que, pour le cerveau frappé de maladie ou de démence, le son d'un mot appelle un autre mot analogue comme aspect, mais n'ayant aucune analogie comme sens et comme valeur dans le langage.' ('It should be pointed out that, for the brain attacked by illness or dementia, the sound of a word calls up another analogous word as an aspect, but lacking any similarity in meaning or linguistic value').[16] This puts the stress on a passive echolalia, but the process can be more dynamic, as described by Eastman:

> There are forms of insanity in which . . . a 'flight of ideas' occurs, which is like the racing of a motor disgeared from the machine it was intended to move, and in this condition puns are sometimes seen to fly off in the most extraordinary swarms and galaxies.[17]

It was Hermann Oppenheim who coined the term 'Witzelsucht' to describe what Jastrowitz had formerly termed 'Moria'. (Centuries before, Sir Thomas More had already punned on the coincidence of his name with the Greek words *moria*: folly and *moros*: stupid.) 'Witzelsucht' is defined as 'a morbid tendency to pun . . . while being oneself inordinately entertained thereby'.[18] For some, it is associated with frontal lobe tumours. Koestler reports the phenomenon of compulsive punning, known as 'Förster's syndrome', first observed by Förster, a German surgeon in 1929,

> when he was operating on a patient suffering from a tumour in the third ventricle – a small cavity deep down in the phylogenetically ancient regions of the mid-brain, adjacent to structures intimately concerned with the arousal of emotions. When the surgeon began to manipulate the tumour affecting those sensitive structures, the (conscious) patient burst into a manic flight of speech, quoting passages in Latin, Greek, and Hebrew. He exhibited typical sound associations, and with every word of the operator broke into a flight of ideas . . . 'Messer, messer, Metzer, Sie sind ein Metzel' [all words to do with knives and butchery].

Koestler comments on 'this gruesome kind of humour coming from a man tied face down to the operating table with his skull open'.[19] This phenomenon was actually observed. Psychologists like Brill disagree.

> ['Witzelsucht' is] not a special phenomenon characteristic of brain tumours, as is commonly believed. Rather it is nothing but an unconscious reaction of the individual to a mental disintegration, of which he is unconsciously aware.[20]

Given the terms, this can be only a supposition, but it widens the theatre of operation.

The phenomenon commodiously known as schizophrenia would seem especially suited to doubling up, or splitting, verbally. At the purely playful end, there is what has been called 'schizoverbia' (e.g. a comment on an income-tax return: 'the most rigged-up marole that had ever been seen').[21] It often seems as if schizophrenia were the most word-haunted state. For Freud,

> if we ask ourselves what it is that gives the character of strangeness to the substitutive formation and the symptom in schizophrenia, we eventually come to realise that it is the predominance of what has to do with words over what has to do with things.[22]

More specifically, Max Levin diagnoses:

> impairment of the ability to differentiate symbol and object, abstract and concrete, figurative and literal, relevant and pseudo-relevant. Much of it can be summed up by saying that the patient confuses form and substance.

(As does the wilful punner.) '"Don't count your chickens before they're hatched" is, to the schizophrenic, a precept for poultrymen.'[23] As Arieti expresses it, 'the attention of the patient is often focussed not on the connotation or denotation of the term but on the word as a word.'[24] For Neale and Oltmanns, in some experiments, 'schizophrenics more often indicated that two words were conceptually similar on the basis of mere association.' Their problems in communication 'may be attributed to their excessive misinterpretation of double-meaning words'.[25] This sounds like folk etymologists and punsters, though the questions of volition and control are crucial. R. Bastide uses wordplay to evoke the trap-situation of such people:

> Le schizophrène qui s'est enfermé dans la carapace de ses systèmes de concepts ne peut briser ces résistances que par le jeu de mots qui peut les rendre perméables – mais comme ces systèmes sont des systèmes 'personnels,' donc non communicatifs, les jeux de mots deviennent des 'mots de je.'

> (The schizophrene who has locked himself under the carapace of his conceptual systems can break down these barriers only by wordplay which can render them permeable, but, as these systems are strictly 'personal', and so non-communicative, wordplay becomes ego-play.)[26]

Not surprisingly, some analysts have found that schizophrenics have a special difficulty in understanding humour, since many jokes depend on double meanings, and hence an ability to focus on both primary and secondary, strong and weak meanings of a word, an area in which, as we have seen, they tend to be defective.[27] Perhaps the point is that some can create puns, but few appreciate those of others: a one-way traffic which does little to alter the isolation. Until very recently in human history those not labelled as mad must frequently have found the mentally ill funny, to the extent that the word 'funny' itself was, and still is, used as a synonym for mentally unbalanced. To the labelled, the illness and such attitudes are no joke. Expectably they strike back, though more commonly, it seems to be agreed, among manic–depressives than schizophrenics (e.g. '"Punning speech": A form of embolophrasia characterized by pathological play on words of the same sound but of different meaning. It is sometimes manifest in the manic phase of manic–depressive psychoses').[28] Arieti notes:

> In this incessant logorrhea, the [manic–depressive] patient makes jokes. The propensity towards association leads to repeated clang associations, which the patient uses to make jokes, puns, etc. In some rare cases the lack of thought inhibition facilitates a certain artistic propensity, which does not, however, lead to achievement because of the lack of concentration.[29]

Such wordplay is often aggressive in intent, a revenge for being mocked or condescended to. One chronic mental patient loved making incomprehensible requests for a visiting pianist to play 'Mother's Stove'. Eventually it emerged that he wanted 'Home on the Range'. He was pulling the pianist's leg.[30] Other instances suggest lucid self-referentiality. One patient believed that Jesus, cigar-boxes and sex were identical. The connection? All these are encircled (as of course the patient is): with a halo, a tax-band, and a woman by the erotic attention of men.[31] When von Domarus on the same page moves away from sympathetic observation to link the schizophrenic's laws of logic with those of primitive people, he lays himself open to the attack of R. Brown, which we would all do well to keep at the forefront of our minds:

> Research workers believe in the psychological unity of children, in the mind of primitive man, in the animal mind. They believe in disease entities called schizophrenia and aphasia. And so they are disposed to unify each category through the use of a common descriptive term. All of these categories are fallen away from the healthy, civilized, human adult. Each category lacks one attribute of the category to which the researcher himself belongs. There is a beautiful simplicity in the notion that all departures from ourselves are basically the same kind of departure.[32]

What of wordplay within the practice of psychoanalytic investigation? Ernest Jones tells us that Freud found 'that the patients' utterances, and their play with words, commonly centre on some part of their body, so that Freud speaks of their "organ language" . . . Their symptoms also are often built on resemblances between words instead of ideas.'[33] Freud found that an entire neurosis could take the form of an elaborate pun, best exemplified by the 'Rat Man' case.

Here, at the outset, the patient himself, having already read *The Psychopathology of Everyday Life*, 'had come across the explanation of some curious verbal associations which had so much reminded him of his own "efforts of thought" in connection with his ideas that he had decided to put himself in my hands'.[34] In other words, the subject was already linguistically predisposed towards Freud's likely 'solution' to his dilemma. The 'verbal bridge' that Freud located, or threw, across this divided consciousness was the term *Spielratte*: play-rat, gambler (the father's debts were shameful to the son). Further complex links between rats, money and anal eroticism (*Ratten*: rats; *Raten*: instalments) team up with the 'screen association' – *heiraten* (to marry: the question of legacies and settlements). This sounds plausible, if over-convenient. Given the patient's readiness to acquiesce to Freud's method, this 'solution' must be right, successful, for the subject agrees to and with it. Freud clearly felt that humour helps us to be our own psychoanalysts, to handle our own conflicts, but he was equally alert to the converse possibility, that humour could be a sign of, as well as therapy for, neuroses.

> We get an impression that the subjective determinants of the joke-work are often not far removed from those of neurotic illness – when we learn, for instance, of Lichtenberg that he was a severely hypochondriacal man, with all kinds of eccentricities.[35]

In comparison, Adler seems positively tetchy: 'Actually a large number of nervous symptoms seem like a poor joke. They try to trip us up, and sometimes surprise us as a joke does.' Perhaps seeking revenge at being thus unseated, Adler goes on to explain that he sometimes used jokes as therapy, 'to clarify his error to the neurotic'.[36] He had ways of making him talk straight. While it might well be dangerously counter-productive to try wordplay on a would-be suicide, there seems to be a place for the sensitive use of humour in therapy. But it remains as much of a minefield as the question of the wilfulness of patients' joking. Bergson, as we saw, viewed humour as a normative operation, a *correction*. In both French and English, this word has both pedagogical and penal connotations.

Neologisms, too, enter into this complex equation. According to Ball, they are much commoner in persecution-mania patients than others.[37] With a far greater sense of inwardness, the poet Henri Michaux reports after his plunges.

> Certains aliénés pour qui il est des impressions majeures, empoignantes, s'imposant sans contrôle, abordant la conscience avec impétuosité et 'ensemble' et ne la quittant pas, font, par nécessité intérieure, un mot nouveau de leur double ou multiforme misère. Ainsi une malade se dit constamment 'pénétroversée', c'est-à-dire pénétrée en même temps que traversée. Ce mot en elle s'impose. Mot pour ses besoins nouveaux. Elle n'a pas étudié pour le fabriquer.

(Certain inmates, who are grabbed by traumas which take them over totally and which attack their consciousness impetuously and 'simultaneously', and will not let go, are forced by inner necessity to coin a word for their double or multiform misery. Thus, one sick woman said constantly that she was 'penetroversed', that is, penetrated and traversed at the same time. This word forces itself upon her. A word for her new needs. She didn't need to read books in order to make it up.)[38]

No wonder that one of Jung's patients called her coinages 'power-words'.[39] Even Nonsense, as Lewis Carroll was fully aware, can be a way of maintaining a kind of balance. Perhaps this is what is meant by 'the higher lunacy'. On a more everyday level, many jokes, of both children and adults, include answers or punch-lines that both make sense and no sense at the same time. In this respect, jokes inhabit a world where, as in madness, an internal logic rules: that is, the joke means something in its own created universe but not in the wider world of reality. Max Miller told a yarn of meeting a desirable nude woman on a narrow cliff-ledge: 'I didn't know whether to edge past her or to toss myself off there and then.' The suicidal second meaning is nonsense; and yet the whole makes sense, when we recall the Anglo-Saxon keeping of sex at arm's length.

In the section, 'Puns of a Diseased Brain', of his study of Shakespeare's puns, Bather cites Edgar (as Mad Tom), replying with 'Pillicock sat on Pillicock Hill' to Lear's cry about 'These pelican daughters', and Hamlet feigning madness in mistaking Polonius.[40] Not only creations but creators also simulate. Eluard and Breton try to conjure up 'manie aiguë' by a series of puns and assonances:

> Ma mère s'est mariée avec le Shah de Perse, ils ont loué une boutique à Passy, une sorte de maison de passe à passage à niveau pour les hommes seuls. Le Shah arrive tôt dans la château; ma mère est chatoyante.
>
> (My mother married the Shah of Persia. They have leased a shop in Passy, a sort of *maison de passe* [brothel] on a level-crossing for lonely men. The Shah arrives early at the chateau; my mother is shatteringly beautiful.)[41]

But this is merely stringing words, and us, along. Sartre detects a greater existential necessity for such simulation in Jean Genet:

> En parlant, Genet *se surveille* ... Les mots peuvent avoir des sens secrets, une phrase dite sérieusement peut déchaîner l'hilarité et sans le savoir mettre les rieurs contre lui. Il n'y a qu'un moyen d'éviter les embûches: faire rapidement et avant les autres la revue de tous les sens possibles, au besoin briser les mots, associer les syllabes entre elles de toutes les façons, comme font les collégiens qui veulent découvrir des vers pornographiques dans *Polyeucte*. Bref, prendre vis-à-vis du langage l'attitude du paranoïaque vis-à-vis du monde, y chercher tous les symboles, tous les signes, toutes les allusions, tous les calembours, pour pouvoir,

le cas échéant, les reprendre à son compte et les faire passer pour l'effet de sa volonté.

(As he speaks, Genet keeps a watch on himself. Words can have secret meanings, a sentence uttered seriously can unleash a gale of laughter and unwittingly set the laughters against him. There is only one way to avoid being ambushed: quickly and ahead of everybody else, to run through all the possible meanings, and if need be dislocate words, link syllables up every which way, like schoolboys trying to find pornographic lines in Corneille's *Polyeucte*. In short, to adopt towards language the attitude of the paranoiac towards society: to hunt out all the symbols, all the signs, all the allusions, all the puns, so as to be able, should the need arise, to claim them for his own and pass them off as deliberate.)[42]

This is the gun-jumping tactic of Mine Own Executioner, with which all convinced punners are necessarily familiar.

A state akin to mental derangement with which all human beings are familiar is dreaming. Here some seem, or pretend, to have absorbed Freud into their very unconscious: 'Now I even dream in puns. Like last night I dreamed of a female deer chasing a male deer in the mating season . . . A doe trying to make a fast buck.'[43] In chapter 4 we saw Lewis Carroll, well before Freud, fully aware of the links between dream and punning. Freud himself found these elements to be common to jokes and to 'dream-work': 'Displacement, faulty reasoning, absurdity, indirect representation, representation by the opposite'.[44] J. Hillis Miller stresses Freud's demonstration, in the *Psychopathology of Everyday Life* and in *Jokes and their Relation to the Unconscious*,

> of the way wordplay in all its forms is superficial. Wordplay is the repression of something more dangerous. This something, however, interweaves itself with that wordplay and forbids it to be merely verbal or merely play.[45]

In dreams, metaphors come true. 'Le rêve est l'état de réalité des figures' ('dreaming is where rhetorical figures come true'), said Valéry, and again spoke of 'le rêve aveugle, littéral – comme si tout comptait au même titre ('the blind, literal dream – as if everything there were equally valid')'.[46] Such a view, however, keeps the phenomenon on a level of passivity. The true punner exploits dreaming. Thomas Pynchon writes with more passion of 'the dreamer whose puns probe ancient fetid shafts and tunnels of truth . . . Worlds no man had seen if only because there was that high magic to low puns'.[47]

A state perhaps akin to that of dreaming, and that can be induced, is intoxication, more interestingly by drugs than by alcohol. Baudelaire on the effects of hashish (on *some* people):

> Il arrive quelquefois que des gens tout à fait impropres aux jeux de mots, improvisent des enfilades interminables de calembours, des rapprochements

d'idées tout à fait improbables, et faits pour dévoyer les maîtres les plus forts dans cet art saugrenu.

(It can happen that people quite unfitted for wordplay improvise endless strings of puns, highly unlikely associations of ideas, enough to drive crazy the greatest masters of this preposterous art.)

Unfortunately, he offers no examples. In fact, he gives off the odour of someone trying to outdo experience by words: 'Les équivoques les plus singulières, les transpositions d'idées les plus inexplicables ont lieu. Les sons ont une couleur, les couleurs ont une musique' ('The most amazing equivoques, the most inexplicable transpositions of ideas come about. Sounds get a colour, colours become musical'). In this way synaesthesia enters punning, and it sounds very close to a state of possession:

Des ressemblances et des rapprochements incongrus, impossibles à prévoir, des jeux de mots interminables, des ébauches de comique, jaillissent continuellement de votre cerveau. Le démon vous a envahi; il est inutile de regimber contre cette hilarité, douloureuse comme un chatouillement.

(Similarities and incongruous analogies, totally unexpected, interminable plays on words, comic sketches, leap continuously from your brain. The demon has got into you; it is no use resisting this hilarity which is as irksome as an itch.)[48]

This may be exhilaration invented in tranquillity. More persuasively, since, even when not writing under the influence of mescalin, he coins both imaginary creatures and new words, Michaux writes of the effect of drugs on his production: 'Pressé par le temps, le temps vivacissime, les mots parfois seront écourtés, par une fatale coalescence, deux tronçons étrangers, subitement soudés en un mot nouveau' ('Harried by time, hurtling time, words will sometimes be cut short and by a fateful coalescence two foreign stumps will be suddenly soldered into a new word').[49]

Let us examine the cases of two strange writers who neither simulated nor induced madness. The first, Christopher Smart, was forcibly confined for his religious mania at intervals over seven years; the second, Jean-Pierre Brisset, lived an outwardly unremarkable existence. In both cases, we meet a logocentric world.

I am inclined to think that instead of pointing to a coherent body of religious thought and sentiment, Smart's multilingual punning points to a mad, philological vision of reality. It is as if Smart's obsession with the sound, texture, and meaning of words in various languages has transformed the concrete reality of sanity into the philological reality of madness.[50]

In *Jubilate Agno* (B2.269), Smart speaks of the common Greek preposition $\varkappa \alpha \tau$

as being identical in sound with 'cat': 'The power and spirit of a CAT is in the Greek ... The pleasantry of a cat at pranks is in the language ten thousand times over' (B2. 628 and 630). Dearnley glosses: 'For all its oddity, the metaphorical and punning image of the cat is obviously meant to express the protean quality of the Greek language' (p. 164). Latin is also brought in: 'For the power of some animal is predominant in every language! ... For the Mouse (Mus) prevails in the Latin, for edi-mus, bibi-mus, vivimus – ore-mus' (B. 638–9). As for English, 'All the words ending in ble are in the creature. Invisi-ble, incomprehensi-ble, ineffa-ble, A-ble' (B2 646). Smart thus plays cat-and-mouse with Greek and Latin, and charges at us with a load of bull in English. Atheists would agree: 'For BULL in the first place is the word of Almighty God' (B2 676). Commenting on such passages, Frye writes: 'It is possible that similar sputters and sparks of the fusing intellect take place in all poetic thinking.'[51] Welsh argues on similar lines; '*Jubilate Agno* is a poem gone mad among names ... And often the names led him through underground passages of sound to perceive hidden relationships in the divine order he was praising.' We have seen something comparable in Donne, Hopkins, and indeed in the Biblical prophets. Welsh goes on to stress:

> Smart's belief that all creation had been named in a way that reflected a divine order and the poem is a record of a search for names that still reveal this hidden internal design uniting all creation. It is, finally, a religious rather than a magical sense of the word: 'For all good words are from GOD, and all others are cant' (B1 85). He trusted, probably too much, that any relationship between the sounds of words was not just fortuitous.[52]

Here again we witness the strange use of the fortuitous phenomenon, homonymy, to combat randomness in experience. Throughout *Jubilate Agno*, we hear the reiteration, the anvil-chorus, of 'Let X rejoice'. This is wordplay as jubilation, as climax, as congress. (D5): 'Let Crook, house of Crook rejoice with Ophites black-spotted marble – Blessed be the name of the Lord Jesus by crook.' Shepherd's crook, deviousness and determination (by hook or by crook). 'The Lord enable me to shift.' God, the supreme and clandestine punster, aids Smart to follow in his footsteps, to bend things and names to his way.

Brisset combated randomness from a different angle, though the Bible often lends him also support and rhythms. Unearthed by the Surrealists, rescued from them by Queneau and again by Foucault, he worked with the railway police at Angers and, in his writings, to make lunatic sense of chaos. As so little is known of his life, we must assume that it was obsessively spent in speculating and writing on the origins of mankind and of language. His brief moment of renown came when a young Jules Romains, Apollinaire and student cronies invited him up to Paris as a jape to give a speech and to be crowned Prince of Thinkers.[53] Brisset tells us in his *Grammaire logique* (p. 121) that from early adolescence he was obsessed with decomposing and reconstituting language, reversing phrases and coining palindromes: a centripetal activity. Also from childhood he observed frogs with fascination, and moved from the unexceptionable comparison of spawn with sperm to an elaborate analogy between frogs and man: an extended visual pun. Frogs, gods, demons, mankind – this is Brisset's version of history. Frogs spoke to him: 'Coa, coa . . . quoi, quoi?': the primordial question.

Initially a religious *illuminé*, he became virulently anticlerical, concentrating on the rump-waggling motions of priests at the altar during Mass. His own sexuality curiously linked fellatio and sodomy in a self-contained and retroactive system, a kind of acrobatic tail-chasing. Like the palindrome. His interest in words was frankly oral: 'Tous les mots ont été sucés, têtés, aspirés, léchés et il n'y en est aucun qui ne soit entré dans la bouche par une de ces actions' ('All words have been sucked, imbibed, lapped up, licked, and every single one has entered the mouth by one of these means') (*Origines humaines*, p. 310). With typical narcissism, he claims in *La Grammaire logique* that the verb *être* is reflexive (p.5).

For him, all ideas expressed in similar-sounding words have identical origins and refer to the same object. He calls this *à-peu-près* 'l'euphonie', and it enabled him to shuttle between French, Latin, German, English, Italian, Sanskrit and Breton, in search of comprehensive corroboration for his intuitions. In *Les Origines humaines* he quotes *Corinthians*: 'But God hath chosen the foolish things of this world to confound the wise.' The pun is precisely 'ce jeu d'esprit, cette chose méprisée'. Language tells us all we want to know (pp. 102–3): 'Voyons où ces ancêtres étaient logés: l'eau j'ai, loge ai, l'auge ai. On fut donc dans le principe logé dans l'eau' ('Let us see where these ancestors were lodged: water I have, lodging I have, trough I have. They were thus in the beginning lodged in water') (p.89).

Brisset once confided to a local reporter: 'Depuis plus de seize ans que notre pensée ose pénétrer dans le temple de Dieu, nous n'y avons jamais trouvé de non-sens' ('For the sixteen years or more that our thoughts have dared to penetrate the temple of God, we have never found there any non-meaning').[54] A totally signifying universe, the antithesis of the Absurdist view. In seeking to abolish chance and chaos, Brisset erects the truly fortuitous – i.e. the assimilability of separate words – into his own system of connected meaning. As Foucault said of this scheme: 'Dans le language en émulsion, les mots sautent au hasard, comme dans les marécages primitifs nos grenouilles d'ancêtres bondissaient selon les lois d'un sort aléatoire. Au commencement étaient les dés' ('At the slimy stage of language, words leapt about at random, just as in the primeval swamps our frog ancestors jumped about according to the laws of an experimental fate. In the beginning were dice').[55] It is easy to see why Breton and other Surrealists championed Brisset. Yet Breton, as so often, defused the originality of Brisset by talking of 'un humour de réception', involuntary humour (this sounds rather like 'objective guilt' in Stalinist Russia).[56] This would be another bonus in the field of 'le hasard objectif', that rather comfy set-up where the material world plays ball with our innermost desires by granting joyous coincidences. In fact, anything but involuntary, Brisset was fully aware of his own quirky wordplay. Talking of Esau, in *Les Origines humaines*, for example: 'Le pelu plut tant qu'il plut, mais quand il devint méchant il ne plut plus' ('The hairy one pleased as long as he was popular, but when he became evil he no longer pleased') (p. 109). On the other hand, there were accidental puns in Brisset's home environment: a nearby village was famous for its frogs and its inhabitants were nicknamed 'les grenouillards'; Brisset was born at Noé, and the sons of Noah built Babel.

Marcel Duchamp called Brisset the Douanier Rousseau of philology. In reworking human history, Brisset rewrites etymology, which, as we have seen, is tightly linked with punning. Since the start of time, both popular and learned etymologists have come up with inspired daftness. It is the Cratylist tradition, the belief in a necessary connection between the phonic or orthographic form of words and what they designate. This is teleological etymology, but it rarely strays far away from the more purely ludic variety. Thus in *Origines humaines* Brisset, again on Esau, can write: 'Esaü était bien l'aîné, étant lainé ou couvert de laine dès sa naissance' ('Esau was truly the firstborn, being woolly or covered with wool from birth') (p. 108). Human descent from frogs (*raine* being one of the French words for this creature) is backed up by an amazing list: Lorraine, Touraine, *marraine* (pp. 98–101). The oldest god is Uranus: '*Ure anus* signifie qui urine par l'anus, ce qui est le propre de la grenouille' (p.21).

Brisset juggles with *sexe* and *excès*. The phenomenon of language, for him, is heavily eroticized. No wonder Foucault pricks up his ears. In return, like a 'plagiaire par anticipation' (as 'Pataphysicians call their precursors), Brisset can sound like Lacan: 'Le diable étant un père sévère criant: Persévère! C'était aussi un père vert, le vieux pervers.'[57] Brisset has a totalizing mania and a ragbag methodology. As with folk-etymology, we see in him the craving for symmetry and likeness. Thus, in *La Grammaire logique*, the Latin verb *ire* explains all infinitive endings in Romance languages (pp. 94–5). Some distortion of the evidence is necessary to prove the point. Such a universal language would indeed be Pan-glossism. Breton said: 'Les mots font l'amour.' Brisset's version is 'La parole est née de la force sexuelle' (*Les Origines humaines*, p. 85).

It has been suggested by Cullard, on the basis of his writings and odd statements, that Brisset was a paraphrenic – one of the multiple forms of schizophrenia. The apparent signs are: delirious inventiveness, systematization, yet a continuing grip on the real world: the mind on high but the feet on the ground. One clinical study of the *délire d'interprétation* by Paul Guiraud tells how a woman patient reported that her husband left a *horn* snuff-box on her bedside table in order to hint to her that she was a cuckold. This reasoning is logical, 'puisque les malades croient que cette allusion par calembour est faite volontairement par des personnes mal intentionnées' ('since patients believe that punning allusions are made deliberately by malevolent people'). Another patient thought she was Jesus made woman, and the Republic: 'En effet, je me suis livrée à de nombreux amants, donc la raie de mon fondement a été publique, donc je suis la République' ('Indeed, I have given myself to many lovers, and so the crack in my arse has been made public, and therefore I am the Republic').[58] As with Brisset, such delirious interpretations seek to explain otherwise fortuitous events. More soberly, however, Brisset in his *Grammaire logique* was able to recognize that 'on ne découvre que ce qu'on cherche' ('we discover only what we are looking for') (p.145). He knew he was inventing a new world-history, but no doubt preferred his alternative reality.

Undoubtedly, the demon analogist Brisset is better to think about than to read. At times, he seems to have taken French leave of his senses. He is manically repetitive. After conducting his lengthy researches into nineteenth-century literary and scientific 'hétéroclites', Queneau concluded with waspish magnanimity: 'Des hyperinconnus qui prétendent à la paraméconnaissance. Bref, on aura tout vu. Effectivement, il faut avoir tout vu' ('Supernonentities who lay claim to hyperneglect. In short, we've seen the lot. Truly, we need to have seen everything').[59] Thus speaks the true encyclopaedist. Brisset, besides, can counter-attack for himself. He accuses naturalists of having been 'devant la grenouille, comme le linguiste devant le calembour: pétrifiés et aveugles' ('confronted by the frog, like linguists confronted by the pun: petrified and blind').[60] Frogs begat Man; the Logos speaks French. We are in an umbilicism characteristic of Brisset, but also of his nation.

Bending over the time-warp of Brisset's lucubrations, we may well experience vertigo. His head buzzes with words, and he makes ours do so too. Cocteau said that we all bear a schizophrenic within us, and Pierre Bourgeade, writing on Queneau, claimed that 'le calembour introduit la folie dans le langage.'[61] But perhaps Brisset was right, and it was there all the time. He escapes from Emerson's imprisoning, static view of language as 'fossil poetry'. Finally, a doubting voice should be raised against Brisset, over whom it is easy to get excited. On Brisset's claim to abolish exceptions from grammatical rules, Jean Paris comments:

Il devient impossible de distinguer la règle de sa transgression. En s'étendant au lexique entier, en conférant son statut propre à tout vocable, le composite perd des traits distinctifs et, du coup, exempte le langage de sa menace. La victoire, paradoxalement, désarme une subversion qui ne trouve plus d'objet dont se nourrir.

(It becomes impossible to distinguish the rule from its infringement. By covering the whole lexis and conferring its own status on every word, the composite loses any distinguishing features and, in the process, frees language from any threat. Paradoxically, victory disarms a revolt which can no longer find any object to feed on.)[62]

This overstatement of the case against must be in turn contested, since anarchy need not self-destruct, revolution can be permanent; Brisset remains troubling, and cannot be safely catalogued.

Lapsus

'It is the surface of language that is the concern of the puzzle-solving psychoanalyst, its punning possibilities.'[63] Feeney expands on a comparable idea:

A pun is only surface humour. Real humour consists in seeing an incongruity between the fact and an imitation of the fact, between the truth and an almost truth. The incongruity observed is not complete, but only partial; because a likeness as well as an unlikeness must exist in the bogus that pretends to be real before it becomes funny. When both are presented to the mind in contrast, we laugh. Why we laugh is a mystery. It seems that the intellect is submitted to some sort of hot and cold douche in one shower. The mind half accepts, half rejects, what is being offered to it for recognition. At one and the same moment it sees a darkness and a light, a nothingness and a somethingness; it becomes simultaneously aware of its own madness and its own sanity.[64]

This strikes me as one of the sanest statements on the subject, in that it stresses oscillation, instead of freezing the adventure at one pole. We do indeed remember, just as the paraphrenic manages to keep one foot on the ground, that such enforced or fortuitous coincidences as puns need have nothing paranormal about them, although wordplay often features centrally in the communication of mystical experience. They are most often down-to-earth, and often their job is to cut pretensions down to size and, by reminding us of the literal buried within the figurative, to resee things as they are. If the mad make us question what it means to be sane, parapraxes of all kinds remind us of our unstable footing or control. Let us look, to borrow Freud's telling title, at the psychopathology of everyday life. 'The lip can slip, the eye can lie, but the nose knows.'[65] Let us, like a fetishist, have a good sniff at slips.

The very phrase 'words tripped off his lips' catches the ambiguity of our stance towards the trustworthiness of our mental and physical equipment, for it suggests both fluency and errors. Linguistics has a term for unstable vowels: 'off-glide'. We often liken speech to bodily movements: race, trip, slip, slide, *faux pas*, blunder, *la langue lui a fourché*. The pun has been compared often to a forked, split, or double, tongue. As regards slips, we are all postlapsarian. We do not live in Indian file. We jabber and jam. We are always liable to pun by doubling up, or overlapping. In reading, too, we race ahead or backtrack and focus only with effort. 'In fact, if one assumes that the origin of man and the origins of language and speech were simultaneous, then ... "spoonerisms" began with Adam.'[66] Such familiarity is perhaps what induced humility in Freud on this subject: 'Sometimes we cannot avoid an impression that everything that can be said about forgetting and about parapraxes is already ... self-evident to everyone.' Along with dreams, parapraxes enabled him to extend to general mental life the discoveries he had already made in connection with neuroses. An example of mis-laying: an elderly man marries a very young girl but forgets to take his wallet on the honeymoon. He is thus without means (*ohne Vermögen*). During the wedding night he was *unvermögend* (impotent).[67] The French counterpart of 'Freudian slip' ('acte manqué') seems particularly appropriate here. Helen McNeil writes in this connection:

> I suspect puns are rejected because it is neater and less threatening to believe that every word has a reliable signification, that it is not suddenly taking on a will of its own and attaching itself ad lib to other suppressed meanings. The high analogies of meaning seem tarnished by the low analogies of sound. Thus 'Freudian slips', a subgroup of sexual puns, endanger the speaker because they communicate more about his secret associations than he wants others to know.[68]

The Spoonerism, or 'tangle-talk', is related to the pun because it creates a new meaning, as in the one about the kitten that fell off a balcony and survived by popping on its drawers. There are 'whole-phrase' variants, such as: 'Alimony: bounty from the mutiny'.[69] And the American extension ('carp-to-carp walleting').[70] Such forms are obviously deliberate metatheses, controlled skids. The French have 'un art du contrepet'. It is an in-game: 'Le pouvoir créateur du verbe suscite entre ces initiés, par la seule conjuration tacite des lettres et des syllabes, une franc-maçonnerie mystérieuse' ('The creative power of the word gives rise amongst initiates, by the mere tacit incantation of letters and syllables, to a mysterious freemasonry'). It affords a decent way of being obscene, between what Etienne engagingly terms 'contrepétomanes'. On the French Radio from London in 1942, the speaker slipped in some pointed ones: 'Duce, tes gladiateurs circulent dans le sang' (s'enculent dans le cirque) ('Duce, your gladiators parade amid blood/bugger each other in the arena').[71] Rabelais had already coined some excellent *contrepèteries* ('A Beaumont le vicomte' – 'A beau con le vit monte').[72] Perceau offers: 'Pour entrer aux Carmélites, il faut savoir utiliser le mot de guichet' ('le godemiché') ('To enter the Carmelites, you need to know the password at the gate/bring a dildo'), and 'la jeune fille toussait en se mouchant' ('moussait en se touchant') ('The girl coughed as she blew her nose/frothed where she stroked herself').[73] Any more complicated chiasmuses become truly perverse, that is: long-winded. Perhaps to counter such a danger, Desnos spells out his spoonerisms: 'Rrose Sélavy n'est pas persuadée que la culture du moi puisse amener la moiteur du cul' ('Rrose Sélavy is not convinced that egomania produces a moist groin').[74] Finally, jokes about absent-mindedness are akin to spoonerisms in that they involve transposition of context or action; they are situational puns: 'The absent-minded showman got married and sent out press invitations to the first night.'[75]

The malapropism is a related form, and, likewise, while apparently aiming to record fallibility, manages to celebrate the wit of the recorder. 'Just as the spoonerism is a slip of the tongue, the malapropism is a slip of the vocabulary.'[76] This is true of their least usual and least innocent forms. Angus Ross says of Smollett's *Humphry Clinker*:

> The past experience of Tabitha and Win Jenkins form [sic] part of what they see in the unfamiliar and the new. Their malapropisms suggest this. In the last letter in the book, the religious ideas and the sacrament of marriage are given physical, kitchen dress in Win's language: 'We were yesterday three kiple *chined*, by the *grease* of God, in the holy bands of *mattermoney*.' Here is, of course, the sexual innuendo with which Smollett puts himself as author in the joke. But 'providinch' and the 'comely pear' are different. Here Smollett's fun with inventiveness play a part in the structure of the book as a whole.[77]

As Charney argues, 'malapropisms require a certain genius, and . . . they are always the ironic fomulations of a sophisticated author for his "low" characters.'[78] The whole phenomenon is tied up with the *approximation* we have so often found characteristic of punning. Whatever happens to characters in books, we are all of us prone to such near-misses. Adrian Room calls these confusibles:

> A confusible, basically, is a word that not only resembles another in spelling and pronunciation, but one that additionally has a similar or associated meaning. Put rather more formally, it is a word having a lexical and semantic (but not necessarily etymological) affinity with another. It is thus rather more than a malapropism – as in Mrs. Malaprop's famous 'nice derangement of epitaphs' – and closer, perhaps, to a paronym, e.g. fraction/faction.[79]

Howlers are to connoisseurs of puns what 'ready-mades' can be to artists: creative accidents, like the unwittingly sceptical spelling 'crucifiction'. Kenner defines the inadvertent pun as 'a word bringing to one context its affinities for another'.[80] 'An eavesdropper is an icicle' is a perfect pun. 'A paradox is a four-sided triangle': an accidental paradox itself. False etymology is seen productively at work in 'A hare-lip is where two parts of the upper lip have failed to unite. It is so called because they came within a hair of being united.'[81] Slips can be acts of commission or omission, just as 'sins of omission are those we have forgotten to commit.' The howler can bifurcate like a conundrum: 'What does a bat do in winter? It splits if you don't oil it.'[82] The rhythm of inertia can be felt in 'Les trois grandes époques de l'humanité sont l'âge de la pierre, l'âge du bronze et l'âge de la retraite' ('The three great epochs of mankind are the Stone Age, the Bronze Age and Pensionable Age').[83]

Pupils can slip when tested. The Press, and the world of business, also put themselves on show, and thus often show their slips, as in the report of a pop-group guitarist who was 'charged with the sexual battery of a woman'. The newspaper headline, 'Incest more common than thought in British Isles', the result of an over-compressed message, goes a long way towards explaining the anti-intellectual bias of modern British life. The sub-reporter, instructed to be concise, telescoped thus the escape of a mental inmate who raped a woman: 'Nut Bolts and Screws'.[84] An example of fortuitous juxtaposition of titles: 'SEXUAL RESPONSE IN HUMANS. 15 INJURED IN BIG PILE-UP'. And of unconscious gallows-humour: 'TWO CONVICTS EVADE NOOSE: JURY HUNG'.[85] Notices can have the opposite effect to the one intended, as in the Acapulco hotel sign: 'The Manager Has Personally Passed All the Water Served Here.' Tourist menus in particular provide much by way of mistranslation, semantic calques (cf. 'Fractured French'): 'Mussels in a seamanlike manner'.

Mishearing, like any other kind of mistake, can be wilful or involuntary. I have discussed earlier the sixteenth-century expression 'faire de l'entend-trois', for somebody feigning not to understand what is being said and answering aside. This is *fausse naïveté*. Yet there are clearly aural illusions, as well as optical ones. Carroll's illustration of this, while patently set up, makes the point. A tutor tests, and torments, his student by conducting the tutorial at a distance, through closed doors and using various college servants as intermediaries.

> Tutor: What is twice three?
> Scout: What's a rice tree?
> Sub-scout: When is ice free?
> Sub-sub-scout: What's a nice fee?
> Pupil (timidly): Half a guinea.[86]

The following could be a splendid example of dumb insolence: an exchange between a medical officer and a new recruit in the second world war:

M.O.: How are your bowels working?
   R.: Haven't been issued with any, sir.
M.O.: I mean, are you constipated?
   R.: No, sir, I volunteered.
M.O.: Heavens, man, don't you know the King's English?
   R.: No, sir, is he?[87]

As Ayres says of *Alice in Wonderland*, this exemplifies 'the rich possibilities arising not from misunderstandings, but from parallel understandings of a single continuity of uttered sounds'.[88]

Here lies the body of John Mound,
Lost at sea and never found;

'Where will you find any modern building that has lasted so long as the ancient?'; a Cork paper, describing an interlude of peace in a stormy public meeting, said: 'For some time a great calm raged.'[89] Sydney Smith sagely opines: 'A bull is exactly the counterpart of a witticism: for as wit discovers real relations that are not apparent, bulls admit apparent relations that are not real.' Like all neat polarities, this sounds spurious, but he goes on more enterprisingly: 'The pleasure arising from bulls proceeds from our surprise at suddenly discovering two things to be dissimilar in which a resemblance might have been suspected.'[90] This is not the first time we have found wordplay reminding us of divergence rather than congruence. The Irish Bull has affinities with mixed metaphor and, like paradox, is a self-contradicting proposition. According to Walter Jerrold, the word 'bull' comes from the Icelandic, where it signifies nonsense.[91] We might also think of bull-shit and army bull (meaningless sheen). For Eastman,

an Irish Bull may very well be defined as any remark which appears rotund and meaningful enough, until our apprehension actually arrives upon it, when there is simply nothing there. Its plausibility is the only thing to distinguish it from pure nonsense.[92]

This is to see it more negatively than is necessary. An alternative stance is adopted by Marshall Brown:

The bull proceeds, not from the want, but the superabundance of ideas, which crowd each other so fast in an Irishman's brain that they get jammed together, so to speak, in the doorway of his speech, and can only tumble out in their ordinary disorder.[93]

The last word should go to Sir John Pentland Mahaffy, who is said to have distinguished the Irish and the English bull thus: 'The Irish Bull is pregnant, whereas the English Bull is sterile.'[94]

Slips of mind, tongue or pen, catch the perpetrator out, but, as elsewhere, they can have the same effect on the receiver. There is much *fausse naïveté*, or just simple *fausseté*, in many collections of howlers. Wordplay sets traps, as in the wilfully misleading advert for 'Une machine à écrire et une machine à coudre, en parfait état de marche, 500 francs' ('Machines for writing and sewing, in perfect working order, 500 francs'): the crook sent his suckers a pencil and a needle. Quoting this, Olbrechts-Tyteca comments: 'L'escroc, comme l'homme d'esprit, compte sur l'oubli de certaines propriétés du langage' ('The crook, like the man of wit, counts on people forgetting certain properties of language').[95] As Peeters notes: 'Le jeu de mots est en fait un croc-en-jambe aux mécanismes linguistiques, et par là même met en cause le caractère référentiel du langage articulé en montrant la nature arbitraire du signe linguistique' ('Play on words throws language's mechanisms out of gear, and thus it questions the referential character of articulated language by demonstrating the arbitrary notion of the linguistic sign').[96] In a footnote, after quoting Abel's views on Egyptian phonology – that in the oldest languages words denoting opposite qualities are often identical – Freud stated:

> It is plausible to suppose, too, that the original antithetical meaning of words exhibits the ready-made mechanism which is exploited for various purposes by slips of the tongue that result in the opposite being said of what was consciously planned.

This strikes me as a dubious analogy, a kind of wordplay in itself. Indeed, Freud himself referred to the 'heads I win, tails you loose' tactic he was once accused of using in his analyses (cf. also dreams where, for Freud, things may also stand for their opposites).[97] But perhaps punning reminds us that all comparisons are as odious as they are inevitable. It can be an unprovoked, or an engineered, accident, a quip as much as a slip. In driving, slips can be controlled. Slippage, flexibility, overlap are at the very heart of wordplay: room for manoeuvre. As Hockett stresses, the pun is the only occasion when two words or phrases can be uttered simultaneously.[98] The only time when, without artificial recording, we can play a duet or fugue with ourselves; when there is truly method in our madness. Then the pun is an anti-parapraxis, sure-footed even when straddling separated concepts. 'Many boners are not as innocent as they seem . . . All the best ones have an air of sophisticated nonsense about them that is a tribute to the ingenuity of wit rather than the hilarious blundering of naïvety,' a sceptical view which Charney then undercuts by quoting this probably genuine misprint: 'McCormick invented the automatic raper, which could do the work of a thousand men in one day.'[99]

The 'superiority' theory of humour probably works best in the realm of slips. Those who know the right answer or the correct form laugh at those who have not realized what they have said or written. But why do we laugh at mistakes? Because we are spared or because we are (potentially) included? Is it a laugh of exclusion or of fellow-feeling? Somehow an adult's regression to duncehood is more engaging than a child's acceleration into cute smartness. Eastman argues that:

> These blunders are beautiful. And naïve absurdities are often more beautiful, even when they are not more humorous, than absurdities of the voluntary kind. They offer us a variety of positive satisfactions which the clown or the deliberate wit-snapper can only simulate – the satisfaction of loving an innocent mind.[100]

Schopenhauer is expectably less charitable: 'The misunderstanding of the word or the *quid pro quo* is the unintentional pun, and is related to it exactly as folly is to wit.'[101] But punning offers the constant lesson that we can keep nothing in neat categories. Slips remind us of the verge of madness, the loss of control. After talking of 'the "clang" of words which are similar in sound but not necessarily in meaning', Koegler goes on to offer this explanation for the disproportionately low esteem in which the pun is held:

> This is because of its close similarity to the loosening of association and 'clang' associations found in the unconscious and openly expressed in schizophrenia. Society protects itself against the threat of being reminded of unconscious processes by downgrading the pun as a form of humour, thus limiting its use.[102]

Puns remind us both of our mastery and of our lack of control over language: this is their primordial ambiguity. We are always in danger of punning.

Backlash

'Freud has explained that humour is a denial of anxiety, so you must understand', says Peter de Vries' alter-ego, 'that these puns of yours arise from one of the most intense forms of belligerence – the belligerence of the insecure.'[103] Playing beautifully on the opposite meanings of the two words, the author declares elsewhere: 'We all have a guilt-edged security.'[104] There are elements of aggression, oneupmanship, in all games, including the conversational one, and puns figure widely in repartee, turning the tables on others. Games need rules. What are those of the pun? Stendhal obliquely suggests one, when he has Mosca say to Gina: 'Vous savez que j'ai fait venir un cuisinier français, qui est le plus gai des hommes, et qui fait des calembours; or, le calembour est incompatible avec l'assassinat' ('You know that I have engaged a French cook, who is the drollest of men and who keeps punning – well, puns and murder do not go together'): a crucial distinction in the conspiratorial world of Parma.[105] Even if stopping short of murder, the punster can exhibit true violence. Thersites, in *Troilus and Cressida*, claims: 'He would pun thee into shivers with his fist,' which recalls the etymological connection with hammering.[106] The brevity and the shock-value of the telling pun makes it more akin to the short-arm jab than to the haymaker.

Such violence can turn inwards. In Sartre's *L'Enfance d'un chef*, there is a delectable moment where the hero, when very young and desperate to make the world of objects kowtow to his will, concludes that an unresponding tree must be, to ignore him so totally, 'de bois' ('wooden-hearted'). Punners often thus beat their heads against recalcitrant reality. They pun out of frustration with language; they exact verbal revenge. In such cases, puns probably relieve tension less than they exacerbate it. Hence all the customary accompaniments to the word 'pun': grinding, excruciating, atrocious; *grinçant, tordant, grimaçant* (grating, twisting, grimacing). No wonder that Queneau spoke of his ambition as being 'élever le calembour à la hauteur d'un supplice' ('to raise the pun to the level of a torture').[107] Puns irritate: 'Le texte, mot par mot, est une sorte de tunique de Nessus en poil à gratter (comme dirait San Antonio): le récit se tortille à l'intérieur sans pouvoir l'enlever ni en mourir' ('The text word by word, is a sort of Nessus' tunic filled with itching-powder (as San Antonio might say): the narrative twists about inside without managing to pull it off or to die').[108] Often the aggression turns outwards, into the delight of seeing others squirm. Like pedagogues, punsters want to teach others a lesson. In Ionesco's *La Leçon*, the professor stabs his young pupil with the word 'knife', and the conclusion is: 'La philologie mène au crime' ('Philology leads to crime').[109] Sartre describes the linguistic vicious circles in which Flaubert entrapped himself as 'le tourniquet'. Many punners are such verbal torturers, practising *Schadenfreude*.

Opposite imprisonment and punishment, release. 'Freedom begets wit, and wit begets freedom,' claims Jean-Paul.[110] But Lessing notes more soberly: 'Not all are free who mock their chains.'[111] Marx uses a ludic chiasmus to make his point that 'The weapon of criticism certainly cannot replace the criticism of weapons'.[112] If not always born of freedom, wordplay can at least betoken freedom. Insofar as it reshapes the language we use to talk of the real world, wordplay can be critical and to that extent a political gesture. 'Le jeu de mots est une petite révolution: il provoque souvent l'explosion d'une vieille structure et y installe, en son lieu, de nouvelles formes possibles' ('Wordplay is a minor revolution; it often brings about the explosion of an old structure and instals in its place new forms of possibility').[113] Similarly, Jean Ricardou speaks of 'le calembour, cet explosif procédé de capture des sens'.[114] Puns contributed to anticlerical propaganda in 1789: 'l'abbé casse, l'abbé gueule' ('the priest breaks/the stupid maid, the priest yells/the prim miss').[115] Laughing with fellow spirits at a common enemy undoubtedly boosts morale and can promote daring action.

Les jeux de mots constituent une des principales armes de la satire politique sous les dictatures. Ils fleurissent pendant les guerres de religion, sous la Révolution, sous l'occupation, et plus près de nous, dans la plupart des régimes policiers.

(Puns are one of the main weapons of political satire under dictatorships. They flourish during wars of religion, the Revolution, the Occupation and, nearer our time, in most police-states.)[116]

One example is provided by the *Flüsterwitze*, or whispered jokes, of Nazi Germany. A German stands before portraits of Hitler, Goebbels and Göring and muses: 'Should one hang them or put them up against the wall?'[117] The pun is always something of an underground mode, like irony, allegory/fable, *faux-naïf* stories. Of course, like parody, its potentiality for charm might help to preserve the very ones whom it seeks to impale; the enemy can be transformed into beautiful butterflies in a special case. Yet, at their best, pointed puns are a way of countering insolently ideological double-talk, an improper gander which, like the Roman ones, can act as watchdog. The pun can be retaliation, Parthian shot, the revenge of the disrespectful Id on the censorious Superego. For Freud,

the grandeur in humour clearly lies in the triumph of narcissism, the victorious assertion of the ego's invulnerability. The ego refuses to be distressed by the provocations of reality, to let itself be compelled to suffer.[118]

One political pun, by Benjamin Franklin at the signing of the Declaration of Independence, serves as a transition to the domain of gallows humour: 'We must all hang together, or assuredly we shall all hang separately.' Such situations reveal punning at its most desperate, though some kind of hope must inhere in the use of language at all at these moments. Such wit sees death as an execution rather than as a natural and ineluctable culmination; an aggression to be countered, not by turning the other cheek, but by returning cheek, as when Thomas Hood complained that he was being pestered by an undertaker who wanted to 'urn a lively Hood'. We saw earlier, in considering Hood, that much ambiguity lies in such responses. Are they an evasion of reality, a denial of the facts, or an answer to those facts? Shakespeare's plays show no reluctance to face up to the realities of dying, but they frequently make room for last-ditch playful language:

How oft when men are at the point of death
Have they been merry! which their keepers call
A lightning before death![119]

Gaunt's obsessive punning on his name, suggests Mahood,

> is not only true to the trivial preoccupations of the dying; it also reminds us of the play's dominant theme, the relationship between names and their bearers. Gaunt is saying in effect: 'I am true to my name, Gaunt, but you are not true to the name you bear of king.' Besides this, *gaunt* in the sense of 'wasted' prepares us for his long speech of remonstrance, in which wordplay underlines that relationship between the spiritual health of the king and the well-being of his kingdom which was a living concept for the Elizabethans.

As she reminds, 'nicely' in Richard's response to such playing on names means 'subtly' as well as 'trivially'.[120] Coleridge's comment on this recurrent phenomenon was: 'Is there not a tendency in the human mind, when suffering under some great affliction, to associate everything around it with the obtrusive feeling, to connect and absorb all into the predominant sensation?'[121]

Lofty personages attract striking last words, for instance the consecrated words of Louis XVIII on his deathbed surrounded by doctors: 'Allons, finissons-en. Charles attend (Charlatans)' ('Come on, let's get it over with. Charles (X) awaits/Quacks!')[122] In such contexts the pun can be spirited, or glum: underlining the defeat. An aged parishioner says to the clergyman he has just beaten at golf: 'Cheer up. Remember, you win in the end. You'll bury me one day.' The preacher replies: 'Even then, it will be your hole.'[123] It can be pure fatalism. The parachute trainee asks what will happen if the chute does not open. 'That', replies the instructor, 'is what is known as jumping to a conclusion.'[124] Swift wilfully and gladly contradicts himself when he has the inveterate punner Tom Ashe exclaim: 'Let punners consider how hard it is to die jesting, when death is so hard in digesting.'[125] Violette Morin stresses that compulsive associative tendency Coleridge spoke of when she says of San Antonio's frequent references to death: 'N'ayons pas peur des néologismes et disons que, du calembourage au moribondage, l'écart est singulièrement irréductible' ('Don't let us be afraid of neologisms and let's say that, from *calembourage* to *moribondage*, the gap is singularly wide').[126] *Moribondage* is a nicely judged coinage, for the *bondage* section suggests stuffing, like the *bour(r)age* section of the other word; the topic and the vehicle are pulled lightly together. Wilde, naturally, illustrates the elegant variety of last words. On his deathbed, hearing his doctors worrying about the payment of their fees, he said: 'It would appear that I am dying beyond my means.'[127] Roland Topor offers as number 55 of his 'cent bonnes raisons pour me suicider tout de suite: parce que j'ai toujours eu envie de posséder une langue morte' ('a hundred good reasons for committing suicide straight off: because I've always wanted to have a dead tongue/know a dead language').[128] Gallows humour can be imposed, as well as self-generated. At the funeral of Marguerite d'Autriche, who died in childbirth, a motto was made: an Aurora bringing light to the world, with these words: 'Dum pario pereo.' The popular ballad recording Billy Budd's execution lends him the words: 'O, 'tis me, not the sentence they'll suspend'.[129] Eastman's attempt at explanation of such humour, while useful in general, seems in this instance inadequate: 'We came into the world endowed with an instinctive tendency to laugh and have this feeling in response to pains presented playfully.'[130] We might wonder, too, what possible consolation can be found in this contemporary example: 'One of the advantages of nuclear warfare is that all men are cremated equal.'[131] It could be argued that such a joke, which offers a false bonus, simply underlines the lunacy of the world it refers to. But the doubt remains, and I am reminded of that form of schizophrenic humour known as *'doomsday* or *calamity humour,* in which some patients laugh hilariously at the daily reports of tragic events; the more mayhem the better, and if they don't find any, they make it up.'[132] It could be that a deeper meaning of the link between joking and death is that what is being celebrated, with morose delectation, is the imminent extinction of language. As Beckett said in his study of Proust: 'The whisky bears a grudge against the decanter.'[133] The dying person wants to take all with him. He uses language to express, and to be consumed in, the ultimate absurdity: death. 'Ordered to help row the lifeboat, the first-class passenger sniffed: "Do I have a choice?" "Certainly, sir," replied a sailor. "Either oar."[134]

Related terms to gallows humour are: black comedy, sick humour, *rire jaune.* In all pain and pleasure are mixed, perhaps the definitive recipe for all punning. Black comedy can be more aggressive, less stoical, as in Allais' superb anecdote about a doctor who stitches his wife and her lover together: it is entitled 'Collage'.[135] It can be truly sinister when we are not sure where the perpetrator stands, as in 'The aim of eugenics is to make the population less dense.'[136] This links, Nazi-fashion, selective breeding and eclectic liquidation; is it a critical comment or a proposal? With Camus we are on surer ground. The fanatical power-worshipper of 'Le Renégat' claims that only rifles have souls (*âme* = soul, and bore); his own soul has transmigrated into this talisman, which helps him to serve the Fetish of the tribe who have captured him. In another story of the collection *L'Exil et le royaume,* the posture of its tragicomic hero Jonas is caught beautifully by the poised pun on *solitaire/solidaire* with which it ends. All such terminal wordplay has a tutorial side, as in Lautréamont's instructions for use of 'le rire mélancolique', a distinct improvement on Pagliacci: 'Riez, mais pleurez en même temps. Si vous ne pouvez pas pleurer par les yeux, pleurez par la bouche. Est-ce encore impossible, urinez' ('Laugh, but cry at the same time. If you can't cry with your eyes, cry through your month. If you still can't manage it, urinate').[137] A wittier, more civilized and less pompous poem on death than Dylan Thomas's 'And Death Shall Have No Dominion' is this splendid piece of intricate sophistry:

If Death do come as soon as Breath departs,
Then he must often die, who often Farts;
And if to die be but to lose one's Breath,
Then Death's a Fart, and so a Fart for Death.[138]

A place apart must be made for the Jews. Both their persecutors and Zionists themselves would agree with this sentiment. They have been collectively battered. They are scarred by a common weal. As Freud remarked, 'I do not know whether there are many other instances of a people making fun to such a degree of its own character.'[139] Concerning Yiddish, Leo Rosten claims that it is 'a tongue that never takes its tongue out of its cheek'. As an example, he quotes the pun on the *mohel* (who circumcises the infant male): 'The rabbi gets the fees, it's the *mohel* who gets all the tips.'[140] Arieti offers a down-to-earth explanation for such self-directed wit: 'It is better to be accused of stinginess and dirtiness than of ritual murder. It is better to be laughed at than to be massacred.'[141] Looking at the question from the opposite end, Irving Kristol stressed that:

> one must bear in mind to what extent the fullness of Jewish life was, for almost two millennia, devoted to what is rationally absurd, to what extent it was a dream-life, a sane type of madness. Jewish existence was grounded in a series of fantastic 'make-believes'. The Jews, seemingly the lowest of the low, were God's chosen people.

The result, for the modern Jewish jokester, is that 'his reason finds itself impotent, and in the circular joke it proceeds to outwit outself.'[142] But surely the age-old subversive stoicism remains in many Jewish jokes.

One danger of this variety of wordplay *in extremis* is that it can become mechanical, unexamined, a mere reflex. As Mary Douglas suggests, 'The sick joke plays with a reversal of the values of social life; the hearer is left uncertain which is the man and which the machine, who is the good and who the bad, or where is the legitimate pattern of control.'[143] Sick humour is, in every sense, the most offensive form of gallows humour. As Demott says: 'The sicknik cannot open the gimcrack gates of the palace of irony without losing his audience; he cannot keep his audience unless he calls down a plague on every visible house outside.'[144] This is the perennial risk of mutual congratulation societies. But the backlash calls forth chastisement. One slang meaning of 'pun' is punishment.[145] The punishment can be made to fit the pun. Whereas Carroll ('"It's a pun!" the King added in an angry tone, and everybody laughed')[146] is accommodating, another legendary king told his jester that only if he ceased his incessant punning would his life be spared. The jester commented: 'No noose is good news', so they hanged him.[147] Thus can punsters be made to pay, in this cautionary tale, the ultimate price for their addiction.

Nietzsche placed the highest value on the iconoclastic powers of wit: 'Not by wrath does one kill but by laughter. Come, let us kill the spirit of gravity.'[148] Others have reservations about the real power of such verbal play. For Mary Douglas,

> needless to say, a successful subversion of one form by another completes or ends the joke, for it changes the balance of power. It is implicit in the Freudian model that the unconscious does not take over the control system. The wise sayings of lunatics, talking animals, children and drunkards are funny because they are not in control; otherwise they would not be an image of the subconscious. The joke merely affords opportunity for realising that an accepted pattern has no necessity. Its excitement lies in the suggestion that any particular ordering of experience may be arbitrary and subjective. It is frivolous in that it produces no real alternative, only an exhilarating sense of freedom from form in general.[149]

Mahood puts even more emphasis on the more reassuring side of wordplay:

> Time and again the wordplay of Shakespeare's personages lends support to Freud's contention that the function of verbal wit is to afford a safe outlet for repressed impulses. The impulse to be irrational gives us the type of harmless, pointless punning represented by Beatrice's 'civill as an orange', in which our pleasure comes from the verbal ingenuity itself, and the impulses to be aggressive, exhibitionist or sceptical give us pointed, tendentious puns which please speaker and hearer because they act as a safety valve for the antisocial instincts.[150]

Such views are balanced but, to my taste, just too measured. Punning escapes such categories and patterns. It is, as Sollers says of Ponge, 'semantic kidnapping'.[151] It is always on the run from capture.

7

Puns Out and About

Guano of the Mind: Puns in Advertising

What is the status of wordplay within the trade of advertising? I wrote to twenty of the largest international agencies to find out. The most common reaction was to claim that it was out of date to pun in adverts. Was professional deformation compelling them to have me on? A more charitable explanation would be that they were reflecting the age-old embarrassment connected with puns. Punsters in company habitually apologize for their activity. In addition, some practitioners stand on the dignity of the profession. Claude C. Hopkins said, in *My Life in Advertising*: 'Frivolity has no place in advertising. Nor has humor. Spending money is usually serious business . . . People do not buy from clowns.'[1] Somebody should inform McDonald's. A standard warning in guides to copywriting states: Do not be 'clever'; it is distracting. There clearly is a danger of in-jokes, of mutual congratulation societies being formed between a witty sloganeer and a small body of like-minded consumers. But what of the other possibility: that humorous adverts might function like the jollities of a dentist as he extracts painfully from your gums and your pocket? One further point: it may well be that the supposed untranslatability of many puns deters advertisers, who often want to standardize their campaigns over various countries. (There is the warning example of Pepsi-Cola's motto: 'Come alive – You're in the Pepsi Generation.' In its Chinese version this emerged as 'Pepsi brings your ancestors back from the dead.')[2]

But the arguments for the usefulness of wordplay are stronger than such doubts. Advertising space is costly. Economy is essential, and puns are highly economical (two meanings for the price of one word or phrase), and in fact much more of a labour-saving device than many of the products they seek to promote. The mode of advertising is telegraphic, lapidary, as in journalism. 'In Tabloid English, the thematic pun becomes a semantic substitute for syntax. It signposts the narrative structure of a brief story more clearly than any other verbal device known to literate man.'[3] Not only constraints of space, but also the need to spare possible buyers brain-fag or eye-strain, these too lead to foreshortened texts. Since the fundamental message of all advertising is known to everyone in advance, there is a need for diversification. Wordplay, with its distortions, bifurcations and re-creations, introduces variety and refreshment into saturation. Puns, the devious ones, are a way round those rather stuffy rules of the advertising watchdogs: adverts should be legal, decent and true. A recipe for mass-produced boredom. The words of adverts are double-talk, necessarily. If adverts told only the verifiable truth, they would be pedantic and tedious. And so they have to approximate; they have to say one thing and suggest another. Obliqueness is all. So why not make a virtue out of necessity, and a silk purse out of a sow's ear? Enjoy the compulsion. Make business into a fête, combine business with pleasure. Thus many adverts come to be prized as art-work or as social entertainment. While still remaining sceptical of the ends being served, surely we can profit from the means.

Puns are undeniably used as attention-grabbers, e.g. 'Population down 30 per cent!' in an advert for Kellogg's 30 per cent Bran Flakes. We are caught and led to read on. An even more blatant instance of misleading headlines (from the nineteenth century): '*A Beautiful Young Girl Strangled* a cry of admiration when she saw our new blouses.'[4] McLuhan wrote:

> A lush car features a baby's rattle on the rich rug of the back floor and says that it has removed unwanted car rattles as easily as the user could remove the baby's. This kind of copy has really nothing to do with rattles. The copy is merely a punning gag to distract the critical faculties while the image of the car goes to work on the hypnotised viewer.[5]

Is he not insulting the viewer? Need we be dupes to that extent? We recognize, besides, the wisdom but also the other-worldliness of the Jewish proverb: 'They say to fruit-bearing trees: "Why do you not make any noise?" and the trees reply: "Our fruits are sufficient advertisement".'[6]

Advertising is all about association: associating a particular product with a particular firm and with an idea of quality; and so word and thought associations (echoes, jingles, puns) obviously come into useful play. There is a kind of situational punning in many adverts which forces distinct things together, e.g. the one for White Horse Whisky. There is no inevitable link between horses and whisky, but the slogan establishes one, to punch home by baroque juxtaposition the message 'You can take a white horse anywhere.' By this process, the whisky is naturalized, made a part of our mental, and gustatory, landscape. As one practitioner stated: 'It is difficult to find many words in the English language that possess only one meaning.'[7] Anthony Burgess expands on this basic phenomenon:

> Ambiguity is a vice of words . . . A scientific age like ours tends to worry about this aspect of language . . . Meaning should be mathematical, unambiguous. But this plurality of reference is in the very nature of language, and its management and exploitation is one of the joys of writing.[8]

And, we should add, of reading. Ambiguity has obviously become a hurrah-word. Perhaps this stems from the teachings of Freud, and the whole concept of complex motivation. Ambiguous behaviour is felt to be richer than clear conduct. Behind all this skulks no doubt an unsureness about values. Since God died or was pensioned off, plurivalency reigns. We are all mugwumps. All wit, and (some would maintain) all mental creativity, entail the ability to think on at least two planes at once, by a kind of semantic and lexical diphthong. We are always on the look-out for doubles (to the extent of doubling up in both laughter and pain). Many people give punning names to their children or their homes (e.g. 'Kutyurbelyakin', which I took globally for a possibly Armenian word, until I broke it down into its constituent sounds). Think of the long list of double-barrelled terms we use: double-talk, double-meaning, double-cross, double-decker, double-edged, double-take, seeing double.

Just like double-meaning, or even more so double entendre, the neutral word 'suggestive' has come to have predominantly erotic connotations. In fact, despite the tactic of supplying scholarly equivalents, in order to sterilize or at least to cool what is being discussed, it is the most general words that can secrete the greatest amount of innuendo. As Maurice Charney explains:

> Double entendres, some planned but most fortuitous, lurk everywhere in the English language, whose loss of declensions, conjugations, and exact syntax make it vulnerable to sexual ambiguity. Any unsecured use of 'it' in English is almost automatically sexual and a vague 'do' has similar connotations . . . This gives the English language a quality of phonetic innuendo that may not be present in other, more exactly inflected language systems.[9]

(The author is here guilty of linguistic chauvinism, for the verb 'faire' in French lends itself to very similar exploitation.)[10] The suggestiveness can be brutal, as in 'Unzipp a Banana' (though note the extra p as a nervous preliminary to consummation). But equally, taboos can be circumvented, as with the firm who asked its potential customers whether weeds were a pain in their grass.[11] Much advertising relies on this practice of nudging and winking, although in the area of erogenous zones, like that of parking zones, a stern warden keeps in check those who would violate the limits. The calculation must be exact, otherwise the joint stimulation offered (to buy and to jubilate) might get confused, to the detriment of the former. Hence perhaps what has been called the 'provocative serenity' of many faces in adverts.[12] The models' desires are already satisfied, because they have enjoyed the product. Now it is up to us to sample it with the same kind of controlled licentiousness.

But one man's licence is another man's veto. In order to lacerate the consciences of licence-dodgers, the BBC coined the slogan: 'NO LICENCE. NO LIFE ON EARTH'. This was advertising as terrorism. The mere removal of distinguishing punctuation produced arresting ambiguity. No TV = living death. In a sense, this message was even truthful. If, as a result of being detected and in order to pay the hefty fine, you have to sell your set or return it to the rental company, you have, so to speak, no longer any 'world about you', no 'life on earth' at your disposal. The message of course tells us something we already know, but it drives the meaning in; our dependence on TV is literally brought home to us. This skirts tautology, but in a more telling way than in another announcement from a public utility, the telephone service. This invented a very talkative little bird called Buzby. One of the accompanying slogans was: 'A ring keeps the family circle together.' This could mean: legalized marriages last longer; the family that prays together stays together (as the priest on the *Titanic* declared); and, of course, call your folks regularly. All edifying truisms: no shock, no rethinking involved. At best, this slogan reminds us of unwelcome obligations. But traps have to be set better than that. An old advert for Player's cigarettes tricked us with punctuation, like the BBC example. The initial slogan was 'Player's please'. Thus the mere act of politely asking for a packet over the counter acted as a boost for the product; the client is turned into the promoter.

Such twists of familiar phrases are common. The ancient cry of the icecream vendor, 'Stop me and buy one', was transformed by a family-planning campaign to 'Buy me and stop one', which has a kind of brutal charm. A similar example concerns the contraceptive-manufacturer Durex, which has also sponsored racing-cars. The net result of these twin activities was a picture of a sleek speedster with the ironic motto: 'The small family car'. If car adverts habitually equate ownership of their particular make with sexual possession, this version at least introduces an element of caution into the rapture. 'Bottle', in criminal slang, means guts. Newcastle Brown Ale, supposedly a stronger beer than most, chooses the slogan 'Even in a can it's got bottle' – the implication being that different packaging in no way impairs the strength of the brew. One of the most famous of all British adverts for many years was the Guinness series for their stout: the very simple phrase 'My Goodness, My Guinness'. The rhyming message is obvious. The means varied inventively, but all featured a potential consumer exclaiming on seeing his beloved beverage being taken from his grasp: a zoo-attendant gazes at the shape of his glass inside the long neck of an ostrich; a construction worker watches his drink lifted from his grasp on a girder hoisted by a crane, etc. Moving from beer to milk, let us see how this 'goodness' ploy is exploited. In recent years, the Milk Marketing Board has featured a young, fresh, fair-haired girl, raising a glass of milk towards her lips, accompanied by the slogan 'I'm full of natural goodness.' This could signify: 'I'm drinking milk, which is good for my healthy development'; 'I'm virginal'; 'I'm good-hearted'; 'I'm liberal with my favours' (for goodness implies generosity); and (because the glass is held at chest-height) 'My breasts are full of milk.' This last is somewhat spoilt as a suggestion by the fact that the girl is under-endowed. A pretty complex, and possibly self-contradictory, set of meanings. The girl, in addition, has the heel of her shoe lodged in her crotch. Boot in puss, for a change. The technical advertising term 'body copy' (i.e. the main text of an advert after the headline or slogan) takes on its full import here. We might also call this 'knocker copy'. A further series makes the underlying suggestions of the first one more explicit: 'Some Like It Hot'. A more exciting and excited girl, lips pursed, raises to her mouth a glass of steaming milk, in which floats upright a stick of dark flake chocolate. Both series, incidentally, have the narcissistic quality of that old underwear advert of a young lady announcing: 'Next to myself I like Vedonis'.

An example of commercial counter-advertising. At the turn of the century a popular myth held that pedalling a sewing-machine could endanger the baby of a pregnant woman. Singer put out a poster on which a healthy mother-to-be, in the centre of a capital S (*gros S*) sewed happily away: 'Grossesse heureuse avec une machine à coudre Singer' ('A safe pregnancy with a Singer sewing-machine').[13] Another specimen of effective advertising concerns selling an idea, a social ideal, not a product; and it is in fact aimed precisely at the by-products of industry. 'The effluent society: how can we help to clean it up?' – with a picture of a drain discharging into a river. This is a truly pointed pun, whereas so many are blunt, and a tight twist, as the word 'society' consorts well with both the near-identical qualifiers, affluent and effluent.

Puns do not always work, of course, or work only dubiously, which is perhaps fitting for such an ambiguous mode. Another Guinness motto was 'There's a lot of it about.' This is simultaneously a truism about the ubiquitousness of this beer, a wry comment on the clichéic nature of everyday conversation (for this is the stock response in Britain if you mention you have been ill), and thus finally an unfortunate assimilation of Guinness to a noxious virus. Less efficient again was the slogan in the Queen's Jubilee Year: 'We've poured throughout her reign.' This is strictly meaningless and certainly pointless, for no other liquid (except acid?) falls in company with rain. 'Even advertisers call meaningless copy "resounding non-statements".'[14] Then there are unintentional puns, like the pharmacy that claimed: 'We dispense with accuracy.' When the secondary meaning was pointed out to him, the manager simply changed it to 'We do not dispense with accuracy,' and thus compounded the felony. Or the educational establishment, desperate to recruit students, putting this advert in the papers: 'You'll be in a class of your own.' I like also the T-shirt on sale in the Far East: 'If you're tired of life, visit Sri Lanka.' The age of package suicides? In the desperate verbal skirmishes of ad wars, leading British cigarette companies in 1901, under threat from the American Tobacco Company, used a slogan: 'Don't be gulled by Yankee Bluff,/Support John Bull with every Puff,'[15] which, with its use of bull and puff, was almost self-defeating.

'You can tell the ideals of a nation by its advertisements,' said Norman

Douglas, who was wrong about a lot of other things, too.[16] If only things were so simple. In case what I go on to say seems to treat the French as whipping-boys, I should stress that, if advertising appears to be still in its infancy in France, in Britain and the USA it often seems to be in its second childhood. One French student of advertising language in fact underlines the relative rarity of wordplay in French adverts. He reasons that most clients there are flattered to be addressed in a tone which is 'noble, éloquent, oratoire ou poétique'.[17] Similarly, Reboul makes some unexamined claims in his study of wordplay in political watchwords, which he says is practically nonexistent on the classical Left, for three reasons:

> D'abord les idéologies de gauche se veulent rationnelles et méprisent ces techniques de persuasion visiblement infantiles . . . Ensuite, internationalistes par définition, les idéologies de gauche recourent à des formules traduisibles . . . Enfin, la première fonction du cri de ralliement est d'ordre expressif: il s'agit d'unir en frappant; or la pensée de gauche préfère s'affirmer par des formules universelles et rationnelles, du moins en apparence.

> (Firstly, leftwing ideologies aim at being rational and scorn such visibly infantile techniques of persuasion. Next, internationalist by definition, leftwing ideologies use translatable formulae. Finally, the major function of a rallying-cry is expressivity. The goal is to unite people by striking home; now leftwing thought prefers to assert itself by universal and rational formulae, on the surface at least.)[18]

Gallic rhetorical snobbery obviously permeates all levels of culture there, but who has not noticed the inanity of the famous 'Dubo, Dubon, Dubonnet' series? As if in recognition of the infantile nature of many of their slogans (e.g. 'C'est Shell que j'aime', which sounds like a drunkard's mispronunciation of 'C'est celle que j'aime', or perhaps a Club Méditerranée advert: 'Seychelles que j'aime'), the French often repeat the same poster dozens of times in close contiguity, literally papering the walls with some brand-image. A centripetal variant of this is the advert for the cheese 'Vache qui rit', whose image is reiterated internally to infinity. Here the onlooker's eye is coaxed to burrow into one placard instead of skating across dozens of the same. Perhaps the best hope for wit in advertising in France lies in the involuntary kind, as in this supermarket sign: 'Slips à la portée de toutes les bourses' ('Underpants to suit all pockets/balls'). A recent globetrotting researcher into advertising language claims he found twice as much wordplay in English or American adverts as in French ones. In more detail, he saw in Britain more extensive punning and alliteration, but little rhyme, which was commoner on the Continent. His conclusion was that such adverts were in direct line of descent from the English wordplay tradition – Shakespeare and the Metaphysicals through to Joyce.[19]

As rhetoric is the art of persuasion, we can justifiably talk of advertising language as a rhetoric.[20] We all pun; we all sell images of ourselves (including modest, underplayed images). Norman Mailer is just more blatant than most of us in talking of 'Advertisements for Myself'.[21] Language itself is narcissistic in this way. As Jean Paulhan has pointed out, the very word 'etymology', signifying 'the authentic meaning', acts as its own advertisement.[22] Etymology, like Coca-Cola, is the real thing. Self-advertising also favours the oblique approach. Conundrums, charades, rebuses (graphic charades) and puns are all inter-related and of like ancestry. All involve the recipient in that their coded message needs to be deciphered. The object is to impress the receiver with the cleverness of the person seeking to publicize himself in this way and, incidentally, to let the receiver congratulate himself on his astuteness in correctly reading the puzzle. Heraldry, for instance, provides many examples of punning in armorial bearings and family badges. Sir Walter Scott, in his notes to *Waverley*, calls the motto of the Vernon family a perfect pun: 'Ver non semper vivat'. The Spring will not last forever, or Vernon will last forever. On the Via Appia near Rome, the tomb of one Publius Maximus Philo*mus*us contains two bas-reliefs of mice. (And notice how the joke cowers within the name, in a mouselike fashion.) Shop-signs continue this tradition, as in this French example: 'Au p'tit chien' (Opticien). 'Not only did our ancestors pun during their lives, but endeavoured, as much as possible, to convey the idea that they would do so in the world to come, for many of their epitaphs are replete with puns.'[23] Here is one such for a dentist:

> Stranger, tread
> This ground with gravity:
> Dentist Brown is filling
> His last cavity.[24]

Of course, as regards comic epitaphs, there are many more spurious than genuine ones, so much so that the epitaph itself has been described, in a pun, as 'a monumental liar'.[25] Today, of course, we have punning T-shirt mottoes, lapel-badges, car-stickers, trade-names (a food company named its delicate blend of tea, orange peel and spices 'Subtle Tea'), banners at demonstrations and public events, a whole plethora of means whereby we can seek attention and admiration, affirm ourselves, and provide free entertainment for others. Punning book-titles, too, e.g. a book on millinery design, *Talking Through My Hat*, or one on gardening, *A Sense of Humus*. On a more elevated level, Eugene O'Neill's play-title, *The Ice-Man Cometh*, alludes to the traditional amorousness of the ice-vendor but, coming from O'Neill, it does so under the shadow of impending death. Doubts have, naturally, been raised by the democratization of such humour, e.g.:

the almost ritualized comic antithesis shown by 'fun cards'. One is under no obligation to cultivate his individual sense of humor so long as he carries or shows a sign, like a certifying badge. As it were, he has a credit card in American humor. He may defer payment in this respect endlessly . . . In this light, he is unabashedly announcing himself.[26]

Graffiti, in particular, are self-advertisements, even though mostly anonymous or pseudonymous. They are one of the very few means for the great majority of unrecognized writers and draughtsmen to reach a public. That least snobbish of writers, Raymond Queneau, once said: 'Les graffiti, qu'est-ce que c'est? tout juste de la littérature.'[27] Such wall-writing has been described as the 'I-was-here' syndrome. 'It is the ego at work, the self-accolade of achievement as well as a kind of recognition that maybe history has been made and posterity should be informed.'[28] What will future generations, if there are any, think of our contemporary anti-nuclear graffito: 'The only safe fast breeders are rabbits'? Or the splendid Spoonerism in 'Psychology is producing habits out of a rat'? Many graffiti, of course, show scant concern for social utility and are purely, or more often impurely, personal. It is not surprising to find puns so often among graffiti in that home of strain and release, the latrine. As one team has said:

> The combination of antisocial thought, antisocial language to express it, and antisocial disfigurement of someone else's property enables the graffitist to discharge in one 'emotional orgasm' many of the deep-seated emotions he may be harbouring and thus helps him to regain his composure.[29]

I cannot help feeling that there is an element of wishful thinking in this analysis even stronger than that of the graffiti in question. There is also the phenomenon of cross-traffic, as when a graffitist amends a commercial poster, e.g. the comment added to an advertisement for a duplicator: 'Xerox never comes up with anything original.'[30] Simple tearing or obliteration would do as a purely destructive response. Adverts disfigure and enliven our environment. Amended slogans capitalize on this capitalist phenomenon (we might coin: 'Take laxative X and get a run for your money') and act as a critique, as in the feminist emendation of the notorious Fiat advert 'If it were a lady it would get its bottom pinched': 'If this lady were a car she'd run you down.' Slogans seek to inculcate mindless, unquestioning behaviour, as in BEANZ MEANZ HEINZ, which underlines its dictatorial designs by rewriting English grammar and spelling. BEANZ MEANZ FARTZ seems a justifiable riposte to the verbal rip-off, this catch-phrase. Advertising is always trying to catch us out, off-guard or on a good day. The pun, 'le seigneur du langage truqué' ('the lord of dodgy language'),[31] is the weapon of attack and retaliation. By a simple displacement

('Bar Hershey'), it can act as a veto. The scrawl on the contraceptive vending-machine, 'This is the worst chewing gum I have ever tasted', is a kind of semantic pun, and peculiarly apt in that condoms and chewing-gum contain comparable substances: latex and chicle. In fact, chicle is the latex (i.e. milky ooze) from the sapodilla. By an obscure association of ideas, some might be reminded of the old popular song: 'Does your chewing-gum lose its flavour on the bedpost overnight?'

Wordplay recycles language. 'So many puns in modern advertising copy depend on a familiarity with the hackneyed in our language.'[32] We might add that we are all familiars of this particular sabbath, this common place where we are all experts. While we all use clichés, not everybody knows how to reuse what have been called 'duck-billed platitudes'.[33] Here is one twist which I have not yet inscribed anywhere: 'The meek shall inherit the earth. But the brazen shall contest the will.' It has been remarked that, in advertising, such shifts are almost always from the metaphorical to the literal, since advertisers are promoting things.[34] But I think this view could itself be tilted around, for it is no less true that advertisers are selling an *idea* of things, as a prelude to the purchase of the article itself. I suspect, rather, that most advertising language plays, like puns, between the two levels of the spirit and the letter, and would not wish to be closely tied to one or the other. 'There is no one-way traffic between the literal and the metaphorical.'[35]

McLuhan suggests there is an innate comedy in the very phenomenon of advertising:

> Will Rogers discovered years ago that any newspaper read aloud from a theatre stage is hilarious. The same is true today of ads. Any ad put into a new setting is funny. [Hence those TV comics who have only to quote a slogan to procure a conditioned response of laughter.] This is a way of saying that any ad consciously attended to is comical. Ads are not meant for conscious consumption. They are intended as subliminal pills for the subconscious in order to exercise an hypnotic spell, especially on sociologists.[36]

Inevitably, punning adverts do draw attention to themselves as such, as artifacts. Even though oblique (not everyone will see their point), they are in this way less insidious than the 'subliminal seduction', the 'hidden persuaders', of advertising images. You need to be fully conscious to rumble a pun. Such self-conscious adverts give the game away, blow the gaff, on the whole process of publicizing.[37] In addition, such adverts of course free themselves to some extent from purely commercial utilitarianism and offer themselves as wit, poetry or art. It has long been recognized that advertising is a branch of the entertainments industry, show business, to the extent that today many adverts seem hardly to be connected with a product at all, but rather to exist in their own right, as an object of amusement, puzzlement or aesthetic pleasure. Some series (the

Benson and Hedges cigarette one, for instance, with the gold packet only one item in a luxuriantly golden roomscape) are in fact sold as décor. As Hayakawa has suggested: 'The task of the copywriter is the poeticising of consumer goods.' He calls this 'sponsored poetry'.[38] Obviously, the whole phenomenon is highly ambivalent. Such rhetoric is in a kind of straddle-position, between true art and commerce. As such, it is perhaps an indication, or a reductio ad absurdum, of the enforced position of the writer or artist in the contemporary world.

There is, too, the element of opportunism. The neologism 'actuavity' has been coined to define this: 'Actuavity, from *actua*lity and *vitality*, could in basic terms be described as the riding of a wave generated by the media for secondary purposes.'[39] Ours is after all the society of side-effects, spin-offs and bandwaggoning. In 1977, Wall's advertised their sausages with the message, 'I'm meaty. Fry me!' – which was a skilful exploitation, the second time round, of National Airlines' slogan: 'I'm Mandy. Fly me.' Another kind of opportunism is visible in the mattress manufacturer's poster during a French election: 'Pour tous les candidats qui se feront étendre le 12 mars'. ('For all the candidates who will be laid out on the 12th March'). We live now largely by approximation. 'In the increasingly budget-conscious world of advertising, products and campaigns will more and more have to rely on the riding of waves of sympathetic acknowledgement, near-recognition and imminent acceptance.'[40] We have seen how clichés may be recycled. There is no need for us to be sniffy about such apparent parasitism, such salvage-operations, for they are inherent in all art: 'Cliché, or a standardised subsystem, is the necessary element for creation, since all inventions consist of the reassociation of previous material.'[41] Advertising is an enterprise of montage. It places 'des bouteilles de Pepsi sur les lourds pavés d'une barricade ("Révoltez-vous, dit le slogan, pensez Pepsi")' 'Bottles of Pepsi on the heavy cobblestones of a barricade ("Revolt" reads the slogan, "think Pepsi")'.[42] Advertising design annexes the latest experiments of contemporary art. While no doubt such recuperation can degrade or trivialize, it can also help to give currency to what might otherwise remain marginal.

It has been maintained that advertising does not create needs, but responds and gives a direction to needs; it articulates them.[43] Perhaps this is why an agency could advertise itself as 'ghostwriters for the masses'.[44] Even so, this is scarcely the posture of the public servant; it is more that of the *éminence grise*. Advertising simultaneously treats its consumers as intelligent (they must see the joke, make the connection, seize the allusion) and gullible, in that the satisfaction afforded by the former exercise will assist the ulterior aim of selling the product.[45] How persuasive can wordplay be in this? Traditionally, the pun makes you wince, flinch, grimace: all of these are movements away. But it can also incite to complicity, clubbability: a movement towards. (*Réclame* and 'slogan' both derive from rallying-calls.) It is both centrifugal and centripetal.

Thus some reworked sayings are paradoxical, as in 'Conservation is strictly for the birds,' which is simultaneously dismissive and supportive of the ecological endeavour. Perhaps there is elitism in all this. It is well known that advertisers divide their potential public up into distinct classes. It could be that witty adverts, acting like passwords, are meant to appeal only to one section and to exclude the rest. But, then, why play this in-game of shibboleth on hoardings and TV screens, where it is viewed by millions of people? It has been argued, indeed, that bad puns may serve the purposes of attention-grabbing better than subtle ones, for 'what copywriter, one imagines, could afford to be desperately unassuming?'[46]

McLuhan accords to all of us the same democratic privilege of being moulded by the media:

> The old belief that everybody really saw in perspective, but only that Renaissance painters had learned how to paint it, is erroneous. Our first TV generation is rapidly losing the habit of visual perspective as a sensory modality, and along with this change comes an interest in words, not as visually uniform and continuous, but as unique worlds in depth. Hence the craze for puns and wordplay, even in sedate ads.[47]

Is this prevalence a sign of decadence? Flaubert agonized over words; we toy with them (but Flaubert was also an inveterate punner). 'Les réclamiers', comments Grandjouan, 'sont nos Précieux à nous' ('Advertisers are our Précieux').[48] Is this world of verbal and iconographic narcotics going to pot? Are we making a hash of our lives, and, with more haste, is there less speed? The grass is always greener in another joint. We could continue this excruciating acid-test for ages, but it is surely self-evident that much poppycock is talked about decadence. Near the end of Petronius' *Satyricon*, that splendid portrait of a society revelling in its death-throes, a boy hands round the feasters a jar containing puns and conundrums (besides, all the food at this feast is stuffed with other food). The consummate conspicuous consumption of a consumer-society? As the whole phenomenon of wordplay in advertisements is so highly hybrid, perhaps we should simply exploit in our turn this state of affairs, enjoy what Pascal, in another context, called 'the hovering between veracity and salacity'.[49] Provided that 'media audiences are conditioned never to forget the *con* in *con*fidence or the *sin* in *sin*cere'.[50] Raymond Williams is understandably less sanguine than I, when he talks of:

> the development of a knowing, sophisticated, humorous advertising, which acknowledged the [critical scepticism] and made claims either casual and offhand or so ludicrously exaggerated as to include the critical response ... Thus it became possible to 'know all the arguments' against advertising, and yet accept or write pieces of charming or amusing copy.[51]

I have been talking about something that assails us every day, if often out of the corner of our eyes or through half-closed lids and switched-off minds: language (slogans become household words) is being used to sell us. To sell us short, to sell us a pup, to sell us down the river – or to sell us the goods (a conveniently ambiguous phrase)? Selling and deception have long been synonymous. 'He failed with the hard sell. So he's trying the soft peddle.'[52] An advert for Bulova Accutron watches claims: 'Once people see them, they're sold.'[53] This plays on the ambiguity of 'they', so that the client and the object are fused. To be sold on something, to be totally won over, is obviously the ideal state for a consumer in the eyes of the seller. No doubt words can be like the food (or even the bell substituted for food) provided for Pavlov's dog. They can manipulate us, but we all know how pleasant manipulation can be. Puns are especially well suited for the advertising job, for they are usually delivered with the requisite ambivalent mixture of false apology and only too real aggression. We need to remember, of course, that the tigers in our tanks, a few years back, were merely paper ones.

Victor Hugo says in *Les Misérables*: 'Le calembour est la fiente de l'esprit qui vole' ('The pun is the guano of the winged mind').[54] A fittingly equivocal metaphor to end on, for Hugo may be either boosting a fertilizer, or pooh-poohing a waste-product.

The Press

The Press, always in a hurry, and alternately short of room or filling spaces, keen to divert while informing, provides a natural home for the pun (although one leading perpetrator, the *Guardian*, officially disclaims its approval of them).[55] We have seen in the previous section Roy Harris's remarks on Tabloid English, and in 'Lapsus' I gave examples of unwitting puns in headlines. It is time to consider the deliberate variety in newspapers, aptly termed by Louis Veuillot 'feuilles de joie' ('joy-rags/whores').

The very title of *Le Canard enchaîné* is a play on words, for it embraces the ideas of a harmless domestic creature and a scandal-mongering, satirical rag. It betrays a lasting fondness for 'le calembour-massue' (cudgel puns), and appropriately it was founded during the first world war to combat official brainwashing of the common soldier or citizen ('le bourrage de crâne'). It boasts of its counter-offensive: 'le calembourrage de crâne'. Nowadays, in the age of jetting popes, it reminds His Holiness to take with him on the journey his Holy ejector-See.[56]

The advertising slogans of papers are aptly subject to come-backs. Between the wars, the French daily *L'Oeuvre* had a slogan: 'Les imbéciles ne lisent pas L'Oeuvre,' to which the riposte soon came: 'Ils l'écrivent'.[57] (A British equivalent would be: 'Top people read *The Times*' – 'Bums write in it'.) Within the text of papers themselves, the danger, as always, is that of facetiousness. For Keith Waterhouse, a fine comic writer but a stern moralist when it comes to newspaper prose, words are often used solely 'to keep the wordplay bouncing along, to prevent the text flagging for even a tenth of a second'. He considers journalists' humour to be often schoolboyish, and terms it 'The Third Form of the Fourth Estate'. Some of his strictures would abolish punning altogether, as when he declares that 'a sentence that obliges the reader to revise his opinion of what it is saying should be recast.' No double-takes, then. His overall view is that:

> there will always be room for a really good pun or ingenious play on words in a headline, which is where the pun started its long and mainly undistinguished career in journalism . . . There is hardly any place for it in the text . . . Automatic punning is a tedious schoolboy game.

Yet surely, in celebrating the popular Press's movement away from aping the posh dailies, he should have stressed more the part played by punning in this emancipation. After all, there is a pun in the technical jargon ('a literal' is a printing error. To be unrelievedly literal is certainly another mistake). Who can lament those particular old days?

> When the *Daily Mirror* first gave voice it spoke in the celluloid collar English then common to all newspapers. In those penny-a-lining days, policemen were upholders of the law, criminals were denizens of the underworld, goalkeepers were custodians of the citadel – and journalists were gentlemen of the Press. They wrote like counting-house clerks forging their own references.[58]

We will show later how puns serve precisely to sabotage such clichés.

Visual

With advertising and the Press, we have been moving nearer the domain of the visual pun, a category I had not thought of until Hughes and Hammond's *Upon the Pun*, with its bilateral thinking, introduced me to it. Although their study of verbal punning should make us listen more acutely to what we and others say, their sections on pictorial puns really open our eyes. They rightly equate visual puns with metaphors, in that both coalesce tellingly things normally kept distinct. Their running attempt to link verbal and iconographic punning (they call Salvador Dali the Thomas Hood of fine art) is a variety of wordplay itself. For example, they talk frequently of a 'continuum' between canvas and printed page, by which I take it that they mean overlap and approximation, those nebulous constituents of all punning. Undoubtedly, we are slower on the uptake with images (how many of us have walked into the wrong lavatory because signs are less distinctive than words!): hence the need for captions, or other verbal clues such as labels, in most cartoons. This is not to deny the occasional existence of the 'pantomine strip' without a text; and, after all, bodies and faces can speak volumes. More often the drawing elicits the double meaning of a verbal statement, as in the cartoon of a legless man on crutches arriving at his gate, where there is a sign reading 'Chien méchant'. On the other side of the gate waits his dog, a pair of slippers in his mouth.[59] Their illustrations of puns in the plastic arts embrace the whole gamut from seaside postcards (a prime source of double entendre) to Arcimboldo and Dürer ('The Men's Bath' of the latter, where a nude male stands suggestively in close conjunction with a tap). The longest section in the book ('Visual Puns on the Face, Breasts, Posterior and Penis') is naturally fascinating, e.g. Magritte's ladylike hand grasping a factory chimney. In general, the authors are better, because less nit-picking about definitions, more slap-happy and free-wheeling in their interpretations, on visual than on verbal puns. And fresher too, for, as they correctly claim, the territory is well-nigh uncharted. 'A visual pun is made when someone notices that two different things have a similar appearance, and constructs a picture making this similarity evident.'[60] This remark by Hughes and Hammond is made more explicit by Geoffrey Strickland, when he spoke to me of 'the shock, in a visual pun, of a dual identity, or a shift from one to the other'. Thomas Hood's woodcuts were often visual puns, or as More puts it, 'play in forms' just as his practical jests were 'amphibology in act'.[61] As well as Dürer's juxtaposition, there is in Hogarth's 'Evening' a cuckold, not wearing the symbolic horns, but standing 'accidentally' in front of a bull whose horns seem to be protruding from his head.[62] As with the optical puns in Freudian dreams – broomsticks for phalluses – the visual pun is 'one visual form bisociated with two functional contexts'.[63]

Though James Brown states confidently that 'there is no such thing as a perceptual pun,'[64] the trick-pictures beloved of experimental psychologists of perception indicate that we see what we elect to see, just as we hear in puns what we want to hear. Objects can be puns in that they are capable of plural interpretation. Kökeritz compares the pun to 'the optical illusion created by certain geometrical designs which the mind of the viewer can at will arrange in two different patterns'.[65] Is Wittgenstein's famous duck/rabbit a pun of perception? Not strictly, or even laxly, as the two animals are alternatives, not simultaneities, and they do not create a meaningful synthesis. We are in the area of *trompe-l'oeil*, 'cet équivalent visuel du calembour'.[66] (The uttered pun is a *trompe-l'oreille* or, in fractured French, an ear-trumpet.)

Metaphysical poets recognised the kinship between verbal and visual wit and knew that readers would also, for the seventeenth century marvelled at optical ingenuity of all kinds – in anamorphic images, perspective boxes, mirrors and lenses, telescopes and prisms – and at the tricks of perspective in such diverse fields as landscape gardening and theatrical design.

In the previous century, Gilman cites the example of Arcimboldo's painting 'Summer', where from a distance the human head is natural but from close up is a still life composed of fruit and vegetables – though this is of course still 'natural'.[67] (The very term 'still life' is a visual paradox or oxymoron.) As Odilon Redon commented on his fellow-artist, as an empirical fantasist Arcimboldo is one of the supreme masters of 'that sense of mystery which is always to be found in the equivocal, in double and triple aspects, in hints of aspects and in the existence of an image within an image'.[68] Trickery and truth are not immutable opposites, of course, and such miscegenation as Arcimboldo practised opens eyes as much as it temporarily deceives the mind. His painting of Herod, in which the face is constructed entirely of the flesh of the children he has had slaughtered, draws this commentary from Jencks and Silver:

> Here the satire extends beyond the wit of combining previously separated systems to an ironic comment on the embarrassing repetition of nature. The naked human bodies which make up this portrait are divested of any individual qualities to become a squirming mass of biological tissue.[69]

Here, instead of an anthropocentric landscape we see a human-all-too-human monster. As with puns, a slight recoil is necessary to gauge fully the abyss that is being bridged. One of the erotic postcards selected by Paul Eluard, on the other hand, which features a face made up of nude women, does not work, for the nudes distract too much for the viewer to see the face straight off; we see it second, and the double-take nose is thus put out of joint.[70]

Puns, Spoonerisms, chiasmuses, all involve reshuffling of material, as does such double-exposure art. Arcimboldo's precursor, Bosch, was adept too at untying 'les liens rattachant entre elles les parties d'un tout', then dispersing the pieces and finally reassembling them in a different order.[71] As with wordplay, the new meanings are hidden but discoverable. Like jokes, the plastic artist can remind us that anything is possible: 'Objects formed by man – man formed by objects: the "reversed world", another favourite fantasy with artists of the time'.[72] Gilman links trompe-l'oeil and wit:

> Shifts of perspective . . . reveal the limits of the ordinary means of methodising nature by making unauthorised short-circuits across rational boundaries, and in that sense they lie . . . but they repay these trespasses by skilfully juggling the ordinary into the witty.[73]

The commonplace that literature can achieve only consecutive linearity whereas painting, like music, can offer simultaneity, is of course belied by the existence of puns, which provide the chance for coexistent meanings.[74]

A more naïve – though it has often appealed to sophisticated minds – linkage between word and image can be found in the long tradition of emblematic, or figured, verse. The shape of the poem is allied to its subject-matter, but in a literal-minded way which seems poetic only at an unadvanced level. It is a kind of visual analogue which finds a physical, or at least iconographic, equivalent for an idea or metaphor. It has been called 'art chirography' and it is perhaps suited to children's, or child-based, contexts, such as *Alice in Wonderland* with the mouse's long caudal *tale*. A related item is the 'pun tableau', e.g. 'Monuments of Greece', illustrated by two tallow candles; or again, Bruce McMillan's 'Punography': he plays it straight in a pleonastic literalism. 'Chain-smoking' is pictured by somebody puffing at some links.[75] In the eighteenth century, the painter Constantin had the idea of publishing 'calembours figurés', representing *équivoques* to be decoded by the viewer, and inspired by the Marquis de Bièvre. One featured a thick letter S and an A in bed: 'la grossesse et l'accouchée' ('*gros S et l'A couché*/pregnancy and the woman delivered of child').[76] In addition to heraldry, already noted, punning rebuses were also common in painted glass windows, decorated Gothic architecture and the title-pages of early printed books, and were often known as 'painted poesies'.[77] A more original kind of emblematic verse is that of Francis Ponge or Marianne Moore. Of the later, Kenner writes: 'In her poems, things utter puns to the senses . . . Her poems deal in many separate acts of attention, all close-up; optical puns, seen by snapshot.' Miss Moore does not worry any more about congruousness, in such comparisons, than Braque does about perspective. In the same text, Kenner remarks that when Marianne Moore compares a snake's skin to rose petals, it is 'neither as a fancy nor as a simile, but as a virtual identity of tactile sensation: a species of wit gone into the fingertips: a tactile pun'.[78] The pun is a constant reminder of the inseparability of anything from the physical.

As well as phonic or orthographic puns, there are, then, the kinetic or gestural.[79] In the film, *A Mad Mad Mad World*, Jimmy Durante, as he expires, physically dislodges a bucket with his foot. The 'sight gag' offers the chance for *double voir* as well as double entendre. McLuhan wittily remarks that Mae West, 'a visual pun', impersonated a female impersonator. 'This may have obtained for her the unexpected honor of having an environmental garment named after her. The "Mae West" was no matter of mere levity, but a protection against graver depth charges.'[80] The TV satire programme, *That Was The Week That Was*, as a comment on television's desperate habit of backing up all news items with images, mentioned the Lord Privy Seal. In quick succession were flashed up pictures of an aristocrat, an outdoor lavatory and an animal balancing a ball on its snout. This splendid conjunction of Establishment, excrement and animal-act both deflated the official function and the news medium itself.

Puns, paradoxes and riddles do to language what pies do to faces and pratfalls to bottoms – destroy its dignity. R. B. Blackmur has called punning 'the onomatopoeia of meaning', or we might say that punning is sound whacking sense.[81]

Zen teachers, *Punch* or *Le Canard enchaîné* would agree with this last phrase. A gaffe can be a pratfall in speech.[82] Attributed variously to Christopher Fry or Christopher Morley is the description of a show-off speaker as 'coruscating on thin ice'. Think also of the kinetic bathos of Icarus' fall. More deliberate, clearly, are practical jokes, beloved of Flaubert and the Surrealists: plastic turds, for instance: 'What seems, but is not'.[83] There is an age-old longing that language should have some real power over events, a more total link with action, as reflected in these words of the painter Closon:

> C'est le geste du verbe qu'il nous faut aller chercher dans tout mot: j'aimerais alors que fesser soit l'origine gestuelle de professer et de confesser. La confession serait la fessée que nous nous donnons pour redresser nos torts, c'est-à-dire, toujours gestuellement parlant, pour rectifier le tortueux, remettre droit le tordu: ce que fait aussi le professeur.

> (It's the gesture in language that we must look for in every word. I would like *fesser* (to spank) to be the gestural origin of profess and confess. Confession would then be the spanking we give ourselves to atone for our wrongdoings, that is, and still speaking in terms of gesture, our attempt to straighten the tortuous, to put right the twisted – which is what a professor does.)[84]

Here again we see that pedagogic urge so frequent among punners, though all would-be pedagogues might remember that charades, the acting out of puns, like all puzzles and bees, die once they have used their sting.

Puns mix up, mix together – like collages, and these latter have comparable parodic intent. Likewise, the Surrealist game of 'l'un dans l'autre' suggests both the superimposing and telescoping found in all punning, and, inevitably, a miniature analogue to the sexual act. As Fadiman points out, Surrealist punning 'has a certain feverish, almost delirious quality. Thus there are wordplays that *almost* make sense, teasing the mind as after-images tease the optic nerve.' He goes on to link Surrealist language and painting: 'The candid lover of puns . . . will cheerfully confess to a perversion, to a preference for language under stress, as Dali prefers a melted watch to the correct time.'[85] Notoriously, Dali, and other Surrealists, aped schizophrenia or paranoia. Just as there are neologisms in schizophrenic language, so there are neomorphisms in schizophrenic art. Turning aside, or sequestered from, everyday reality, schizophrenics deviate, blend, contaminate. Rudolf Arnheim comments:

Remnants of thoughts and experiences are organised, not according to their meaningful interaction in the world of reality, but by purely formal similarities and symmetries. There is visual 'punning' – the fusion of heterogeneous contents on the basis of external resemblance.

Lest the rest of us should feel superior or left out, Arnheim goes on to stress that:

> it is no accident that similar characteristics are found in the 'doodles' of persons whose minds are concentrated on some train of thought while the sense of form directs the hands and eyes with no guiding idea or experience left in control. Geometric shapes generate each other, sometimes adding up to well-organised wholes but more often to chance agglomerations of elements.[86]

This is akin to dreaming, or slips of the tongue, which likewise give us away. The 'droodle', on the other hand, entirely wilful, is defined by Hughes and Hammond as a generally 'lewd visual metathesis'.

'The pun has been the homunculus of humour, its hunchback of Notre Dame.'[87] Surrealism and madness lead on to the grotesque. In fact, a stock French dictionary example of the pun emphasizes the grotesque element: 'Un effet de l'art (un nez fait de lard)' ('An artistic effect (a nose made of bacon)'). Visual puns recur in caricature. Kris and Gombrich quote the famous cartoon of King Louis-Philippe as a pear (*poire* = fathead).[88] The actual monarch's head housed this potentiality. It needed an artist to recognize the like in the unlike and to bring them rudely together. The resultant shape, or misshapen form, speaks directly, though doubly, to us. Auden expresses this phenomenon quite beautifully:

> Every face is a present witness to the fact that its owner has a past behind him which might have been otherwise, and a future ahead of him in which some possibilities are more probable than others. To 'read' a face means to guess what it might have been and what it may still become. Children, for whom most future possibilities are equally probable, the dead, for whom all possibilities have been reduced to zero, and animals who have only one possibility to realise and realise it completely, do not have faces which can be read, but wear inscrutable masks. A caricature of a face admits that its owner has had a past, but denies that he has a future. He has arrested his features up to a certain point, but now they have taken charge of him so that he can never change; he has become a single possibility completely realised. That is why, when we go to the zoo, the faces of the animals remind one of caricatures of human beings. A caricature doesn't need to be read; it has no future. We enjoy caricatures of our friends because we do not want to think of their changing, above all, of their dying; we enjoy caricatures of our enemies because we do not want to consider the possibility of their having a change of heart so that we would have to forgive them.[89]

We have seen already, in the section on gallows humour, the verbal grotesque. As the grotesque depends so heavily on the physical (bodily deformity, especially) and seeks a physical impact (a disorienting jolt to the recipient's system), it is even more at home in the plastic arts, where its tendency to exaggerate, to run away with the whole scene, can have free play. The term originated in painting.[90] Hugo did more than most to acclimatize it to literature with his insistence on the fruitful mingling of genres. With that more drily intellectual mode, irony, you need time to think twice, to twig the real message. In the case of the grotesque, we see double, troublingly, as in drunkenness, hallucinations or concussion. Like punning, it remains profoundly ambivalent, for the tensions it sets up, the incompatibles it deals in, are never fully resolved. As a result, it cannot be clearly liberating, nor indeed imprisoning, but rather *shocking*, in its effect. Like taking medicine, it is hard to swallow. It can make strange, or, as Hugo always argued, it can simply reflect what is strange in supposedly normal life. Ambidextrously it can offer both a distortion and a correction of vision. As Freud noted, the ugly 'must be brought forward and made obvious, so that it lies clear open to the light of day'.[91]

Children and Folk-Wisdom

Children love the absurd and the mixture of different levels, the unseating of the comfortably installed. For Kris and Gombrich, the deliberately simple lines of caricature can be taken to resemble the unprofessional scrawls of children, just as in wordplay, according to Freud, we return to the childlike pleasure of mastering the art of language.[92] As Molly Mahood observes,

> Freud's contention that punning releases a desire to talk nonsense which was suppressed in the nursery gains support from the experimental psychologists, who have shown that in the process of verbal association children generalise by homophones (*style* to *stile*) more easily than grown-ups, who prefer semantic generalisation (*style* to *fashion*). Perhaps the Victorians were ashamed of puns because they had received an ultra-rational education from the English Rousseauists who tried to 'inculcate the principles of Reason and Morality' at a tender age. Puns let us be unprincipled about both.[93]

Obviously, in their addiction to word-association, children are trying to see, or to force, connections, to link all the multitudinous bits of experience: it is a serious game. As with their toys, children fondle and fool around with words; they dislocate and reassemble them. Max Levin makes this point persuasively:

> If play were not pleasurable, kittens would never chase each other's tails, and so would lack practice in the motor skills needed for survival. If there were no

pleasure in the appreciation of the absurd, if there were no fun in playing with ideas, putting them together in various combinations, and seeing what makes sense or nonsense – in brief, if there were no such thing as humor – children would lack practice in the art of thinking, the most complex and most powerful survival tool of all.[94]

In her Freudian study of the subject, Martha Wolfenstein distinguishes several stages in the process of playing with language. She sees name-play as an important prelude. One child attributing to another a name different to the one he or she in fact bears is clearly on the attack. Toying with another's meaning 'has the underlying implication: You are not what you think you are. Similarly the transformation of one's own meaning suggests: I am not what you think I am. This also has initially an unsettling effect.' At a later stage, more elaborate joke-façades are set up in order to get 'the sexual or hostile theme past inner and outer censorship'. Children love bringing together the high and the low, as in the advertising slogan for toilet-paper quoted earlier: 'Tops for bottoms'. Wolfenstein stresses the importance of the age of the child in all this, because though 'many children enjoy the discovery of sound similarities, when a shift of meaning is forced on them they are more apt to be distressed'.[95]

That children do not merely imitate but adapt and originate, in the field of language, is obvious to any receptive observer. As Stephen Leacock says, children make words work overtime; they put them to uses which words should be able to fulfil but had not previously to the child's extension of their range. He quotes the example of the boy declaring that he would love to eat more of the food but that he had 'run out of stomach' – by analogy with running out of food, money, petrol.[96] Children are down to earth, of this earth: 'Even simple puns tie a physical action or object to a mental concept or thought, such as the man taking a ruler to bed to see how long he slept.'[97] While recognizing the schoolchild's 'love of puns and word mutilation', the Opies still characterize the pun as 'that pick-pocket of wit', and talk of 'the corruptive influence of the pun on language and custom', though, to be fair, what they mean mainly by this description is the variants (often creative) on expressions, arising as much by accident as by design.[98] The archetypal adult's tendency to apologize for committing a pun ('No pun intended') is presumably due to his imagining that puns are a primitive form of humour reserved for children and thus beneath the dignity of grown-ups.

Koestler indeed makes the tired old link of children and 'primitives' when he asserts that for both groups 'name and object form an almost indivisible unity, shown in the universal practices of word magic, incantations and verbal spells,' and again, together with rhyme, assonance and rhythm, 'puns are deeply rooted in primitive and infantile forms of thought and utterance, in which sound and meaning are magically interwoven.'[99] We move from jokelore to folklore (often fakelore). Eric Partridge states, over-categorically:

Proverbs are instances of racial wisdom, whereas clichés are instances of racial inanition. It is perhaps not irrelevant to note that with the rapidly decreasing popularity of proverbs among the middle and upper classes, clichés are, there, becoming increasingly popular.[100]

This is too selective a conception of clichés, though the decline of proverbs in urban society is undeniable. What we do practise extensively in our age is the twisting of proverbs to suit new purposes, though this activity is in fact as old as burlesque itself. (Isaac Disraeli mentions *The Crossing of Proverbs* of 1616.)[101] As Jacobs recognizes, 'a proverb, being a highly conventionalised, fixed formulation, lends itself to distortion.'[102] The high incidence of assonance and metaphors in proverbs is a further condition for punning reworkings; proverbs are parables writ small. Any verbal situation in which a contrast can be made between full and empty, inert and lively, literal and figurative, is similarly likely to provoke the urge to adapt. Furthermore, as many proverbs no longer have any clear meaning to our minds, the possibility of misinterpreting them, fortuitously or on purpose, is that much greater. Updating does not automatically entail a loss of something valuable. As the folklorist C. Grant Loomis points out concerning perverted proverbs (sometimes called 'perverbs'),

> the preservation of a considerable segment of proverbs, even in indirect fashion, is well worth recognition, since historians of the genre do not seem to have noted the maintenance of tradition by the way of parody.[103]

Jacobs quotes as an example 'Many are called but few get the right number.' He adds that:

> the literal significance of a common phrase or proverb can also be evoked by placing it in an unexpected context; as Hamlet's 'O that this too, too solid flesh should melt' sometimes found on weighing scales.

Conversely, 'something concrete can be suddenly shunted into the abstract.' For example, on Procrustes and the iron bed to which he tied his victims and then stretched or cut off their legs to adapt them to its length: 'A giant with a keen sense of the fitness of things'.[104]

'As Boers would say, two blacks don't make a white.' The Wellerism is related to the perverb and to quotation in general. It is named after Sam Weller ('Coaches, Sammy, is like guns – they requires to be loaded with very great care, afore they go off').[105] An American variant is the 'Yankeeism': '"After you've been ironed, you'll be hung up to dry", as the sheriff pleasantly remarked to the criminal.'[106] A cousin is the Tom Swifty, punning adverbs of manner, which, despite its name, is an elephantine mode: '"I'll chop the tree down", he said, lumberingly.' At its best, the Wellerism itself, a yoking of different contexts to make a telling point, is a rhetorical device of real value: 'The Democratic Party is like a mule – without pride of ancestry or hope of posterity.'[107] Similes can play on words, as in 'I feel as horny as a rhinoceros' – which relies in addition on the reference to the supposed aphrodisiac qualities of this appendage, when ground up. Like any humour, the Wellerism can be callous: '"I am just throwing out a feeler" remarked the saloon keeper, as he put the blind man into the street.'[108] It often uses a proverb attached to a far-fetched situation, or dexterously misapplied, as in '"Virtus in medio", said the Devil as he seated himself between two old whores.'[109]

Proverbs and their relatives pose as worldly-wise, and are often wise-acre. Unless they are recycled they tend to petrify, apart form the few powerfully indisputable ones. Clichés, too, are petrified language and thought. To balance the study of poetics, we need one of prosaics. They have few champions, and so a few words need to be said on behalf of these congealed words which have lost their telling power. It must be the case that we can hardly speak or write a sentence without using a cliché of some kind. Speech and writing would be enormously fatiguing, and probably often incomprehensible for the receiver, if they sought novelty at every turn. The *four banal* is a communal oven, which in medieval times there was a feudal obligation to use. 'Banality' was, and is, the common lot. We know that language speaks us as much as we speak it.

> All speech is potentially speech with two tongues – the unique physical tongue of the individual giving utterance, and the generally prevailing mother tongue that was outside and prior to the individual, but now takes up residence in his singular tongue.[110]

This permanent take-over of the individual by the collective voice is one of Flaubert's chief lessons. As Hugh Kenner expresses it:

> Art tending towards the general and human behaviour tending towards the cliché, we are back again to the fact that the supreme artist is the cliché expert and cannot do better than to imitate, as closely as he can, the procedures of the hack.[111]

The logic here is dubious in its very plausibility. I feel that Sartre gets nearer to the heart of the matter when he links clichés and puns.

> Cet *on* heideggérien, c'est le commun des hommes, qui emploient le langage à servir leurs fins triviales. Si le style loin d'être un meilleur usage poétique des mots n'en était qu'un *autre* usage? Depuis l'enfance, Gustave, écrasé sous le poids des phrases toutes faites et des lieux communs, semble s'en être douté. Je ne puis expliquer que par une obscure prescience l'acharnement lourd et laborieux avec lequel, depuis l'enfance, il s'exerce aux calembours.

(This Heideggerian 'One' is the mass of men, using language to serve their trivial goals. But what if style, far from being a *better* poetic use of words, was only a *different* one? From childhood on, bowed down under the weight of ready-made phrases and commonplaces, Gustave seems to have suspected this. I cannot explain except by such a faint foresight the ponderous and laborious ruthlessness with which, from childhood on, he tried his hand at puns.)[112]

According to this reading, Flaubert turned to puns – wilfully bad puns – as his way of accentuating the clichéic nature of all language, a desperate Absurdist tactic. In his urge to accuse Flaubert of passivity on all levels Sartre equates the registering of commonplaces with the largely mechanical process of proof-correction (though, surely, totally mindless editing is unthinkable): 'Pour découvrir un lieu commun, il faut le subir et non le dépasser par l'utilisation qu'on en fait ('To locate a commonplace you must undergo it and not move beyond it by your use of it'). Flaubert remains, in this view, passive even when he *hunts out* clichés in his study of human *bêtise*, because he isolates them, taking no account of the 'synthesising activity or the real intentions' of the speaker. Stupidity thus becomes a bottomless pit over which Flaubert leans in a state of vertigo. As a result, Flaubert's 'Dictionary of Clichés' is a rag-bag: 'idées reçues, locutions, calembours et jeux de mots, "perles"' ('clichés, set expressions, puns and wordplays, "howlers"'): it attacks nobody in particular.

> Tout ce qu'il peut faire, c'est de les opposer pour qu'ils montrent d'eux-mêmes leurs contradictions et dans l'espoir qu'ils se détruiront les uns les autres: c'est le type même de l'activité passive.

> (All he can do is set them face to face so that they themselves reveal their contradictions, in the hope that they will destroy each other. This is the very essence of passive activity.)

Perhaps it was Flaubert's persistent doubt that originality was possible that made him guilty, in Sartre's eyes, of 'la fuite constante de l'idée ou, plus exactement, la fuite *devant l'idée* ('The constant flight from ideas or, more exactly, flight from the very idea of ideas').[113] Sartre is harsh on Flaubert and clichés. Barthes, an admitted disciple of Sartre, is more accommodating, finding even in the banalized language of advertising causes of non-alarm.

> Les figures du langage publicitaire sont ceux-là mêmes de la poésie: figures rhétoriques, métaphores, jeux de mots, tous ces signes ancestraux, qui sont des signes *doubles*, élargissent le langage vers des signifiés latents et donnent ainsi à l'homme qui les reçoit la puissance même d'une expérience de totalité.

> (The tropes of advertising language are those of poetry itself: rhetorical figures, metaphors, wordplay – all those ancestral signs, which are double signs, set free

language's latent signifieds and thus give the receiver the very powerful experience of totality.)

Commonplaces can thus enlarge and set free (*élargissent*). The self-avowed 'demoralizer' Flaubert did not allow for this spin-off from the verbal vertigo. Barthes goes on:

> L'excellence du signifiant publicitaire tient ainsi au pouvoir, qu'il faut savoir lui donner, de *relier* son lecteur à la plus grande quantité de 'monde' possible: le monde, c'est-à-dire: expérience de très anciennes images, obscures et profondes sensations du corps, nommées poétiquement par des générations, sagesse des rapports de l'homme et de la nature, accession patiente de l'humanité à une intelligence des choses à travers le seul pouvoir incontestablement humain: le langage.

> (The excellence of the advertising signifier rests on the power, which we need to know how to give it, of linking its reader to the greatest possible amount of 'world': that is, the experience of very ancient images, obscure and profound bodily sensations which have been named by generations of poets, the wisdom of the relationship between man and nature, the patient access of mankind to an understanding of things through the only unarguably human power there is: language.)[114]

The great debunker and demythologizer Barthes here edges towards endorsing 'la sagesse des nations' (worldly wisdom), and reminding us of what Sartre prefers to forget: the necessity of familiarity to make life livable. Along a parallel path, I presume that by 'slang' Chesterton means mechanical and shop-worn figurative speech when he makes this spirited defence of it: 'The world of slang is a kind of topsy-turveydom of poetry, full of blue moons and white elephants, of men losing their heads, and men whose tongues run away with them – a whole chaos of fairy tales.'[115]

Other rejoinders to clichés than Flaubert's raging passivity, Sartre's pitying scorn and Barthes' lordly latitudinarianism are available and widely practised. I would resume them under the heading of 'twisting', and there is an obvious tie-up with 'perverted proverbs'. The most obvious motive for twisting clichés, proverbs or any other products of 'la sagesse des nations' is the desire to be a wise guy, undeceived or less deceived: showing off. Less obviously but more crucially, when we make a pun, when we play with words, we are making them our own. The twist we effect wrenches them out of their comfortable, hallowed context and sets them up. Not for us alone, of course, as we can then display them as trophies to others, as proofs of that mastery over language about which we need to reassure ourselves every bit as much as the child apprentice. We may not aspire to the sophisticated perfectionism of Don Marquis's 'stroke a platitude until it purrs like an epigram,' but our lesser efforts can still be a highly useful act of linguistic ecology.[116] The re-use of the consecrated to attack the established can act as a boost to morale, as when my English teacher used to annex Miltonic lines to describe his unlovable colleagues: the chemistry teacher: 'that sciential sap', the fat religious knowledge teacher: 'that foul worm'. This dismasting of masters gave us inklings of how to master our awe of them. Similarly, the priest-hating drunk in Prévert's poem filches the famous line from Corneille's *Horace* – 'Rome, l'unique objet de mon ressentiment' – and injects it with a fresh anticlerical impetus. Prévert rejuvenates a cliché by using a term for a stock phrase literally, thereby solidifying for our inspection the hollowness of official speechifying: 'Le grand homme d'Etat trébuchant sur une belle phrase creuse/tombe dedans' ('The great statesman stumbling over a hollow rhetorical flourish drops himself in it').[117]

We talk in fact of an 'original turn of phrase', as if the existent form needed to be swivelled in order to rebecome interesting. G. B. Milner illustrates what he prettily calls a 'morphological syntagmatic reversal' by this phrase of a voter writing to his MP: 'I assure you that you are, Sir, my obedient servant,' which puts a whole unbalanced relationship back in its proper place.[118] Revitalized idioms can make us sit up and take notice, as in Ronald Knox's 'Any stigma will do to beat a dogma.'[119] As well as reactivating, such distortions can serve to denude pomposity of its pretensions. As Pascal might have said (for he was punning already on the 'face' of the world), if Cleopatra's nose had been a different shape, she would have been Jewish (or Roman). Exploiting the literal level of tired metaphorical phrases can reveal a subtext; here again the pun unearths: 'An atheist is a man with no invisible means of support.'[120] In the film *Kiss Me Stupid*, Ray Walston strokes Kim Novak's knee and whispers: 'What's a beautiful joint like this doing in a girl like you?' – thus reducing the age-old seducer's spiel, while telling the same old story. Berloquin detects the strength of the pun as lying in 'l'écart entre la banalité de ce qui est dit et le choc de ce qui est évoqué' ('the gap between the banality of what is said and the shock of what is hinted').[121]

The decomposition or reconstituting of set expressions is, as Jean Paulhan has remarked, akin to etymology, as in this play on 'sens commun': 'Le sens commun est moins commun qu'on ne dit' ('Common sense is less common than is thought'); or:

'A force de peloter les uns et les autres, il est arrivé à faire sa pelote; il s'agit en vérité d'une étymologie: *pelote, pilotta*, c'est également la petite balle que l'on manie et caresse, et le trésor qui s'arrondit.

(By dint of flattering everyone, he managed to make his pile. There is indeed an etymological link: *pelote, pilotta*, is both the little ball we can handle and caress, and the lucre rounded up.)[122]

In this way the past is made to prefigure the future utilization; it is what the adepts of OULIPO term 'plagiat par anticipation', or topsy-turveydom. In the present, as we saw with advertising language, such recycling capitalizes on what is already acquired. As does parody, with its· take-offs from a consecrated platform. Trite words can act as trampolines and thus the elasticity of speech is reconfirmed. The whole phenomenon is a reminder that we necessarily live off each other, like fleas, in an infinite regress, and progress. Some threadbare formulations are already, in themselves, puns, as in the ritual French saying about foregone conclusions or immutable laws: 'C'est réglé comme du papier à musique,' or the English 'he is as nutty as a fruit-cake.' But the pun here is itself, of course, consecrated and thus refrigerated.

It is commonly felt that clichés occur by parthenogenesis (as indeed they do under my pen as I write). Zijderveld first chastises us, then pats us reassuringly when he writes in his study of clichés:

> The manipulation of clichés in mirth has itself become a cliché, not in the least for commercial reasons . . . Yet in our mirthful playing with traditional and routinised meanings . . . we have a chance to subdue clichés to our ingenuity and wit, and thus to relativise their power.[123]

As we move from the relative safety of 'la sagesse des nations' to that notoriously unwise area of 'national characteristics', we will start with this possible corruption of punning twists – where else? – in the United States. As in comparative literature, however, we will be looking for differences as much as similarities, for if the impulse to pun is universal, its forms take local variants, habitations and names.

8

Across the Rivers and into the Trees

Anglo-Saxon and French

Any visitor to the United States is likely to concur with at least the first part of this statement of Bier:

> Since much of the American mentality itself battens on simplifications – on clichés, on shibboleths, on proverbs, on slogans, on formulas – an equal amount of our humor is in the service of unholy complication.[1]

The second part is true, to the extent that twisting complicates any thread. Nor is this a product of a cynical twentieth century, for such parodic subversion of all forms of pious rhetoric dates back to the literary comedians of the nineteenth, like Mark Twain and Ambrose Bierce, and to the contrariness of thinkers like Thoreau. Marcus Cunliffe widens the attack by observing that:

> '*idées reçues* are [held to be wrong] – dead wrong, so to speak ... Expressed geometrically, the proposition would mean that a truly original hypothesis or artifact ought to be at 180° from its antecedent, i.e. a complete opposite.

From this urge stems also the habit of reversal in critical discourse (e.g. 'Marx stood Hegel on his head'). The danger, of course, as Cunliffe stresses, is that:

> this relentless formulaic inversion, with its unearned, knowing 'novelty', threatens to be as trite, hackneyed, etc., as the clichés it battens upon ... The demand for 'turnover' in the economic order causes a craving for 'turnover', or rather 'overturn' in the realm of imagination and the intellect.

The result is that 'too many joke-reversals are parasitic rather than truly parodistic.'[2] There is much truth in the complaint. Many such twists update a well-known reference to no real end, as in 'King Midas had a gilt complex,' or go in for wilful misunderstanding by again importing a contemporary allusion: 'Eli Whitney invented the cotton gin, but at first it didn't sell because nobody wanted a fluffy martini,' though the latter has a quality of surrealist nonsense.[3]

Sometimes we are offered an unlikely double helping, as in the Hollywood anecdote of the Jewish writer who went to the plastic surgeon. One of her friends remarked: 'I see you've cut off your nose to spite your race.' 'Yes,' replied the writer, 'Now I'm a thing of beauty and a goy forever.'[4] The only shortcoming in Bier's and Cunliffe's critique is that both seem to think they are talking of a recent phenomenon, whereas the reversible world, 'Mundus Inversus', is ancient and transcultural. Upturning is adult play, a negation used to create a space for freer manoeuvres.

Reversals, like etymologies, work backwards. You think of the twisting punchline and then devise a narrative situation which will lead up to it; you provide a home for these strays of language. Bier regrets the mass-production of such wit, on cards, lapel-badges and so on, but he might have added that other American invention: the script-writer, whose existence turns the comedian into a performer or salesman for somebody else's labour. The professionals are thus spared what Bier calls 'the burden of origination' just as much as the rest of us amateurs.[5] Neither he nor Cunliffe pays attention to the salvaging aspect of such wit. Ingenuity and the finding of new use for old objects are surely desirable civic qualities in an age of vanishing resources. Spitzer puts a much more positive gloss on the whole phenomenon when he argues: 'Freedom of speech involves a concept of non-finality of speech. In America the human word is thought of only as having a provisional value. One word may be undone, and outdone, by another.'[6] This allows for the built-in obsolescence of all aspects of US life, the competitiveness of its people, and the constant desire for improvement, for going one better. Punning twists can introduce vitality, ruin unthinking expectations, reverse the inertia of language.

Naturally, Americans wanted to dissociate themselves from the British, especially in so personal a matter as the sense of humour. One typical opinion from Kimmins: 'In America, the riddle appears and is never as popular as in England, as it is frequently associated with puns, which fortunately have never taken firm hold in American literature.'[7] Eastman elaborates: 'I count it a point of legitimate pride in my own country . . . that it has, upon the whole, manfully resisted the transplantation and general propagation of the household pun.'[8] Loomis, on the other hand, describes the early nineteenth century, in particular, as being 'especially prolific in word play'.[9] One specifically American innovation in that century was the cult of cacography. 'What the pun was to England bad spelling was to America. A whole generation of Artemus Wards traded on bad spelling. In the end they killed it as dead as the dead pun in England.' Less exclusive than Kimmins or Eastman, Agnes Repplier goes on to give her own view: 'The United States, destitute of kings and courts, lived as humorously as it could on British puns and home-made misspelling.'[10] Josh Billings brings the two themes together when he says: 'The English are better punsters, but i konsider punning a sort ov literary prostitushun in which future happynesz iz swopped for the plezzure ov the moment.'[11] If the pun is artificial, doubly so is cultivated cacography. Bier's explanation for the cult is this:

> The delight in spelling or misspelling was a clear indication of the newly acquired character of mass literacy, accelerative but unsure of itself yet and needing to laugh at the next lowest level from which most of the population were just barely lifting themselves.[12]

This charitable view of an uncharitable mockery leaves out the ancient tradition of posing as a clod for comic effect.

A truly distinctive feature of American humour is clearly leg-pulling exaggeration, noted a century and a half ago by an English visitor, Captain Marryat:

> The Americans are often themselves the cause of being misrepresented; there is no country perhaps where the common habit of deceiving for amusement, or what is termed hoaxing, is so common. Indeed, this and hyperbole constitute the major part of American humour.[13]

The big sell and the con-trick are indeed central to the American tradition, together with what Bier calls 'the overwhelmingly verbal cast of American humor'.[14] The Marx Brothers, confidence-men, exaggerators, ring all the changes on language in its various guises: 'Groucho's brazenly nasty double-talk, Chico's artfully stupid malapropisms, Harpo's startling physical horseplay'. In more detail,

> Groucho's 'logic' is really the manipulation of pun, homonym and equivocation. He substitutes the quantity of sound and the illusion of rational connection for the theoretical purpose of talk: logical communication.

Chico's relationship to language:

> also substitutes sound for sense and the appearance of meaning for meaning . . . He alone can puncture Groucho's verbal spirals by stopping the speeding train of words and forcing Groucho to respond to his own erroneous intrusions.

In this way, we see pseudo-'dumb' language showing up pseudo-smart language. But Harpo caps it all; he makes only sounds:

> The irony that a bumbling foreign speaker (Chico) renders a mute clown's honks, beeps and whistles into English so it can be understood by the supreme verbal gymnast (Groucho) plays a role in every Marx Brothers film.[15]

An unholy alliance of the verbal and the gestural play with language is the Marx Brothers' contribution to American humour.

Turning to Britain, I found fewer examples than I expected of explicit statements about puns, though of course partial attitudes to this subject are scattered throughout this study. This paucity might reflect British hypocrisy and snobbery: the pretence that, though puns pullulate at all levels of British life, we should pretend they do not exist; the famous British anti-theoretical bent; or the notorious laziness of the race: a phenomenon so everyday needs no analysis or comment. We take puns for granted, as indeed they are by our munificent language. The fact remains that, in the area of twists for one, it was British writers like Shaw, Chesterton and Oscar Wilde ('Work is the ruin of the drinking classes') who perfected what the American literary comedians had started.[16] The recent spate of collections of graffiti reveals both a widespread practice and a large-scale response. One such editor points to:

> the nature of the English language itself. Because of its richness and variety the language lends itself to playfulness. Most of the graffiti in this book are based on puns or other forms of word play. Wherever English is spoken, the same kind of jokes arise, as if by spontaneous combustion.[17]

This has more to do with ease of travel, the technology of mass-production and distribution, and imitative modes of behaviour, but the general interest remains valid. 'The pun is the power-unit that drives, and that has always driven, the lifeboat of English humour.'[18] As an example of the traditional British enjoyment of the double-meaning joke, the former film-censor John Trevelyan cites the case of Marie Lloyd changing the words of her song 'She Sits Among the Cabbages and Peas', after complaints from a watchdog committee, to 'She Sits Among the Cabbages and Leeks'.[19] At the other end of the social scale, Harold Nicolson describes the English love of associating sounds as 'a simultaneous awareness of doubleness and singleness' (and in its sounds his sentence enacts his meaning). But he goes on to castigate:

> No mental effort is needed or attempted: the reaction is, if not entirely physiological, is [sic] certainly not one by which the higher cortices of the brain are affected. It is thus a primal, or infantile, reaction.[20]

Empson betrays a less snobbish and more clear-headed mind when he writes of modern English:

> Always without adequate means for showing the syntax intended, it is fast throwing away the few devices it had; it is growing liable to mean more things, and less willing to stop and exclude the other possible meanings.

English, the universal language, is (we might say) all things to all men. Empson does not view this development with dismay, for he welcomes the increasingly fluid and adaptable nature of English grammar and sees it as a source of possible reinvigoration of the language.[21]

Whether or not English (British or American varieties) has more homophones or homonyms than French, both those varieties are clearly the product of a greater long-term linguistic melting-pot. One significant outcome is the availability of numerous similar monosyllabic words (e.g. pat, pet, pit, pot, put), which obviously facilitate approximate wordplay. It is no doubt more a matter of morphological observation than of numeracy that makes people claim that X language has more homophones than another. For one side, 'French and Spanish seem to allow much less phonetic and phonological manipulation in puns than does English.'[22] For the other:

> Le calembour fait partie intégrante, non seulement de l'esprit, mais encore de l'humour français. Il serait absurde de le mépriser, plus encore de l'ignorer, même si les autres nations le pratiquent moins fréquemment, et donc plus maladroitement que nous.
>
> (The pun is an integral part of both French wit and humour. It would be absurd to look down on it, or even more to ignore it, even if other peoples practise it less frequently and therefore less skilfully than we do.)[23]

Bièvre, who was better qualified than most to comment, states categorically that 'de toutes les langues de l'Europe, la française ... est la plus abondante en homonymes.'[24] An Englishman joins the chorus: 'The number of final letters, which among the French are mere ciphers in pronounciation, has always given them a decided advantage in puns of mere words than every other nation.'[25] A more measured line is taken by Stephen Ullmann:

> The simple syllabic structure peculiar to French even in polysyllables makes it into a favourite playground for *calembours* ... In contradistinction to the more conservative German, Spanish and Italian, French and English owe the frequency of homonymy in their structure principally to the speed and scope of their phonological evolution ... Acceleration in the rhythm of development would thus go hand in hand with the spread of homonymity and with increased aliveness to its pitfalls.[26]

Obviously, a distinguo is needed. French may, or may not, offer more opportunities for wordplay than English, but it does not follow that they are seized with the same alacrity. Yaguello fairly criticizes the widely held assumption, even amongst the supposedly well-informed, that 'le français, plus que toute autre langue, est propre au mot d'esprit, au calembour, au jeu de mots. Toutes les langues autorisent le jeu' ('French, more than any other language, is suited to the witticism, the pun, the play on words. All languages permit play').[27]

'Notre langue, nous ne saurions trop le dire, est essentiellement ennemie de toute affectation, de tout jeu de mots puéril' ('Our language, we can hardly overstate this, is essentially hostile to all affectation, all puerile play with words') is a statement at once severely puritanical and inaccurate.[28] Listen to Balzac's vaunting puerility in this passage about the key-term *plâtre* which figures in a law-suit:

> Les plaisants de la ville dirent qu'on avait *replâtré* l'affaire, que l'accusateur public avait *gâché* sa position et que les Simeuse devenaient blancs comme *plâtre*. En France, tout est du domaine de la plaisanterie, elle y est la reine: on plaisante sur l'échafaud, à la Bérésina, aux barricades, et quelque Français plaisantera sans doute aux grandes assises du jugement dernier.

> (The town wits said the affair had been *whitewashed*, that the public prosecutor had *plastered* his incompetence everywhere and that the Simeuse family were as white as *chalk*. In France, everything can be turned to a joke, for the joke is king. Men joke on the scaffold, at the Beresina, on the barricades, and some Frenchman will no doubt crack a joke at the Great Assizes of the Last Judgement.)[29]

For something less galumphing, more balletic, we should turn to Musset's Fantasio: 'Un calembour console de bien des chagrins, et jouer avec les mots est un moyen comme un autre de jouer avec les pensées, les actions et les êtres. Tout est calembour ici-bas' ('A pun consoles you for many woes, and playing with words in one way of playing with ideas, actions, people. Everything on earth can be a pun'). At another point the hero boasts: 'Je suis en train de bouleverser l'univers pour le mettre en acrostiche' ('I am in the midst of turning the world upside down to make an acrostic from it').[30] There is something quintessentially French about this pseudo-metaphysical posturing and claims of elegance. I am reminded of the Absurdist tactic of Camus's Caligula when Adele King comments: 'God's word has created a meaningless world . . . If the world is a pun, one asserts oneself by punning against it.'[31] I prefer the no less Gallic but franker insolence of Laurent Tailhade's pun on *crachats* (in slang: military decorations): 'Leurs poitrines reluiront des crachats que méritent leurs visages' ('Their chests will glisten with the gongs/gobs of spit that should land on their faces').[32] Or this variant on the sacred *charlatan* pun: Talleyrand saying of the carriage commissioned by Napoleon to crown the Arc de Triomphe, 'Le char l'attend.'[33] It seems indisputable that, like other peoples, 'depuis toujours, les Français se sont amusés à bousculer les mots, à envoyer des tartes à la crème sur les phrases, à mettre des peaux de banane sous les adjectifs pour provoquer leur chute' ('The French have always enjoyed knocking words about, throwing custard pies at sentences, slipping banana-skins under adjectives to trip them up').[34] San Antonio illustrates this with engaging frankness when he admits that the phrase 'décamouiller les bagoules' 'ne correspond à aucune expression argotique. C'est une espèce de tachisme littéraire, un superlatif poussé jusqu'à l'absurde, une mise en demeure du lecteur. Je remplace les mots par les sons' ('does not correspond to any slang expression. It's a kind of literary tachism, a superlative pushed to absurd lengths, a challenge to the reader. I replace words with sounds').[35]

Why then are the French in general sniffier than the British about puns? A leading Shakespeare and Sterne scholar and translator, Henri Fluchère, holds that the French separate sharply high literature and 'le Café de Commerce' – that mythical locus of average French discourse.[36] Another separation would be that between the factual and the comic, as if reality could not be funny in itself. It's as though Cartesian dualism operated also here, severing not only the mind from the body, but also the comic from higher truths. This would leave mainly *invented* humour (wit at one extreme and *le loufoque*, the French form of whimsy, at the other). If French is, as its champions proclaim, expert in abstraction, this might reduce the play between the literal and the figurative, on which punning so heavily depends. No people write so abstractly about the body as they. They cannot even decide whether to call the genitals ('the private parts', as the British say reasonably, for they are generally covered up) 'les parties honteuses' ('the shameful parts') or 'les parties nobles' ('the noble parts'). It may be too, that the golden (and tautological) rule of French composition: 'Une idée par paragraphe et un paragraphe par idée' militates against multi-layered meanings, as does the national trait, devised by Anon, that 'le lecteur français est peu enclin à comprendre deux pensées à la fois' ('the French reader is disinclined to understand two ideas at the same time'). On the other hand, the French might be better at twisting, as they have a firmer sense of tradition, of what has already been said on the subject. This obviously produces a more incestuous and drier kind of wordplay. The French can be economical (hence perhaps their reputation for wit, so reliant on brevity). The difference is between 'la fable-express' typified by Alphonse Allais, a brief story or poem with a punchline punning on a set expression, and the longer-winded 'Upon My Word' type of shaggy-dog story. English humour blows cold (the deadpan, the poker-face), and warm. This is what John Weightman terms 'whimsy', which, he argues, 'supposes that the jester is performing a self-deprecating act in front of a society with which he is fundamentally in harmony and in front of a God whose benevolent, paternal authority he ultimately accepts'.[37]

But all interracial comparisons are odious, and none more so than those which equate, like Koestler, punning with children, lunatics and savages. As well as in sophisticated societies, wordplay is at home in so-called 'primitive' groups. R. Bastide, earlier quoted on the wordplay prevalent in African cosmologies, points out that 'Le Dahomey lui-même a été fondé en tant que nation politique . . . sur un jeu de mot éclaboussé de sang' ('Dahomey itself was founded as a political state on a play on words spattered with blood').[38] One of the reasons is spelled out by Charney:

> In an oral culture, the sounds are literally the basic units of meaning, with almost unlimited possibilities of punning. The awareness of spelling tends to restrict the free play of the comic imagination.[39]

In more detail, G. B. Milner mentions that Polynesian languages:

> have a small inventory of segmental phonemes, and this, in addition to certain other features, such as phonemic length and glottalisation, greatly facilitates punning and other forms of language-based humour.[40]

Comparably, 'a monosyllabic language, like the Chinese, is but, as it were, a cluster of homonyms.'[41] There are, however, prophylactics against puns. John Orr mentions:

> the ingenious devices of tone, key-words, and pseudo-diminutives which the Chinese are obliged to employ to ovecome this destruction of their phonetic material. Otherwise, life would just be one long pun to the poor creatures.[42]

For R. H. Blyth, this fate is in fact gladly shouldered:

> That Chinese language is quite often ambiguous as written and very often as heard is not merely an assistance to the would-be humorist; it is an expression of the Chinese mind, which sees the universe *sub specie facetiarum*, as something paradoxical, indeterminate, incoherent, significantly insignificant, in a word, humorous.[43]

According to Huizinga, the natives of Central Buru in Indonesia practise ceremonial antiphony, a ritualized wordplay: 'Allusion, the sudden bright idea, the pun, or simply the sound of words themselves, where sense may be completely lost'.[44] The 'sudden bright idea': as good a definition as any of the pun, which is the opposite of verbal hindsight, 'l'esprit de l'escalier'. That the ideas are not unfailingly bright is proved by the categorization in Aarne/Thompson's compendious study of folklore, 'Stupid Stories Depending on Puns'.[45]

Interlingua

'A consciously created, artificial language would allow no homonymic clashes,' states John Orr.[46] I checked with an Esperanto specialist and met a contradiction. Not only are they possible, but this created tongue has arranged for a range of rhetorical terms to cover the varieties: *vortludo*, *mistrancô* (a miscut or slice, and a second word for 'pun'), *sonalterno* (Spoonerism), *proksimumo* (an *à-peu-près*), *senco-turno* (wordplay), *pintumo* (*pointe*).[47] Esperanto, by definition, straddles existing languages. The fork-tongued pun is by essence translingual. In its imperial days, Vienna was a linguistic melting-pot, and I have sometimes wondered whether Freud's, and his patients', interest in punning is connected with this social fact of life. Earlier, the polyglot scholars of the Middle Ages and the Renaissance maintained the ancient macaronic tradition. But anyone with more than a smattering of another language can throw false bridges across the gap and create the true universal idiom, punning. 'Ubi benny, ibi patria', as the drug-addict said. A Frenchman might typify buggery as 'vice a tergo'. Swift opined: 'Life is but a vapour, car elle va pour la moindre chose.'[48] Eleanor Roosevelt, discussing democracy with an oriental ambassador, asked: 'And when did you last have an election?' The diplomat, with some embarrassment, answered, 'Before blekfast'.[49] The game of 'fractured French' extracts from that language phrases which could be read as English ('coup de grâce': lawnmower). Conversely, we can find, or more strictly project like a cuckoo, meanings in other tongues which are not there to its native speakers. Among the four types of interpretation of the Torah comes *sod*, 'the secret, mystical, esoteric meaning contained beneath the surface of a word or passage'.[50] In the teeth of plural meanings, many of us mortals have similarly uttered 'Sod'. We find buried treasures in alien tongues.

> The word *pun*, in Malay, is 'literally untranslatable'. It is an emphasising word that 'lights up' the semanteme that goes before . . . There is no single meaning for *pun*, and it is hard to get at its roots and origin; its correct use is incredibly difficult to learn.[51]

Quite so.

Punning appeals particularly to exiles (whether external or inner) for, having two homes and languages, the exile has a binary, split perspective (or strabismus) on his adopted culture: Ionesco, Beckett, Nabokov, Joyce – but not, I think, Conrad. It is hard to be entirely serious in your non-native tongue – or even, unrelievedly, in the maternal. You see the second language from the outside, and its mechanisms, its automatisms, are that much more apparent to you. As Brigid Brophy's ambivalent Irish 'hero' puts it:

I was, perhaps, ripe for . . . defoliation by linguistic leprosy. I had many branches but no root. Transplanted, I had become derooted and derouted. I have no – I haven't quite a – native language.[52]

This process of estrangement can thus happen also within a native language, as Sartre spotted in Flaubert. Your own tongue, as we all know, can feel thick in your mouth.

Linguistic exile can be immensely productive. Nabokov was warned by Edmund Wilson when starting on the American scene: 'Do please refrain from puns, to which I see you have a slight propensity. They are pretty much excluded from serious journalism here.'[53] Luckily, Nabokov ignored this unsound advice, to the extent that the hero of his novel *Despair* toys with the idea of calling his memoirs *Crime and Pun*, thus rejoining the notion of the pun as outrage. As Ciancio remarks: 'Nabokov forces us to "earwitness" – another of his neologisms – the primal sonorities of the grotesque.' For Ciancio, Nabokov is not out merely to amuse, but to heighten 'the artificiality of language and, as the puns pile up, [to strain] the sense of his world to the bursting point'.[54] Eric Korn puts a similar idea more gastronomically:

> Nabokov's puns, echoes and chimes are not inserted currants but the texture of the poetry itself; and the resulting confection is a miraculous millefeuille or, if you prefer, a madeleine . . . Polyglottery becomes not a stumbling-block but a springboard, and the pun is restored to a structural rôle in prose.[55]

Jean Arp chose to write in French instead of his own German: 'Je me suis décidé à rédiger directement en français parce que maîtrisant moins cette langue, je m'y dépaysais davantage' ('I decided to write directly in French because as I had less control over this language I was more adrift in it').[56] Samuel Beckett also elected French for very similar reasons: he wanted to escape the facile momentum, the contemptible familiarity, of his native language. Writing in French has assisted him in his quest for lessness; he is a whispering barker offering amazing reductions. Just as he breaks down the movement of his figures in a landscape into hobbling on crutches, falling over, crawling and terminal stasis, so he decomposes the set expressions of his adopted language. The French form 'ne pas savoir à quel saint se vouer' ('not to know which saint to devote oneself to/to be at one's wit's end') is made over to 'connaître le saint, tout est là, n'importe quel con peut s'y vouer' ('finding the saint, that's the sod of it, any twat can devote himself to that'),[57] His residual people are at their wit's end, and the foreign, analytic gaze and ear underline the situation. He views life as a bad joke, to be answered with understandable unkindness, in kind. 'What but an imperfect sense of humour could have made such a mess of chaos. In the beginning was the pun.'[58] Just before this passage, a reference is made to Joe Miller. Beckett cannot keep his mind off bad jokes, and so the seeming criticism of the pun here is probably tongue-in-cheek. Ackerley comments on this passage:

> And so on, in fact, until the end, when 'excellent gas superfine chaos', brings Murphy's body to its ultimate stasis, its final quiet. The pun implied in Murphy's death (gas creating *chaos*) may or may not be a good joke, but in Murphy's progress from young aspirant to old suspirant the puns reveal more than simply Beckett's imperfect sense of humour; rather they create within the novel a deeper complexity which leads the reader to a more humane understanding of the mess of chaos which is Murphy's life (and death).

I jib at the last sentence, and Beckett himself has disclaimed that 'deeper complexity' which critics are forever foisting on his work. ('Gas', by the way, is widely accepted as having been suggested by the Greek χάος, and so Murphy's guess is as good as the professionals'). Etymology, too, operates interlingually. Ackerley teams up with some of the better views on the pun when he writes:

> As a figure of language, the pun combines the extremes of both the rational and the irrational. Its insistence upon the syzygy of ideas normally distinct offers to our rational understanding a challenge not dissimilar to that of the Cartesian duality: on the one hand, the yoked components are the 'same'; on the other hand, they are 'different' . . . Janus-like, the pun faces both creation and chaos . . . the light and the dark.[50]

That Cartesian duality is another magnet for Beckett in choosing French as an alternative language. His gallows humour is perhaps best typified by the pun implicit in much of his work, on *asile*/asylum: his creatures find that any shelter is another madhouse, and that goes for the brain inside the skull.

Of Beckett's mentor, James Joyce, it seems safe to say that *Finnegans Wake* is 'the most thoroughgoing example of multilingual word play ever devised by man'.[60] Joyce has left his mark on the landscape:

> Today at the foot of the path to the summit of Howth where Poldy and Molly lay in that memorable light amid the rhododendrons, a sign evidently placed in all innocence enjoins tourists not to Disturb the Blooms.[61]

The *Wake* is a continuous purple passage, yet blocked by sinusitis, or sinuosity. It is a work of literary and linguistic Stakhanovism, and it encourages matching behaviour in its critics. McLuhan quotes Joyce's retort to one critic of his puns: 'Yes, some of them are trivial and some of them are quadrivial,' and then expatiates on the expatriate patriot:

He means literally that his puns are crossroads of meaning in his communication network, and that his techniques for managing the flow of messages in his network were taken from the traditional disciplines of grammar, logic, rhetoric, on one hand, and of arithmetic, music and astronomy, on the other.[62]

Is it Joyce, or the pun, that makes pedants of us all? I wonder myself whether such unrelenting punning as propels, or clogs, *Finnegans Wake* leads, as its champions claim, to a weird monumentalization, or rather to a mechanical trivialization. What is clear is that Joyce sought to fabricate a synthetic language, expressing in puns and approximations countless similarities transcending language barriers: an international echolalia. Benstock summarizes the orthodox defence:

> Joyce's puns usually have three levels of significance: as serious linguistic manipulations they allow the author to include various concepts, overlapping themes, and levels of meaning in compressed form; as humorous concoctions they grate against our dulled senses – they are the stumbling blocks that make us conscious of every step we take through the *Wake*; as a poetic device they are controlled by a rhythmic logic that creates individual sound patterns at once familiar in rhythm and new in sound.[63]

The whole of *Finnegans Wake* is a vast neologism born of the desire to make new, to make strange. But the new needs the old, the strange needs the familiar to play against, if you want to make your own mother-tongue look and sound foreign, to be xenophonous. Stephen Hero flees the obvious ('The hell of hells') like the plague. It seems to me strange that Joyce's defenders do not see the obvious: that Joyce forces himself, in his polylingual allusiveness, into the most obvious choices. On Joyce's parodies of jingles, Mercier comments: 'The more familiar the underlying jingle, the more extravagantly can Joyce counterpoint his puns against it without the experienced readers losing the melodic line altogether.'[64] Kenner illustrates the danger. After quoting a long passage from the *Wake*, he goes on:

> This is musical bric-à-brac in God's plenty, again recognizable (and the passage readable) to the extent that its components are reducible to dead lists whose members prompt their neighbours into visibility. 'Let every sound of a pitch keep still in resonance' says 'Let every son of a bitch keep still in reverence', reverence being defined as a state of being overwhelmed by this piece that passeth understanding, the only parts of which that we can read are the parts we have somehow read before.[65]

This strikes me as abdication of the critical faculties; I could not concur less. Allusiveness and corniness are blood brothers; Joyce is hag-ridden by what he is avowedly rejecting. He is repeating, with variations, not creating. 'Joyce creates "tautautologically" and in so doing makes the word "tautologically" become what it describes.'[66] The danger – and in present circumstances this is no joke – is redundancy. Joyce's magistrate-like verdict – 'Every word will be bound over to carry three score and ten toptypsical readings' – sounds like penal servitude for life.[67] I hear more jingling than jangling, unlike David Nokes, who says of Joyce's 'epiphanies' that they are 'acts of verbal magic that give old words a rub and make them new, offering not a jingle of words, but a jangle of ideas'.[68]

McAlman cannot be wrong when he ventures that it is 'possibly necessary to "trance" oneself into a state of word intoxication, flitting-concept inebriation, to enjoy this work to the fullest'.[69] I must ask whether Clive Hart fully realizes how damning and daunting he is being when he writes of the *Wake*:

> The word-play creates, in the long run, no emotionally charged atmosphere at all. It comes to be accepted, just as the ordinary reader of an ordinary book accepts the usual conventions of language. After a few hundred pages we are so saturated with puns that nothing surprises, nothing shocks; the mind's ear takes part-writing for granted, the mind's eye is fixed in a permanent state of multiple vision.[70]

I can see the logic of Joyce's position. When a culture is felt to be atomized, then a habit of punning may well come into its own as a piously optimistic means of imposing some kind of order, however artificial. That is, if you cannot have sequential order, you can at least try for superimposed or parallel equivalents. Then you achieve chimes, refrains, variations, if not the straightforward music of logic. Mayoux talks of 'une métaphysique du calembour', by which he means 'un monde où la diversité et l'unicité des phénomènes ne sont que l'illusion sous laquelle se dissimule l'éternelle répétition de quelques combinaisons simples' ('a world where the diversity and uniqueness of phenomena are merely the illusion beneath which is hidden the endless repetition of a few simple combinations').[71] This apparently abstract and arid analysis seems to me to get closer to the bleak heart, or heartlessness, of Joyce's vision than the chummy, hanging-on glosses of his admirers. Hugh Kenner's verve is of this kind:

> The *Wake* is ideally a book for perhaps twelve people (more get unruly), not people keeping silence either but shouting out the words. It is part of the Irish perception of the unnaturalness of reading, that written stuff trances people into a solitude of sitting very still and keeping very mum, which is no way to be; and it is that ideal reader, remade into a multitude, who is meant, like the old languages of Ireland, to leap up shouting, 'Did ye think I was dead?'[72]

It sounds like Christ reincarnated, what with the *twelve* disciples. Twelve is also a seminar number and the *Wake* must be more often read in this context than in the private chair. But multitudes, no. As Mario Praz says of Joyce's synthetic tongue: 'the juxtaposition of different languages was for Joyce a first step towards the creation of an ultrasonic language, a language that falls on deaf ears as far as common mortals are concerned.'[73] Joyce cannot escape his circle, and fittingly I end this section with the phrase of one of his neophytes with whom I started it, for Joyce is circular. Brigid Brophy says: 'We are in the grips of compunsion.'[74] The translingual pun disappears up its own Erse. Shem the Penman is too unremittingly Shem the Pun-man, even for my bad taste.

Translingualism suggests translation (and *Finnegans Wake* has recently been made over into French). Puns (in this respect as in several others like poetry) are often held to be untranslatable. Poets and punners try, like a Tokyo subway official, to cram in ever more, and thus the normal, weighty enough problems, of matching one language by another are compounded. Addison's confident test has all the often spurious logic of the Age of Reason, wishing to condemn one kind of wit by using another:

> The only way . . . to try a Piece of Wit is to translate it into a different language, if it bears the Test you may pronounce it true; but if it vanishes in the Experiment, you may conclude it to have been a Punn. In short, one may say of a Punn as the Country-man described his Nightingale, that it is *vox et praeterea nihil*, a Sound, and nothing but a Sound.[75]

All that this test proves in fact is that even languages have an area of privacy and idiosyncrasy. For his part, Voltaire, in his report on English comedy, links the ideas of translating and of explicating: 'La plaisanterie expliquée cesse d'être plaisanterie: tout commentateur de bons mots est un sot' ('A joke once explained ceases to be a joke. Every commentator on witticisms is a fool').[76] Max Eastman puts it more picturesquely: 'You cannot enjoy an explained joke for the same reason that you do not laugh when tickled by an ant – namely, that the ant is serious and so are you.'[77] But frontiers can be crossed and moods shared. Voltaire is equally famous for the episode in *Candide*, in the Eldorado section, where the benevolent king's interpreted jokes remain amusing to the visitors, which astonishes the hero more than anything else he encounters. And the proponents of the superiority-theory of laughter can even agree on this point. 'When we understand a joke in a foreign language, we show teeth with more than usual insistence, because we celebrate a twofold triumph – that of understanding the joke and that of understanding the language.'[78] I cannot seriously deny that many puns *are* untranslatable, though I remain convinced that this fact proves nothing against the pun as such. As they are so often approximations, we can exact on occasion a rough justice. For example, Cocteau's comment on Rousseau's account of being spanked by the sister of the Protestant pastor who was his guardian, 'Le postérieur de Jean-Jacques est-il le soleil de Freud qui se lève? J'y distingue plutôt le clair de lune romantique,' goes not too protestingly into: 'Is this portrait of Jean-Jacque's backside the first rosy light of Freudian psychology? Or is it rather the moonshine of Romanticism?' This improves upon the original in one sense if not in another.

Curiosa et Erotica

As Alice might have said. One place where tongues do actually meet is in lovers' mouths, the area Queneau called 'la languistique'.[79] Brigid Brophy rejoyces: 'It is a very daycent class of fellatio you meet travelling Aer Cunnilingus.'[80] The sweet (or sour) smell of suck-sex. Like fleas and puns, sex gets everywhere; it crosses all frontiers, invades all zones, whether erogenous, topographical or semantic. Legman, on the whole hostile to puns, knows how to find them in the unlikeliest places:

> The word 'Horn Book' originally referred to a sort of kindergarten battledore on which was tacked a slip of paper with the alphabet and the Lord's Prayer printed on it, and covered with a strip of transparent horn to protect the print from children's grimy hands. By extension, the term has come to mean any primer . . . of sex-technique, with a pun on the word 'horn'.[81]

Already in the nursery children have dirty hands, and minds. As Ellis reminds, 'wit' has had the meanings of pudendum and penis as well as its intellectual signification.[82] The links are inescapable. 'Sex is the mode of social adhocism,' for it is 'after all the putting together of a purposeful hybrid'.[83] According to Guiraud: 'Une énorme partie, sans doute la plus grande partie des mots de la langue, comporte, en puissance, une image sexuelle que le moindre contexte suffira à actualiser' ('A huge proportion, no doubt the greatest part of the words of a language, contain potentially a sexual image which any context can bring to the fore'). The verb is a copula: 'L'acte sexuel est le mode de représentation de la relation transitive d'où il résulte que tout verbe transitif contient en puissance une image sexuelle' ('The sexual act is the mode of representation of the transitive relationship, and so any transitive verb contains a potential sexual image').[84] Language has great potentiality. As Ponge writes of words: 'C'est leur copulation que réclame l'écriture (véritable ou parfaite): c'est l'orgasme qui en résulte, qui provoque notre jubilation' ('It is their copulation that writing (actual or ideal) calls for; it is the ensuing orgasm which makes us exult').[85] Here are three examples of such celebration (of language and of sexuality):

'L'acte sexuel, acte gratuit à la portée de toutes les bourses' ('The sexual act, a gratuitous/free-of-charge act to suit all pockets/balls'); 'It wasn't so bad living in my old man's scrotum, as far as I can recall. It was warm and humid, and there was lots of companionship. I had a ball' (a nice joke about ante-natal memories); a toast to a lesbian couple: 'Nos félicitations aux deux cons joints' 'Our congratulations to the happy couple/linked cunts').[86] Barthes talks of Sade's 'arithmetic of pleasure', as in this proliferation of words for the same fundamental act: 'Me voilà à la fois incestueux, adultère, sodomite.'[87] (I am reminded here of the lapsing headline: 'Population of US broken down by age and sex'.)[88]

After this frank opening, we move to innuendo, the field of the equivoque, and run the risk, as I have gladly throughout, of being thought to belong to the 'critical Playboy Club' with its many members.[89] It may be disappointing that terms like 'suggestive' or 'innuendo' itself should have come to have almost uniquely erotic connotations, for it limits their deployment. After all, religious and political parables or fables are also double-meanings, and they are seeking to convey complex spiritual or seriously practical messages. Freud quotes Lipps on this question of the understatement which packs in extra:

> A joke says what it has to say, not always in few words, but in *too* few words – that is, in words that are insufficient by strict logic or by common modes of thought and speech. It may actually say what it has to say by not saying it.

Suggestion, we might say, means making the import of an utterance conspicuous by its absence. Freud calls this 'allusion by means of omission'.[90] Fill in the details yourselves. As Duisit says of eighteenth-century French libertine writing: 'L'emploi de mots innocents comme *guitare*, *sarabande*, est toujours susceptible d'abriter des interprétations scabreuses. En fait, le jeu de mots existe partout, mais il n'est jamais affiché'. ('The use of innocent words like *guitar, saraband*, is always liable to let in bawdy interpretations. Indeed wordplay is ubiquitous but never blatant').[91] There is a splendid scene in Laclos' *Liaisons dangereuses*, in which the rake uses a courtesan's naked back as a writing-desk on which to compose a letter to his prudish target. He describes the ready flesh as if it were a wooden object, referring to it as the 'holy altar' of his love.[92] The whole sequence is a pun, a double entendre in action. It is naked to the reader but clothed to the recipient. The active receiver of any text, as we saw in the previous section, can plant meanings where they were not intended. Stanford writes:

> It is the duty of the legislator to take all possible precautions to avoid such uncertainties, just as a poet must, as far as he can, choose his words so that no incongruous-sounding meaning may intrude. In some ways, it is beyond the

powers of even the most ingenious writers to accomplish this, for there are refinements of *doubles entendres* that only one in a million will excogitate, and also, no matter what the poet does he cannot control the semantic development of words after his death.

He adduces Ausonius' obscene twists on Virgil's 'innocent phrases'.[93] It is that one in a million excogitating, and even more the millions who do it as against the one who feels pure enough to complain, that makes me doubt whether legislation has any role in this matter. I find 'pornography' a dirty word, though there is a place for 'obscenity'. 'Deliberate distortion and deformation of words and expressions, which is so dear to vulgar minds, has the sole purpose of exploiting innocent occasions for hinting at forbidden topics.'[94] Nobody can deny the aggressive purpose behind such tactics. As Freud charges:

> Smut is thus originally directed towards women and may be equated with attempts at seduction. If a man in a company of men enjoys telling or listening to smut, the original situation, which owing to social inhibitions cannot be realised, is at the same time imagined. A person who laughs at smut that he hears is laughing as though he were the spectator of an act of sexual aggression.[95]

The only objection to make to this hypothesis is to question why Freud confines such behaviour to the one sex, when both practise it. By analogy with Tacitus' famous maxim 'Omne ignotum pro magnifico' (we over-populate the empty space of our ignorance), someone coined once the counterpart: 'Omne ignotum pro obscaeno' (we sully what is beyond us). Obscene innuendo, feigning reserve, provokes a visible response. It enables us to have it, like the actress with the bishop, both ways. The more openly obscene, of course, steps up the aggression, but is clearly more than this.

> The mechanics of metaphorical obscenities are similar to the mechanics of dreams, wit and other more or less dissociated states of mind. In all these activities the mind manipulates comparisons, symbols, and verbal displacements to identify objects and acts subject to underlying feelings of hostility, anxiety, and desire, and to achieve pleasure in that expression.[96]

In addition, as Kirk indicates, 'obscenity, of course, was common ritual practice, useful for keeping away evil spirits or for promoting fertility.'[97] In all these ways, obscenity is *necessary*, and is stifled only at great cost.

Strongest of all the verbal aggressions is the scatological. What Freud reserves for infancy or neurotics should probably be extended to us all: 'Throughout the whole range of the psychology of the neuroses, what is sexual includes what is excremental, and is understood in the old, infantile sense.'[98] One of the very words for double entendre, 'cacemphaton' (called also 'turpis locutio'), has a scatological ring to it: caca + fart. Zola's novel, *La Terre*, in which one of his peasants lets off resoundingly on many pages, illustrates the splendid gratuitousness of much scatology: fart for fart's sake. A countryman of 'Le Pétomane' is ideally suited to link this whole natural if antisocial phenomenon with comedy itself when he writes: 'Liés aux deux extrémités du tube digestif, le rire, qui est le pet de la bouche et le pet, qui est le rire de l'anus' ('Tied to the two opposite ends of the digestive tube, laughter, which is a mouth-fart, and fart, which is anus-laughter').[99] Beckett even extends it to his own art: 'My work is a matter of fundamental sounds (no pun intended).'[100] I have quoted earlier Hugo's remark that 'le calembour est la fiente de l'esprit qui vole,' which would suggest that the pun itself is faecal by nature. It certainly can be in its context (cf. Dundes' term 'latrinalia' to distinguish lavatorial inscriptions from other and more public graffiti), and in its practice, as in Desnos' anti-religious jibe: 'La Trinité: l'émanation des latrines'.[101]

After the heavy breathing and the straining, the breath can finally come, more boyscoutishly, in short pants, as I turn to the less warlike and more consensual forms of eroticism. I talked earlier of the 'armed rapport' between Shakespeare's lovers, their war-games. Huizinga attaches the concept of play not so much to the sexual act itself (though this has its moments of high and low comedy, as befits any activity forever threatened by fiasco) as 'the road thereto, the preparation for and introduction to "love", which is often made enticing by all sorts of playing'.[102] Foreplay, by-play, wordplay. Most of us read books at half-arm's length, just about the right distance. I would describe this not as scepticism, but rather as that delectable state of mind which leads us to say to a person we find attractive but disconcerting: 'You're having me on' (or, less passively, 'I take your point'). The sexual undertones seem to me essential. Double meanings are often akin to verbal seduction, if made subtly, or, if uttered brutally, to verbal rape. Teasing or flirting is a stimulating experience, and it does not rule out the possibility of going beyond the brink and taking the plunge. I am talking of partnerships (however unstable). Puns are the coupling of things that do not customarily cohabit. Coleridge expresses all this beautifully when he says of puns that they are:

> analogous to sudden fleeting affinities of mind. Even as in a dance, you touch and join and off again, and rejoin your partner . . . They too not merely conform to, but are of and in and help to form the delicious harmony.[103]

It takes two to love: it takes two (words or phrases) to pun. I said in the section on advertising that we double up in both pain and laughter. When short of space, we also double up by sharing a bed, and of course when we accelerate our pace. In all this, the erotic and the verbal collaborate. René Crevel celebrates 'le jeu des idées, quand, enfin, le verbe *jouer* n'est plus un doublet parent pauvre du verbe *jouir*' ('the play of ideas, when at last the word to *play* is no longer the poor relation of the verb to *climax*').[104] This is the erotics of thinking. Tony Tanner would radicalize this:

> We may say that puns and ambiguities are to common language what adultery and perversion are to 'chaste' (i.e. socially orthodox) sexual relations. They both bring together entities (meanings/people) that have 'conventionally' been differentiated and kept apart; and they bring them together in deviant ways, bypassing the orthodox rules governing communications and relationships. (A pun is like an adulterous bed in which two meanings that should be separate are coupled together). It is hardly an accident that *Finnegans Wake*, which arguably demonstrates the dissolution of bourgeois society, is almost one continuous pun (the connection with sexual perversion being quite clear to Joyce).[105]

I doubt myself whether puns will help to wither away the state, but this passage illustrates very well the links between outrage and punning, as well as the dangers of analogy. Such dangers lie not only in punning, however, but in how it is received and judged. On a comparable tack to Tanner, Valesio switches the perspective from the wordplay threatening the state to society rejecting or relegating wordplay:

> Incest is felt as a threat, because it shatters the equilibrium of kinship systems by obscuring the distinction between permissible and non-permissible mates; in an analogous way, verbal folklore, as realized in figure of speech, is felt as a threat, because it shatters the formal equilibrium of language by obscuring the relationship between related and unrelated words; more specifically by relating words above and beyond the framework of etymological kinships and grammatical paradigms. In both threats lurks the danger of madness.[106]

The incubus of analogy plagues all of us, and who is the madder, he who puns or he who fears punning?

Conclusion

To forge a picture that will pass for true.
Robert Graves, 'The Devil's Advice to Story-Tellers'

Non veritas sed verba amanda!
(Words are more lovable than truth.)[1]

Why defend wordplay? Play is indefensible. It simply is. Perhaps nothing else simply is quite so exquisitely and wholeheartedly as play. In studying the ludic element in culture, literary and everyday, I should logically also posit a similar element in those who receive and respond to wordplay: that is, all of us. Punning is a free-for-all available to everyone, common property; it is a democratic trope. It is the stock-in-trade of the low comedian and the most sophisticated wordsmith: James Joyce and Max Miller (and who comes first?). It is and always has been. God was the first logonaut ('Tu traverses le lexique avec la prestesse d'une fusée interstellaire en véritable logonaute que tu es' ('You traverse the lexis with all the velocity of a space-rocket like the true logonaut you are') is the accolade granted to one of Queneau's figments).[2] As God's figments we have followed the lead: 'One of the first uses to which man put his gift of speech was to play upon words and bring them into a connexion, often arbitrary and fanciful, on the ground of some superficial resemblance between them.'[3] Even while acknowledging its eternity, students of punning yet feel constrained to temper their enthusiasm by doubts and qualifications.

> Le jeu de mots, toujours métaphorique, est une petite paraphrase, c'est un jeu de cache-cache, ou de 'cherchez le trésor' . . . Mais ce non-dit demeure peut-être en fin de compte un vide, un non-sens, une absence de profondeur.
>
> (Wordplay, always metaphorical, is a miniature paraphrase, a game of hide-and-seek or treasure-hunt. But this unsaid statement maybe remains, when all is said and done, a void, a non-meaning, an absence of depth.)[4]

I could in fact construct a set of parallel antitheses, which might seem suitable for the highly contestable pun, but it seems more interesting to observe one such student in the act of apparent self-contradiction, which is even more fitting for so self-evidently ambivalent a mode. Friedrich Schlegel placed an each-way bet on this barb. At one moment, 'the original form of poetry is wordplay'; at another, 'there is a form of wit which is like the excrement of the mind.'[5] Koestler, too, vacillates: 'Most puns strike one as atrocious, perhaps because they represent the most primitive form of humour; two disparate strings of thought tied together by an acoustic knot.' (As always with Koestler, the reader needs to resist the hectoring but dubious clarity of the image used.) A further mechanistic recipe is: 'Any two frames of reference can be made to yield a comic effect of sorts by hooking them together and infusing a drop of malice.' Then his historical sense makes him concede that:

> games based on sound-affinities have exercised a perennial attraction on the most varied cultures; anagrams, acrostics, and word-puzzles; incantations and verbal spells; hermeneutics and Cabala, which interpreted the Scriptures as a collection of the Almighty's hidden puns, combining letter-lore with number lore.[6]

Where does he finally stand? In a straddle-position, no doubt, like the pun itself. Koestler, however, would no doubt agree that a real danger for any free association is that it may degenerate into automatic amalgams. False linkages are constructed daily by overlords and underdogs, and by the chief sinner in all human affairs, and in this sentence: generalization.

Some critics of punning sound like the probably apocryphal Congressman who 'proposed a constitutional amendment to ban puns; but Prohibition should have taught him that such evils as drinking, gambling, whoring and punning, cannot be eliminated by edict.'[7] His no less unlikely French counterpart, the minister Aspiquet, wanted to put a tax on puns.[8] When I myself talk of the oblique pun, of glancing wit, I must never forget that many dislike epidermic humour: brittle, smart-aleck, 'clever-clever', or even 'clever' wordplay. Nor that there are balletic puns and galumphing ones. It must be the second kind that made Proust himself ('Je n'ai pas l'art du calembour') and one of his heroines, Mme de Guermantes, go on the defensive. It is said of her that 'elle détestait les calembours et n'avait hasardé celui-ci ["quand on parle du Saint-Loup"] qu'en ayant l'air de se moquer d'elle-même' ('she loathed puns and had only ventured this one ("When you talk of Saint-Loup/the devil") with an air of self-mockery').[9] But doubts can cut far deeper: 'Can the profoundest truths about Man', asks a reviewer of Lacan's *Ecrits*, 'be expected to come from minds distinguished in the main by wit, by combinatory cleverness?'[10] I hope the answer (leaving Lacan out of it) is 'yes', but the suspicion is entirely reasonable. Such sceptics accuse inveterate punners of letting language do their thinking for them, of playing possum while feigning to be tigerish, of capitalizing on the cheap.

The pun is often charged with parasitism, but fleas go *ad infinitum*; it is a continuum. Art is parasitic on daily life, all artists on their predecessors, thinkers on thinkers and scientists on scientists; and children on parents. We are all up to our ears in debt. The pun recognizes this fact of life. Language itself is indebted, interconnected. Like synaesthesia, where the senses cross boundaries, there is phonaesthesia (which embraces consonance and assonance): 'Words sounding alike suggest a common general meaning.'[11] These are isophonic words, eminently confusible. We are all conscious of this fact. How often in ordinary conversation, broadcasting or in public speaking, do we utter or hear these significant qualifiers, these tokens of linguistic self-consciousness? 'If you take my meaning', 'Sorry I'll read that again', 'If I may rephrase that', 'So to speak', 'Or words to that effect', 'In more senses than one'. Even if we don't all gaily do it, we are very aware of its existence. Perhaps the best defence of wordplay is to do it. Having punned on 'raisonnement/résonnement' (which encapsulates the ambiguity of wordplay: logical meaning/sound echoes), Ponge was rebuked by Jean Paulhan: 'De plus en plus creux, tu n'exprimes plus que l'orgueil' ('You're getting hollower every day and totally vain'). To which Ponge retorted: 'Mais bien sûr! Qu'est-ce qui résonne mieux que ce qui est creux? Les tuyaux d'orgue sont aussi creux' ('But of course! What resounds better than a hollow object? Organ-pipes are hollow, too').[12] Wordplay suits those unconvinced that rational argument suffices. These would include: advertisers, ironists, religious leaders, politicians, liars, writers of all kinds, madmen – and all of us at some moments of our lives. Puns appeal to those who want to say several things at once, and for whom unambiguous utterance is too linear and restricting. Double-talk is not necessarily mendacious. Sometimes, if we wish to amuse, to preserve but share secrecy, to convince the doubting, it is the only way to communicate. Hood lent to Dr Johnson these words: 'Sir, if a man means well, the more he means the better.'[13] Double talk can be plain speech, Christ knew. Not only the Portuguese God of the proverb dear to Claudel can write straight in crooked lines.

Besides, it is good for you, though punning, like laughter itself, need not involve explosive noise nor even moving the muscles of eyes, cheeks, lips, chest or stomach, for we can laugh in the mind.

> As for health of a body, I look upon punning as a nostrum, a *Medicina Gymnastica*, that throws off all the bad humours, and occasions such a brisk circulation of the blood, as keeps the lamp of life in a clear and constant flame.[14]

Such puffs are useful, since the tendency is to regard punning as a disease. Coleridge writes very fair-mindedly against this facile temptation:

> In the Scriptures themselves these plays upon words are to be found as well as in the best works of the ancients and in the most delightful parts of Shakespeare; and because this additional grace, not well understood, has in some instances been

converted into a deformity – because it has been forced into places where it is evidently improper and unnatural, are we therefore to include the whole application of it in one general condemnation?[15]

The defence, however valid, smacks perhaps too much of sanity. Another poet, Valéry, plumps brazenly for lauding the very falsity of 'false wit':

Nous serions peu de chose, et nos esprits bien inoccupés, si tous ces mythes, ces fables, ces religions, ces allégories, ces calembours sanctifiés, ces hypothèses, ces figures de langage et ces pseudo-problèmes de métaphysique, n'existaient point. C'est le faux qui colore et fait vivre le vrai.

(We would not be worth much, and our minds would be underemployed, if all these myths, fables, religions, allegories, sanctified puns, hypotheses, figures of speech and metaphysical pseudo-problems did not exist. It is falsity that gives colour and life to truth.)[16]

Those graven images of truthfulness, children, do not hold the monopoly, for 'la vérité sort de la bouche des calembours' ('truth comes out of the mouth of puns').[17] Like it or not, 'the pun is at the heart of language.'[18] Though often classified with tongue-twisters, acrostics and other verbal sports, their natural place lies with metaphor, irony: the very foundations of all rhetoric. They are not a device, an instrument to be grasped or spat upon at will, but a whole way of feeling, seeing, thinking and expressing. Nietzsche loved puns; Hartman reveres Nietzsche, and makes the most outrageous claim of all: 'There is no such thing as a good pun. Puns are the only thing beyond good and evil.'[19] This seeks to transcend the for/against syndrome, but this giant step leaves too many interesting questions behind.

Opposites do exist, powerfully, and we have to live in relation to them – for instance, freedom and constraints. The second first. What Wilson says of jokes in general could very plausibly be argued of puns in particular:

It seems that joking is a powerful conservative. Its effects reinforce existing ideology, power, status, morality, norms and values within a society. These conservative functions are achieved most effectively in tribal societies, where joking is demanded in clowning or as a matter of everyday manners. Comparable patterns of joking arise in industrial societies, but are developed by the jokers themselves to serve personal rather than social functions. Through its pleasures and personal utility humour recruits and bribes us to become laughing conservatives. Joking reflects and partially compensates for our failings, dissatisfactions and self-alienation. Freed from ignorance, inhibitions, fear and prejudice, the super-psyche would have no use for humour. You will recognise a Utopia by the complete absence of humour; you will spot superman by his unmitigated, infuriating seriousness.[20]

But what of the zany Big Rock Candy Mountains? Jacob Levine adduces Freud: 'the opposite of humour is not being serious but reality . . . The humour illusion is but one form of the aesthetic illusion . . . In humour, we can both commit sin and enjoy it.'[21] Both these arguments stress the harmlessness of licensed fooling. I have spoken myself of the distance necessary for the proper registering of puns. Is that distance one of safety? Are puns buffer-states against the more unpleasant realities they apparently face up to? Is the displacement-technique so typical of the pun merely a shuffling of the feet? We raised the question especially in the case of Hood, but it has general application. I would say we have seen many examples of subversive, desacralizing puns, and it would be inaccurate to describe them, or humour in general, as inevitably conserva-tive, though, like parody, there seems to be some element of preservation in all forms of witty attack. The rogue socialist, Jules Vallès, who punned for his life, saw no contradiction between this and militancy; in his view, puns do not mean that you do not mean it.

The pun, which spares time, space and effort, if properly aimed, spares no one. Nobody, in his physical or moral person, even in his name, is proof against it. 'Red stern', my English teacher rebaptized me, on raising the cane to punish my temerity in jumping a class. The triumph of the chastiser depends on the discomfiture of the target; the freedom of the one entails the acquiescence of the other. But not only conflict is involved. Simply in terms of the individual, wordplay offers the chance of seeing or hearing double, or of having a second glance, second thoughts. We can all have a second go. Puns are all about entertaining possibilities – a pun itself, where 'entertaining' is both an adjective and a transitive present participle. And this, in turn, is surely what both writing and reading, indeed any thinking, is all about. 'La littérature est le discours construit par excellence, d'où son affinité avec le jeu de mots.'[22] *Construit*: there's the rub. However dependent, as we have seen, on fortuitousness, puns involve effort, if only that of adroit placing and timing. The freedom to pun is always limited, constrained, as Lévi-Strauss stresses in this analogy between *bricolage* (a form of manual punning) and myths:

> Comme les unités constitutives du mythe, dont les combinaisons possibles sont limitées par le fait qu'elles sont empruntées à la langue, où elles possèdent déjà un sens qui restreint la liberté de manoeuvre, les éléments que collectionne et utilise le bricoleur sont 'précontraints'.

> (Like the constituent parts of a myth, whose possible combinations are limited by the fact that they are borrowed from language, where they already have a meaning which restricts their freedom of manoeuvre, the materials which the *bricoleur* collects and uses are 'pre-conditioned'.)[23]

Puns, too, use the means to hand. Like a good crypto-scientist, Todorov exclaims rhetorically: 'Comment systématiser les jeux de mots?' He would clearly love to do so, but is forced to concede that 'les jeux de mots forment une série ouverte'.[24] All attempts to catch wordplay in the web of words are doomed to self-destruction. Perhaps this is why post-structuralists and deconstructionists are so given to it. As well as being verbicide (as O.W. Holmes called it), punning can be suicide. But there are less extremist ways of transgressing our own limits.

The pun demands close collaboration or complicity between reader and author, listener and speaker. Even when exhibiting antisocial animus it animates sociability, albeit on a small scale. This is why Ludovici's description sounds so one-sided: 'To show teeth, therefore, is to make a claim of superior adaptation.'[25] Oneupmanship leaves no space for shared wit. In his chapter on *argot* in *Les Misérables*, Hugo writes: 'Le propre d'une langue qui veut tout dire et tout cacher, c'est d'abonder en figures' ('The characteristic of a language which wants to say everything and conceal everything is to revel in figures of speech').[26] Wordplay communicates to some and withholds from others; or, like a clinging dress, it tells all while showing nothing. The pun is versatile and encourages versatility in its receivers, who identify with the deliverer if the process succeeds. This *esprit de corps* can of course degenerate into *esprit de chapelle* or *esprit de clocher*, mere parochialism.

These French terms do not exclude the British from the phenomenon they designate. Just as wordplay turns on overlap, so there is no final distinction to be made between French and Anglo-Saxons in the matter of punning. We are, of course, more empirical ('Let sleeping dogmas lie', says Anthony Burgess, punning twice in four words, and Lewis Carroll writes, ' "Why," said the Duchess, "the best way to explain it is to do it" ').[27] But Queneau's Duc d'Auge cannot be alone in claiming, 'Moi pas être un intellectuel', in mock-pidgin.[28] Spitzer generalizes, but not unfairly, 'that basic mistrust of language itself which is one of the most genuine features of the Anglo-Saxon character, as opposed to the trust in words by which the Romance peoples are animated'.[29] Even if this were verifiable, how would it explain the greater Anglo-Saxon tolerance of punning? Could it be that uncertainty favours playfulness and confidence solemnity? Whatever the final solution of these posers, the strategy I have adopted throughout has been that of turning, indifferently, to one or the other side of the Channel (and of the Atlantic) for leads or illustration. Even if many puns defy translation, attitudes to them can be shared internationally.

If you keep them to yourself, you risk madness, and we have on numerous occasions veered towards that area. That way madness lies. As Vendryès commented: 'S'il était vrai qu'un mot se présentât toujours avec tous ses sens à la fois, on éprouverait sans cesse dans la conversation l'impression agaçante que produit une série de jeux de mots' ('If it were true that a word always offered all its meanings at the same time, we would experience nonstop in conversation the irritating impression produced by a string of puns').[30] A buzzing, blooming confusion would undoubtedly set in. Even in less extreme hypotheses, the links are there, as Todorov glosses Curtius' view of medieval wordplay: 'Le jeu de mots voisine l'anormal: c'est la folie des mots' ('Wordplay borders on the abnormal: it is madness in language').[31] But it is a 'madness' that *can* be chosen. 'Pour certains individus, le calembour est un violon dingue' ('For some people, the pun is a hobbyhorse/demented violin').[32] After crediting Nabokov with restoring the pun to a structural role in prose, Eric Korn goes on:

> The Victorians banished puns to the parlour or the nursery, and we are still sheepish about serious wordplay. Joyce may have made it respectable, but for Joyce the pun is a universal solvent, all language fused by the 'abnihilization of the etym'. And Paul Schiller's *Psychoanalytic Remarks on 'Alice in Wonderland'* offers a pretty sticky prognosis for Dodgson. The punster is dislocated from the real and can only manipulate its shell. Violence to language expresses murderous feelings. To clinch it: schizophrenics make puns, you make puns, therefore you are schizophrenic.[33]

There are other ways of boldly going where few dare. 'In making puns and jokes, a man behaves in a way that is different from that of the humorless man. He is teetering near the outer edge of our linguistic existence.'[34] He may even fall off the end, as McLuhan demonstrates in describing Echoland, 'the world of acoustic space whose center is everywhere and whose margin is nowhere, like the pun'.[35] Renou manages to keep his feet on the ground when analysing the otherworldly wordplay of Indian religion:

> Ces calembours ne sont pas des fantaisies, si déconcertants qu'ils nous paraissent; ils sont faits en vue d'atteindre une réalité suprasensible. Quand le nom du dieu Indra est expliqué par le verbe *indh* – 's'enflammer', c'est pour dégager une vérité ésotérique, à savoir qu'Indra grâce à son pouvoir inné (*indriya*) 'enflamma' les souffles vitaux à l'origine des temps: c'est pourquoi on l'appelle Indra cryptiquement, 'car les dieux aiment ce qui est cryptique'.
>
> (These puns are not fantasies, however disconcerting they appear to us; they are made so as to attain a reality not of this world. When the name of the god Indra is explained by the verb *indh* – 'to burst into flame', it is so as to release an esoteric truth, namely that Indra, thanks to his innate power (*indriya*) 'inflamed' the vital breath of life at the origin of time. That is why he is cryptically called Indra, 'for the gods love all that is cryptic'.)[36]

The phrase 'more than words can say' (whether this entails gestures, telepathy, silence or Interflora) is a very necessary reminder that, while language may well be all we have, there are times when it simply, or even doubly, is not enough. 'Une thème ludique par excellence, c'est celui de Janus.'[37] Throughout this study, we have met this each-way figure. He is utilized as a pejorative analogy ('Le Janus à deux fronts, l'hébété calembour' – 'The two-faced Janus, the punch-drunk pun'),[38] or the reference to him is meant to suggest enrichment, the bonus of the double ('La nature c'est l'éternel *bifrons*').[39] If Nature itself is double, then the double-dealing pun mimes it. Tanner writes:

> 'Duplicity' is latent in the very nature of the phenomenon of language. The German words used by Freud [in *Jokes and their Relation to the Unconscious*] are *Doppelseitigkeit* and *Doppelzüngigkeit*, the latter meaning literally the 'two-tongued' quality of speech/language.[40]

But is miming only reflection, reiteration? After quoting the currently fashionable view that we humans exert little control over our language ('The *system*, repository of the community's verbalized knowledge about the world, is logically prior to, and more important than, the individual lexical item, which is no more than an agreed form attaching to a selected cluster of semes'), S. J. Newman counter-attacks:

> Now it is the nature of comic art (like Dickens's) to come apart at the semes . . . The novel, like reality itself, isn't a passive monster awaiting exegesis, but alive, perpetually renewing or unmaking itself in the reader's mind. Interpretation is constantly baulked by its linguistic play. No system will contain it . . . Modern Europe . . . has applied comic theory like a tourniquet and waits numbly for the last laugh.[41]

Wordplay, like comic art in general, turns mimesis into an active response, undoing certainties, making them 'come apart at the semes'. The ancient doctrine of homeopathic medicine, 'similia similibus curantur', works here, too. The often painful pun reacts to the pains of living; it can make them more manageable. The pun, or life itself, is the double-cross, or criss-cross, that we have to bear, with a grin. It is neither exclusively conservative nor subversive, but contestatory. Like herbal remedies or palliatives, it extracts from nature (i.e. from the usual run of language) to combat natural ills.

Whatever I say, punning will, for many, remain in bad taste, in bad odour, – stink in their nostrils. 'C'est l'enfant gâté de l'oisiveté et du mauvais goût' ('It is the spoilt child of idleness and bad taste').[42] But bad taste is where we mostly live, and perhaps most honestly live; it is what we most often have in our mouths, just as the commonplace is where the majority live. We are more frequently in a mid-way state than in extreme ones, in excruciation rather than tragedy. The pun is the weapon of those trapped in the middle: the defensive/offensive weapon of ambiguity and scepticism. 'Pourquoi', asks Luc Etienne, 'le mauvais goût ne serait-il pas aussi raffiné que le bon? plus peut-être' ('Why should bad taste not be as refined as good? More so, perhaps?').[43]

Baudelaire rounds off the argument with dandy insolence: 'Ce qu'il y a d'enivrant dans le mauvais goût, c'est le plaisir aristocratique de déplaire' ('What is intoxicating about bad taste is the aristocratic delight in being unpopular that it affords').[44] More mildly, Freud says: 'We do not insist upon a patent of nobility from our examples.'[45] The epitome of bad taste, of course, is to talk of oneself, which I now will do in order to close the circle started by my introduction to this study.

But first, if I favoured Cambridge with quotations pro and con at the outset, I must now redress the balance on behalf of Oxford, or, rather, let it speak for itself. Nicholas Amhurst, of St John's, Oxford, somewhat spoils his eulogy of his university (O! Oxford! thou British paradise!) by some unintentional double meanings: 'What egregious children hast thou to boast of! ... How was I pleased ... to hear my jovial companions display their ambiguous capacities against one another?'[46] Like most I probably prefer such unwitting puns, and, in conversation at least, the extempore variety. 'The best puns depend on spontaneity – a printed, annotated anthology of puns is unreadable.'[47] This is not literally true, as I, for one amongst millions, have read many such. I take the point, however; I calculated that in Crosbie's *Dictionary of Puns*, I was impressed by 15 out of 3,500: ½ per cent. The trouble with all such compilations is that we do not there see the puns in context, or, if we do, it is introduced laboriously. My own enterprise is a four-part brew: part anthology, part gloss, part invention, part speculation. I have thus only sporadically remembered the old warning: 'Critic: stowaway on the flight of someone's imagination'.[48] Among the imaginable defects of my book are that it simultaneously or alternately tells you more than you want to know, or less. It takes in adjacent or distant areas like stray dogs. It protracts key terms beyond danger-point, by a long stretch of the gelastic. (My favourite title for a pop-group would be 'Gutta Percha and his Gelastic Band'). At times I pun to beat the band. (In conversation, I myself rarely pun, but place a pen in my hand, and I can hardly write two sentences without playing on words.) My tone swivels between academic pedantry, journalese and the gutter; between the pedestrian and the jaywalker. This study has been a rough draft in more senses than one: it is a ragbag (or more flatteringly a glory-hole) of random ideas; it may taste to readers like moonshine; but its intention is to let in some bracing air on a cloistered topic. Such an approach has, like elephants' foreskins, enormous drawbacks.[49] Here, there is a bit of everything. I make no apologies. The pun *is* a bit of everything: logic and illogicality, reason and madness, gratuitousness and pointedness. A bastard, a melting-pot, a hotchpotch, a potlatch, pot-luck. There is here, too, a good deal of slippage, but then approximation, *l'à-peu-près*, is of the essence. Some of my harangues are undoubtedly pickled. You may feel that there is too much theory and commentary, and a paucity of practice, of examples. I have a confession to make. I do not actually like many of the puns I encounter, in

Shakespeare or on the streets. I sometimes wonder whether it is not some Platonic Idea of the pun that I am pursuing (Mallarmé: 'L'absente de tous bouquets').[50] I suspect that most of the better puns in this book are 'popular' rather than derived from 'high' literature. There's a turn-up for the book. Pascal was right in speaking of 'opinions du peuple saines'.[51] In addition, of course, I have a weakness for one-liners (and have often mused on how many books could be thus usefully miniaturized). Like the baby demanding its dummy, I'm a sucker for the gag. Just as Huizinga was criticized for subsuming virtually all human activity under the heading 'play', my study must seem at times to be implying that everything is wordplay; that I am Dr. Pun-gloss; that, as Swift ironically noted, puns get everywhere, like fleas; that pun = *pan*. I do not believe this. The pun is not the whole world; only the whole world is that. What I am asking is that if, like flagellation, punning is *le vice anglais*, it should be given its fair crack of the whip, and not be confined to the closet of curiosities. On the other hand, as Marianne Moore said of poetry, I could say of puns: 'There are things that are important/beyond all this fiddle,'[52] – where, as I cannot resist glossing, 'fiddle' evokes the antisocial Nero, nervous compulsion, counterfeit and daylight robbery.

Even so, what I am implicitly recommending throughout is a less solemn, more ludic approach to matters of importance, and I trust that by now nobody any longer translates 'playful' as 'frivolous'. (Some puns are kill-joy, the sort of gags that silence laughter.) Athletes and children play hard, work hard at play. In the north-east of England, 'serious' means 'off the rocker'. Erasmus put it beautifully: 'Rien n'est plus sot que de traiter avec sérieux de choses frivoles; mais rien n'est plus spirituel que de faire servir les frivolités à des choses sérieuses' ('Nothing is more foolish than to talk of frivolous things seriously; but nothing is wittier than to make frivolities serve serious ends').[53] The serio-comic is my preferred mode. I wanted to avoid writing in a style so sober as to teeter on the verge of the teetotal. Without levity there is no true gravity, and freedom from gravity has been a persistent dream since man first tried to fly. If it cannot fly, with its hidden recesses the pun can bound, like a marsupial. I endorse what Eastman calls 'the importance of not being earnest'.[54]

You would expect familiar quotations in any study of Shakespeare. I can make no honest apology if readers have heard of many of the puns and related forms here examined. Just as the pun itself is a salvage-operation on language, so I am trying to rehabilitate the convicted pun. I hope I have given a name, a home and honourable employment to this poor bastard, but I have no desire to domesticate it. My aim has been not to belittle the pun, but to aggrandize it; not to defuse it, but to suggest its range of fire-power. My hobby-horse may well have a spavined gait. If necessary, they shoot horses, don't they? I started with an epigraph from Montaigne, where he dismisses the charge that he is too figurative a writer and proudly accepts that what he writes, he is. Apart from pious intentions, there are giveaways. 'Your favourite joke is your psychological signature. The "only" joke you know how to tell, is you.'[55] I have been another playboy of the western word. The alternative title of this study (apart from the temptation of adding *Kama Sutra II* to the present one) was at one stage: *More Senses Than One*. We should be grateful, indeed, that we enjoy more senses than one, that we have at our disposal more ways than one out (escape-routes) and in (penetration). I second Chesterton's remark: 'I am almost certain that many moderns suffer from what may be called the disease of the suppressed pun.'[56] Like the deeply ambivalent, arrogantly pathetic Humbert Humbert, I end with the despairingly triumphant: 'Oh my Lolita! I have only words to play with.'[57]

Notes

Introduction

1 M. E. de Montaigne, *Essais*, ed. M. Rat. Paris, Garnier, 1958, vol. 3, p. 99.
2 J.-P. Sartre, *L'Idiot de la famille*. Paris, Gallimard, 1971, vol. 2, p. 1978.
3 R. Steele, *Spectator*, ed. D. Bond. London, Oxford University Press, 1965, vol. 3, p. 483.
4 Swift, 'A Modest Defence of Punning', *Collected Writings*, ed. H. Davis and L. Landa. Oxford, Blackwell, 1957, vol. 4, p. 206.
5 B. Blackmantle, *The Punster's Pocket-Book*. London, Sherwood, 1826, p. 10.
6 J. Henley, 'An Oration on Grave Conundrums', *Oratory Transactions*. London, 1728, no. vi, p. 12.
7 J. Addison, *Spectator*, ed. D. Bond. London, Oxford University Press, 1965, vol. 2, p. 261.
8 From Boghouse, Trinity College, Dublin. In R. Reisner and L. Wechsler, *Encyclopaedia of Graffiti*. New York, Macmillan, 1974, p. 70.
9 S. Beckett, *Murphy*. New York, Grove, 1957, p. 65.
10 M. Charney, *Comedy High and Low*. New York, Oxford University Press, 1978, p. 24.
11 E. Kris and E. Gombrich, *Psychoanalytic Explorations of Art*. London, Allen & Unwin, 1953, p. 200.
12 E. Colman, *The Dramatic Use of Bawdy in Shakespeare*. London, Longman, 1974, p. 36.
13 G. Legman, *No Laughing Matter*. London, Granada, 1978, p. 166.
14 G. Lichtenberg, *Reflections*. 1799.
15 P. Guiraud, *L'Argot*. Paris, PUF, 1956, pp. 50, 59.
16 B. Rodgers, *The Queens' Vernacular*. San Francisco, Straight Arrow, 1972, Introduction and pp. 29, 126.
17 O. W. Holmes, 'A Visit to the Asylum for Aged and Decayed Punsters', *Soundings from the Atlantic*. Boston, Ticknor & Fields, 1864, p. 349.
18 Blackmantle, *Punster's Pocket Book*, p. 3.
19 T. Sheridan, 'The Original of Punning from Plato's Symposiacs', in T. Ruddiman, *A Collection of Scarce, Curious and Valuable Pieces*. Edinburgh, 1785, pp. 358–9.
20 J. Dryden, 'Defence of the Epilogue', *Essays*, ed. W. Ker. Oxford, Clarendon, 1926, vol. 1, p. 237.

21 L. Duisit, *Satire, parodie, calembour*. Saratoga, Anma Libri, 1978, pp. 1, 89, 91.

22 C. Baudelaire, 'De l'essence du rire', *Curiosités esthétiques*. ed. H. Lemaître. Paris, Garnier, 1962, p. 263.

23 E. Gilman, *The Curious Perspective: Literary and Pictorial Wit in the Seventeenth Century*. New Haven, Yale University Press, 1978, p. 234.

24 S. Freud, *Jokes and their Relation to the Unconscious*. Harmondsworth, Penguin, 1976, p. 46.

25 L. G. Heller, 'Towards a General Typology of the Pun', *Language and Style*, 7, 1974, p. 272.

26 E. Bergler, *Laughter and the Sense of Humour*. New York, International Medical Book Co., 1956, p. 180.

27 E. Esar, *Comic Encyclopaedia*. New York, Doubleday, 1978, p. 627.

28 R. Colie, *Paradoxia Epidemica*. Princeton University Press, 1966, pp. 44–5.

29 M. Mahood, *Shakespeare's Wordplay*. London, Methuen, 1979, p. 19.

30 E. Esar, *The Humor of Humor*. London, Phoenix House, 1954, p. 70.

31 G. Orwell, *Nineteen Eighty-Four*. Harmondsworth, Penguin, 1956, p. 32.

32 M. Yaguello, *Alice au pays du langage*. Paris, Seuil, 1981, p. 141.

33 P. Valéry, *Oeuvres*. Paris, Gallimard, 1959, vol. 1, p. 687,

34 S. Barnet, 'Coleridge on Puns', *Journal of English and Germanic Philology*, 56(4), 1957, p. 603.

35 See S. Turkle, *Psychoanalytic Politics*. London, Burnett/Deutsch, 1979, p. 244.

36 P. Hughes and P. Hammond, *Upon the Pun*. London, W. H. Allen, 1978, unpaged.

37 Aristotle, *De Sophisticis Elenchis*. 1, 615a, 11.

38 See Barnet, 'Coleridge on Puns', p. 602; and J. Snyder, *Puns and Poetry in Lucretius' 'De Rerum Natura.'* Amsterdam, Grüner, 1980, pp. 62–3.

39 G. Meredith, 'An Essay on Comedy', in W. Sypher (ed.), *Comedy*. New York, Doubleday, 1956, p. 4.

40 Montaigne, *Essais*, p. 1096.

Chapter 1: Shaky Foundations

1 G. de Rocher, *Rabelais' Laughers and Joubert's 'Traité du Ris'*. Alabama University Press, 1979, p. 81.

2 M. Müller, *Biographies of Words*. London, Longman, 1898, p. X.

3 E. Augier, *Gabriella*, II. 4, in *Théâtre complet*. Paris, Calmann-Lévy, n.d., p. 318.

4 L. G. Kelly, 'Punning and the Linguistic Sign', *Linguistics*, 66, 1971, pp. 5, 6.

5 Duisit, *Satire*, p. 60.

6 R. Barthes, *Roland Barthes par Roland Barthes*. Paris, Seuil, 1975, p. 76 (on pp. 76–7 he lists such amphibologies).

7 N. Jacobs, *Naming-Day in Eden*. London, Gollancz, 1958, p. 150.

8 T. Tanner, *Adultery in the Novel*. Baltimore, Johns Hopkins University Press, 1979, p. 335.

9 Mallarmé has an intriguing prose-poem with this title in *Igitur*, ed. Y. Bonnefoy. Paris, Gallimard, 1976, pp. 75–7.

10 F. de Saussure, *Course in General Linguistics*. London, Peter Owen, 1960, pp. 126–7.

11 Charney, *Comedy High and Low*, p. 20.

12 Freud, *Jokes*, p. 41.

13 R. Queneau, *Bâtons, chiffres et lettres*. Paris, Gallimard, 1965, p. 69.

14 F. Paulhan, 'Psychologie du calembour', *Revue des Deux Mondes*, 142, 15 August 1897, pp. 864–5, 881.

15 A. Koestler, 'Humour and Wit', *Encyclopaedia Britannica*, 15th edn, Chicago, Benton, 1974, vol. 9, p. 5 ('Since the step from the sublime to the ridiculous is reversible, the study of humour provides the psychologist with clues for the study of creativity in general').

16 C. Jencks and N. Silver, *Adhocism*. New York, Anchor, 1973, p. 65. (Edward de Bono, in *Lateral Thinking*, Harmondsworth, Penguin, 1977, pp. 110–11 and 34, and in related works, sidesteps along similar paths.)

17 Jencks and Silver, *Adhocism*, p. 70.

18 J. Huizinga, *Homo Ludens*. London, Granada, 1970, pp. 21, 65, 37.

19 E. Benveniste, 'Le Jeu comme structure', *Deucalion*, 2, 1947, p. 164.

20 Swift, 'A Modest Defence of Punning', p. 206.

21 B. Brophy, letter of 12 November 1981.

22 J. Stedmond, *The Comic Art of Laurence Sterne*. Toronto University Press, 1967, p. 44.

23 Sade, quoted in G. Gorer, *The Life and Ideas of the Marquis de Sade*. London, Peter Owen, 1962, p. 153.

24 *The Portable Nietzsche*, ed. W. Kaufmann. New York, Viking, 1975, p. 153.

25 V. Morin, 'Avec San Antonio, un humour en miettes', in *Une Nouvelle Civilisation?* Paris, Gallimard, 1973, pp. 418, 422. (The reference to the 'sens traître' is to the cinematic meaning of *doubler*, to dub, where translation is often, indeed, betrayal.)

26 J. Vendryès, *Le Langage*. Paris, Renaissance du Livre, 1921, p. 209.

27 Duisit, *Satire*, p. 129.

28 M. Winston; 'Black Humor', in M. Charney (ed.), *Comedy: New Perspectives*. New York Literary Forum, 1, 1978, p. 39.

29 W. Jackson, *The Four Ages* (1798), quoted in R. Tuve, *Elizabethan and Metaphysical Imagery*. Chicago University Press, 1947, p. 258.

30 M. Eastman, *Enjoyment of Laughter*. London, Hamish Hamilton, 1937, p. 133.

31 M. Douglas, 'The Social Control of Cognition', *Man*, 3, 1968, p. 373 (cf. 'How do you get four elephants in a Mini? – Two in the back, two in the front').

32 Reader Guide no. 7, British Library, 1980, p. 9.

33 J. Peignot, *Le Petit Gobe-mouches*. Paris, Bourgois, 1979, p. 73; J. Delacour,

Dictionnaire des mots d'esprit. Paris, A. Michel, 1976, p. 56; 'Noctuel', *Dictionnaire franco-rosse*. Paris, Calmann-Lévy, 1965, p. 170; E. Esar, *Comic Dictionary*. New York, Horizon, 1960, p. 28.

34 *OED*, and Skeat's *Concise Etymological Dictionary of the English Language*.

35 L. Spitzer, *Linguistics and Literary History*. Princeton University Press, 1948, p. 7.

36 P. Guiraud, *Le Jeu de mots*. Paris, PUF, 1976, p. 121.

37 See A. Couvray, *Calembours et jeux de mots des hommes illustres anciens et modernes*. Paris, Aubry, 1806, preface.

38 See E. Littré, *Supplément au Dictionnaire de la langue française*. Paris, Hachette, 1873, p. 59.

39 C. Nodier, *Examen critique des dictionnaires de la langue française*. Paris, Delangle, 1828, p. 85.

40 C. Bally, *Linguistique générale et linguistique française*. Berne, Francke, 1950, p. 178.

41 Guiraud, *Jeu de Mots*, p. 97.

42 F. Caradec, 'Le Calembour', in R. Alleau (ed.), *Dictionnaire des jeux*. Paris, Tchou, 1964, p. 85.

43 J. Franklin, *Which Witch?* London, Hamish Hamilton, 1966, p. xviii.

44 R. Barthes, 'L'Ancienne Rhétorique', *Communications*, 16, 1970, p. 174.

45 J.-P. Grousset, *Si t'es gai, ris donc!* Paris, Julliard, 1963, p. 29.

46 J. Crosbie, *Dictionary of Puns*. New York, Harmony, 1977, p. 245.

47 B. Dupriez, *Gradus: les procédés littéraires*. Paris, Union Générale d'Editions, 1980, pp. 332–4.

48 H. Rowley, *More Puniana*. London, Chatto & Windus, 1875, p. 257.

49 Crosbie, *Dictionary of Puns*, p. 13.

50 J. B. Watson, *Behaviourism*. London, Kegan Paul, 1930, pp. 247–8.

51 P. Jennings, *Pun Fun*. Feltham, Hamlyn, 1980, p. 81.

52 C. Bayet, *Victor Hugo s'amuse*. Paris, Atlas, 1955, p. 53.

53 Charney, *Comedy High and Low*, p. 24.

54 H. W. Fowler, *A Dictionary of Modern English Usage*. Oxford, Clarendon, 1965, p. 492.

55 P. Hughes and G. Brecht, *Vicious Circles and Infinity*. Harmondsworth, Penguin, 1971, p. 1.

56 P. H. Davison, 'Popular Literature', *Encyclopaedia Britannica*, 15th edn., vol. 14, p. 806.

57 C. Fadiman, 'Small Excellencies: A Dissertation on Puns', in *Appreciations*. London, Hodder & Stoughton, 1962, p. 174.

58 W. B. Stanford, *Ambiguity in Greek Literature*. New York, Johnson, 1972, p. 72.

59 Tanner, *Adultery in the Novel*, p. 324.

60 M. Corvin, *Petite Folie collective*. Paris, Tchou, 1966, p. 15.

61 E. Auboin, *Technique et psychologie du comique*. Marseilles, n.p., 1948, p. 136.

62 Quoted in Hughes and Brecht, *Vicious Circles*, p. 46.

63 A. Burgess, *Joysprick*. London, Deutsch, 1973, p. 136.

64 J. Wright (ed.), *The English Dialect Dictionary*. Oxford, Frowde, 1905.
65 Eastman, *Enjoyment of Laughter*, p. 133.

Chapter 2: The Motions of Puns

1 J. Garvey, 'Laurence Sterne's Wordplay', PhD thesis, University of Rochester, New York, 1974, p. 135.
2 J.-O. Grandjouan, *Les Jeux de l'esprit*. Paris, Scarabée, 1963, p. 11.
3 Benveniste, 'Le Jeu comme Structure', p. 162.
4 J. Ricardou, *Pour une théorie du nouveau roman*. Paris, Seuil, 1971, p. 122.
5 H. A. Ellis, *Shakespeare's Lusty Punning in 'Love's Labour's Lost'*. The Hague, Mouton, 1973, p. 86.
6 G. B. Milner, 'Homo Ridens', *Semiotica*, 1(V), 1972, p. 18.
7 L. Carroll, *The Annotated Alice*, ed. M. Gardner. Harmondsworth, Penguin, 1978, p. 95.
8 B. DeMott, 'The New Irony', *American Scholar*, 31(1), 1961–2, p. 115.
9 G. Puttenham, *The Arte of English Poesie*. Cambridge University Press, 1936 (1589), p. 206.
10 Jacobs, *Naming-Day in Eden*, pp. 134–5.
11 A. Schopenhauer, *The World as Will and Idea*, in P. Lauter (ed.), *Theories of Comedy*. New York, Doubleday, 1964, p. 358.
12 J. Gross, *Joyce*. London, Fontana/Collins, 1971, p. 80.
13 J. Sherzer, 'Oh, That's a Pun and I didn't mean it', *Semiotica*, 22(3/4), 1976, p. 342.
14 Crosbie, *Dictionary of Puns*, p. 173.
15 R. Crevel, *Le Clavecin de Diderot*. Paris, Pauvert, 1966, p. 30.
16 J. Batlay, 'Les Jeux de mots et de l'art dans *Rock-Monsieur*', in N. Arnaud and H. Baudin (eds), *Boris Vian*. Paris, Union Générale d'Editions, 1977, vol. 2, p. 241.
17 V. Hugo, *Les Misérables*. Paris, Hetzel, n.d., vol. 7, pp. 59–60. (*Faire partir* can mean to inspire, to give a climax, and to cause to run away. The last sense contradicts, but gives point to, the first two.)
18 J. Clubbe, *Victorian Forerunner: The Later Career of Thomas Hood*. Durham, North Carolina, Duke University Press, 1968, p. 67.
19 Crosbie, *Dictionary of Puns*, p. 184.
20 O. W. Holmes, 'A Modest Request', *Poetical Works*. London, Sampson Low, 1891, vol. 1, p. 98.
21 R. Queneau, *Les Fleurs bleues*, Paris, Gallimard, 1978, p. 69.
22 W. Shakespeare, *Troilus and Cressida*, II 1.42.
23 C. Hyers, *Zen and the Comic Spirit*. London, Rider, 1974, p. 136.
24 Legman, *No Laughing Matter*, p. 30.
25 Esar, *Comic Encyclopaedia*, p. 367.
26 Crevel, *Diderot*, p. 112.
27 W. Y. Tindall, *The Literary Symbol*. New York, Columbia University Press, 1955, p. 206.

28 See Thomas Sheridan's poem, in Introduction.
29 Legman, *No Laughing Matter*, p. 859.
30 P. Valéry, *Tel Quel 1*. Paris, Gallimard, 1971, p. 193.
31 A. Duchene, 'No Phrase Left Unturned', *Guardian*, 25 September 1969, p. 8.
32 G. W. Turner, *Stylistics*. Harmondsworth, Penguin, 1975, p. 224.
33 Freud, *Jokes*, p. 79.
34 J. Y. T. Greig, *The Psychology of Laughter and Comedy*. London, Allen & Unwin, 1923, pp. 214–16.
35 Freud, *Jokes*, pp. 167, 174, 211, 210.
36 Batlay, 'Jeux de mots', p. 243.
37 A. Bierce, *The Enlarged Devil's Dictionary*. London, Gollancz, 1967, p. 254.
38 Douglas, 'Social Control of Cognition', p. 366.
39 G. Mikes, *Humour in Memoriam*. London, Routledge & Kegan Paul, 1970, p. 82.
40 Jennings, *Pun Fun*, p. 7.
41 Greig, *Laughter and Comedy*, p. 211.
42 S. Mallarmé, 'Ses purs ongles', *Poésies*. Paris, Gallimard, 1945, p. 127.
43 H. Kenner, *The Stoic Comedians*. London, W. H. Allen, 1964, p. 37.
44 Valéry, *Tel Quel 2*, p. 63.
45 M. McLuhan and E. Carpenter, *Explorations in Communication*. Boston, Beacon, 1960, p. 125.
46 J. R. Lowell, 'Humor, Wit, Fun and Satire', *The Function of the Poet*. Boston, Houghton Mifflin, 1920, pp. 48–9.
47 P. De Vries, *Without a Stitch in Time*. Boston, Little, Brown, 1972, p. 160.
48 A. Moger, *The Complete Pun Book*. Secaucus, New Jersey, Citadel, 1979, pp. 135, 148.
49 Crosbie, *Dictionary of Puns*, p. 169.
50 Dowden, quoted in W. Clemen, *The Development of Shakespeare's Imagery*. London, Methuen, 1951, p. 180.
51 Letter from L. Helbin, 18 September, 1979.
52 Grousset, *Si t'es gai*, p. 21.
53 Jennings, *Pun Fun*, p. 7.
54 Mahood, *Shakespeare's Wordplay*, p. 29.
55 Batlay, 'Jeux de mots', p. 244.
56 Blackmantle, *Punster's Pocket-Book*, p. 11.
57 M. Grotjahn, *Beyond Laughter*. New York, McGraw-Hill, 1966, pp. 79–80.
58 A. Ludovici, *The Secret of Laughter*, London, Constable, 1932, p. 78.
59 Koestler, 'Humour and Wit', p. 5.
60 M. Eastman, *The Sense of Humor*. New York, Scribner, 1921, p. 69.
61 Reisner and Wechsler, *Encyclopaedia of Graffiti*, p. 394.
62 Corvin, *Petite Folie Collective*, p. 19.
63 L. Olbrechts-Tyteca, *Le Comique du discours*. Editions de l'Université de Bruxelles, 1974, p. 62.
64 R. Frost, quoted in Moger, *Complete Pun Book*, p. 80. (A nice play, as the

verb 'to euchre' means to outwit, which is what Frost is doing here.)
65 Freud, *Jokes*, p. 41.
66 A. Bain, *English Composition and Rhetoric*, London, Longman, 1869, p. 31.

Chapter 3: Making History I

1 W. Gass, *On Being Blue*. Boston, Godine, 1976, p. 20.
2 Huizinga, *Homs Ludens*, pp. 23, 152.
3 R. Blyth, *Oriental Humour*. Tokyo, Hokuseido, 1959, pp. 5–6.
4 P. Clastres, *Society Against the State*. New York, Urizen, 1972, pp. 108–9, 127. (R. Bastide reports similar findings in African cosmologies, in 'Le Rire et les courts-circuits de la pensée', in J. Pouillon and P. Miranda (eds), *Echanges et communications*. The Hague, Mouton, 1970, vol. 2, p. 959.)
5 O. Barfield, *Poetic Diction*. London, Faber, 1952, p. 74.
6 V. Mercier, *The Irish Comic Tradition*. London, Oxford University Press, 1962, p. 6.
7 C. Lévi-Strauss, *La Pensée sauvage*. Paris, Plon, 1962, p. 26.
8 M. Müller, *Lectures on the Science of Language*. London, Longman, 1866, p. 12.
9 S. N. Kramer, *Mythologies of the Ancient World*. New York, Doubleday, 1961, p. 8.
10 P. Regnaud, 'Le Caractère et l'origine des jeux de mots védiques', *Revue de l'Histoire des Religions*, 16, 1887, pp. 166–8.
11 Burgess, *Joysprick*, p. 135.
12 G. Chaucer, *Troilus and Criseyde*, IV.1406.
13 Quoted in C. Kahn, *The Art and Thought of Heraclitus*. Cambridge University Press, 1979, pp. 270–1.
14 A. L. Oppenheim, *Ancient Mesopotamia*. Chicago University Press, 1964, p. 211.
15 G. Contenau, *La Divination chez les Assyriens et les Babyloniens*. Paris, Payot, 1940, p. 90.
16 A. Burgess, *Language Made Plain*. London, Fontana/Collins, 1975, p. 13.
17 *Dialogues of Plato*, tr. B. Jowett. New York, Macmillan, 1892, vol. 1, p. 351.
18 V. Fromkin, 'Slips of the Tongue', *Scientific American*, Dec. 1973, p. 111.
19 Jacobs, *Naming-Day in Eden*, p. 150.
20 G. Caird, *The Language and Imagery of the Bible*. London, Duckworth, 1980, pp. 9, 45.
21 G. Driver, 'Playing on Words', *4th World Congress of Jewish Studies*, 1, 1967, pp. 124, 125, 129.
22 J. Allegro, *The Sacred Mushroom and the Cross*. London, Abacus, 1973, p. 66.
23 R. Frank, 'Some Uses of Paronomasia in Old English Scriptural Verse', *Speculum*, 47(2), 1972, p. 215.
24 E. McCartney, 'Verbal Homeopathy and the Etymological Story', *American Journal of Philology*, 48(4), 1927, pp. 337, 326–7, 335, 337.

25 Note by L. Cellier, in Hugo, *Les Contemplations*. Paris, Garnier, 1969, p. 772, on poem 'Nomen, Numen, Lumen'. (Intriguingly, Cellier describes 'Nomina Numina' as a formula of the Sceptics.)
26 Morin, 'Avec San Antonio', pp. 422–3.
27 P. Valéry, 'Au sujet d'*Adonis*', *Variété 1*, Paris, Gallimard, 1924, p. 53.
28 Dupriez, *Gradus*, pp. 48–9.
29 McCartney, 'Verbal Homeopathy', p. 326.
30 Puttenham, *Arte of English Poesie*, p. 202.
31 V. Hugo, *L'Ane*. Paris, Hetzel, n.d., p. 85.
32 N. Malcolm, *Ludwig Wittgenstein*. London, Oxford University Press, 1958, p. 29.
33 Kahn, *Art and Thought of Heraclitus*, pp. 201, 270–1, 91.
34 M. F. Burnyeat, 'Message from Heraclitus', *New York Review of Books*, 29(8), 13 May 1982, pp. 46–7.
35 Freud, *Jokes*, p. 161; and J. Feibleman, *In Praise of Comedy*. New York, Horizon, 1970, pp. 210–11.
36 Stanford, *Ambiguity*, p. 60.
37 Davis, *Elements of Deductive Logic*, quoted in M. Brown (ed.), *Bulls and Blunders*. Chicago, Griggs, 1893, p. 189.
38 S. T. Coleridge, *Aids to Reflection*, ed. T. Fenby. London, Routledge, 1905, p. xiii.
39 Stanford, *Ambiguity*, p. 18.
40 Snyder, *Puns and Poetry*, pp. 31, 39, 46.
41 P. Valéry, *Eupalinos*, ed. V. Daniel. London, Oxford University Press, 1967, p. 99.
42 Burnyeat, 'Message from Heraclitus', p. 47, quoting Heraclitus.
43 F. Rigolot, *Poétique et onomastique*. Geneva, Droz, 1977, p. 230.
44 R. Wellek, *History of Modern Criticism: The Romantic Age*. New Haven, Yale University Press, 1966, p. 41 (on Schlegel).
45 Rigolot, *Poétique et onomastique*, p. 110.
46 Gratian du Pont, quoted in E. Tabourot, *Les Bigarrures*. Brussels, Mertens, 1866 (1572), vol. 1, p. 139.
47 E. Tabourot, *Bigarrures*, p. 175.
48 *The Annotated Alice*, pp. 279–80. (In *The Field of Nonsense*. London, Chatto & Windus, 1952, p. 36, E. Sewell writes: 'A pun is not simple but it is not ambiguous. It is of the very nature of the pun that its meanings are separate, and are therefore still within the mind's control.' This view depends on the standpoint of Nonsense.)
49 M. Bakhtin, *Rabelais and his World*. Cambridge, Mass., MIT, 1968, p. 413.
50 F. Rabelais, *Gargantua*. Paris, Garnier/Flammarion, 1968, p. 74.
51 Bakhtin, *Rabelais*, p. 409.
52 Colie, *Paradoxia Epidemica*, pp. 21, 44, 5.
53 Ibid., pp. 206, 35, 38.
54 H. Kenner, *Paradox in Chesterton*. London, Sheed & Ward, 1948, p. 18.
55 C. Wilson, *Jokes*. London, Academic, 1979, p. 15.

56 Kenner, *Paradox*, pp. 40, 57.
57 Hyers, *Zen and the Comic Spirit*, pp. 103, 144, 148.
58 J. Paulos, *Mathematics and Humor*. Chicago University Press, 1980, p. 14.
59 Guiraud, *Jeu de mots*, p. 94; letter from L. D. Burnard, 2 June 1980. (On the other hand, a computer at Euratom was christened ZAZIE, after Queneau's pun-aware nymphet. See J. Bens, *Oulipo*. Paris, Gallimard, 1980, p. 54.)
60 *Johnson on Shakespeare*, ed. W. Raleigh. London, Frowde, 1908, p. 24.
61 Mahood, *Shakespeare's Wordplay*, p. 11.
62 W. Empson, *Seven Types of Ambiguity*. Harmondsworth, Penguin, 1973, pp. 110–11.
63 *Hamlet*, V.1.135; and *Richard II*, III.1.83.
64 Gilman, *Curious Perspective*, pp. 110–11, 151.
65 H. Kökeritz, *Shakespeare's Pronunciation*. New Haven, Yale University Press, 1953, p. 54.
66 *Coleridge on Shakespeare*, ed. T. Hawkes. Harmondsworth, Penguin, 1969, p. 250.
67 Mahood, *Shakespeare's Wordplay*, pp. 9, 121.
68 *Coleridge on Shakespeare*, p. 175; K. Muir, 'The Uncomic Pun', *Cambridge Journal*, 3, 1950, pp. 473, 483, 485.
69 *King Lear*, IV.6.150.
70 *Richard II*, II.1.84–5.
71 *Romeo and Juliet*, III.1.98.
72 M. Morgann, *Essay on Falstaff* (1777), quoted in R. Tuve, *Elizabethan and Metaphysical Imagery*, Chicago University Press, 1947, pp. 196–7.
73 Mahood, *Shakespeare's Wordplay*, p. 30.
74 M. Spevack, 'Shakespeare's Early use of Wordplay', in B. Fabian and U. Suerbaum (eds), *Festschrift für Edgar Mertner*. Munich, Fink, 1969, pp. 159–60, 164.
75 *Romeo and Juliet*, II.4.110.
76 C. Ricks, *Milton's Grand Style*. Oxford, Clarendon, 1968, pp. 66, 74.
77 R. Robbins, 'A Prevalence of Paronomasia', *Times Literary Supplement*, 8 May 1981, p. 522.
78 See K. Ruthven, *The Conceit*. London, Methuen, 1969, p. 39.
79 W. S. Landor: *Complete Works*, ed. T. Welby. London, Chapman & Hall, 1927–36, vol. 5, p. 258.
80 Colie, *Paradoxia Epidemica*, p. 132.
81 Ruthven, *Conceit*, p. 7.
82 G. Herbert, 'Jordan', *Penguin Book of English Verse*, ed. J. Hayward. Harmondsworth, Penguin, 1956, p. 107.
83 Ruthven, *Conceit*, p. 46.
84 Empson, *Seven Types*, pp. 227, 131.
85 *Coleridge on Shakespeare*, pp. 253–4.
86 J. Dryden, 'Preface to Annus Mirabilis', *Works*, ed. W. Ker, vol. 1, p. 15; and 'A Discourse concerning the Original and Progress of Satire', vol. 2, p. 95.

87 J. Dennis, *Letters on Several Occasions*. Farnborough, Gregg, 1971 (1696), pp. 68, 66.

88 J. Eachard, *Complete Works*. London, 1773, p. 31 (the text is from 1670).

89 Molière, *Le Misanthrope*, I.2.387–8.

90 Muir, 'The Uncomic Pun', p. 484.

91 W. Wycherley, 'A Panegyric on Quibling', *Works*, ed. M. Summers. Soho, Nonesuch, 1924, vol. 3, p. 165.

92 Addison, *Spectator*, vol. 2, p. 305.

93 J. Sully, *An Essay on Laughter*. London, Longman, 1902, p. 354.

94 Colie, *Paradoxia Epidemica*, pp. 515–16.

95 J. Boswell, *Life of Johnson*. London, Oxford University Press, 1961, p. 1308.

96 Empson, *Seven Types*, p. 111.

97 Delille, quoted in F. de Donville, *Mille et un calembours*. Paris, Garnier, 1978 (1881), p. 5.

98 T. G. Smollett, 'Reproof: a Satire', *Poetical Works of Goldsmith, Smollett, Johnson and Shenstone*. London, Routledge, 1861, p. 26.

99 A. Pope, 'The Art of Sinking', *The Works of Alexander Pope*, ed. W. Elwin. London, Murray, 1886, vol. 10, p. 378.

100 J. Arbuthnot, 'An Heroi-Comical Epistle from a certain Doctor to a certain Gentle-Woman, In Defence of the most Antient Art of Punning', quoted in W. H. Irving, *John Gay*. Durham, North Carolina, Duke University Press, 1940, pp. 145–6.

101 D. Donoghue, *Jonathan Swift*. Cambridge University Press, 1969, pp. 49, 125, 48.

102 C. Probyn, 'Swift and the Human Predicament', in C. Probyn (ed.), *The Art of Jonathan Swift*. London, Vision, 1978, p. 76.

103 D. Nokes, 'Hack at Tom Poley's: Swift's Use of Puns', in Probyn (ed.), *Swift*, pp. 54, 46–7.

104 Swift, 'A Modest Defence of Punning', p. 205.

105 Quoted in P. E. More, 'Thomas Hood', *Shelburne Essays*. New York, Putnam, 1910, p. 53.

106 Marquis de Bièvre, *Biévriana*. Paris, Maradan, an VIII, pp. 109, 120.

107 Marquis de Bièvre, *Vercingentorixe*. Paris, Pauvert, 1961 (1770), p. 30.

108 J. Roudaut (ed.), *Poètes et grammairiens au XVIIIe siècle*. Paris, Gallimard, 1971, p. 184.

109 P. Berloquin, *Dictionnaire de jeux de mots*. Paris, Encre, 1980, p. 28.

110 O. Jespersen, *Language*. London, Allen & Unwin, 1922, p. 173.

111 Kant, quoted in Eastman, *Enjoyment of Laughter*, p. 26.

112 An example of a pathetically limp pun, recorded by Diderot, 'On a déjà fait un calembour sur M. de Maisnon d'Invaux. On a dit: "Nous avons un habile contrôleur général, mais non"'. *Lettres à Sophie Volland*, ed. A. Babelon. Paris, Gallimard, 1930, vol. 3, pp. 153–4.

113 J.-P. Richter, *The Horn of Oberon*, tr. M. Hale. Detroit, Wayne State University Press, 1973, pp. 173–8.

114 *Jean Paul's Werke*, ed. E. Berend. Berlin, n.d., vol. 5, section 44.

115 Richter, *The Horn of Oberon*, p. 138.

Chapter 4: Making History II

1 Empson, *Seven Types*, pp. 134–5, 128.
2 W. Hazlitt, 'Lectures on the English Comic Writers', *Collected Works*, ed. A. Waller. London, Dent, 1903, vol. 8, pp. 19–20.
3 S. Smith, 'On Wit and Humour', *Elementary Sketches of Moral Philosophy*. London, Longman, 1850, pp. 129–30.
4 R. B. Martin, *The Triumph of Wit*. Oxford, Clarendon, 1974, p. 69.
5 H. Rowley, *Puniana*. London, Hotten, 1867, p. 33.
6 Anon. 'The Anti-Punster', in W. Burton (ed.), *Cyclopaedia of Wit*. New York, Appleton, 1858, p. 1011.
7 C. Lamb, *Works*. London, Dent, 1903, vol. 2, pp. 221, 220, 223.
8 Lamb, *Works*, vol. 1, p. 214.
9 Quoted in R. B. Martin, *Triumph of Wit*, p. 35.
10 *The Letters of John Keats*, ed. M. Forman. London, Oxford University Press, 1960, pp. 529, 280.
11 C. Ricks, *Keats and Embarrassment*. Oxford, Clarendon, 1974, p. 69. (For some splendidly far-fetched shaggy-pun stories credited to Keats and Chapman, see Flann O'Brien, *The Best of Myles*. London, Hart-Davis, MacGibbon, 1975, pp. 180–200.)
12 M. West, 'Scatology and Eschatology: The Heroic Dimensions of Thoreau's Wordplay', *PMLA*, 89(5), 1974, pp. 1044–5.
13 S. T. Coleridge, *Anima Poetae*, ed. E. Coleridge. London, Heinemann, 1895, p. 225.
14 Barnet, 'Coleridge on Puns', p. 603.
15 *Coleridge on Shakespeare*, p. 164.
16 Quoted in A. Ainger (ed.), *Humorous Poems of Thomas Hood*. London, Macmillan, 1893, pp. viii–ix (the 'Newgatory' pun is in a poem to Mrs Fry).
17 Mahood, *Shakespeare's Wordplay*, p. 11.
18 Clubbe, *Victorian Forerunner*, p. 5.
19 R. Henkle, *Comedy and Culture, England 1820–1900*. Princeton University Press, 1980, pp. 192–3.
20 Ainger, *Thomas Hood*, p. xiii.
21 M. Sutton, 'Inverse Sublimity in Victorian Humor', *Victorian Studies*, 10(2), 1966, p. 189.
22 Ainger, *Thomas Hood*, pp. xvi–xvii.
23 D. J. Gray, 'The Uses of Victorian Laughter', *Victorian Studies*, 10(2), 1966, p. 169.
24 Empson, *Seven Types* pp. 135–6.
25 Clubbe, *Victorian Forerunner*, pp. 16, 56.
26 E. A. Poe, *Works*, ed. E. C. Stedman and G. E. Woodberry. Chicago, Stone & Kimball, 1896, vol. 8, pp. 283–4. (Poe also wrote: 'Of puns it has been said that most dislike them who are least able to utter them,' which antedates Jack Benny's 'The only reason people complain about puns is that they never thought of them first'.)

27 More, 'Thomas Hood', pp. 58, 62. (The lines are from Hood's 'Ode to Melancholy'.)

28 G. K. Chesterton, 'The Pun', *Lunacy and Letters*. London, Sheed & Ward, 1958, p. 83.

29 W. Kaufman (ed.), *The Portable Nietzsche*. New York, Viking, 1975, pp. 107–10.

30 Henkle, *Comedy and Culture*, pp. 190, 192.

31 Sutton, 'Inverse Sublimity', p. 189.

32 More, 'Thomas Hood', p. 52.

33 Poe, *Works*, p. 284.

34 *The Annotated Alice*, pp. 270, 263, 121.

35 L. Carroll, *The Annotated Snark*, ed. M. Gardner. Harmondsworth, Penguin, 1979, p. 59.

36 *The Annotated Alice*, pp. 224–5.

37 J. Flescher, 'The Language of Nonsense in *Alice*', *Yale French Studies*, 43, 1969, pp. 138–9 (e.g. tail/tale, not/knot, pp. 51–2 of *Annotated Alice*).

38 *The Annotated Alice*, p. 182.

39 Gray, 'Victorian Laughter', p. 170.

40 Burgess, *Joysprick*, p. 136.

41 Sewell, *Field of Nonsense*, pp. 36–7.

42 P. Alexander, 'Logic and the Humour of Lewis Carroll', *Proceedings of the Leeds Philosophical and Literary Society*, 6, 1951, pp. 560, 556, 564.

43 W. Combe, 'Dr. Syntax in Search of the Picturesque', *The Three Tours of Dr. Syntax*. London, Murray, 1871, p. 120.

44 Mahood, *Shakespeare's Wordplay*, p. 11.

45 A. Bierce, *The Enlarged Devil's Dictionary*, London, Gollancz, 1967, p. 232.

46 O. W. Holmes, *The Autocrat of the Breakfast-Table*. London, Sampson Low, 1891, p. 11.

47 H. Thoreau, *Walden*. New York, New American Library, 1960, pp. 147, 94.

48 M. West, 'Scatology', p. 1056.

49 Thorean, *Walden*, p. 216.

50 R. Poirier, *A World Elsewhere*. London, Chatto & Windus, 1967, pp. 85–6 (e.g. 'I fear chiefly that my expression may not be extra-vagant enough, may not wander far enough beyond the narrow limits of my daily experience', *Walden*, p. 215).

51 R. W. Emerson, 'Literary Ethics', *Works*. London, Bell, 1881, vol. 2, p. 214.

52 F. Caradec, 'Le Calembour', in R. Alleau (ed.), *Dictionnaire des jeux*. Paris, Tchou, 1964, p. 86.

53 Commerson, *Pensées d'un emballeur*. Paris, Garnier, 1978, cover page and pp. 19, 32, 45, 44.

54 H., de Balzac, *Correspondance*, ed. R. Pierot. Paris, Garnier 1966, vol. 4, p. 690.

55 Quoted in H. Guillemin, *L'Humour de Victor Hugo*. Neuchâtel, La Baconnière, 1950, p. 29.

56 V. Hugo, *L'Ane*, Paris, Hetzel, n.d., p. 141.

57 A. Rochette, *L'Esprit dans les oeuvres poétiques de Victor Hugo*. Paris, Champion, 1911, p. 165.
58 V. Hugo, *Lucrèce Borgia*. Paris, Charpentier, 1882, p. 53.
59 V. Hugo, *Les Misérables*. Paris, Hetzel, n.d., vol. 7, p. 72.
60 Ibid., vol. 1, p. 185.
61 Flaubert, quoted in Sartre, *L'Idiot*, vol. 2, p. 1974.
62 M. J. Durry, *Flaubert et ses projets inédits*. Paris, Nizet, 1950, pp. 60–1.
63 G. Lukács, *The Historical Novel*. London, Merlin, 1962, p. 194.
64 Tanner, *Adultery in the Novel*, p. 257, 264, 345.
65 Sartre, *L'Idiot*, pp. 1316, 1974–5, 1985.
66 G. Flaubert, *Correspondance*. Paris, Conard, 1926, vol. 2, p. 407.
67 Sartre, *L'Idiot* p. 1974.
68 H. Bergson, *Le Rire*. Paris, PUF, 1975 (1900), p. vi (subsequent references are in brackets after quotations).
69 A. Koestler, *The Act of Creation*. London, Hutchinson, 1964, p. 47.
70 Eastman, *Enjoyment of Laughter*, pp. 46–7.
71 Freud, *Jokes*, p. 104.
72 L. Feinberg, *The Secret of Humor*. Amsterdam, Rodopi, 1978, p. 22.
73 S. Freud, *The Psychopathology of Everyday Life*. Harmondsworth, Penguin, 1975, p. 262.
74 Eastman, *Enjoyment of Laughter*, p. 289.
75 R. Roussel, *Comment j'ai écrit certains de mes livres*. Paris, Pauvert, 1963, pp. 20, 23.
76 M. Foucault, *Raymond Roussel*. Paris, Gallimard, 1963, p. 70.
77 A. Duncan, 'The Novels of Claude Simon, 1945–60'. PhD thesis, Aberdeen University, 1976, pp. 317–18, 320, 324–5, 328, 331.
78 A Breton, *Les Pas perdus*. Paris, Gallimard, 1924, pp. 170–1.
79 D. Sonstroem, 'Making Earnest of Game: G. M. Hopkins and Nonsense Poetry', *Modern Language Quarterly*, 27(2), 1967, p. 197.
80 A. Welsh, *Roots of Lyric*. Princeton University Press, 1978, p. 248.
81 Corvin, *Petite Folie collective*, p. 23.
82 See L. Peeters, *La Roulette aux mots*. Paris, La Pensée Universelle, 1975, p. 45.
83 Crosbie, *Dictionary of Puns*, p. 38.
84 A. Allais, *Allais-grement*. Paris, Livre de poche, 1965, p. 230.
85 J. Prévert, *Spectacle*. Paris, Livre de poche, 1949, p. 35.
86 R. Queneau, unpublished note, quoted by C. Debon-Tournadre: 'Présence d'Apollinaire dans l'oeuvre de Queneau', *Revue d'Histoire littéraire de la France*, 81(1), 1981, p. 75.
87 R. Queneau, *Les Derniers Jours*. Paris, Gallimard, 1963, p. 177.
88 R. Queneau, *Chêne et chien*. Paris, Gallimard, 1968, p. 129.
89 C. Kestermeier, 'Raymond Queneau's *Zazie dans le Métro*'. PhD thesis, University of Wisconsin-Madison, 1982, p. 20.
90 R. Queneau, *Odile*. Paris, Gallimard, 1937, pp. 29–30.
91 M. Leiris, *Mots sans mémoire*. Paris, Gallimard, 1969, p. 110.

92 M. Leiris, 'De la littérature considérée comme une tauromachie', *L'Age d'homme*. Paris, Livre de poche, 1946, pp. 16, 227.

93 M. Leiris, *Le Monde*, 10 January 1975.

94 M. Foucault, *Roussel*, pp. 22–3.

95 C. Lévi-Strauss, *Tristes Tropiques*. Paris, Union Générale d'Editions, 1955, pp. 37–8.

96 F. George, *L'Effet 'yau de poêle*. Paris, Hachette, 1979, p. 148.

97 See Turkle, *Psychoanalytic Politics*, pp. 123–4.

98 M. Bowie, 'Jacques Lacan', in J. Sturrock (ed.), *Structuralism and Since*. London, Oxford University Press, 1979, p. 144.

99 P. Bowles, 'Schizophrenia in the Sewer', *Times Literary Supplement*, 26 June 1981, p. 735.

100 Turkle, *Psychoanalytic Politics*, p. 55.

101 J. Hillis Miller, 'The Critic as Host', in H. Bloom (ed.), *Deconstruction and Criticism*. New York, Seabury, 1979, p. 230.

102 B. Poirot-Delpech, 'Tics', *Le Monde*, 3 January 1975, p.9.

Chapter 5: The Extended Family

1 N. Frye, *Anatomy of Criticism*. Princeton University Press, 1957, p. 276.

2 L. G. Heller, 'Towards a General Typology', p. 271.

3 Steele, *Spectator*, vol. 1, p. 251.

4 Crosbie, *Dictionary of Puns*, p. 90. (A traditional guessing-game toys similarly with the erogenous zones of discourse: 'I get it out, stuff it into a hairy hole, and it's wet at the end . . . It's my pipe.' This answer of course refuels the prurience, for the pipe is archetypically phallic.)

5 C. Gruner, *Understanding Laughter*. Chicago, Nelson-Hall, 1978, p. 71.

6 A. Bain, *English Composition and Rhetoric*. London, Longman, 1869, p. 31.

7 Holmes, 'A Visit to the Asylum for Aged and Decayed Punsters', p. 361.

8 D. Borgmann, *Language on Vacation*. New York, Scribner, 1965, p. 103.

9 C. Tomlinson, 'Ritornello', in L. Michaels and C. Ricks (eds), *The State of the Language*. Berkeley, University of California Press, 1980, p. 34.

10 Quoted by S. Gilbert, in *Our Exagmination*. London, Faber, 1972, p. 49.

11 G. S. Kirk, *The Nature of Greek Myths*. Harmondsworth, Penguin, 1974, pp. 58–9, 135–6, 113–14.

12 Quoted in A. Bergens, *Raymond Queneau*. Geneva, Droz, 1963, p. 196.

13 A. S. Palmer, *The Folk and their Word-Lore*. London, Routledge, 1904, p. 9.

14 J. Orr, *Three Studies in Homonymics*. Edinburgh University Press, 1962, p. 42.

15 Quintilian, *Institutiones Oratoriae*. 1.6.34. (R. Frank, 'Some Uses of Paronomasia in Old English Scriptural Verse', *Speculum*, 47(2), 1972, p. 209, lends support: 'Modern etymological science confirms that *lucus* "sacred grove" and *luceo* "to be bright, shine" are cognates; the original "shining" or "open place" in the woods was later taken to signify the grove itself.')

16 E. Brehaut, *An Encyclopaedist of the Dark Ages*. New York, Franklin, n.d., p. 232.

17 J. Paulhan, 'La Preuve par l'étymologie', *Oeuvres complètes*. Paris, Cercle du livre précieux, 1966–70, vol. 3, pp. 49, 65, 69–70.

18 Y. Belaval, preface to R. Queneau, *Chêne et chien*, Paris, Gallimard, 1968, pp. 25–6.

19 Caird, *Language and Imagery*, p. 45.

20 Palmer, *Folk*, p. 82.

21 M. E. de Montaigne, *Essais*, ed. M. Rat. Paris, Garnier, 1958, vol. 2, p. 691.

22 Jacobs, *Naming-Day in Eden*, pp. 134–5.

23 Stanford, *Ambiguity*, pp. 40–1.

24 I. Goldberg, *The Wonder of Words*. New York, Appleton-Century, 1938, p. 122.

25 P. Guiraud, 'Etymologie et *ethymologia*', *Poétique*, 11, 1972, pp.405–11. (This latter tactic can of course backfire. I recall an adolescent attempt to hide the cliché 'leaden sky' by 'plumbic'.)

26 F. Ponge, *Proêmes*. Paris, Gallimard, 1948, p. 139.

27 F. Ponge, *Méthodes*. Paris, Gallimard, 1961, p. 98.

28 F. Ponge, *Le Parti pris des choses*. Paris, Gallimard, 1967, p. 33.

29 Burgess, *Joysprick*, p. 146.

30 Barthes, *Roland Barthes par Roland Barthes*, p. 88.

31 H. Vetter, *Language Behavior and Psychopathology*. Chicago, Rand McNally, 1969, p. 183.

32 See P. Farb, *Word Play*. London, Cape, 1974, p. 81.

33 Turkle, *Psychoanalytic Politics*, p. 147.

34 E. Partridge, *A Dictionary of Clichés*. London, Routledge & Kegan Paul, 1950, p. 39; L. Larchey, *L'Esprit de tout le monde*. Paris, Berger-Levrault, 1892, vol. 1, p. ix; *Le Canard enchaîné*, 17 July 1970; L. Untermeyer, *Treasury of Great Humor*. New York, McGraw-Hill, 1972, p. 676.

35 Grandjouan, *Jeux de l'esprit*, p. 4. Susan Stewart draws the overlapping lines: 'The pun involves the simultaneity of two or more meanings within one word. Conversely, the portmanteau involves the simultaneity of two or more words within one meaning.' *Nonsense: Aspects of Intertextuality in Folklore and Literature*. Baltimore, Johns Hopkins University Press, 1978, p. 163.

36 A. Rigaud, 'Les Mots-centaures', *Vie et Langage*, 202, 1969, p. 54.

37 Carroll, preface to *The Annotated Snark*, p. 42.

38 Sewell, *Field of Nonsense*, p. 119.

39 A. Finkielkraut, *Ralentir! mots-valises!* Paris, Seuil, 1979 (unpaged).

40 F. Huxley, *The Raven and the Writing Desk*. London, Thames & Hudson, 1976, p. 73.

41 Yaguello, *Alice*, p. 29.

42 R. Queneau, *Saint Glinglin*. Paris, Gallimard, 1981, p. 182.

43 R. Barthes, *Sade, Fourier, Loyola*. Paris, Seuil, 1971, pp. 161, 87.

44 W. Kaufman (ed.) *The Portable Nietzsche*, New York, Viking, 1975, p. 109.

45 J. Henderson, *The Maculate Muse*. New Haven, Yale University Press, 1975, p. 55.

46 S. Ullmann, *The Principles of Semantics*. Oxford, Blackwell, 1963, p. 137.

47 E. Abel and B. Buckley, *The Handwriting on the Wall*. Westport, Connecticut, Greenwood, 1977, p. 73.

48 J. Shipley, *Word Play*. New York, Hawthorne, 1972, p. 59.

49 Farb, *Word Play*, p. 88.

50 E. Leach, 'Anthropological Aspects of Language', in E. Lenneberg (ed.), *New Directions in the Study of Language*. Boston, MIT, 1964, pp. 25, 27.

51 L. Feinberg, *The Secret of Humor*, Amsterdam, Rodopi, 1978, p. 3.

52 Thoreau, *Walden*, p. 215.

53 Freud, *Jokes*, p. 101.

54 Puttenham, *Arte of English Poesie*, p. 191.

55 V. Jankélévitch, *L'Ironie*. Paris, PUF, 1950, p. 95.

56 W. A. Coupe, in A. J. Krailsheimer (ed.), *The Continental Renaissance*. Harmondsworth, Penguin, 1971, p. 416.

57 W. Labov, *Language in the Inner City*. Oxford, Blackwell, 1977, p. 320.

58 Abel and Buckley, *Handwriting on the Wall*, p. 29.

59 Quoted in R. Edouard, *Dictionnaire des injures*. Paris, Tchou, 1967, pp. 11, 57.

60 L. Cazamian, *The Development of English Humor*. New York, AMS, 1965, p. 13.

61 W. H. Auden, 'Notes on the Comic', *The Dyer's Hand*. New York, Random House, 1962, p. 383.

62 C. Abastado, 'Situation de la parodie', in 'La Parodie', *Cahiers du XXe Siècle*, 6, 1976, pp. 11, 17.

63 D. Macdonald, *Parodies*. New York, Random House, 1960, pp. xiii, xv, 560.

64 D. Donoghue, *Jonathan Swift*. Cambridge University Press, 1969, p. 48.

65 G. Flaubert, *Madame Bovary*. Paris, Cluny, 1938, pp. 278, 118.

66 V. Hugo, *Chansons des rues et des bois*. Paris, Hetzel, n.d., p. 99.

67 J. Dubois, et le groupe μ, *Rhétorique générale*. Paris, Larousse, 1970, p. 120.

68 Colie, *Paradoxia Epidemica*, p. 26.

69 A. Hershkowitz, 'The Essential Ambiguity of, and in, Humour', in A. Chapman and H. Foot (eds), *It's a Funny Thing, Humour*. Oxford, Pergamon, 1977, p. 140.

70 Jacobs, *Naming-Day in Eden*, p. 150. (An adynata is an impossibility.)

71 Ruthven, *Conceit*, p. 20.

72 W. C. Booth, *A Rhetoric of Irony*. Chicago University Press, 1975, p. 26.

73 Puttenham, *Arte of English Poesie*, p. 189.

74 D. Muecke, *The Compass of Irony*. London, Methuen, 1980, p. 29.

75 Ibid., p. 15.

76 J. Brown, 'Eight Types of Pun', *PMLA*, 62, 1956, p. 18.

77 Mercier, *Irish Comic Tradition*, p. 83.

78 Huizinga, *Homo Ludens*, p. 23.

79 Welsh, *Roots of Lyric*, p. 245.

80 D. L. Bolinger, 'Metaphorical Aggression', in D. and A. Nilsen (eds), *Language Play*. Rowley, Mass., Newbury House, 1978, pp. 260–1.
81 Caird, *Language and Imagery*, pp. 16–17.
82 T. Hawkes, *Metaphor*. London, Methuen, 1972, p. 7.
83 J. Cocteau, quoted in G. Elgozy, *De l'humour*. Paris, Denoël, 1979, p. 111; A. Thau, 'Play with Words and Sounds in the Poetry of Max Jacob', *Revue des Lettres Modernes*, 336–9, 1973, p. 127.
84 Ponge, *Méthodes*, p. 274.
85 Ibid., p. 41; and *Pour un Malherbe*. Paris, Gallimard, 1965, p. 134.
86 Colie, *Paradoxin Epidemica*, p. 132.
87 P. Moloney, *A Plea for Mersey*. Liverpool, Gallery, 1966, p. 52.
88 Ruthven, *Conceit*, pp. 53, 69, 9.
89 R. Heppenstall, *Raymond Roussel*. London, Calder & Boyars, 1966, p. 45; and Koestler, *Act of Creation*, pp. 65, 314.
90 M. Edwards, 'Exercise in Queneau', *Prospice*, 8, 1978, p. 45; and Untermeyer, *Treasury of Laughter*, p. 672.
91 Prévert, *Paroles*, Paris, Livre de poche, 1948, p. 12.
92 Caird, *Language and Imagery*, pp. 47–8.
93 B. Dupriez, *Gradus*, p. 404.
94 According to F. Caradec, 'Vers olorimes', in R. Alleau (ed.), *Dictionnaire des jeux*. Paris, Tchou, 1964, p. 519, this pair, usually attributed to Hugo, was coined by Marc Monnier.
95 J.-C. Carrière (ed.), *Humour 1900*. Paris, J'ai lu, 1980, p. 148.
96 V. Hugo, *La Dernière Gerbe*. Paris, Hetzel, n.d., p. 15.
97 Lord Byron, *Don Juan*, ed. T. Steffan. Harmondsworth, Penguin, 1978, p. 220.
98 Auden, 'Notes on the Comic,' p. 380.
99 Rochette, *L'Esprit dans les oeuvres*, p. 159.
100 Untermeyer, *Treasury of Laughter*, p. 673.
101 G. K. Chesterton, quoted in B. Hillier, *Punorama*. Andoversford, Whittington, 1974, p. 6.
102 Jankélévitch, *L'Ironie*, pp. 125–6.
103 Welsh, *Roots of Lyric*, p. 245.
104 J. Lipton, *An Exaltation of Larks*. Harmondsworth, Penguin, 1977, pp. 91–2.
105 R. Jakobson, *Essais de linguistique générale*. Paris, Minuit, 1963, p. 86.
106 R. Queneau, *Zazie dans le Métro*. Paris, Gallimard, 1972, p. 115.

Chapter 6: Rounding Up

1 Or, with more apparent assurance, 'C'est mon opinion et je la partage.' Henry Monnier, *Mémoires de Joseph Prudhomme*. Paris, Librairie Nouvelle, 1857.
2 M. Gutwirth, 'Réflexions sur le comique', *Revue d'Esthétique*, 17, 1964, p. 33.

3 C. F. Keppler, *The Literature of the Second Self.* Tucson, Arizona University Press, 1972, p. 10.

4 See note 62 to chapter 2.

5 J. Paris, 'L'Agonie du signe', *Change*, 11, 1972, p. 167. (The reference is to Carroll's portmanteau-name based on Richard/William.)

6 Thoreau, *Walden*, p. 94.

7 R. Barthes, *S/Z.* Paris, Seuil, 1970, p. 151.

8 Empson, *Seven Types*, p. 90.

9 E. Esar, *Humorous English.* New York, Horizon, 1961, p. 100.

10 G. Lanson, *L'Art de la prose.* Paris, Fayard, 1909, p. 32; and J. Cocteau, quoted in H. Parisot, 'Pour franciser les jeux de langage d'*Alice*', *Cahiers de l'Herne*, 1971, pp. 81–2.

11 Jennings, *Pun Fun*, p. 8; and Esar, *Comis Encyclopaedia*, p. 623.

12 Mahood, *Shakespeare's Wordplay*, p. 40.

13 Paulhan, 'Psychologie du calembour', p. 868.

14 *Coleridge on Shakespeare*, p. 175.

15 J. Jackson, 'An Address on the Psychology of Joking' (1887), *Selected Writings.* London, Hodder & Stoughton, 1932, pp. 359–60.

16 P. Régnard, *Les Maladies épidémiques de l'esprit.* Paris, Plon-Nourrit, 1887, p. 413.

17 Eastman, *Sense of Humor*, p. 69.

18 *Stedman's Medical Dictionary.* Baltimore, Williams & Wilkins, 1966, p. 1784.

19 Koestler, *Act of Creation*, pp. 315–16. (The full account is in 'The Hypothalamus and Central Levels of Autonomic Function', *Association for Research in Nervous and Mental Disease*, 20, 1939. Reprint 1966, New York, Hafner.)

20 A. A. Brill, 'The Mechanism of Wit and Humor in Normal and Psychopathic States', *Psychiatric Quarterly*, 14, 1941, p. 748.

21 E. Sagarin, *The Anatomy of Dirty Words.* New York, Lyle Stuart, 1962, pp. 150–1, quoting F. Packard.

22 S. Freud, 'The Unconscious', Standard edn, London, Hogarth, 1957, vol. 14, p. 200.

23 M. Levin, 'Wit and Schizophrenic Thinking', *American Journal of Psychiatry*, 113, 1957, pp. 917–19.

24 S. Arieti, 'New Views on the Psychology and Psychopathology of Wit and the Comic', *Psychiatry*, 13, 1950, p. 47.

25 J. Neale and T. Oltmanns, *Schizophrenia.* New York, Wiley, 1980, p. 112.

26 Bastide, 'Le Rire et les courts-circuits de la pensée', p. 960.

27 L. Chapman, J. E. Chapman and G. A. Miller, 'A Theory of Verbal Behaviour in Schizophrenia', *Progress in Experimental Personality Research*, 1, 1964, p. 74.

28 S. D. Robbins, *A Dictionary of Speech Pathology and Therapy.* London, Peter Owen, 1962, p. 86.

29 S. Arieti (ed.), *American Handbook of Psychiatry.* New York, Basic, 1959, p. 428.

30 J. Levine, 'Humor and Psychopathology', in C. Izard (ed.), *Emotions in Personality and Psychopathology*. New York, Plenum, 1979, pp. 59–60.

31 E. von Domarus, 'The Specific Laws of Logic in Schizophrenia', in J. S. Kasanin (ed.), *Language and Thought in Schizophrenia*. Berkeley, University of California Press, 1944, pp. 108–9.

32 R. Brown, *Words and Things*. Glencoe, Illinois, Free Press, 1958, p. 297.

33 E. Jones, *Life and Work of Sigmund Freud*. London, Hogarth, 1955, vol. 2, p. 364 (re 'The Unconscious').

34 In *Case Histories II*. Harmondsworth, Penguin, 1979, p. 40.

35 Freud, *Jokes*, p. 193.

36 *The Individual Psychology of Alfred Adler*, ed. H. and R. Ansbacher. London, Allen & Unwin, 1958, p. 252.

37 B. Ball, *Leçons sur les maladies mentales*. Paris, Asselin & Houzeau, 1890, p. 485.

38 H. Michaux, *Connaissance par les gouffres*. Paris, Gallimard, 1967, p. 128.

39 E. Bleuler, *Dementia praecox*. New York, International Universities Press, 1950, p. 152.

40 F. A. Bather, 'The Puns of Shakespeare', in C. Hawkins (ed.), *Noctes Shaksperianae*. London, Castle & Lamb, 1887, pp. 77–8.

41 P. Eluard and A. Breton, 'L'Immaculée Conception', in P. Eluard, *Oeuvres complètes*. Paris, Gallimard, 1968, pp. 320–1.

42 J.-P. Sartre, *Saint Genet, comédien et martyr*. Paris, Gallimard, 1953, p. 275.

43 P. De Vries, *Without a Stitch in Time*, Boston, Little, Brown, 1972, p. 65.

44 Freud, *Jokes*, pp. 130–1.

45 J. Hillis Miller, 'The Critic as Host', in H. Bloom (ed.), *Deconstruction and Criticism*. New York, Seabury, 1979, p. 249.

46 P. Valery, *Cahiers*. Paris, CNRS, 1958, vol. 4, pp. 528, 585.

47 T. Pynchon, *The Crying of Lot 49*. Harmondsworth, Penguin, 1974, p. 97. (This novel carries a running pun on 'lots': car-lots, stamp-lots, auctions.)

48 C. Baudelaire, *Oeuvres complètes*, ed. Y. le Dantec. Paris, Gallimard, 1963, pp. 336, 338, 357.

49 Michaux, *Connaissance par les gouffres*, p. 128.

50 M. Dearnley, *The Poetry of Christopher Smart*. London, Routledge & Kegan Paul, 1968, p. 163.

51 N. Frye, *Anatomy of Criticism*. Princeton University Press, 1957, p. 276.

52 Welsh, *Roots of Lyric*, pp. 246–8.

53 The few biographical details on Brisset come from P. Cullard, 'Un Paraphrène au XIXe siècle, J.-P. Brisset', thesis, Faculté de Médecine, Strasbourg, 1980.

54 Ibid., p. 17.

55 M. Foucault, preface to *Les Origines humaines* and *La Grammaire logique*. Paris, Tchou, 1970, p. viii. (I quote Brisset from the Paris, Baudoin editions of these two texts.)

56 A. Breton, *Anthologie de l'humour noir*. Paris, Livre de poche, 1966, p. 308.

57 J.-P. Brisset, *La Science de Dieu*, quoted in Cullard, 'Brisset', p. 65. (Re

'plagiat par anticipation', see OULIPO: *Atlas de littérature potentielle*. Paris, Gallimard, 1981, p. 167.)

58 P. Guiraud, 'Les Formes verbales de l'interprétation délirante', *Annales médico-psychologiques*, 1, 1921, pp. 396–406.

59 R. Queneau, preface to 'Les Hétéroclites et les fous littéraires', *Bizarre*, 4, April 1956, p. 2.

60 Brisset, *La Science de Dieu*, quoted in Cullard, 'Brisset', p. 65.

61 J. Cocteau, quoted in M. Blanc, M. Bourgeois, B. Favarel-Garrigues and J.-F. Bargues, 'A propos d'une paraphrène', *Annales médico-psychologiques* 1(3), 1967, p. 418; and P. Bourgeade, *Le Monde*, 26 October, 1968, p.v.

62 Paris, 'L'Agonie du signe', p. 152.

63 J. Horvat, 'Freud in France', *Cambridge Quarterly*, 7(4), 1977, p. 353.

64 L. Feeney, 'The Menace of Puns', in P. Phelan (ed.), *With a Merry Heart*. London, Longman, 1943, p. 169.

65 Esar, *Comic Encyclopaedia*, p. 618.

66 V. Fromkin (ed.), *Speech Errors as Linguistic Evidence*. The Hague, Mouton, 1973, p. 215.

67 S. Freud, *The Psychopathology of Everyday Life*. Harmondsworth, Penguin, 1975, pp. 213, 264.

68 H. McNeil, in Jencks and Silver, *Adhocism*, p. 191.

69 J. Paulos, *Mathematics and Humor*. Chicago University Press, 1980, p. 58. (One that might especially appeal to our European partners is: 'Britannia waives the rules'.)

70 J. Bier, *The Rise and Fall of American Humor*. New York, Holt, Rinehart & Winston, 1968, p. 107.

71 L. Etienne, *L'Art du contrepet*. Livre de poche, 1972, pp. 15–16, 95.

72 Rabelais, *Pantagruel*, II, XXI.

73 L. Perceau, *La Redoute des contrepèteries*. Paris, Briffaut, 1949, pp. 45, 69.

74 R. Desnos, *Domaine public*. Paris, Gallimard, 1963, p. 43.

75 Esar, *Comic Encyclopaedia*, p. 5.

76 Hughes and Hammond, *Upon the Pun*.

77 A. Ross, preface to T. Smollett, *Humphry Clinker*. Harmondsworth, Penguin, 1975, p. 16.

78 Charney, *Comedy High and Low*, p. 34.

79 A. Room, *Dictionary of Confusibles*. London, Routledge & Kegan Paul, 1979, pp. 2–3.

80 H. Kenner, 'The Jokes at the Wake', *Massachusetts Review*, 4, 1981, p. 724.

81 A. Abingdon (ed.), *Second Boners Omnibus*. New York, Blue Ribbon, n.d., pp. 19, 27, 204.

82 C. Hunt (ed.), *My Favourite Howlers*. London, Benn, 1951, pp. 21–2.

83 Jean-Charles, *La Foire aux cancres*. Paris, Calmann-Lévy, 1974, p. 20.

84 Sagarin, *Anatomy of Dirty Words*, p. 133.

85 E. Tempel (ed.), *Humor in the Headlines*. New York, Pocket Books, 1969, pp. 16, 133.

86 L. Carroll, *Letters*, ed. M. Cohen. London, Macmillan, 1979, vol. 1, p. 31.

87 G. Brandreth, *Wordplay*. London, Severn House, 1982, p. 224.

88 H. Ayres, *Carroll's Alice*. New York, Columbia University Press, 1936, p. 65.

89 Brown, *Bulls and Blunders*, pp. 161, 164, 196.

90 S. Smith, 'On Wit and Humour', *Elementary Sketches of Moral Philosophy*, London, Longman, 1850, p. 141.

91 W. Jerrold (ed.), *Bulls, Blunders and Howlers*. London, Brentano, 1928, p. 5.

92 Eastman, *Sense of Humor*, p. 61.

93 M. Brown (ed.), *Wit and Humor*. Chicago, Griggs, 1883, p. 112.

94 Esar, *Humorous English*, p. 166.

95 L. Olbrechts-Tyteca, *Le Comique du discours*, Editions de l'Université de Bruxelles, 1974, p. 62.

96 Peeters, *Roulette aux mots*, p. 10.

97 S. Freud, 'The Antithetical Meaning of Primal Words', Standard edn, vol. 11, London, Hogarth, 1957, p. 161.

98 C. Hockett, 'Where the Tongue Slips, There Slip I', in *To Honor Roman Jakobson*. The Hague, Mouton, 1967, vol. 2, p. 931.

99 Charney, *Comedy High and Low*, pp. 35–6.

100 Eastman, *Sense of Humor*, p. 66.

101 Schopenhauer, quoted in Lauter, *Comedy*, p. 358.

102 R. Koegler, 'In Defense of the Pun', *American Imago*, 16, 1959, p. 234.

103 De Vries, *Without a Stitch in Time*, p. 67.

104 P. De Vries, *No, But I Saw the Movie*. London, Panther, 1966, p. 74.

105 Stendhal, *La Chartreuse de Parme*. Paris, Nelson, n.d., p. 491.

106 W. Shakespeare, *Troilus and Cressida*. II.1.42.

107 R. Queneau, *Les Oeuvres complètes de Sally Mara*, Gallimard, 1962, p. 349. Following on, Evert van der Starre talks of this work as *une calembourrasque* (*bourrasque* = squall), and its author as *un calembourreau* (*bourreau* = executioner): *Temps mêlés*, 150, 20–21, 1983, pp. 99–100.

108 Morin, 'Avec San Antonio', p. 423.

109 Ionesco, *La Leçon*, in *Théâtre*. Paris, Gallimard, 1954, vol., 1, p. 89.

110 Richter, *Horn of Oberon*, p. 24.

111 Lessing, *Nathan der Weise*, IV, 4.

112 K. Marx, *Critique of Hegel's 'Philosophy of Right'*. Cambridge University Press, 1970, p. 137.

113 Batlay, 'Jeux de mots', p. 241.

114 J. Ricardou, *Pour une théorie du nouveau roman*. Paris, Seuil, 1971, p. 52.

115 *Le Dessin d'humour du XVe siècle à nos jours*. Paris, Bibliothèque Nationale, 1971, p. 152.

116 Guiraud, *Jeu de mots*, p. 96.

117 E. Larsen, *Wit as a Weapon*. London, Muller, 1980, p. 53.

118 S. Freud, 'Humour', Standard edn, vol. 21, London, Hogarth, 1961, p. 162.

119 Shakespeare, *Romeo and Juliet*, V.3.88–90.

120 Mahood, *Shakespeare's Wordplay*, pp. 81–2.

121 *Coleridge on Shakespeare*, p. 263.
122 Quoted in *Grand Larousse Universel du XIXe sièle*. Paris, 1867, vol. 3, p. 131.
123 T. Masson, *Book of Wit and Humor*. New York, Sears, 1927, p. 2.
124 R. L. Woods, *The Modern Handbook of Humor*. New York, McGraw-Hill, 1967, p. 436.
125 Seift, 'The Dying Speech of Tom Ashe', *Collected Writings*, ed. M. Davis and L. Landa, Oxford, Blackwell, 1957, vol. 4, p. 265.
126 Morin, 'Avec San Antonio', p. 431.
127 O. Wilde, quoted in Brill, 'Mechanism of Wit and Humor', p. 748.
128 J. Sternberg, *Roland Topor*. Paris, Seghers, 1978, p. 116.
129 Du Marsais, *Traité des tropes*. Paris, Le Nouveau Commerce, 1977, p. 199; H. Melville, *Billy Budd*. New York, Signet, 1961, p. 87.
130 Eastman, *Enjoyment of Laughter*, p. 61.
131 Crosbie, *Dictionary of Puns*, p. 58.
132 Levine, 'Humor and Psychopathology', p. 58. (According to Bleuler, *Dementia Praecox*, p. 12, an undercurrent of gallows humor is common in delierium tremens.)
133 S. Beckett, *Proust*. London, Calder, 1965, pp. 20–1.
134 Crosbie, *Dictionary of Puns*, p. 163.
135 A. Allais, 'Collage', Oeuvres authumes. Paris, Table Ronde, 1970, vol. 1, pp. 16–18.
136 Esar, *Comic Encyclopaedia*, p. 367.
137 Quoted in Elgozy, *De l'humour*, p. 101.
138 W. Penkethman, *Penkethman's Jests*. London, Warner, 1721, vol. 2, p. 132.
139 Freud, *Jokes*. p. 157. (Some of the French call the funny-bone 'le petit juif', presumably a compliment, for once, to the Jewis sense of humour, even in the midst of pain.)
140 L. Rosten, *The Joys of Yiddish*. Harmondsworth, Penguin, 1978, pp. xvii, 260.
141 Arieti, 'New Views', p. 61
142 I. Kristol, 'Is Jewis Humor Dead?', *Commentary*, 12(5—, 1951, p. 435.
143 Douglas, 'Social Control of Cognition', p. 366.
144 B. DeMott, 'The New Irony', *American Schola*, 31(1), 1961–2, p. 112.
145 E. Partridge, *Penguin Dictionary of Historical Slang*. Harmondsworth, Penguin, 1978, p. 733. (From Harrow School, mid-nineteenth-twentieth century: 'Pun-paper': ruled sheets for impositions.)
146 Carroll, *The Annotated Alice*, p. 160.
147 Crosbie, *Dictionary of Puns*, p. 160.
148 *The Portable Nietzsche*, ed. W. Kaufman. New York, Viking, 1975, p. 153.
149 Douglas, 'Social Control of Cognition', p. 365.
150 M. Mahood, *Shakespeare's Wordplay*, p. 29.
151 P. Sollers, *Ponge*. Paris, Seghers, 1963, p. 51.

Chapter 7: Puns Out and About

1 New York, Harper, 1927, p. 179.
2 N. Rees, *Slogans*. London, Allen & Unwin, 1982, p. 105.
3 R. Harris, 'The Dialect of Fleet Street', *Times Literary Supplement*, 22 May, 1981, p. 560.
4 G. Dyer, *Advertising as Communication*. London, Methuen, 1982, pp. 154–5, 30.
5 M. McLuhan, *Understanding Media*. London, Routledge & Kegan Paul, 1964, p. 231.
6 L. Rosten, *Treasury of Jewish Quotations*. New York, Bantam, 1977, p. 160.
7 W. Weir, *On the Writing of Advertising*. New York, McGraw-Hill, 1960, p. 50.
8 Burgess, *Language Made Plain*, pp. 105–6.
9 Charney, *Comedy High and Low*, p. 20.
10 See P. Guiraud, *Sémiologie de la sexualité*. Paris, Payot, 1978, p. 110.
11 P. Kolin, 'Paronomastic Announcements', *American Speech*, 52(1–2), 1977, pp. 35–6.
12 V. Morin, 'Erotisme et publicité', *Communications*, 9, 1967, pp. 105–6.
13 J. Boullet, *Symbolisme sexuel dans les traditions populaires*. Paris, Payot, 1961, p. 206.
14 Dyer, *Advertising*, p. 151.
15 Ibid., p. 41.
16 N. Douglas, *South Wind*. New York, Dodd, Mead, 1930, p. 62.
17 M. Galliot, *Essai sur la langue de la réclame contemporaine*. Toulouse, Privat, 1955, p. 472.
18 O. Reboul, *Langage et idéologie*. Paris, PUF, 1980, p. 124.
19 H. Kirschner, 'Word Play in English Advertising', in R. Ligton and M. Saltzer (eds), *Studies in Honor of J. Alexander Kerns*. The Hague, Mouton, 1970, pp. 75–8.
20 We should not be shy of mentioning rhetoric in connection with everyday speech-habits. As the rhetorician Du Marsais pointed out: 'Il se fait dans un jour de marché plus de figures qu'en plusieurs jours d'assemblées académiques.' Quoted in O. Reboul, *Le Slogan*. Brussels/Paris, Complexe, 1975, p. 77.
21 Cf. the anecdote of Beau Nash going out in gorgeous attire and being asked his destination. 'Why, I'm going to advertise myself, for that's the only use of fine coat.' Quoted in W. Jerrold, *A Book of Famous Wits*. New York, McBride, Nast, 1913, p. 184.
22 Paulhan, 'La Preuve par l'etymologie', p. 12.
23 J. André, 'Puns and Rebuses in History and Archaeology', *Reliquary*, 23, 1882–3, pp. 170, 169, 170. (In Latin, *arma cantantia*, in English Canting, or Allusive, Arms.)
24 *Comic Epitaphs*. Mount Vernon, New York, Peter Pauper, 1957, p. 35.
25 Esar, *Comic Encyclopaedia*, p. 619.

26 Bier, *Rise and Fall of American Humor*, p. 339.
27 R. Queneau, *Les Fleurs bleues*. Paris, Gallimard, 1978, p. 95.
28 R. Reisner, *Graffiti: Two Thousand Years of Wall Writing*. New York, Cowles, 1971, p. 70.
29 Abel and Buckley, *Handwriting on the Wall*, p. 74.
30 Reisner and Wechsler, *Encyclopaedia of Graffiti*, p. 162.
31 Corvin, *Petite Folie collective*, p. 14.
32 E. Sheldon, 'Some Pun among the Hucksters', *American Speech*, 31, 1956, p. 14.
33 C. Wordsworth, *Guardian*, 16 October 1980, p. 8.
34 Sheldon, 'Some Pun', p. 15.
35 Caird, *Language and Imagery*, p. 15.
36 McLuhan, *Understanding Media*, p. 228, (a nice sting in the tail).
37 See J. Kelly and P. Solomon, 'Humor in Television Advertising', *Journal of Advertising*, 4, 1975, p. 35.
38 S. Hayakawa, *Language and Thought in Action*. London, Allen & Unwin, 1965, pp. 263–4.
39 R.-J. Hérail and E. Lovatt, 'Actuavity: the harnessable linguistic workhorse of media projection', *Admap*, September 1978, p. 436.
40 Ibid., p. 437.
41 Jencks and Silver, *Adhocism*, p. 65.
42 J. Dubois, 'Publicité et fonctions du langage', in *Significations de la publicité*. Liège, 1974, p. 41.
43 Reboul, *Langage et idéologie*, p. 65.
44 Fuller, Smith, Ross. In W. Summers, *American Slogans*. New York, Paebar, 1949, p. 11.
45 Duisit, *Satire*, p. 113, 'Si le calembour est consommé quotidiennement par les masses, en échange, il force les masses à consommer.' Thus Duisit runs *une douche écossaise* on the whole phenomenon.
46 Sheldon, 'Some Pun', p. 15.
47 *Understanding Media*, p. 288.
48 Grandjouan, *Jeux de l'esprit*, p. 264.
49 B. Pascal, 'De l'esprit géométrique', *Pensées et opuscules*, ed. L. Brunschvicg. Paris, Hachette, 1957, p. 187. ('Le balancement douteux entre la vérité et la volupté.')
50 W. B. Kay, *Subliminal Seduction*. New York, New American Library, 1974, p. 26.
51 R. Williams, 'Advertising: the Magic System', *Problems in Materialism and Culture*. London, NLB, 1980, p. 181.
52 Letter from A. Clark, 16 September 1979.
53 R. Callary, 'The Literalization of Idioms', *American Speech*, 45, 1970, p. 303.
54 V. Hugo, *Les Misérables*. Paris, Hetzel, n.d., vol. 1 p. 185. (In vol. 7, p. 115, on the Paris sewers, Hugo says 'Il n'est aucun guano comparable au détritus d'une capitale'.)
55 Letter from *Guardian*, 14 March 1978.

56 *Le Canard enchaîné*, 3 June 1970 and 25 November 1970.
57 Reboul, *Langage et idéologie*, p. 27.
58 K. Waterhouse, *Daily Mirror Style*. London, Mirror Books, 1981, pp. 42, 25, 87, 9.
59 Cartoon by Reisner, *Magazine littéraire*, 63, 1972, p. 14.
60 Hughes and Hammond, *Upon the Pun*.
61 More, 'Thomas Hood', p. 52.
62 E. H. Gombrich, *Meditations on a Hobby Horse*. London, Phaidon, 1965, p. 122.
63 Koestler, *Act of Creation*, p. 179.
64 Brown, 'Eight Types of Pun', p. 14.
65 H. Kökeritz, *Shakespeare's Pronunciation*. New Haven, Yale University Press, 1953, p. 58.
66 Duisit, *Satire*, p. 114. (Hughes and Hammond, after plausibly linking puns with the chiasmus, mention the 'chiasmic nerve' in the eye.)
67 Gilman, *Curious Perspective*, pp. 1, 56.
68 Redon, quoted in B. Denvir, 'Arcimboldo', in J. Hadfield (ed.), *The Saturday Book*, No. 24. London, Hutchinson, 1964, p. 217.
69 Jencks and Silver, *Adhocism*, p. 23.
70 P. Eluard, 'Les plus belles cartes postales', *Minotaure*, 3–4, 1933, p. 89.
71 F.-C. Legrand and F. Sluys, *Arcimboldo et les arcimboldesques*. Paris, La Nef de Paris, 1955, p. 71.
72 P. Wescher, 'The "Idea" in Giuseppe Arcimboldo's Art', *The Magazine of Art* (New York), 43(1), 1950, p. 8.
73 Gilman, *Curious Perspective*, p. 80.
74 As regards puns in music, Brigid Brophy in a letter of 12 January 1981 speaks of a 'three-dimensional or indeed mixed-media pun: Mozart's use of the horns to accompany Figaro's "Aprite un po' quegli occhi", because the audience has both to recognize the instrument and know it is (in several languages) called a horn, even though the musical kind no longer looks very like an animal's/cuckold's horn'. It is fitting, then, that Brophy's *In Transit* 'uses words and even syllables as musical notes (hence the puns, as the syllables fly about and copulate in odd pairs and triplets)'. I. Shenker, *Words and their Masters*. New York, Doubleday, 1974, p. 107.
75 Esar, *Comic Encyclopaedia*, p. 629; and B. McMillan, *Punography*. Harmondsworth, Penguin, 1978.
76 Mareschal de Bièvre, *Le Marquis de Bièvre*. Paris, Plon-Nourrit, 1910, pp. 327–8.
77 M. Lower, *The Curiosities of Heraldry*. London, J. R. Smith, 1845, p. 125.
78 H. Kenner, *A Homemade World*. New York, Knopf, 1975, p. 92.
79 Heller, 'Towards a General Typology', p. 273.
80 M. McLuhan, *From Cliché to Archetype*. New York, Viking, 1970, p. 168.
81 B. Fussell, 'A Pratfall Can Be a Beautiful Thing', in Charney, *Comedy: New Perspectives*, p. 248.
82 C. Hockett, 'Jokes', *The View from Language*. Athens, Georgia, Georgia University Press, 1977, p. 257.

83 Jencks and Silver, *Adhocism*, p. 194.
84 J. Billot (ed.), *Entretiens avec Closon sur l'art, l'homme et la vie*. Paris, Société française de presse, 1964, p. 11.
85 Fadiman, 'Small Excellencies', p. 172. (See *Minotaure*, 3, 1931, p. 40, for a representation of Dali's 'visage paranoïaque' à la Picasso – in fact a photo of a tribal hut viewed on its side).
86 R. Arnheim, *Art and Visual Perception*. London, Faber, 1956, p. 104.
87 Hillier, *Punorama*, p. 5.
88 See E. Kris and E. H. Gombrich, 'The Principles of Caricature', *British Journal of Medical Psychology*, 17, 1938, pp. 337–8.
89 Auden, 'Notes on the Comic', p. 383.
90 P. Thomson, *The Grotesque*. London, Methuen, 1972, p. 57. (I am indebted to this study for several fillips to ideas.)
91 Freud, *Jokes*, p. 40, quoting K. Fischer.
92 Kris and Gombrich, 'Principles of Caricature', p. 197.
93 Mahood, *Shakespeare's Wordplay*, p. 30.
94 Levin, 'Wit and Schizophrenic Thinking', p. 921.
95 M. Wolfenstein, *Children's Humor*. Glencoe, Illinois, Free Press, 1954, pp. 15, 79, 81, 159, 170, 182.
96 S. Leacock, *Humor: Its Theory and Technique*. New York, Dodd, Mead, 1935, p. 36.
97 S. McCosh, *Children's Humour*. London, Granada, 1979, p. 52.
98 I. and P. Opie, *The Lore and Language of Schoolchildren*. London, Granada, 1977, pp. 99, 49, 28.
99 Koestler, *Act of Creation*, pp. 187, 313.
100 E. Partridge, *A Dictionary of Clichés*. London, Routledge & Kegan Paul, 1950, p. 3.
101 I. Disraeli, *Curiosities of Literature*. London, Routledge, 1858, vol. 3, p. 41.
102 Jacobs, *Naming-Day in Eden*, pp. 134–5. (See also the Surrealist *152 proverbes mis au goût du jour*, in Eluard, *Oeuvres complètes*, pp. 153ff.)
103 Loomis, 'Traditional American Word Play', p. 352.
104 Jacobs, *Naming-Day in Eden*, pp. 135, 138, 137.
105 C. Dickens, *Posthumous Papers of the Pickwick Club*. London, Dent, 1931, p. 316.
106 Loomis, 'Traditional American Word Play', p. 12.
107 C. Gruner, *Understanding Laughter*. Nelson-Hall, 1978, p. 108, quoting E. Storrs (particularly apt as this party's emblem is a donkey).
108 B. Whiting, 'American Wellerisms of the Golden Age', *American Speech*, 20(1), 1945, p. 9.
109 Jacobs, *Naming-Day in Eden*, p. 135.
110 Tanner, *Adultery in the Novel*, pp. 335–6.
111 H. Kenner, *The Stoic Comedians*. London, W. H. Allen, 1964, p. 19.
112 Sartre, *L'Idiot*, vol. 2, p. 1973.
113 Ibid., vol. 1, pp. 620, 621, 626–39, 646.
114 R. Barthes, 'Le Message publicitaire', *Cahiers de la Publicité*, 7, 1963, p. 95. (Note the very necessary proviso, 'qu'il faut savoir lui donner'.)

115 G. K. Chesterton, 'In Defence of Slang', *The Defendant*. London, Dent, 1907, p. 146.

116 Don Marquis, quited in Esar, *Comic Encyclopaedia*, p. 553.

117 J. Prévert, *Paroles*, Paris, Livre de poche, 1948, pp. 108, 215. (This is what Genette calls 'un calembour intertextuel', *Palimpsestes*. Paris, Seuil, 1982, p. 24.)

118 G. Milner, 'Homo Ridens', *Semiotica*, 1(v), 1972, p. 18.

119 Quoted in Hughes and Hammond, *Upon the Pun*, but also credited to Philip Guedalla.

120 Crosbie, *Dictionary of Puns*, p. 121 (credited to John Buchan).

121 Berloquin, *Dictionnaire de jeux de mots*, p. 20.

122 Paulhan, 'La Preuve par l'etymologie', pp. 68–9, 75–6.

123 A. Zijderveld, *On Clichés*. London, Routledge & Kegan Paul, 1979, p. 102.

Chapter 8: Across the Rivers and into the Trees

1 Bier, *Rise and Fall of American Humor*, p. 3.

2 M. Cunliffe, 'Newness as repudiation', *Times Literary Supplement*, 30 May 1980, pp. 615–16.

3 Crosbie, *Dictionary of Puns*, p. 97.

4 Moger, *Complete Pun Book*, p. 80.

5 Bier, *Rise and Fall of American Humor*, p. 339.

6 L. Spitzer, 'American Advertising Explained as Popular Art', *A Method of Interpreting Literature*. Northampton, Mass., Smith College, 1949, p. 146.

7 C. Kimmins, *The Springs of Laughter*. London, Methuen, 1928, p. 132.

8 Eastman. *Sense of Humor*, p. 70.

9 Loomis, 'Traditional American Word Play', p. 2.

10 A Repplier, *In Pursuit of Laughter*. Boston, Houghton Mifflin, 1936, pp. 174, 208.

11 From *Josh Billings on Ice* (1868), quoted in Bier, *Rise and Fall of American Humor*, p. 115.

12 Ibid., p. 100.

13 Quoted in L. Feinberg, *The Secret of Humor*, Amsterdam, Rodopi, 1978, p. 43.

14 Bier, *Rise and Fall of American Humor*, p. 99.

15 G. Mast, *The Comic Mind: Comedy and the Movies*. Indianapolis, Bobbs-Merrill, 1973, p. 282.

16 Cunliffe, 'Newness as Repudiation', p. 615.

17 N., Rees (ed.), *Graffiti 4*. London, Allen & Unwin, 1982, pp. 5–6.

18 Franklin, *Which Witch?*, p. xi.

19 J. Trevelyan, *TV Times*, 23–9 May 1981, p. 5.

20 H. Nicolson, *The English Sense of Humour*. London, Dropmore, 1946, pp. 48–9.

21 Empson, *Seven Types*, p. 273.

22 Sherzer, 'Oh! That's a Pun', p. 344.
23 Carrière, *Humour 1900*, p. 128.
24 *Biévriana*, pp. 132–3.
25 Blackmantle, *Punster's Pocket-Book*, p. 7.
26 Ullmann, *Principles of Semantics*, p. 136.
27 Yaguello, *Alice*, p. 16.
28 P. Fontanier, *Les Figures du discours*. Paris, Flammarion, 1968 (1821–7), p. 349.
29 H. de Balzac, *Une Ténébreuse Affaire*. Paris, Livre de Poche, 1960, pp. 203–4.
30 A. de Musset, *Fantasio*, in *Théâtre complet*, ed. M. Allem. Paris, Gallimard, 1958, pp. 302–3, 300.
31 A. King, 'The Significance of Style in *Fantasio*', *Language and Style*, 4, 1971, p. 305.
32 L. Tailhade, *Imbéciles et gredins*. Paris, Laffont, 1969, p. 222.
33 Quoted in Davis, *Fine Art of Punning*, p. 113.
34 C. Revi (ed.), *Anthologie de l'humour Vermot*. Paris, Société parisienne d'édition, 1977, p. 5.
35 San Antonio, *Je le jure*. Paris, Stock, 1975, p. 134.
36 H. Fluchère, letters of 13 January 1981 and 18 March 1981.
37 J. Weightman, 'Humour and the French', *Twentieth Century*, 170, 1961, p. 126. (On p. 120, he says: 'The French language is much more riddled with phonetic ambiguities than the English, with the result that puns are almost unavoidable and are willingly accepted as a source of entertainment'.)
38 Bastide, 'Le Rire', p. 959. (Perhaps not surprisingly, my request for elucidation received no reply from Dahomey.)
39 Charney, *Comedy High and Low*, p. 19.
40 G. Milner, 'Homo Ridens', *Semiotica*, 1(v), 1972, p. 3. (Only sixteen in Samoan and even fewer in Hawaiian.)
41 T. Le Marchant Douse, *Grimm's Law*. London, 1876, section 17.34.
42 Orr, *Three Studies*, pp. 23–4.
43 R. Blyth, *Oriental Humour*. Tokyo, Hokuseido, 1959, p. 15.
44 Huizinga, *Homo Ludens*, pp. 144–5.
45 A. Aarne, *The Types of the Folktale*. Helsinki, Suomalainen Tiedakatemia, 1961, p. 399.
46 Orr, *Three Studies*, p. 23.
47 G. Waringhien, 'Modesta Kontribuo pri la Sercologio', *Eseoj 1*, La Languna, J. Régulo, 1956, pp. 33–8.
48 Swift, 'The Dying Speech of Tom Ashe', pp. 265–6.
49 Crosbie, *Dictionary of Puns*, p. 75.
50 L. Rosten, *Treasury of Jewish Quotations*. New York, Bantam, 1977, p. 67.
51 Burgess, *Language Made Plain*, p. 184.
52 B. Brophy, *In Transit*. London, Macdonald, 1969, p. 29.
53 *The Nabokov–Wilson Letters (1940–1971)*, ed. S. Karlinsky. London, Weidenfeld, 1979, p. 29.

54 R. Ciancio, 'Nabokov and the Verbal Mode of the Grotesque', *Contemporary Literature*, 18(4), 1977, pp. 525, 520. ('Ear-witness' is from *Lolita*. London, Corgi, 1961, p. 153.)
55 E. Korn, 'Optical Illusions', *Times Literary Supplement*, 18 April, 1975, p. 417.
56 J. Arp, quoted in Peeters, *Roulette aux mots*, p. 163.
57 S. Beckett, *Molloy*. Paris, Union Générale d'Editions, 1963, pp. 33–4.
58 S. Beckett, *Murphy*. New York, Grove, 1952, p. 65.
59 C. Ackerley, 'In the beginning was the pun: Samuel Beckett's *Murphy*', *AUMLA*, 55, 1981, pp. 16, 19.
60 Mercier, *Irish Comic Tradition*, p. 103.
61 Kenner, 'Jokes at the Wake', p. 723.
62 M. McLuhan, *The Interior Landscape*. New York, McGraw-Hill, 1969, p. 23.
63 B. Benstock, *Joyce-Again's Wake*. Seattle, Washington University Press, 1965, p. 124.
64 Mercier, *Irish Comic Tradition*, p. 230.
65 Kenner, 'Jokes at the Wake', p. 732.
66 M. Bowie, 'Jacques Lacan', in J. Sturrock (ed.), *Structuralism and Since*. London, Oxford University Press, 1979, p. 144.
67 J. Joyce, *Finnegans Wake*. London, Faber, 1975, p. 20.
68 Nokes, 'Hack at Tom Poley's', p. 46.
69 R. McAlman, 'My Joyce Directs an Irish Word Ballet, in S. Gilbert, *Our Exagmination*. London, Faber, 1972, p. 114.
70 C. Hart, *Structure and Motif in Finnegans Wake*. Evanston, Illinois, Northwestern University Press, 1962, p. 34.
71 J.-J. Mayoux, *James Joyce*. Paris, Gallimard, 1965, pp. 139–40. For the argument that each pun in *Finnegans Wake* is a microcosm of the whole work, see Umberto Eco, *L'Oeuvre ouverte*. Paris, Seuil, 1965, pp. 264–5.
72 Kenner, 'Jokes at the Wake'. p. 733.
73 M. Praz, *Mnemosyne*. London, Oxford University Press, 1970, p. 194.
74 Brophy, *In Transit*, p. 35.
75 Addison, *Spectator*, vol. 1, p. 263.
76 Voltaire, *Lettres philosophiques*, ed. F. A. Taylor. Oxford, Blackwell, 1970, p. 83. (In an addition of 1756, he said: 'et un commentateur de bons mots n'est guère capable d'en dire'.)
77 Eastman, *Enjoyment of Laughter*, p. 58.
78 Ludovici, *Secret of Laughter*, p. 79.
79 R. Queneau, *Les Fleurs bleues*. Paris, Gallimard, 1978, p. 48.
80 Brophy, *In Transit*, p. 35. (After punning on 'coney-linctus' in chapter 2, I found out that 'linctus' comes from the Latin *lingere*, to lick.)
81 G. Legman, *The Horn Book*. New York, University Books, 1964, p. 48.
82 Ellis, *Shakespeare's Lusty Punning*. pp. 103–5.
83 Jencks and Silver, *Adhocism*, p. 197.
84 P. Guiraud, *Sémiologie de la sexualité*. Paris, Payot, 1978, pp. 110, 107.
85 F. Ponge, *La Fabrique du Pré*. Geneva, Skira, 1971, p. 23.

86 G. Elgozy, *L'Esprit des mots*. Paris, Denoël, 1981, p. 173; J. Heller, *Something Happened*. London, Corgi, 1976, p. 491; Grousset, *Si t'es gai*, p. 113.

87 R. Barthes, *Sade, Fourier, Loyola*. Paris, Seuil, 1971, p. 161.

88 E. Tempel, *Humor in the Headlines*. New York, Pocket Books, 1969, p. 149.

89 Robbins, 'A Prevalence of Paronomasia', p. 522.

90 Freud, *Jokes*, p. 44, quoting T. Lipps; and p. 118.

91 Duisit, *Satire*, p. 97.

92 Laclos, *Les Liaisons dangereuses*, ed. R. Pomeau. Paris, Garnier/Flammarion, 1962, p. 104.

93 Stanford, *Ambiguity*, pp. 28–9. (Corneille in France and Shakespeare in England have suffered similar fates at the hands of generations of schoolboys.)

94 S. Freud, *The Psychopathology of Everyday Life*. Harmondsworth, Penguin, 1975, pp. 125–6.

95 Freud, *Jokes*, pp. 140–1.

96 J. Henderson, *The Maculate Muse*. New Haven, Yale University Press, 1975, p. 41.

97 G. S. Kirk, *The Nature of Greek Myths*. Harmondsworth, Penguin, 1974, p. 199.,

98 Freud, *Jokes*, p. 141.

99 Bastide, 'Le Rire', p. 955.

100 S. Beckett, a letter to A. Schneider of 29 December 1957. See 'Beckett's Letters on *Endgame*', *the village VOICE*, 19 March 1958, pp. 8, 15.

101 A. Dundes, quoted in Abel and Buckley, *Handwriting on the Wall*, p. 47.

102 Huizinga, *Homo Ludens*, p. 63.

103 S. T. Coleridge, *Anima Poetae*, ed. E. Coleridge. London, Heinemann, 1895, p. 108.

104 R. Crevel, *Le Clavecin de Diderot*. Paris, Pauvert, 1966, p. 146.

105 Tanner, *Adultery in the Novel*, p. 53.

106 P. Vallesio, 'The Language of Madness in the Renaissance', *Yearbook of Italian Studies*, 1, 1971, p. 229.

Conclusion

1 R. Graves, *Poems*. Harmondsworth, Penguin, 1957, p. 83. The Latin tag is a grammatical play, for *amanda* here is both neuter plural and feminine singular.

2 R. Queneau, *Contes et propos*. Paris, Gallimard, 1981, p. 203.

3 A. Palmer, *Folk and their Word-Lore*, p. 5.

4 J. Batlay, 'Jeux de mots', pp. 270–1.

5 F. Schlegel, *Literary Notebooks*. London, Athlone, 1957, pp. 245, 115. (Cf. Hugo on puns as guano. Great minds think alike, i.e. lavatorially.)

6 Koestler, 'Humour and Wit', p. 8, for the first two quotations, and *Act of Creation*, p. 315, for the third.

7 E. Espy, *An Almanac of Words at Play*. New York, Potter, 1975, p. 42.

8 G. Ferdière, 'Mes mots-maux-bile', *Bizarre*, 32–3, 1964, p. 139.

9 M. Proust: letter to Mme Straus, January 1917; and *Le Côté de Guermantes*. Paris, Gallimard, 1954, vol. 2, p. 254.

10 J. Horvat, 'Freud in France', *Cambridge Quarterly*, 7(4), 1977, p. 353.

11 A. Room, *Dictionary of Confusibles*. London, Routledge & Kegan Paul, 1979, p. 4.

12 F. Ponge, *Pour un Malherbe*. Paris, Gallimard, 1965, pp. 180, 215.

13 T. Hood, quoted in H. Orel (ed.), *The World of Victorian Humor*. New York, Appleton-Century-Crofts, 1961, p. 20.

14 T. Birch, 'A Modest Apology for Punning', *The Tatler and The Guardian* (*Guardian*, no. 36, 22 April 1713). Edinburgh, Nimmo, 1880, p. 53. (The present-day *Guardian* rather more guardedly keeps alight this particular torch.)

15 *Coleridge on Shakespeare*, p. 255.

16 P. Valéry, 'Autres Rhumbs', *Tel Quel 2*. Paris, Gallimard, 1971, p. 154.

17 P. Nizan, *Aden Arabie*. Paris, Maspero, 1960, p. 151.

18 M. Edwards, 'Sublunary Language', *Prospice*, 11, 1981, p. 90.

19 G. Hartman, *Saving the Text*. Baltimore, Johns Hopkins University Press, 1981, p. 46.

20 Wilson, *Jokes*, pp. 230–1.

21 J. Levine, 'Humour as a Form of Therapy', in A. Chapman and H. Foot (eds), *It's a Funny Thing, Humour*. Oxford, Pergamon, 1977, pp. 134–5.

22 T. Todorov, *Les Genres du discours*. Paris, Seuil, 1978, p. 296.

23 C. Lévi-Strauss, *La Pensée sauvage*. Paris, Plon, 1962, p. 29.

24 Todorov, *Genres du discours*, pp. 304, 306.

25 Ludovici, *Secret of Laughter*, p. 70.

26 V. Hugo, *Les Misérables*. Paris, Hetzel, n.d., vol. 5, p. 222.

27 Burgess, *Language Made Plain*, p. 110; and Carroll, *The Annotated Alice*, p. 48.

28 R. Queneau, *Les Fleurs bleues*. Paris, Gallimard, 1978, p. 25.

29 L. Spitzer, *A Method of Interpreting Literature*. Northampton, Mass., Smith College, 1949, p. 120.

30 J. Vendryès, *Le Langage*. Paris, Renaissance du Livre, 1921, p. 209.

31 T. Todorov, *Genres du discours*, p. 294.

32 Grousset, *Si t'es gai*, p. 21.

33 E. Korn, 'Optical Illusions', *Times Literary Supplement*, 18 April 1975, p. 417.

34 P. van Buren, *The Edges of Language*. London, SCM, 1972, p. 103. (Not all have been hostile to 'pulpit-wit'. Amhurst wrote: 'The poor sinner was mightily awaken'd to his duty by a pretty pun, and oftentimes owed his salvation to a quibble or conundrum; the devil was jested out of his dominions, and heaven was croud'd with religious punsters and witals.' *Terrae-Filius*. London, Francklin, 1754, p. 204.)

35 McLuhan, *From Cliché* to Archetype, p. 35. This much-munched phrase

originated with Alan of Lille, who was talking of God. (Elsewhere McLuhan likened the reverberations of our new world-tribal drums to the pun, though I confess I do not know why.)

36 Renou, 'Art et religion dans la poétique sanskrite', p. 284.
37 R. Barthes, *Système de la mode*. Paris, Seuil, 1967, p. 223.
38 A. Chénier, *Oeuvres complètes*, ed. G. Walter, Paris, Gallimard, 1950, p. 448.
39 V. Hugo, *William Shakespeare*. Paris, A. Michel, 1937.
40 Tanner, *Adultery in the Novel*, p. 335.
41 S. Newman, *Dickens at Play*. London, Macmillan, 1981, pp. 122–5, quoting R. Fowler.
42 C. Rozan, *Petites Ignorances de la conversation*. Paris, Durocq, n.d., p. 41.
43 L. Etienne, quoted in P. Guiraud, *Jeu de mots*, p. 116.
44 C. Baudelaire, *Le Spleen de Paris*, ed. Y. le Dantec. Paris, A. Colin, 1958, p. 121.
45 Freud, *Jokes*, p. 84.
46 Amhurst, *Terrae-Filius*, p. 205.
47 L. Untermeyer, quoted in Moger, *Complete Pun Book*, p. 77.
48 Esar, *Comic Dictionary*, p. 76.
49 I lift this delectable Wellerism from the generally anti-punning Legman, *No Laughing Matter*, p. 957.
50 S. Mallarmé, 'Crise de vers', *Igitur*, ed. Y. Bonnefoy. Paris, Gallimard, 1976, p. 25.
51 Pascal, *Pensées et opuscules*, ed. L. Brunschvicg. Paris, Hachette, 1957, pp. 475–6.
52 M. Moore, 'Poetry', *Penguin Book of Modern American Verse*, ed. G. Moore, Harmondsworth, Penguin, 1954, p. 114.
53 D. Erasmus, *Eloge de la folie*. Paris, Garnier/Flammarion, 1964 (1511), p. 14.
54 Eastman, *Enjoyment of Laughter*, p. 35.
55 Legman, *No Laughing Matter*, p. 16.
56 G. K. Chesterton, *The Well and the Shallows*. London, Sheed & Ward, 1935, p. 10.
57 V. Nabokov, *Lolita*. London, Corgi, 1961, p. 35.

Select Bibliography

I have boiled down a bibliography several times this size, retaining the most useful, and especially including collections of puns. Many other interesting items can be found in the notes.

Abel, E.L. and Buckley, B.E., *The Handwriting on the Wall: Towards a Sociology and Psychology of Graffiti*. Westport, Greenwood, 1977.

Ackerley, C.J., '"In the Beginning was the Pun": Samuel Beckett's *Murphy*', *AUMLA*, 55, 1981, pp. 15–22.

Addison J., *The Spectator*, ed. D. Bond. London, Oxford University Press, 1965.

Aimard, P., *Les Jeux de mots de l'enfant*. Villeurbanne, Simep, 1975.

Alexander, P., 'Logic and the Humour of Lewis Carroll', *Proceedings of the Leeds Philosophical and Literary Society*. 6, 1951, pp. 551–66.

Alleau, R. (ed.), *Dictionnaire des jeux*. Paris, Tchou, 1964.

André, T.L.: 'Puns and Rebuses in History and Archaeology', *Reliquary*, 23, 1882–3, pp. 169–73.

Angotiana, ou suite des Calembourgs comme s'il en pleuvait. Paris, Barba, 1803.

Arieti, S., 'New Views on the Psychology and Psychopathology of Wit and the Comic', *Psychiatry*, 13, 1950, pp. 43–62.

Ashton, J. (ed.), *Humour, Wit and Satire of the Seventeenth Century*. London, Chatto & Windus, 1883.

Auden, W.H., 'Notes on the Comic', in *The Dyer's Hand*. New York, Random House, 1962.

T.B. and T.C., *The New Pun Book*. New York, Carey-Stafford, 1906.

Barnet, S., 'Coleridge on Puns', *Journal of English and Germanic Philology*, 56, 1957, pp. 602–9.

Bastide, R., 'Le Rire et les courts-circuits de la pensée', in Pouillon, J. and Maranda, P. (eds) *Echanges et communications*. The Hague, Mouton, 1970, vol. 2, pp. 953–63.

Bather, F.A., 'The Puns of Shakespeare', in Hawkins C. (ed.), *Noctes Shakesperianae*. London, Castle & Lamb. 1887, pp. 69–91.

Batlay, J.H., 'Les Jeux de mots et de l'art dans *Rock-Monsieur*', in Arnaud, N. and Baudin, H. (eds), *Boris Vian*. Paris, Union Générale d'Editions, 1977, vol. 2, pp. 239–74.

Baudelaire, C., 'De l'essence du rire', *Curiosités esthétiques*, ed. H. Lemaître. Paris, Garnier, 1962.

Baudoin, D., 'Jeux de mots surréalistes, l'expérience du proverbe', *Symposium*, 24(4), 1970, pp. 293–302.

Baum, F., 'Chaucer's Puns' and 'A Supplementary List', *PMLA*, 71(1). 1956, pp. 225–46, and 73(1), 1958, pp. 167–70.

Bayet, C., *Victor Hugo s'amuse*. Paris, Atlas, 1955.

Benveniste, E., 'Le Jeu comme structure', *Deucalion*, 2, 1947, pp. 161–7.

Bergson, H., *Le Rire*. Paris, PUF, 1975 (1900).

Berloquin, P., *Dictionnaire de jeux de mots*. Paris, Encre, 1980.

Bier, J., *The Rise and Fall of American Humor*. New York, Holt, Rinehart & Winston, 1968.

Bièvre, G.M.de, *Le Marquis de Bièvre*. Paris, Plon-Nourrit, 1910.

Bièvre, Marquis de, *Vercingentorixe*. Paris, Pauvert, 1961(1770).

Bièvre, Marquis de, *Bièvriana*. Paris, Maradan, an VIII.

Bièvre Marquis de, 'Kalembour', *Encyclopédie* (Supplément). Paris, Briasson, 1777.

Birch, T., 'A Modest Apology for Punning', *The Tatler and The Guardian*. Edinburgh, Nimmo, 1880.

Blair, W. and Hill. H., *American Humor*. New York, Oxford University Press, 1978.

Boyer, R., 'Mots et jeux de mots chez Prévert, Queneau, Boris Vian, Ionesco', *Studia Neophilologica*, 40(2), 1968, pp. 317–58.

Brandreth, G. *Wordplay*. London, Severn House, 1982.

Bridges, R., 'On English Homophones', *The Society for Pure English*. Tract no. 2, 1919.

Brisset, J.-P., *Les Origines humaines*. Paris, Baudoin, 1980 (1913).

Brisset, J.-P., *La Grammaire logique*. Paris, Baudoin, 1980 (1883).

Brophy, B., *In Transit*. London, Macdonald, 1969.

Brown, J., 'Eight Types of Pun'. *PMLA*, 71, 1956, pp. 14–26.

Brown, M. (ed.), *Bulls and Blunders*. Chicago, Griggs, 1893.

Brunetiana. Paris, Barba, 1862.

Burgess, A., *Joysprick*. London, Deutsch, 1973.

Burgess, A., *Language Made Plain*. London, Fontana/Collins, 1975.

Caird, G.D., *The Language and Imagery of the Bible*. London, Duckworth, 1980.

Des Calembourgs comme s'il en pleuvait. Paris, Barba, 1800.

Canel, A., *Recherches sur les jeux d'esprit*. Evreux, Hérissey, 1867, 2 vols.

Carrière, J.-C., *Humour 1900.*, Paris, J'ai lu, 1980.

Carroll, L., *The Annotated Alice*, ed. M. Gardner. Harmondsworth, Penguin, 1978.

Carroll, L., *The Annotated Snark*, ed. M. Gardner. Harmondsworth, Penguin, 1979.

Casanowicz, I.M., *Paronomasia in the Old Testament*. Boston, Norwood, 1894.

Caws, M.A., 'Jean-Pierre Brisset et la grammaire des grenouilles', *Nineteenth-Century French Studies*, Fall 1972, pp. 43–60.

Cerf, B., *Bennett Cerf's Treasury of Atrocious Puns*. New York, Harper & Row, 1968.

Charney, M., *Comedy High and Low*. New York, Oxford University Press, 1978.

Charney, M. (ed.), *Comedy: New Perspectives*. New York Literary Forum, 1, 1978.

Cherrier, C., *Polissonniana*. Amsterdam, Schelt, 1725.

Chesterton, G.K., 'The Pun', *Lunacy and Letters*. London, Sheed & Ward, 1958.

Chevalier, J.-C., 'La Poésie d'Apollinaire et le calembour', *Europe*, 451–2, 1966, pp. 54–76.

Clubbe, J., *Victorian Forerunner: The Later Career of Thomas Hood*. Durham, North Carolina, Duke University Press, 1968.

Coleridge, S.T., *Coleridge on Shakespeare*, ed. T. Hawkes. Harmondsworth, Penguin, 1969.

Colie, R., *Paradoxia Epidemica*. Princeton University Press, 1966.

Commerson, *Pensées d'un emballeur*. Paris, Garnier, 1978 (1851).

Corvin, M., *Petite Folie collective*. Paris, Tchou, 1966.

Couvray, A., *Calembours et jeux de mots des hommes illustres anciens et modernes*. Paris, Aubry, 1806, 2 vols.

Cricriana, ou recueil des Halles. Paris, Cavanagh, 1803.

Crosbie, J., *Crosbie's Dictionary of Puns*. New York, Harmony, 1977.

Cullard, P., 'Un Paraphrène au X1Xe siècle: J.-P. Brisset "Prince des Penseurs"', thesis, Faculté de Médecine, Strasbourg University, 1980.

Cunliffe, M., 'Newness as repudiation: styles in modern American thought', *Times Literary Supplement*, 30 May 1980, pp. 615–16.

Curtius, E.R., *European Literature and the Latin Middle Ages*. London, Routledge & Kegan Paul, 1953.

Daubercies, C., 'Le Jeu de mots chez Raymond Queneau', Thèse de Diplôme d'Etudes Supérieures, Lille University, 1960.

Davis, H.T., *The Fine Art of Punning*. Evanston, Principia, 1954.

Davoine, J.-P., 'Calembour surréaliste et calembour publicitaire', *Studi francesi*, 57, 1975, pp. 481–7.

Delacour, J., *Dictionnaire des mots d'esprit*. Paris, A. Michel, 1976.

Donville, F. de, *Mille et un calembours*. Paris, Garnier, 1978 (1881).

Douglas, M., 'The Social Control of Cognition: Some Factors in Joke Appreciation', *Man*, 3, 1968, pp. 361–76.

Driver, G.R., 'Playing on Words', *4th World Congress of Jewish Studies*, 1, 1967, pp. 121–9.

Ducháček, O., 'Les Jeux de mots du point de vue linguistique', *Beiträge Zur Romanischen Philologie*, 9, 1970, pp. 107–17.

Ducret, E. (ed.), *Les Farceur parisien: choix de calembours*. Paris, Guyot, 1901.

Duisit, L., *Satire, parodie, calembour*. Saratoga, Anma Libri, 1978.

Dupriez, B., *Gradus: les procédés littéraires*. Paris, Union Générale d'Editions, 1980.

Eastman, M., *The Sense of Humor*. New York, Scribner, 1921.

Eastman, M., *Enjoyment of Laughter*. London, Hamish Hamilton, 1937.

Edwards, M., 'Exercise in Queneau', *Prospice*, 8, 1978, pp. 44–50.

Edwards, M., '"Renga", Translation and Eliot's Ghost', *PN Review*, 16, 1980, pp. 24–8.

Edwards, M., 'Sublunary Language', *Prospice*, 11, 1981, pp. 66–96.

Elgozy, G., *De l'humour*. Paris, Denoël, 1979.

Ellis, H.A., *Shakespeare's Lusty Punning in 'Love's Labour's Lost'*. The Hague, Mouton, 1973.

Empson, W., *Seven Types of Ambiguity*. Harmondsworth, Penguin, 1973.

Esar, E., *The Comic Dictionary*. New York, Horizon, 1960.

Esar, E., *The Comic Encyclopaedia*. New York, Doubleday, 1978.

Espy, W., *An Almanac of Words at Play*. New York, Potter, 1975.

Etienne, L., *L'Art du contrepet*. Paris, Livre de poche, 1972.

Fadiman, C., 'Small Excellencies: A Dissertation on Puns', *Appreciations*. London, Hodder & Stoughton, 1962.

Farb, P., *Word Play*. London, Cape, 1974.

Feeney, L., 'The Menace of Puns', in Phelan, P.J. (ed.), *With a Merry Heart*. London, Longman, 1943.

Finkielkraut, A., *Ralentir! mots-valise!* Paris, Seuil, 1979.

Foucault, M., *Raymond Roussel*. Paris, Gallimard, 1963.

Franklin, J., *Which Witch?* London, Hamish Hamilton, 1966.

Freud, S., 'Humour', Standard edn, vol. 21. London, Hogarth, 1961.

Freud, S., *The Psychopathology of Everyday Life*. Harmondsworth, Penguin, 1975.

Freud, S., *Jokes and Their Relation to the Unconscious*. Harmondsworth, Penguin, 1976.

Funny Bone. Hannibal, Hannibal Printing Co., 1880.

Garvey, J.W., 'Laurence Sterne's Wordplay'. PhD thesis, Rochester University, New York, 1974.

George, F., *L'Effet 'yau de poêle: de Lacan et des lacaniens*. Paris, Hachette, 1979.

Gervais, A., 'Le Jeu de mots'. *Etudes françaises*, 7(1), 1971, pp. 59–78.

Gilman, E.B., *The Curious Perspective: Literary and Pictorial Wit in the 17th Century*. New Haven, Yale University Press, 1978.

Gordon, H.C., *PUNishment*. New York, Warner, 1980.

Gordon, H.C., *Grime and Punishment*. New York, Warner, 1981.

Grandjouan, J.-O., *Les Jeux de l'esprit*. Paris, Scarabée, 1963.

Grant, M.A., *The Ancient Rhetorical Theories of the Laughable*. Madison, University of Wisconsin, 1924.

Gray, D.J., 'The Uses of Victorian Laughter'. *Victorian Studies*, 10(2), 1966, pp. 145–76.

Greet, A.H., *Jacques Prévert's Word Games*. Berkeley, University of California Press, 1968.

Greig, J.Y.T., *The Psychology of Laughter and Comedy*. London, Allen & Unwin, 1923.

Greven, H., *La Langue des slogans publicitaires en anglais contemporain*. Paris, PUF, 1982.

Grousset, J.-P., *Si t'es gai, ris donc!* Paris, Julliard, 1963.

Guiraud, P., *Le Jeu de mots*. Paris, PUF, 1976.

Guiraud, P., 'Etymologie et *ethymologia*', *Poétique*, 11, 1972, pp. 405–13.

Guiraud, P., 'Typologie des jeux de mots', *Le Français dans le monde*, 151, 1981, pp. 36–41.

Hausmann, F.J., 'Studien zu einer Linguistik des Wortspiels: das Wortspiel im "Canard enchaîné"' *Beihefte zur Zeitschrift für romanische Philologie*, 143, 1974, pp. 1–166.

Hazlitt, W., *Lectures on the English Comic Writers, Collected Works*. London, Dent, 1903, vol. 8.

Heller, L.G., 'Towards a General Typology of the Pun', *Language and Style*, 7, 1974, pp. 271–82.

Henkle, R.B., *Comedy and Culture, England 1820–1900*, Princeton University Press, 1980.

Henley, J., 'An Oration on Grave Conundrums', *Oratory Transactions*, 6, London, 1728.

Hillier, B. (ed.), *Punorama, or The Best of the Worst*. Andoversford, Whittington, 1974.

Hockett, C.F., 'Where the Tongue Slips, There Slip I', in *To Honor Roman Jakobson*. The Hague, Mouton, 1967, vol. 2, pp. 910–36.

Hoke, H., and Randolph, B. (eds), *Puns, Puns, Puns*. New York, Watts, 1958.

Holmes, O.W., 'A Visit to the Asylum for Aged and Decayed Punsters', *Soundings from the Atlantic*. Boston, Ticknor & Fields, 1864.

Hood, T., *Humorous Poems*, ed. A. Ainger. London, Macmillan, 1893.

Houtzager, M.E., *Unconscious Sound- and Sense-Associations*. Amsterdam, Paris, 1935.

Hughes, P., *More on Oxymoron*. New York, Penguin, 1983.

Hughes, P. and Hammond, P., *Upon the Pun*. London, W.H. Allen, 1978.

Huizinga, J., *Homo Ludens*. London, Granada, 1970.

Hunt, C. (ed.), *My Favourite Howlers*. London, Benn, 1951.

Hutchinson, P., *Games Authors Play*. London, Methuen, 1983.

Hyers, M.C., *Zen and the Comic Spirit*. London, Rider, 1974.

Jacobs, N.J., *Naming-Day in Eden*. London, Gollancz, 1958.

Jencks, C. and Silver, N., *Adhocism*. New York, Anchor, 1973.

Jennings, P. (ed.), *Pun Fun*. Feltham, Hamlyn, 1980.

Jespersen, O., 'Punning of Allusive Phrases in English', *Selected Writings*. London, Allen & Unwin, n.d.

Joe Miller's Jests. London, Whittaker, 1846.

Kellett, E.E., 'The Puns in Milton', *London Quarterly Review*, 159. 1934, pp. 469–76.

Kelly, L.G., 'Punning and the Linguistic Sign', *Linguistics*, 66, 1971, pp. 5–11.

Kenner, H., *Paradox in Chesterton*. London, Sheed & Ward, 1948.

Kenner, H., 'The Jokes at the Wake', *Massachusetts Review*, 22(4), 1981, pp. 722–33.

Kirshenblatt-Gimblett, B. and Sherzer, J. (eds), *Speech Play on Display*. Philadelphia, University of Pennsylvania Press, 1976.

Koegler, R.R., 'In Defense of the Pun'. *American Imago*, 16, 1959, 231–5.

Koestler, A., *The Act of Creation*. London, Hutchinson, 1964.

Koestler, A., 'Humour and Wit', *Encyclopaedia Britannica*. Chicago, Benton, 1974, vol. 9, pp. 5–11.

Kredel, E., *Studien zur Geschichte des Wortspiels im französischen. Beiträge zur romanischen Philologie*, 13, 1923.

Lamb, C., 'Popular Fallacies, IX: That the Worst Puns are the Best', *Works*, ed. W. McDonald. London, Dent, 1903, vol. 2.

Landheer, R., 'Les Règles du jeu de mots en français contemporain', in Sciarone, A.G., van Essen, A.J. and van Raad, A.A. (eds), *Nomen*. The Hague, Mouton, 1969, pp. 81–103.

Larchey, L., *L'Esprit de tout le monde*. Paris/Nancy, Berger-Levrault, 1892–3, 2 vols.

Larudee, P.S., 'Puns as Speech Acts and Speech Acts in Grammatical Theory', PhD thesis, Georgetown University, 1974.

Lauter, P. (ed.), *Comedy*. New York, Doubleday, 1964.

Leech, E., 'Anthropological Aspects of Language: Animal Categories and Verbal Abuse', in Lenneberg, E.H. (ed.), *New Directions in the Study of Language*. Boston, MIT, 1964.

Le Comte, E., *A Dictionary of Puns in Milton's English Poetry*. London, Macmillan, 1981.

Legman, G., *Rationale of the Dirty Joke*. London, Panther, 1976, 2 vols.

Legman, G., *No Laughing Matter*. London, Granada, 1978.

Leiris, M., *Mots sans mémoire*. Paris, Gallimard, 1966.

Levin, M., 'Wit and Schizophrenic Thinking', *American Journal of Psychiatry*, 113, 1957, pp. 917–23.

Lewis, A.F.G.L., *A Pun My Soul*. High Wycombe, 1977.

Liede, A., *Dichtung als Spiel*. Berlin, De Gruyter, 1963, 2 vols.

Loomis, C.G., 'Traditional American Word Play', *Western Folklore*, 8, 1949, pp. 1–21, 235–47 and 348–57; and 9, 1950, pp. 147–52.

Ludovici, A., *The Secret of Laughter*. London, Constable, 1932.

McCartney, E.S., 'Puns and Plays on Proper Names'. *Classical Journal*, 14(6), 1919, pp. 342–58.

McCartney, E.S., 'Verbal Homeopathy and the Etymological Story', *American Journal of Philology*, 48(4), 1927, pp. 326–43.

McCosh, S., *Children's Humour*. London, Granada, 1979.

McEuen, K.A., 'Lowell's Puns', *American Speech*, 22, 1947, pp. 24–33.

McLuhan, M. *From Cliché to Archetype*. New York, Viking, 1970.

McMillan, B.A., *Punography*. Harmondsworth, Penguin, 1978.

Mahood, M., *Shakespeare's Wordplay*. London, Methuen, 1979.

Margolin, R. (ed.), *Peter's Pauper's Pun Book*. Mount Vernon, Peter Pauper, 1962.

Margolin, V., 'The Pun is Mightier than the Sword', *Verbatim*, 7(1), 1980, pp. 1–4.

Martin, R.B., *The Triumph of Wit*. Oxford, Clarendon, 1974.

Mast, G., *The Comic Mind: Comedy and the Movies*. Indianapolis, Bobbs-Merrill, 1973.

The Memoirs of Martinus Scriblerus, ed. C. Kerby-Miller. New Haven, Yale University Press, 1950.

Mendelsohn, C.J., *Studies in the Word-Play in Plautus*. Winston, University of Pennsylvania, 1907.

Mercier, V., *The Irish Comic Tradition*. London, Oxford University Press, 1962.

Milburn, G. (ed.), *A Book of Interesting and Amusing Puns*. Girard, Haldeman-Julius, 1926.

Milner, G.B., 'Homo Ridens: Towards a Semiotic Theory of Humor and Laughter', *Semiotica*, 1(V), 1972, pp. 1–30.

Sr Miriam Joseph, *Shakespeare's Use of the Arts of Language*. New York, Columbia University Press, 1947.

Moger, A., *The Complete Pun Book*. Secaucus, Citadel, 1979.

Moloney, P., *A Plea for Mersey*. Liverpool, Gallery, 1966.

More, P.E., 'Thomas Hood', *Shelburne Essays*, 7th series, New York, Putnam, 1910.

Morin, V., 'Avec San Antonio: un humour en miettes', in *Une Nouvelle Civilisation?* Paris, Gallimard, 1973, pp. 417–32.

Muecke, D.C., *Irony*. London, Methuen, 1973.

Muecke, D.C., *The Compass of Irony*. London, Methuen, 1980.

Muir, F. and Norden, D., *Upon My Word*. London, Eyre Methuen, 1974.

Muir, K., 'The Uncomic Pun', *Cambridge Journal*, 3, 1950, pp. 472–85.

Nokes, D., '"Hack at Tom Poley's": Swift's Use of Puns', in Probyn, C. (ed.), *The Art of Jonathan Swift*. London, Vision, 1978, pp. 43–56.

O'Connor, J.D., 'Phonetic Aspects of the Spoken Pun', *English Studies*, 33(3), 1952, pp. 116–24.

Olbrechts-Tyteca, L., *Le Comique du discours*. Editions de l'Université de Bruxelles, 1974.

Opie, I. and P., *The Lore and Language of Schoolchildren*. London, Paladin, 1977.

Orr, J., *Three Studies on Homonymics*. Edinburgh University Press, 1962.

Palmer, A.S., *The Folk and their Word-Lore*. London, Routledge, 1904.

'La Parodie', *Cahiers du XXe siècle*, 6, 1976.

Partridge, E., *Shakespeare's Bawdy*. London, Routledge, 1947.

(Passard, F.L.?), *Musée drolatique des calembours*. Paris, Passard, 1853(?).

Paulhan, F., 'Psychologie du calembour', *Revue des Deux Mondes*, 142, 15 August 1897, pp. 862–903.

Paulhan, J., 'La Preuve par l'étymologie', *Oeuvres complètes*. Paris, Cercle du Livre précieux, 1966–70, vol. 3.

Peake, M., *Figures of Speech*. London, Gollancz, 1954.

Peeters, L., *La Roulette aux mots: la parodie et le jeu de mots dans la poésie française du symbolisme au surréalisme*. Paris, La Pensée Universelle, 1975.

Peignot, G., *Amusements philologiques*. Dijon, Lagier, 1842.

Peignot, J., *Le Petit Gobe-mouches*. Paris, Bourgois, 1979.

Penkethman, W., *Penkethman's Jests*. London, Warner, 1721, 2 vols.

Philips, S.U., 'Teasing, Punning and Putting People On', *Working Papers in Sociolinguistics*, 28, 1975, pp. 1–21.

Pierrsens, M., *La Tour de Babil*. Paris, Minuit, 1976.

Pointe, Baron de la and le Gai, E., *Dictionnaire des calembours*. Paris, 1884.
Pope, A., 'God's Revenge against Punning', *Prose Works*, ed. N. Ault. Oxford, Blackwell, 1936, vol. 1.
Probyn, C., 'Swift and the Human Predicament', in Probyn, C. (ed.), *The Art of Jonathan Swift*. London, Vision, 1978, pp. 57–80.
The Punster's Last Legacy. London, Langley, 1803.
Puttenham, G., *The Arte of English Poesie*, ed. G. Willcock. Cambridge University Press, 1936 (1589).
Quirk, R., 'Puns to Sell', *Studia Neophilologica*, 23, 1951, pp. 81–6.
Rees, E., *Pun Fun*. London, Abelard-Schuman, 1965.
Rees, N., *Slogans*. London, Allen & Unwin, 1982.
Reisner, R., *Graffiti: Two Thousand Years of Wall Writing*. New York, Cowles, 1971.
Reisner, R. and Wechsler, L., *Encyclopaedia of Graffiti*. New York, Macmillan, 1974.
Renou, L., 'Art et religion dans la poétique sanskrite: le "jeu de mots" et ses implications', *Journal de Psychologie Normale et Pathologique*, 44 (1–2), 1951, pp. 280–5.
Richter, J.-P., *Horn of Oberon: Jean-Paul Richter's School for Aesthetics*. Detroit, Wayne State University Press, 1973.
Riffaterre, M., 'Fonction du cliché dans la prose littéraire', *Essais de stylistique structurale*. Paris, Flammarion, 1971.
Rigolot, F., *Poétique et onomastique*. Geneva, Droz, 1973.
Robbins, R., 'A Prevalence of Paronomasia', *Times Literary Supplement*, 8 May 1981, p. 522.
Robbins, R.H., 'The Warden's Wordplay: Towards a Redefinition of the Spoonerism', *Dalhousie Review*, 46, 1966, pp. 457–65.
Rochette, A., *L'esprit dans les oeuvres poétiques de Victor Hugo*. Paris, Champion, 1911.
Rodgers, B., *The Queens' Vernacular: A Gay Lexicon*. San Francisco, Straight Arrow, 1972.
Rousséliana. Paris, Cavanagh, 1803.
Rowley, H., *Puniana*. London, Hotten, 1867.
Ruthven, K., 'The Poet as Etymologist'. *Critical Quarterly*, 11, 1969, pp. 9–37.
Ruthven, K., *The Conceit*, London, Methuen, 1969.
Sacks, H., 'On Some Puns with Some Intimations', in Shuy, R.W. (ed.), *Report of the 23rd Annual Round Table on Linguistics and Language Studies*. Washington, Georgetown University Press, 1973, pp. 135–44.
Safian, L.A., *Just for the Pun of It*. London, Abelard-Schuman, 1966.
Sartre, J.-P., *L'Idiot de la famille*. Paris, Gallimard, 1971, 3 vols.
Schultz, J., 'Psychologie des Wortspiels', *Zeitschrift für Aesthetik und allgemeine Kunstwissenschaft*, 21, 1927, pp. 16–37.
Sewell, E., *The Field of Nonsense*. London, Chatto & Windus, 1952.
Sheridan, T., 'The Original of Punning, from Plato's Symposiacs', in Ruddiman, T. (ed.), *A Collection of Scarce, Curious and Valuable Pieces*. Edinburgh, 1785.

Sheridan, T., *The Art of Punning*. Dublin, Carson, 1719.

Sherzer, J., 'Oh! That's a pun and I didn't mean it', *Semiotica*, 22(3/4), 1978, pp. 335–50.

Shipley, J., *Word Play*. New York, Hawthorne, 1972.

Smart, C., *Jubilate Agno*, ed. W. H. Bond. London, Hart-Davis, 1954.,

Smith, S., *Elementary Sketches of Moral Philosophy*. London, Longman, 1850.

Snyder, J.M., *Puns and Poetry in Lucretius' 'De Rerum Natura'*. Amsterdam, Grüner, 1980.

Spevack, M., 'Shakespeare's Early Use of Wordplay: *Love's Labour's Lost*', in Fabian, B. and Suerbaum, H. (eds), *Festschrift für Edgar Mertner*. Munich, Fink, 1969, pp. 157–68.

Spitzer, L., 'Pun', *Journal of English and Germanic Philology*, 49(3), 1950, pp. 352–4.

Stanford, W.B., *Ambiguity in Greek Literature*. New York, Johnson, 1972.

Stillman, D. and Beatts, A. (eds), *Titters: the First Collection of Humor by Women*. New York, Macmillan, 1976.

Swift, J., 'A Modest Defence of Punning', *Collected Writings*, ed. H. Davis and L. Landa. Oxford, Blackwell, 1957, vol. 4.

Tabourot, E., *Les Bigarrures*. Brussels, Mertens, 1866 (1572), 2 vols.

Tanner, T., *Adultery in the Novel*. Baltimore, Johns Hopkins University Press, 1979.

Thau, A., 'Play with words and sounds in the poetry of Max Jacob', *Revue des Lettres Modernes*, 336–9, 1973, pp. 125–56.

Thomson, P., *The Grotesque*. London, Methuen, 1972.

Thoreau, H.D., *Walden*. New York, New American Library, 1960.

Todorov, T., *Les Genres du discours*. Paris, Seuil, 1978.

Turkle, S., *Psychoanalytic Politics*. London, Burnett/Deutsch, 1979.

Ullman, S., *The Principles of Semantics*. Oxford, Blackwell, 1963.

Van Gennep, A., 'Wellérismes français', *Mercure de France*, 248, 1933, pp. 700–4, and 253, 1934, pp. 209–15.

Vittoz Canuto, M.-B., *Si vous avez votre jeu de mots à dire*, Paris, Nizet, 1983.

Voss, A., 'Lowell, Hood and the Pun', *Modern Language Notes*, 63(5), 1948, pp. 346–7.

Walle, B. van de, *L'Humour dans la littérature et dans l'art de l'ancienne Egypte*. Leiden, Nederlands Instituut voor Het Nabije Oosten, 1969.

Walsh, W.S., *Handy-Book of Literary Curiosities*. London, Gibbings, 1893.

Waterhouse, K., *Daily Mirror Style*. London, Mirror Books, 1981.

Weis, H., *Jocosa: Lateinische Sprachspielereien*. Munich, Oldenborg, 1952.

Weis, H., *Spiel mit Worten: deutsche Sprachspielereien*. Munich, Oldenborg, 1954.

Wellek, R., *A History of Modern Criticism: The Later 18th Century*, and *The Romantic Age*. London, Cape, 1964 and 1966.

Welsh, A., *Roots of Lyric*. Princeton University Press, 1978.

West, M., 'Scatology and Eschatology: The Heroic Dimensions of Thoreau's Wordplay', *PMLA*, 89(5), 1974, pp. 1043–64.

Wilson, C.P., *Jokes*. London, Academic, 1979.

Wimsatt, W.K., 'Verbal Style: Logical and Counterlogical', *PMLA*, 65(2), 1950, pp. 5–20.

Withington, R., 'Plays upon Language', *Atlantic Monthly*, 166, 1940, pp. 506–8.

Wolfenstein, M., *Children's Humor*. Glencoe, Illinois, Free Press, 1954.

Wolf-Rottkay, W.H., 'Tongue in cheek: A Recent Harvest of Punny Language from Lōs Angeles', *Neusprachliche Mitteilungen*, 25, 1972, pp. 170–5.

Woods, W.L., 'Language Study in Schizophrenia', *Journal of Nervous and Mental Disease*, 87(3), 1938, 290–316.

Yaguello, M., *Alice au pays du langage*. Paris, Seuil, 1981.

Zijderveld, A.D., *On Clichés*. London, Routledge & Kegan Paul, 1979.

Index

Ackerley, C. J., 166
Addison, Joseph, 2, 52, 169
Adler, Alfred, 109
advertising (*see* slogans)
Ainger, Alfred, 62
Alexander, Peter, 66
Allais, Alphonse, 77, 93, 127, 162
allegory (and parable), 82, 96–7, 125, 150, 171
Amhurst, Nicholas, 183, 216n
amphibology, 7, 10, 43, 143
anagram, 17, 70, 83
analogy, 11, 75, 98, 99, 114, 116, 118, 174
antigram, 83
Arcimboldo, Giuseppe, 143, 144
Arieti, Silvano, 107, 108, 128
Aristotle, 7, 82
Arnheim, Rudolf, 146–7
Auden, W.H., 93, 100, 147

Bain, Alexander, 31, 32, 82–3
Bakhtin, Mikhail, 43–4
Balzac, Honoré de, 30, 68, 71, 161
Barthes, Roland, 10, 18, 80, 87, 90, 104–5, 152–3, 171, 181
Bastide, Roger, 107, 163, 192n
Batlay, Jenny, 24, 27, 30, 124, 175
Baudelaire, Charles, 4, 37, 111–12, 183
Beckett, Samuel, 2, 127, 164, 165–6, 173
Benveniste, Emile, 13, 23
Bergler, Edmund, 5
Bergson, Henri, 22, 30, 71–4, 109

Bible, 37–8, 49, 50, 86, 113, 114, 177
Bier, Jesse, 136–7, 156, 157, 158
Bierce, Ambrose, 27, 66–7, 156
Bièvre, Marquis de, 4, 55–6, 145, 160
Billings, Josh, 157–8
Blackmantle, Bernard, 2, 3, 30, 160
Blyth, R.H., 33
Bowie, Malcolm, 81, 168
Breton, André, 75–6, 110, 115
bricolage, 12–13, 34, 139, 179, 184
Brisset, Jean-Pierre, 81, 112, 113–17
Brophy, Brigid, 164–5, 169, 170, 210n
Browne, Sir Thomas, 4, 49
Burgess, Anthony, 21, 66, 87, 131, 164, 180
Byron, Lord, 61, 66, 100

Caird, G.D., 37, 85, 97, 99
Cambridge, 1–2, 183
Camus, Albert, 127, 161
Canard Enchaîné, le, 88, 141, 146
Caradec, François, 17, 67
Carlyle, Thomas, 61, 64
Carroll, Lewis, 21, 41, 43, 46, 48, 60, 64–6, 88, 89, 110, 111, 120–1, 128, 145, 180, 181, 203n
Charney, Maurice, 2, 19, 119, 122, 132, 163
Chaucer, Geoffrey, 35–6
Chester-le-Street, 85
Chesterton, G.K., 45, 64, 95, 101, 153, 159, 185
chiasmus, 23, 124, 144, 210n
children, 110, 148–9, 162, 170

Chinese, 36, 163
Chomsky, Noam, 6
Cicero, 4, 82
circumlocution, 90, 97
cliché, 90, 94, 138, 139, 142, 150–5, 156, 165, 182, 200n
Clubbe, John, 62, 63
Cocteau, Jean, 105, 116, 170
Coleridge, Samuel Taylor, 41, 47, 51, 61, 66, 105, 126, 173, 177–8
Colie, Rosalie, 5, 44–5, 50, 52, 86
Commerson, 68
computers, 46
conceits, 50, 51, 87, 95, 98–9
conundrum, 35, 41, 44, 53, 58, 82–3, 90, 97, 120, 136, 140, 146, 157, 176, 216n
Corneille, Pierre, 51–2, 111, 154, 215n
Corvin, Michel, 31, 76, 137
Cretin, Guillaume, 43
Crevel, René, 24, 25, 76, 173–4
Crosbie, John, 18–19, 25, 127, 128, 156, 164, 183
Cullard, Philippe, 114, 115
Cunliffe, Marcus, 156–7, 159

Dali, Salvador, 142, 146, 211n
Dearnley, Moira, 112–13
DeMott, Benjamin, 128
Desnos, Robert, 119, 173
De Vries, Peter, 111, 123
Dickens, Charles, 62, 150, 182
Diderot, Denis, 5, 26, 195n
Donne, John, 4, 50, 101, 113
Donoghue, Denis, 54, 94
doubles, 103–4
Douglas, Mary, 128, 129
dreams, 11, 12, 66, 73, 105, 106, 111, 118, 122, 143, 147
drugs, 111–12
Dryden, John, 4, 51
Duchamp, Marcel, 76, 105, 115
Duisit, Lionel, 4, 10, 15, 139, 143, 171
Duncan, Alastair, 74–5

Dupriez, Bernard, 39
Dyer, Gillian, 131, 134
dysphemism, 26, 92

Eachard, John, 51
Eastman, Max, 15, 31, 73, 74, 106, 121, 123, 127, 157, 169
Edwards, Michael, 99, 178
Eliot, T.S., 12, 32
Eluard, Paul, 110, 144
Emerson, Ralph Waldo, 9, 67, 116
Empson, William, 46, 50–1, 53, 58, 62–3, 105, 159–60
epigram, 27, 153
epitaphs, 13, 136
Erasmus, Desiderius, 44, 184
eroticism, 18, 20, 75, 90–1, 93, 100, 115, 119, 132, 133–4, 143, 146, 149, 170–4, 199n
Erskine, Henry, 7–8
Esar, Evan, 5, 16, 105, 117, 136, 183
Esperanto, 164
Etienne, Luc, 118, 182
etymology, 11, 38, 39, 42, 67, 83–7, 100, 107, 115, 120, 136, 154, 157, 166
etymology of 'pun' and *calembour*, 16–17
euphemism, 9, 26, 90–2, 96
exaggeration, 92, 93, 148, 158

Fadiman, Clifton, 20, 146
Farb, Peter, 88, 91
Feeney, Leonard, 117
Feibleman, James K., 41
Finkielkraut, Alain, 88–9
Flaubert, Gustave, 43, 69–71, 73, 95, 101, 124, 140, 146, 151–2, 153, 165
Foucault, Michel, 76, 79, 80, 113, 114, 115
Fowler, H.W., 19
Franklin, Benjamin, 6, 125
Franklin, Julian, 17–18, 159
Freud, Sigmund, 5, 11, 22, 26–7, 31, 32, 41, 73–4, 92, 105–6, 107,

Freud, Sigmund, continued
108–9, 111, 117, 118, 122, 123, 125, 128, 129, 132, 143, 148, 149, 179, 182, 183
Frost, Robert, 32, 102, 192n
Frye, Northrop, 82, 113

Gardner, Martin, 43, 65
Genet, Jean, 71, 110–11
Gilman, Ernest B., 4, 64, 143–4
Gombrich E.H., 2, 147, 148
graffiti, 2, 137–8, 159
Granjouan, Jacques-Olivier, 22, 140
Grands Rhétoriqueurs, 43, 86
Gray, Donald J., 62, 65
Greig, J.Y.T., 27, 28
Grimm, Melchior, 55–6
Gross, John, 24
grotesque (and caricature), 95, 147–8
Grotjahn, Martin, 31
Grousset, Jean-Paul, 30, 181
Guiraud, Paul, 116
Guiraud, Pierre, 2, 17, 46, 86, 125, 132, 170

Hammond, Paul and Hughes, Patrick, 5, 7, 17, 18, 19, 28, 84, 99, 142–3, 147
Hart, Clive, 168
Hartman, Geoffrey, 178
Hazlitt, William, 58
Hebrew, 50
Heller, L.G., 82
Henkle, Roger B., 62, 64
Henley, John, 2
Heraclitus, 10, 36, 40–2, 103
heraldry, 39, 136, 145
Herbert, George, 50, 52
heteronym, 18, 28
Hockett, Charles F., 122
Holmes, Oliver Wendell, 3, 25, 67, 83, 180
homeopathy, 14, 38, 39, 182
homograph, 18
homonym, 7, 17–18, 32, 47, 90, 113, 158, 160

homophone, 7, 17, 28, 148, 160
Hood, Thomas, 25, 61–4, 101, 125, 142, 143, 177, 179
Hopkins, Gerard Manley, 76, 113
Horvat, J., 176
Hughes, Patrick (see Hammond)
Hugo, Victor, 4, 19, 24, 38, 40, 68–9, 89, 100, 101, 141, 148, 173, 180, 182
Huizinga, Johan, 13, 33, 34, 97, 163, 173, 184
humour
   American, 155, 156–9, 180
   British, 157, 159–60, 162, 180
   French, 160–2, 180
   gallows, 30, 48, 60, 92, 120, 125–8, 148, 166
   Jewish, 128
   political, 124–5, 178–9

insult (and flyting), 13, 91–3
Ionesco, Eugène, 75, 124, 164
irony, 9, 26, 90, 93, 97, 125, 133, 148, 177, 178
Isidore of Seville, 84

Jackson, John, 105–6
Jacobs, Noah Jonathan, 10, 37, 85, 95, 150, 151
Jakobson, Roman, 102
Jencks, Charles (and Silver, Nathan), 12, 144, 170
Jennings, Paul, 28, 30, 105
Johnson, Samuel, 4, 46, 52–3, 55, 98–9, 177
Jonson, Ben, 4, 50
Joyce, James, 4, 13, 15, 24, 54, 60, 67, 87, 88, 101, 164, 166–9, 174, 175, 181

Kahn, Charles H., 40
Kant, Immanuel, 56, 92
Keats, John, 60, 61, 196n
Kelly, L.G., 9–10
Kenner, Hugh, 28, 45, 119–20, 145, 151, 166, 167, 168

kinetic pun (and pratfall), 84, 145–6, 158–9
Kirk, Geoffrey Stephen, 83–4, 172
Koegler, Ronald R., 123
Koestler, Arthur, 12, 31, 73, 99, 106, 143, 149, 162, 176, 188n
Kökeritz, Helge, 47, 143
Korn, Eric, 165, 181
Kris, Ernst, 2, 147, 148
Kristol, Irving, 128

Lacan, Jacques, 6–7, 80–1, 85, 88, 98, 115, 176
Laclos, Choderlos de, 171
Laforgue, Jules, 77, 90
Lamb, Charles, 59–60, 61
Lautréamont, 127
Leach, Edmund, 91
Leacock, Stephen, 145
Lear, Edward, 66
Legman, Gershon, 2, 25, 26, 93, 170, 185, 217n
Leiris, Michel, 78–9
Lévi-Strauss, Claude, 34, 79–80, 179
Levin, Max, 107, 148–9
Levine, Jacob, 127, 179
Lichtenberg, Georg, 2, 109
limerick, 44, 83
Lipton, James, 101–2
litotes, 26, 52, 90–1, 92, 96
Liverpool, 1, 3
Loomis, C. Grant, 150, 157
Lucretius, 41–2
Ludovici, Anthony, 31, 169, 180

macaronic, 44, 164
McCartney, Eugene S., 38, 39
Macdonald, Dwight, 94
McLuhan, Marshall, 28, 131, 138, 140, 145, 166–7, 181, 217n
Mahood, Molly, 5, 30, 46, 47, 48, 62, 66, 105, 126, 129, 148
Mallarmé, Stéphane, 28, 184
Marquis, Don, 153
Martin, Robert Bernard, 59

Marvell, Andrew, 51
Marx, Karl, 40, 72, 124
Marx Brothers, 12, 158–9
mathematics, 44, 65
Mayoux, Jean-Jacques, 168
mental illness, 20, 30, 73, 81, 87, 88, 103–17, 123, 146–7, 174, 177, 180, 181, 183
Meredith, George, 7
Mercier, Vivian, 34, 166, 167
metanalysis, 39, 56
metaphor, 97–9, 111, 142, 150, 175, 178
Metaphysical Poets, 37, 95, 98
Michaux, Henri, 109, 112
Miller, J. Hillis, 81, 111
Miller, Joe, 166
Miller, Max, 96, 110, 175
Milner, George Bertram, 154, 163
Milton, John, 49–50, 61, 154
Molière, 51, 68, 72, 79
Montaigne, Michel de, 1, 8, 51, 184
Moore, Marianne, 145, 184
More, Paul Elmer, 63, 64, 143
Morin, Violette, 14, 39, 124, 126, 132
Muir, Kenneth, 47–8, 52, 97
Müller, Max, 9, 34–5
Musset, Alfred de, 161
mythology, 11, 33–7, 40, 86, 96–7, 181

Nabokov, Vladimir, 101, 164, 165, 181, 185
names, 37–40, 41, 42–3, 83, 86, 101–2, 113, 126, 132, 136, 149
Nash, Ogden, 19, 100
neologism, 68, 87–90, 109, 126, 139, 167
Newman, S.J., 182
Nicolson, Harold, 159
Nietzsche, Friedrich, 11, 14, 64, 90, 129, 178
Nodier, Charles, 17
Nokes, David, 54, 168
Nonsense, 2, 48, 65, 66, 82, 110, 149

obscenity, 1, 4, 29, 91, 92–3, 113–19, 172–3
Olbrechts-Tyteca, Lucie, 32, 122
oracle (and divination), 35–6, 38, 40, 76, 85
Opie, Iona and Peter, 149
Orr, John, 84, 163, 164
Orwell, George, 6, 45
OULIPO, 87, 155
Oxford, 183
oxymoron, 37, 95–6, 105, 144

palindrome, 114
Palmer, A. Smythe, 84, 85, 175
paradox, 11, 19, 44–5, 50, 67, 71, 95, 120, 144, 146
paragram, 18
Paris, Jean, 103–4, 116–117
parody, 18, 62, 84, 93–4, 125, 146, 150, 155, 156, 167
paronomasia, 18, 51, 82, 101, 102
paronym, 18, 91
Partridge, Eric, 85, 149–50
Pascal, Blaise, 27, 37, 140, 154, 184
'Pataphysics, 5, 95, 115
Paulhan, Frédéric, 11–12, 105
Paulhan, Jean, 84–5, 136, 154, 177
Peeters, Léopold, 122
Petrarch, 42–3
Picasso, Pablo, 12, 14, 94
Plato, 36
Poe, Edgar Allan, 63, 64, 196n
poetry, 7, 11, 42, 47, 101–2, 138, 145, 152–3, 169
Poirier, Richard, 67
Poirot-Delpech, Bertrand, 81
polysemy, 17, 32, 78, 84
Ponge, Francis, 13, 87, 98, 129, 145, 170, 177
Pope, Alexander, 53, 54
pornography, 111, 172
portmanteau-word, 37, 88–90, 104, 105, 200n
press, 120, 130, 141–2
Prévert, Jacques, 77, 99, 154

Probyn, Clive, 54
Proust, Marcel, 11, 43, 94, 127, 176
proverb, 94, 149–51, 153, 156, 163
Puttenham, George, 23, 40, 92, 96

Queneau, Raymond, 11, 14, 25, 46, 77–8, 84, 85, 89–90, 102, 113, 116, 124, 137, 170, 175, 180, 194n
quiproquo, 10, 72, 103, 123
Quintilian, 82, 84

Rabelais, François, 5, 7, 14, 44, 51, 94, 118–19
rebus, 17, 44, 74, 82, 136, 145
Rees, Nigel, 159
Regnaud, P., 35
Reisner, Robert, 137
Renou, Louis, 181
Restoration drama, 52
rhyme, 11, 18, 19, 39, 43, 62, 69, 78, 99–101, 149, 150
Ricardou, Jean, 23, 124
Richter, Jean-Paul, 11, 56–7, 58, 61, 124
Ricks, Christopher, 49, 60
Rigolot, François, 42–3
Robbins, Robin, 49, 171
Rochette, Auguste, 68–9, 100–1
Room, Adrian, 119, 177
Rosten, Leo, 128, 131
Roussel, Raymond, 74–5, 79
Rowley, Hugh, 18, 59
Ruthven, K.K., 50, 98–9

Sade, Marquis de, 14, 171
San Antonio, 14, 39, 124, 126, 162
Sardou, Victorien, 17
Sartre, Jean-Paul, 1, 45, 69, 70–1, 78, 110–11, 124, 151–2, 153, 165
Saussure, Ferdinand de, 11, 83
scatology, 2, 54, 67, 137, 172–3
Schlegel, Friedrich von, 61, 176
Schopenhauer, Arthur, 24, 123
serio-comic, 44, 93, 95, 184

Sewell, Elizabeth, 66, 88, 193n
shaggy-dog stories, 27
Shakespeare, William, 3, 4, 5, 20, 25, 30, 38–9, 46–9, 61, 66, 97, 101, 110, 124, 125–6, 129, 150, 173, 177, 184, 215n
Sheridan, Thomas, 3
Sherzer, Joel, 24, 160
Silver, Nathan (*see* Jencks)
Simon, Claude, 23, 74–5, 88
slang, 2–3, 4, 89, 153, 180
slips (and howlers, Irish Bulls, Spoonerisms), 35, 47, 68, 73, 117–23, 137, 144, 147, 152, 155, 158
slogans, 99, 130–41, 152–3, 156, 177
Smart, Christopher, 112–13
Smith, Sydney, 59, 121
Smollett, Tobias, 53, 119
Snyder, J.M., 41–2
sophistry, 10, 11, 40, 41
Spevack, Marvin, 48–9
Spitzer, Leo, 16, 157, 180
Stanford, William Bedell, 20, 41, 86, 171–2
Steele, Richard, 1, 82
Stendhal, 123–4
Sterne, Laurence, 53
Surrealism, 17, 28, 75–6, 77, 113, 146, 147
Sutton, Max Keith, 62, 64
Swift, Jonathan, 1, 13, 53–5, 66, 94, 126, 164, 184

taboo, 9, 18, 29, 91, 96
Tabourot, Etienne, 43

Tanner, Tony, 20, 69–70, 151, 174, 182
Thau, Annette, 98
Thoreau, Henry David, 67, 92, 104, 156, 197n
Tindall, William York, 26
Todorov, Tzvetan, 179–80, 181
Tom Swifty, 150
translation, 4, 130, 169–70
trompe-l'oeil, 143
Turkle, Sherry, 80–1, 88
Twain, Mark, 156

Ullmann, Stephen, 91, 160
Untermeyer, Louis, 99, 101, 183

Valéry, Paul, 6, 26, 28, 39, 42, 86, 111, 178
Vallès, Jules, 179
Vendryès, J., 14, 180
visual puns, 67, 114, 142–8
Voltaire, 53, 169

Waterhouse, Keith, 142
Weightman, John, 162
Wellerism, 97, 150–1
Welsh, Andrew, 76, 79, 101, 113
West, Michael, 61, 67
Wilde, Oscar, 11, 74, 126, 159
Wilson, Christopher P., 45, 178
Wittgenstein, Ludwig, 40, 143
Wolfenstein, Martha, 149
women, 3, 49

Yaguello, Marina, 6, 41, 160

Zen, 25, 45, 146
zeugma, 94–5, 96